The Rebel World of 1857

The Revolt of 1857 - Region of Estern Uttar Pradesh

MAP – Not According to Scale

The Rebel World of 1857:
Eastern Uttar Pradesh

Syed Najmul Raza Rizvi

KALPAZ

First Published, 2021

Published by

Kalpaz Publications
C-30, Satyawati Nagar,
Delhi – 110052
Ph.: 011-47034999, 9811692060
www.kalpazpublications.com
E-mail: kalpaz@hotmail.com

Printed at: G. Print Process, Delhi

Cataloging in Publication Data—DK
Courtesy: D.K. Agencies (P) Ltd. <docinfo@dkagencies.com>

Rizvī, Syed Najmul Razā, 1950- **author.**
The rebel world of 1857: eastern Uttar Pradesh / Syed Najmul Raza Rizvi.
pages cm
Includes bibliographical references.
ISBN 9789353243043 (HB)

1. Uttar Pradesh (India)—Politics and government—19th century. 2. Revolutionaries—India—Uttar Pradesh. 3. Uttar Pradesh (India)—History—19th century. 4. India—History—Sepoy Rebellion, 1857-1858. I. Title.

LCC DS485.U64R59 2020 | DDC 954.20317 23

Dedicated to

(Late) Professor Sabyasachi Bhattacharya

Former Chairman,
Indian Council of Historical Research,
New Delhi

Contents

Acknowledgement

The present study is an outcome of the Research Project, entitled "The Rebel World of 1857 and Eastern Uttar Pradesh", sanctioned to the author, as a Senior Academic Fellow, by the Indian Council of Historical Research, New Delhi, and the subsequent research work. The author is indebted to the Council for it.

From time to time during the progress of the study, the author received suggestions and co-operation from several learned friends. The foremost name worth mentioning in this regard is that of Professor Saiyid Zaheer Husain Jafri, Department of History, University of Delhi. Through his valuable suggestions, he extended much help in preparing the design of the research. I hereby acknowledge his debt. Among the others who provided suggestions and extended cooperation includes, (Late) Professor Iqbal Hussain (Aligarh Muslim University), Professor N. R. Farooqi (Allahabad), Professor Rashmi Pandey (Lucknow), Dr Vandana Saraswat (Gonda), Dr Manisha Chaudhari (Asst. Professor, Department of History, University of Delhi), Dr Mahendra Pratap (Varanasi), Dr Onkar Nath Upadhyaya (Jaunpur), Dr. Mohd. Arshad (Delhi), Dr Ram Bilas Bharti (Mau), Dr. Ram Pratap (Gorakhpur), Dr Ramdarash Pandey (Librarian, Academic Staff College, D.D.U. Gorakhpur University, Gorakhpur), Sri Dhaneshwar Kumar (Library In-charge, National Archives, New Delhi), Sri Anil Kumar Agnihotri (officer at the Regional Archives) and Ghulam Sarwar (Technical Support, (Persian), Regional Archives, Allahabad). Hereby I heartily acknowledge gratefulness to all these friends.

I received utmost cooperation from my family members during the progress of the study, as they took all care of my needs and comfort and arranged for my travels. I hereby reassert my affections for my sons Syed Mehdi Raza, Syed Mohammed Raza and Syed Abbas Raza Rizvi, for my daughters-in-law Meraj Fatima and Dr Tamheed Fatima, my grandson Ayaan Mehdi and granddaughter Zainab Raza.

At the end, I would like to remember my revered teachers, Professor (Late) Radhey Shyam (Allahabad) and Professor (Late) Hari Shankar Srivastava (Gorakhpur), as well as my late wife, Yasmin Fatima.

Syed Najmul Raza Rizvi
Professor and Former Head,
Department of History,
D.D.U. Gorakhpur University,
Gorakhpur

Preface

The Revolt of 1857 was one of the momentous events of the world during the nineteenth century. The century is regarded to be the most important from the viewpoint of genesis of nationalism. The process led to the rise of Italy and Germany as nations. The ideology of nationalism destroyed the parochial feelings of regionalism among the people and creating the sentiment of a united struggle against the external forces which hampered the growth of nationalism. But no impact of national feeling was visible in the British colonies which were spread all over the world. About India, the British held the categorical position that no feeling of nationalism existed here. They believed that India was no nation but only a "geographical expression." However, going against the British thinking and beliefs, the people of India revolted against the British power in 1857. This revolt was the most powerful and most protracted among the armed struggles, which were launched against the world empire or against colonialism.

Though the revolt was eventually crushed, it produced some immediate as well as long-term impacts which were highly significant. This created a fear psychosis among the British — that the people of India could get united and throw them out anytime. This put a halt to their policy of colonial expansion and compelled the British Government to bring the Company Raj to an end. Thus, it forced the British to take the administration of India in their own hands and to announce some changes in their policies. On the other side of the fence, it led to a rapid growth of nationalism among the Indians. Thus, the popular revolt of 1857 was significant from many angles.

This popular revolt of the nineteenth century was most fatal for the colonialists and imperialists. Therefore, in order to malign it among the people, the British began to present it to the people after distorting its real character. They presented it as a "Sepoy Mutiny", while only 62 regiments of Bengal Army had revolted at various places and over a period. They also dubbed it as "a conspiracy and rebellion of the dethroned kings, feudal lords and zamindars." Shaken to the core by the Hindu-Muslim unity forged during the rebellion, the British described it as a "conspiracy for restoration of the Muslim rule" and thus made an attempt to scare the Hindus away from it. Again, in order to create dissensions among the Hindus, the revolt was said to be motivated by the casteist feelings of the upper caste Hindus. Nay more, from the viewpoint of loss of life and property, someone said it harmed the Muslims and someone else said it was inimical to the Hindus. All these attempts, aimed to hamper the growth of nationalist feeling in India, failed. As was conceded by Sir W. H. Russell, the British sowed the seeds of nationalism in India by their suppression of the revolt of 1857, with the result that the ground for a powerful mass movement was paved in the subsequent years. He wrote in the *London Times* that "we may assume that in the rebellion of 1857, no national spirit was roused, but we cannot deny that our effort to put it down have sown, the seeds of a new plant and thus laid the foundation for more energetic attempts on the part of people in the course of future years".

It was only in the twentieth century that attempts began to assess the real character and significance of the popular revolt of 1857. First of all, in 1909 AD, Vinayak Damodar Savarkar came out with his book the *Indian War of Independence* and described the rebellion as a "war of independence." He wrote "I found to my great surprise the brilliance of a war of Independence shining in the mutiny of 1857". Subsequently, Indian leaders, historians, literary figures and other writers established its significance by describing it as a "national revolt" and "the first war of independence," though Disraeli, a British statesman, and Karl Marx, a great philosopher, had already described it as a "national revolt" even while it was in progress. After the attainment of independence, researches on the revolt were carried out on a large scale in view of its importance. A number of significant works have come out on a national or regional level on the causes of the revolt, its character, the events, its failure, its results and relevance. Of these works, *Eighteen Fifty-Seven* by Surendra Nath Sen is based on the British Government's documents. *The Sepoy Mutiny and the Revolt of 1857* by R. C. Majumdar, *Civil Rebellion in the Indian Mutinies (1857 – 1859)* and *Theories of the Indian Mutiny* (1857-58) by Dr Sashi Bhusan Chaudhuri, *Rebellion 1857: A Symposium,* edited by P C Joshi, *Bahadur Shah II and the War of 1857 in Delhi with its Unforgettable Scenes* by Syed Mahdi Husain, and *Awadh in Revolt* by Rudrangshu Mukherjee are most notable among the English language works. Besides, at the national and regional levels, the number of published researches and articles in English, Hindi, Urdu and other languages are so many that all of these cannot be mentioned here. But a glance upon them makes it crystal clear that the range of historiography of the revolt of 1857 has indeed widened and attention has been paid to the new aspects. As an example, a new dimension which has been added is that of a search of the rebels' vision, their religions and ideals, the role of Dalits and women and more so that of Dalit women, the role of prostitutes in the revolt, and so on. New sources are also coming to light because of articles. Crispin Bates has edited several such articles as *Mutiny at the Margins: New Perspectives on the Indian Uprising of 1857*, in seven volumes. An attempt is being made to assess the role of the Wahabis in a new perspective.

In the seminars and symposia held during the observance of 150th anniversary of the revolt of 1857, attempts were made to view the various aspects of the revolt anew. A little before it, in 2006, William Dalrymple had published his work "*The Last Mughal: The Fall of a Dynasty, Delhi, 1857*". This work made the claim that it was based on certain documents of the National Archives, New Delhi, which research scholars had not even seen. However, in this book, William Dalrymple only presented in a new way the old English thinking which regarded the religious frenzies and racial divisions as responsible for the revolt. This work generated a lot of controversy among the historians. Many scholars edited the papers which were presented in the seminars and symposia. Mentionworthy among these works are "*Rethinking:1857*" edited by Professor Sabyasachi Bhattacharya, "*Facets of the Great Revolt*" edited by Professor Shireen Moosvi, and "*Religion and Ideology of the Rebels of 1857*", a collection of articles, written by Professor Iqbal Husain himself. These works include the papers which throw a new light on new dimensions, ideas and sources. Besides, in Hindi, *Anbhai Sancha* and "*1857: Baghaavat ke Daur ka Itihas*", edited by Murali Manohar Prasad Singh, and "*1857 ka Mahasangram*", jointly edited by Badri Narayan, Rashmi Chaudhari and Sanjay Nath, are also noteworthy.

Though a number of researches have been conducted on the Great Uprising and new dimensions have been explored, the process of studying the rebellion, which took place on a very wide scale, is still incomplete. For example, there has been no independent study about the people of the East, called *Purabiyas* (literally: Easterners), from whom the last Mughal Emperor, Bahadur Shah Zafar, had too many expectations regarding the success of the revolt. About the *Purabiyas*, Bahadur Shah Zafar had written:

Kushta kaamat jitne hain, sab mil-julkar
Ik hashr bapa kar den, kitna achchha ho, kaisa achchha ho!
(Included in the fourth collection)

(All the short-statured people who are here may together wreck a doom. (If it happens) What a good thing it would be!)

It is clear that the Emperor had great expectations from the short-statured people, i.e. the Easterners.

Maulvi Sadruddin Khan 'Azurda,' (the Mufti of Delhi in the pre-1857 days) had also written about the important role played by the Easterners:

Waqt-e-Mauwood se pehle hi qayamat aayi;
Kaale purab se jo aaye to shahr mein aafat aayi.

(The day of doom dawned even before there was dawn on the day; there was trouble in the city when the blacks of the East arrived here.)

The present study is a humble attempt to fill this gap. From the studies that have been made so far, it is evident that there were different reasons in different regions for the revolt against the Company Raj in 1857, and that people of various religions, castes and classes took part in it. Therefore, its nature was not uniform everywhere. Regional level studies in Delhi, Rohilkhand, Bundelkhand, Awadh, Bihar, etc, have corroborated this fact. In the present study, an attempt has been made to find out: What were the reasons of the revolt in Eastern Uttar Pradesh? What was the character of the revolt ? What was the structure of the rebels' world there and who were the main figures in the participants? How did the rebellion come to an end? What was the role of Nepal, the neighbouring country, in this revolt? The necessity of a careful study and analysis of all these issues still remains.

Eastern Uttar Pradesh was never a geographical or administrative unit. At the time of the 1857 revolt, the region included six districts — Banaras, Jaunpur, Ghazipur, Mirzapur, Azamgarh and Gorakhpur. (These have been split into a number of independent districts by now.) By the Treaty of Faizabad in 1775, Nawab Asafuddaulah of Awadh had surrendered the territory known as Banaras Raj (or Suba) to the Company Government; this included Banaras, Ghazipur, Jaunpur and Mirzapur. Then, Nawab Sa'adat Ai Khan surrendered the districts of Azamgarh and Gorakhpur to the Company Government in 1801. In other words, after the Diwani of Bengal, Bihar and Orrisa, eastern Uttar Pradesh was the first territory in North India to come under the Company's tutelage.

The present study is based on contemporary official documents, works by contemporary Indian writers, secondary sources and interviews with persons. The official documents are kept preserved in the National Archives at New Delhi, State Archives at Lucknow and Regional Archives at Allahabad. Information about the events during the revolt is available in the weekly narratives sent by the Commissioners to the Government. Events till the time Gorakhpur was reoccupied may be known from the narrative sent by the Gorakhpur Commissioner, C. Wingfield, to the Secretary to the Government on 5 July 1858. On the other hand, official version of the events which took place and the rebels, who were active in Azamgarh, Ghazipur, Banaras, Jaunpur and Mirzapur districts may be known from the reports "The Rebellion of 1857 in the Province of Benares" sent on 15 October 1858 and "Supplement to the Narrative of Events & c. in the Benares Division" sent on 19 November 1858 by Robert Taylor, the Joint Magistrate of Jaunpur. Besides, the official letters, information and some other papers sent by British officials, commanders and pro-British people are also among the sources used in this study. Some of these prominent documents were edited and published by Syed Athar Abbas Rizvi in six volumes, titled, '*Freedom Struggle in Uttar Pradesh*', in 1959. For the sake of our illumination, the editor has added a number of useful notes to these volumes. Much information about important rebel rajas, zamindars and British supporters of this region has been culled from various settlement reports, district gazetteers and manuals. *Volunteering in India* by John Tulloch Nash provides first-hand account of some happenings in this region.

Apart from the government documents, the most important non-official source used in the present study is *Kashful-Baghaavat*, *Gorakhpur*, written in masnavi style in Urdu and it is metrical poetry. The masnavi was completed on 22 Ziqaad 1274 Hijri (3rd July 1858). But it took the shape of the book in 1859 AD and was published in 1860 AD, from Arifeen Press, Mirzapur. Syed Ahmed Ali Shah, the then caretaker of Imambara of Gorakhpur was its composer. According to him its name was *Kashful-Baghaavat*. Unfortunately, no erudite historian has taken note of this contemporary publication. This work has been used for the first time in the present study. Syed Ahmed Ali Shah, the composer of *Kashful-Baghaavat*, *Gorakhpur*, was a supporter of the British Government and one of the leading personalities who provided protection and support to the British, particularly the English officials, at the time of the crisis; for this reason, he had to face the wrath of the rebels. But he was an eye witness of the events during the rebellion and, therefore, the information provided by him is authentic. His work is full of condemnation of the rebels and sycophancy of the English officers. Apart from the happenings of Gorakhpur district, he has also briefly, presented the rebellious events in Azamgarh, Ghazipur and Jaunpur districts and has said something about some of the rebels and British supporters as well in those districts. According to the governmental sources, the area of Gorakhpur district in 1843 was 7,342 square miles and the population was 12,89,693 (Pre-Mutiny Records, Magistrate's Office, Gorakhpur, Bag No. 141, Serial No. 25, Revenue Letters

Issued, Series 1, From: E. A. Reade, 5 May 1843). The area witnessed the rebels' government for four months and twenty days. Here the rebellion was crushed by the Nepalese Army. The said work presents this kind of significant facts and a first-hand account of the revolt in so wide an area. It also has several pieces of information which are not available elsewhere. Moreover, we may well judge the important role of the rebels from the harsh odious epithets which he has used for them. In sum, this contemporary work is excessively authentic, informative and useful.

The later works in Urdu language include "*Khadang-e-Ghadar*" by Moinuddin Hasan Khan and "*Qaiser-ut-Tawarikh*" by Kamaluddin Haider. These provide important pieces of information. But apart from being pro-British, these writers were no natives of the area. Moreover, they were not present in the country at the time of the rebellion. They completed their works under the patronage of some British officers. As such, much of their descriptions are unreliable and exaggerated. Another later work in Urdu is "*Shajara-e-Shadab*", written by Maulvi Abdul Ghafoor Farooqi in 1901. It gives information about some events which took place during the rebellion in Padrauna Estate which was in the eastern part of Gorakhpur district. Maulvi Abdul Ghafoor Farooqi was manager of the Padrauna Estate which was pro-British. In this study I have also used some Hindi works, viz *Vishwen Vansh Vatika* written by Lal Khang Bahadur Mall, a member of the Majhauli princely estate, and published from Bankipur (Patna) in 1887, and *Nag Kaushalottar*, First Volume, (1909 AD) by Nageshwar Prasad Singh Verma. Some important pieces of information are available in these works.

During my study, I also attempted to explore the Nepalese sources. But the present writer found no such useful document in the Nepal archives in Kathmandu as could tell us about some rebels who had taken refuge in Nepal. Contacts with erudite historians there could not yield any useful letter, information or document either. Only Professor Dinesh Raj Pant provided a booklet titled *Dhading ma Phela Pareka Nepali Kavita* which was published by Rajiv Lochan Joshi Memorial Foundation, Kathmandu, in Vikrami Samvat 2061 (AD 2004). It includes a poem titled "Lakhanao ko Sawai" which was composed in AD 1881 (V.S 1938). The poem contains an exaggerated description of the deeds performed by the Gorkha Army against the rebels in Eastern Uttar Pradesh; for example, it describes the battle of Gagaha, in Gorakhpur, the activities in Azamgarh and in Jaunpur district and in the battle at Chanda in Sultanpur. During the search for oral sources, the writer came in contact with many people living in the Nepalese territory along the Indo-Nepal border, and this yielded some hazy information about Damman Khan of Jhandanagar. Talks with the people of Jhandanagar, Amauli and Chaipurwa villages reveals, that nothing reliable about this rebel leader is now extant in popular memory, nor do they have any interest in knowing about him. In Amauli village, descendants of Damman Khan could not provide any family document about him. About 80 years old Iftikhar Ahmed Khan of Chaipurwa village orally told about many events, which have been mentioned in the British records also. He told me about how Damman Khan came from Bansi tehsil, settled in Jhandanagar, and was accorded the position of Diwan by the Government of Nepal, while another narrative says Damman Khan had come from Utraula tehsil of Gonda district and settled in Jhandanagar.

Liberal use of secondary sources has been made in this study. The work throws ample light on the causes and nature of the revolt in Eastern Uttar Pradesh, on Maulvi Sarfaraz Ali who was the main inspirator behind the revolt, the main happenings in the region, the rebel world and its main figures, and on the limitations, results and significance of the revolt. I hope that the book would add to the information of those interested in the Uprising of 1857.

1st August 2020 **Syed Najmul Raza Rizvi**

Illustrations

Existing condition of the tomb of Maulvi Sarfaraz Ali, situated in Jame Masjid, Nepal (photographed from above)

Existing condition of the tomb of Maulvi Sarfaraz Ali (surrounded by a wall), situated in Jame Masjid, Nepal

Source: The writer's personal collection.

Maulvi Sarfaraz Ali's tomb photographed in 2011 Existing condition of the tomb of Maulvi Sarfaraz Ali, situated in Jame Masjid, Nepal

Source: The writer's personal collection

Existing condition of the tomb of Maulvi Sarfaraz Ali (surrounded by a wall), situated in Jame Masjid, Nepal

Chapter - 1

Resentment and Revolt

Historical researches have brought to light the fact that different regions took part in the revolt of 1857 for different reasons. Regional studies illustrate that though the revolt was directed against a common enemy, different factors were there behind the mobilisation at different places in the expanse of the subcontinent. This fact gets clearly underlined when we glance upon the reasons of revolt in Eastern Uttar Pradesh. Different factors appear to be operating behind the revolt in different districts of this region.

Causes of Revolt

The revenue policy of the Company Government, particularly its land revenue policy and other economic policies, seems to be the most important reason of revolt in this region. Through the Treaty of Faizabad in May 1775, Nawab Asafuddaulah of Awadh surrendered to the Company Government the sovereign rights over the Banaras Zamindari or Banaras Suba (province) which comprised the districts of Banaras, Ghazipur (including Ballia) Jaunpur and Mirzapur.[1] In 1776, in lieu of the revenue of this territory, the Company demanded 23,40,249 *sikka* rupees per annum from Raja Chait Singh of Banaras, which he accepted. After the revolt by Chait Singh, the Company demanded 40 lakh rupees per annum from Maheep Narayan Singh, the new *raja*. Jonathan Duncan, who was appointed Resident of Banaras in 1787, implemented a land revenue settlement for this territory and it was declared permanent in 1795 (with the conditions involved in the Permanent Settlement of Bengal).[2] In the Permanent Settlement, the government's demand of land revenue was so high that its timely payment every year became quite difficult for the zamindars and peasants. Either they were compelled to sell their zamindaris or the Company Government publicly auctioned them in order to realise the pending land revenue. During the Nawab's regime, a zamindari was not auctioned for realisation of the pending land revenue; rather it was somehow extracted by other means. In his study of the Banaras region, B. S. Cohn found that, in all, 283 estates were auctioned by 1850, and 61 of these were purchased by zamindars, 34 by the Raja of Banaras, 66 by *mahajans* (tradesmen and moneylenders) and 46 by government employees. *Mahajans* had thus purchased 26 per cent of the zamindari that was auctioned.[3] B.S. Cohn also demonstrated that between 1795 and 1850, 162 estates were sold in Banaras, 71 in Jaunpur, 21 in Ballia-Ghazipur, and 29 in Mirzapur.[4] Wilton Oldham, the Collector of Ghazipur, has written that by 1871, after the Permanent Settlement in Ghazipur district, as many as 716 estates (zamindaris) alone, whose revenue amounted to 4,37,754 rupees only, had passed into the hands of strangers.[5] In this manner, the zamindari giving one-fourth of the revenue in the district came out of the hands of hereditary zamindars and went to outsiders.[6] Wilton Oldham also wrote that zamindars holding on to their hereditary zamindaris not only remained cool during the revolt of 1857 but also helped the British authorities while the dispossessed zamindars played a notable role in the revolt.[7] About the Zamindars of Jaunpur, Robert Taylor wrote that, "Those who had lost their estates under our rule, thought this a good time to regain them."[8] Thus, the government had deliberately or inadvertently created a powerful opposition in the form of dispossessed zamindars who had been looking for an opportunity to strike against the government.

Through a treaty in 1801, Nawab Sa'adat Ali Khan of Awadh handed over to the Company Government the territory which fell under Chakla Gorakhpur and Chakla Azamgarh;[9] these adjoined the Banaras Suba and formed part of Eastern Uttar Pradesh. Here too, the government had declared its intention to develop agriculture and then implement the Permanent Settlement after ten years. But later the decision was changed, and the Mahalwari System was implemented in the region. This process had not yet completed by the time of the 1857 revolt.[10] The rate of rent was high in the Mahalwari System and it amounted to 66 per cent or two-third of the price of the produce. Professor Irfan Habib has held the Mahalwari System a big cause of the growing restlessness and discontent in the Bengal army. He wrote: "'It was no accident' that the area, the bulk of its sepoys came from, had been turned into the highest taxed part of the country. The peasantry as well as the 'Village Zamindars' here had been made subject to an ever- rising burden of tax under the Mahalwari system established in 1822. In Mahalwari areas, not only were the settlements made for 20 years only, but the revenue rate could be changed at any time."[11] If we put his contention in the context of Eastern Uttar Pradesh, it seems perfectly correct.

While the Banaras Zamindari had the Permanent Settlement, Mahalwari System prevailed in the Ceded Provinces (Gorakhpur and Azamgarh). For this reason, the revolt was more widespread and more severe in the Ceded Provinces.

Amildari System prevailed in the Ceded Provinces during the Nawab's government, and it was marked by intense exploitation and oppression of the weaker zamindars and ryots. This was what British officials raised a big hullabaloo about.[12] According to the available figures, Meer Qazim Ali Khan, the *chakladar* of Gorakhpur, collected the land revenue of 7,40,194 rupees and 10 annas from this territory in Fasli year 1208 (AD 1800).[13] But the Company Government fixed the land revenue of this area at 10,88,577 rupees in 1840 and at 15,53,607 rupees in 1860, which shows the extent of economic exploitation they perpetrated.[14] Similarly, land revenue due in Azamgarh was Rs 6,93,767 in Fasli 1209 (1801), but only Rs 5,89,264 could be collected.[15] But (according to the settlement report, 1837), the Company Government upped it to Rs 12,42,274 in its fifth settlement.[16] Thus, during its rule for 50-55 years in the Ceded Provinces, the Company Government raised its land revenue demand by two to two and a half times. This directly impacted the zamindars and their ryots.

The zamindars of Gorakhpur and Azamgarh districts felt the pinch of this increase in land revenue all the more intentionally, as the Company Government brought the *maafi* (declared to be revenue free), *wiran* (uninhabited or Barren) and *taufir* (overgrown with shrubs) lands too under the purview of land revenue collection. Earlier, the rajas, taluqdars and zamindars used to declare the villages in their zamindaris as *maafi*, *wiran* and *taufir* lands and thus avoided paying land revenue. At the time Gorakhpur district came under the Company rule, in 1802, it had 3,966 *mauzas* (revenue units) as revenue free and their total area was 9,21,061 acres, which was more than half of area of the district. According to the available figures, 1,320 *mauzas* of Gorakhpur district were revenue free in 1802-03, but the number had come down to 134 only in 1861. Similarly, the number of *wiran* and *taufir mauzas* numbered 2,646 but there was none in 1861.[17] According to the records, all the *wiran*, *taufir* and *nankar mauzas* had been brought under the purview of land revenue during the fourth settlement (i.e. Fasli 1224 – 1229 or AD 1816 to 1821), and contracted out.[18] The increased demand of land revenue, therefore, began the process of sale of zamindaris in the Ceded Provinces as well. In Azamgarh district during the ten-year period between 1837 and 1847, 38,398 acres of land were sold out for 48,047 rupees. The process further intensified during the next ten years, from 1848 to 1858, when 61,080 acres of land were sold out for 88,671 rupees. Of this, *mahajans* purchased 59,517 acres.[19] During various settlements in Gorakhpur district, rajas, taluqdars and zamindars refused to enter an agreement with the government and thus articulated their protest. Yet, during the fourth settlement, four estates were alienated for the pending land revenue, while 65 estates with a *jama* (revenue) of Rs 92,842, passed on under *khas* management, i.e., in government's hands, between 1829 and 1835.[20] Several hereditary rajas and zamindars reached the brink of insolvency because of the government's arrears.

The rajas, taluqdars and zamindars of this area, and in particular Gorakhpur district, were discontented with the Company Government for some other reasons as well. The Company Government had issued an order for demolition of the zamindars' mudforts and another to ban the collection of sayer or miscellaneous taxes, and these had put their life as well as income in jeopardy. Hence, they opposed these orders. But the Company Government crushed them by force.[21] They were naturally incensed. The *terai* to the north and east of Ghaghra River was covered with dense forests. Most of the areas of Gorakhpur district were forest-covered at the time.[22] These forests had great importance in the life of the zamindars and peasants. During the Nawab's rule, they used to take refuge in these dense forests to avoid paying the government's revenue. The rajas had even made mudforts in these forests. They also raised forests around their mudforts for the latter's protection.[23] Every zamindar was held to be the owner of the forests in his zamindari's jurisdiction, and also owned the forest produce. These forests were used to save oneself from ailments as well.[24] Hence no zamindar was interested in destroying these forests. But the Company Government's policy was to cut these forests and make their valuable timber available to the shipping industry and to the railways at low prices and thus to promote the timber trade. Therefore, even though the Company did not divest the zamindars of their ownership rights over these forests, it did pressurise them that either they should get these forests cleared and make the timber available for trade or, else, they should contract these forests out to traders for fixed annual fees.[25] Besides, the government was also playing the game of augmenting its own income by imposing a tax of 2.5 per cent on this trade.[26] Transgressing the rights of the zamindars, the government also claimed its right over the forest produce. By issuing an advertisement, it declared the forest produce to be the government property, and invited tenders from the people to get these produced collected. It began issuing the lease deeds for collection of forest produce to the highest bidders.[27] In 1831, the government divested the zamindars of their right to contract the job of forest clearance out, and itself began to lease it out. In 1840, it began to give new forest grants with amended conditions in order to expedite the forest clearance.[28] As many as 64 forest grants were issued in Pargana Haveli alone in Gorakhpur district. The majority of the forest grantees were Europeans. The forest policy of the government naturally angered the zamindars here.

In the settlement of 1835, in order to curb the influence of big rajas and taluqdars, the Company Government directly entered into revenue contracts with the Birtia, and accepted them as independent zamindars.[29] While this new zamindar class became the supporter of the Company Government, the move not only curbed the influence of big rajas and taluqdars but their zamindaris too suffered a contraction. This gave them a shock.

In the Ceded Provinces, there was yet another reason behind the zamindars' seething anger against the Company Government. At the time the district was transferred, the zamindars of Chakla Azamgarh received 82,122 rupees 9 annas and 6 paise while those of Chakla Gorakhpur received 73,077 rupees 1 anna and 3 paise as *nankar*. But the Company Government refused to recognise the right of many zamindars to receive *nankar* and decided to give only 52,938 rupees 7 annas and 9 paise to some of the zamindars as *nankar*.[30] Those who were denied *nankar* turned against the government. As an example, the raja of Shahpur in Dhuriapar in Gorakhpur, who was denied *nankar*,[31] played an active role in the revolt.

Some zamindars of Gorakhpur were angry with the Company Government for personal reasons. For example, a part of the zamindari of the raja of Barhyapar was confiscated in 1818 for non-payment of land revenue. The government gave it, as jagir, to Kareem Khan Pindari who then settled there with all his relatives and followers numbering about 600.[32] Similarly, another Pindari leader, Qadir Bakhsh Khan, was given the Ganeshpur taluka of Nagar pargana in Basti on the condition of payment of land revenue which was only nominal.[33] This turned the rajas of Barhyapar and Nagar against the government.

In medieval period, there was a tradition of allotting *madad-i-ma'ash* (assistance for livelihood) to some of the religious figures, scholars and persons of use for the state. This was given either as cash or as revenue free (*maafi*) land. Mughal emperors and the nawabs of Awadh had issued too many *madad-i-ma'ash* grants in their time. In Gorakhpur district where the population was low and land was in excess, the Nawab's officials and taluqdars had distributed *maafi* lands on a large scale. According to a survey, the *maafi* land amounted to about 5,44,302 *bighas* in this district.[34] Similarly, too much land was *maafi* in Azamgarh district as well.[35] The Company Government stipulated some criteria for the *maafi* lands to be accepted as legitimate, and maintained the *maafi* lands of those who fulfilled these criteria, but confiscated the lands of others and imposed a rent upon them.[36] In the same way, in Azamgarh too, *maafi* lands were confiscated on a large scale and only 9,157 acres remained as *maafi* land.[37] The influential class of *maafidars* thus turned against the government when their *maafi* lands, the means of their livelihood, were taken away. The persons whose grants remained intact proved loyal and helpful to the Company Government or else remained inactive during the Uprising of 1857. Two leading Muslim families of Gorakhpur were the examples.[38]

Ryots or peasants had no place in the Company Government's settlements for land revenue. There was no legal provision about their rights. They were left at the mercy of the zamindars.[39] Their status was almost that of serfs.[40] They were victims of the zamindars' exploitation and oppression. But their relationship with the zamindars continued for generations. Zamindars were their protectors and props in distress. Landless peasants or labourers often worked on the zamindar's *seer* land. These very ryots had to bear the burden of increasing revenue demand of the Company Government. So, they were not happy with the government. Peasants were immediately affected when a zamindari was sold out or auctioned. Because of unfamiliarity, adjustment with the new owner proved difficult. Ryots often opposed the new owners and supported the traditional landowner.[41] Therefore, they sided with their traditional masters when the latter rose against the Company Government.

Industrial and commercial policies of the government were also a major cause of discontent among the people of Eastern Uttar Pradesh and contributed to the rise of the popular revolt. In the Ceded Provinces, the opium and indigo factories belonged to the Britishers. The large-scale import of readymade goods, and particularly of the textiles and machines, had pushed the indigenous handlooms to the brink of a disaster. Weavers, in particular, were seething with anger. The event of Mahua Dabar village in Nagar pargana in Basti district may be seen as a proof of this anger; here the Englishmen who had run away from Faizabad were done to death.[42] The people's attacks on the indigo and opium factories show their discontent and anger. The British had, in a sense, the monopoly of forest clearance and timber trade. That was why the rebels' Proclamation, issued from Azamgarh, had reminded the traders: "The infidel *firangis* have snatched the profitable trade in indigo, opium and cloths, and made it their monopoly, leaving the less profitable trades for you."[43] Similarly, artisans were told that "The British have begun to bring in readymade goods, particularly cloths and machines, on a large scale from their country, which has made it difficult for our artisans to get their livelihood."[44] People also resented the discrimination in government jobs.[45] Local people got very low wages. Getting a government job was difficult in the absence of English education. For their living, almost all the classes had to take loans on interest, which had become a very big cause of increase in their travails.

People of all classes were dissatisfied with the new administrative system of the Company Government, particularly its police and judicial systems. Earlier, panchayats settled the disputes without any cost. Law and order were in the hands of the zamindar who pronounced a nominal punishment and thus kept the situation under control. Panchayats too did not impose any heavy economic punishment. But the village panchayats and other autonomous institutions had no place in the Company's system of governance. The system of justice was now expensive and costly. No case could now be filed without stamp papers, court fee and lawyer's fee. The police could arrest anyone on a flimsy complaint. Bribery and corruption had gone sky-high. As a result, all classes of the people were dissatisfied. The Azamgarh Proclamation drew the people's attention to this aspect in particular and said: "We well know that the British fix the land revenue very high, and this is the cause of your destitution. Moreover, when a case is filed against you, you are summoned to the Britishers' court without any investigation and thus you are insulted and humiliated. Then, when you have to file a case in their court, you are made to get a ticketed paper (stamp paper) written and cough out money, and you are made to pay the court fee, which ruins you."[46]

The rising prices too were ruining the life of the people in Eastern Uttar Pradesh. Prices of grains usually went high whenever crops were destroyed due to natural calamities like heavy rainfall or drought. In such situations, the earlier regimes announced remissions in the rents or revenue, postponed their collection, arranged for grains as *taqavi*, and arranged fodder for the cattle. But nothing like this could be expected from the Company Government. For example, when there was a famine in Gorakhpur district in 1837-38, no step was taken except the announcement of a paltry Rs 208 remission in rent.[47] The grain prices rose sharply because of this famine. Now for one rupee only 15 seers of *chana* (pea gram) was available in place of 60 seers, while the same money now brought 14 seers of wheat instead of 33 seers. There was a partial famine again in 1850.[48] The prices again soared now. In his settlement report, J. R. Reid too has mentioned the rising grain prices in Azamgarh. According to Robert Taylor, prices of daily necessities and grains were soaring high in Banaras as well. This had made the life a hell for the poorer sections.[49]

The profession of moneylending was progressing very fast, due to the economic policies of the Company Government. Contracting loans for payment of the government's rent had become a compulsion for the zamindars as well as the ryots. Artisans and workers were compelled to take loans for daily expenses. The village *banias* and the urban moneylenders or bankers took full advantage of the helplessness of all these sections. No *bania* or moneylender was honest in his dealings. He whimsically charged interest on the loan amounts. In case of non-payment, he added the interest to the principal and thus charged a compound rate of interest. Finally, when a zamindar or ryot failed in repayment, he purchased the defaulter's zamindari or land. If he could not do it himself, he moved to court for loan recovery, contrived a verdict in his favour, and then got the zamindari publicly auctioned. In these auctions, mostly the moneylenders purchased the zamindaris at low prices. William Edward, who was a judge at Banaras at the time of the revolt, wrote that land was acquired for very small loans and this caused distortions in society.[50] The auction of a zamindari not only deprived the concerned zamindar of his livelihood but also caused a severe blow to his prestige in society. Thus, he turned an enemy of the system. In his work *Kashful-Baghaavat*, *Gorakhpur*, Shah Syed Ahmed Ali, the caretaker of Gorakhpur Imambada, who was a partisan and cooperator of the British, even held the moneylenders guilty for the revolt of 1857. Dwelling on the causes of the revolt, Shah Syed Ahmed Ali wrote:[51]

Mahajan hue baais-e-ghadar-e-aam II
Diya jis ko dus us se sau bhar liya, I
Liya karkara jis ko malta diya, II
Siwa es ke nazrana ki hai raqam I
Woh hai saikde panch bekaast-o-kum, II
Tamassuk khun ko naya karte hain. I
Vala mul mein sood ko dharte hain II
Hua asl mein sood jab inzamaam I
Laga sood par sood badhne tamaam II
Na jab sood se dekha apna panaah I
Raha chhaati ko peet kar karz khaah II
Hai yeh bhi unhi ka nihaayat sitam I
Jo karte hain nalish kisi par baham II
Wasooli raqumaat ko zeenahaar I

Nahi dete mujra ve zulmat sheaar II
Mahajan ki illat mein wa hasrata I
Hue mulk neelaam sab barmala II
Hua jis ghadi dakhl neelamdar I
Raha maalik-e-milk ek aah maar II
Biki jinki bhi milkiyat daam mein I
Wohi jaa mile balwa-e-aam mein II
The muddat se jo log az bas tabaah I
Liya milk phir cheen go hai gunaah II
[Mahajan *became the cause of the common revolt,*

Extracted hundred from the one they had given ten,
Took back crisp from the one they had given soggy.
Besides this, is the amount of tax (nazrana)
Which is five on hundred, on uncultivated and scanty land.
They keep renewing the clink of monetary bonds.
Freely they add interest to the principal amount.
When interest became one with the principal amount
Then compound interest over interest multiplied tremendously.
When he did not see appropriate protection from his interest,
The creditor was able to strike wealthy profits.
This also is their extreme oppression
That they ultimately file a legal suit against someone.
On no account on recovery of the total amount
Do these dark-mannered ones ever give any rebate.
Due to the Mahajan's fault unfortunately
All territories are auctioned publicly.
The moment the auctioneer took possession,
The property owner sighed in helpless despair.
Those whose properties were sold for a price
Were the ones who joined in the mass rioting.
People who were ruined since ages
Looted their earlier property back, even though it is sin.]

But Shah Syed Ahmed Ali's contention is only partially true, as the Company Government had created the conducive atmosphere for the *mahajans*.

The Company Government's policy of annexation of the indigenous principalities was one of the main causes of the revolt of 1857. Sir Syed Ahmed Khan held the annexation of Awadh as one of the causes of the revolt.[52] The annexation of Awadh in 1856 on the ground of maladministration became the most important cause of revolt in Eastern Uttar Pradesh. According to J. T. Nash, "The annexation of Oudh was, without a shadow of doubt, primarily and solely, the cause that originated the mutiny."[53] Nash made this comment on the strength of the statement made by Shankar Tewari who was a retired pensioner of the Bengal Army and a resident of Bansi tehsil in Basti district. Because of the annexation of the kingdom of Awadh, numerous courtiers, scholars, *ulema* and those connected with administration became unemployed overnight. In the Awadh army, 60,000 soldiers were laid off. This also impacted the region of Eastern Uttar Pradesh which adjoined the region of Awadh. As an example, Mohammed Hasan, who was the Nazim of Khairabad in Awadh, got unemployed and he joined the revolt after he was appointed as the chakladar of Gorakhpur by Begum Hazrat Mahal. With the help of the rebels, he ran an independent government in Gorakhpur for four months and a half, and he surrendered only after the Begum escaped to Nepal. In his letter to Khairuddin, the magistrate of Gorakhpur who was writing him to surrender, he wrote: "The rebellion arose solely out of the annexation of Oude. Had that not taken place, there would have been no bloodshed because (there would have been) no defection of the chiefs who would have on the contrary inflicted chastisement on mutinous sepoys." He further wrote: "If her Majesty even now acts justly and gives back his Kingdom to the King of Oude, all this disturbance will be brought to an end."[54]

The western boundary of Eastern Uttar Pradesh adjoined the region of Awadh. People of the area had not only industrial, commercial and trade relationship with Awadh but also had family ties there. Many persons of the area had held high positions in Awadh. The Mirza family of Gorakhpur, who was an important collaborator of Mohammed Hasan, belonged to Faizabad.[55] Rani Jagat Raj Kunwari of Amorha also belonged to Faizabad.[56] Similarly, Darshan Singh, the father of Raja Beni Madho of Atraulia in Azamgarh district, had held a high position in the Awadh army. Jailal Singh, Beni Madho's brother, was an employee of the Nawab of Awadh. Beni Madho himself had served in the Awadh army for some time.[57] In brief, the people of Eastern Uttar Pradesh had special affinity with Awadh. Therefore, the annexation of Awadh naturally affected this region. Similarly, people of a number of Muslim villages in Utraula in Gonda district, which was situated on the eastern border of Awadh, had turned jobless and were now in search of employment. Hence, when the rebellion broke out, a large number of these Muslims joined the rebel army.[58] In the Bengal Army too, most of the soldiers belonged to Awadh and Eastern Uttar Pradesh.[59] Not only were they professionally related among themselves, but their villages and families too were mutually connected. So far, they had fought for the Company Government to capture other states. But when the Company Government annexed Awadh without any rhyme or reason (in the people's perception), while the King of Awadh was a friend and co-operator of the British and as Awadh was their own country (state), the move gave a shock to their feelings and they felt injured. From then on, they began to think of ending the Company Raj.[60] As we know, the area of Eastern Uttar Pradesh too was under the Nawabs of Awadh before it passed over to the Company. Therefore, here too the atmosphere was charged with similar feelings. The people here had experienced the difference between the indigenous and alien rulers in a very short time. Hence, they wanted to break free from the English rule. Like the people of Awadh, they too wanted to have a courageous and capable leadership which could raise the banner of revolt against the British. When Begum Hazrat Mahal, wife of Nawab Wajid Ali Shah, the deposed ruler of Awadh, raised the banner of revolt, and formed a government with her minor son, Birjish Qadr, at its head, the people willingly accepted her leadership. Though Begum Hazrat Mahal never visited any part of Eastern Uttar Pradesh, the people were in correspondence with her. They publicly declared acceptance of the Nawab's rule and asked for his help against the British. Nay more, they accepted the persons appointed by his government, like Mohammed Hasan, Raja Beni Madho, Raja Iradat Jehan or Kunwar Singh of Jagdishpur, etc, as their office-bearers, cooperated with them and staged a rebellion under their leadership. In sum, the impressive personality and leadership of Begum Hazrat Mahal was a potent factor of revolt in this area.

Till the time the challenge of the Indian powers had not ended, the Company Government had stuck to the policy of non-interference in social and religious matters. But as soon as there remained no Indian power to challenge it, the Company Government changed its policy. Through the Charter of 1813, the England Government allowed the Christian missionaries to propagate their religion in India. Numerous military and administrative officials of the Company Government began to take interest in religious activities and to misuse their positions and rights for the purpose. Christian missionaries came to India in a spate after 1813. They received open patronage and cooperation from the Company Government. They had adopted a planned policy of religious conversion. They were full of enthusiasm and often they crossed the limits of decency in criticising Hinduism and Islam. Their propaganda materials (pamphlets and booklets) were proof of the fact that they resorted to falsehood and deceit.[61] Therefore, Hindus and Muslims now faced the problem of safeguarding their respective religions. Activities of the Christian missionaries were gradually increasing in Eastern Uttar Pradesh as well. Missionaries opened schools and hospitals here, attracted the poorer and socially excluded sections in the name of philanthropy, and induced them to convert. In Gorakhpur district, Mr R. M. Bird established the Missionary Society in 1821. Reverend M. Wilkinson came here in 1824 and started propagating Christianity. He was granted 1120 acres of land in 1830. Three miles from the city, he settled Mohalla Basharatpur for the Indians who had converted to Christianity, and also established a church there. The London Church Missionary Society opened a school for boys and girls in the city, and teaching Christianity was a part of the syllabus here.[62] Similarly, a school was opened in Azamgarh district too. In 1835, the church missionary society started its activities in the field of education, health and religion. Mr. H. C. Tucker founded Wesley School in 1837 AD. The society took over its management in 1842. Mr. Tucker also started an Anglo-Vernacular school in Azamgarh.[63] In Banaras, a Bengali called Jai Narayan Ghoshal, whom the grapevine said Father Mr Curie of Banaras had almost converted to Christianity, opened a Jai Narayan College in 1825; English and The Bible were taught here. Here, an Anglo-Indian Seminary School was also established in 1830.[64] The Church Mission began its activities in Jaunpur and opened a school and hospital here.[65] In its educational institutions, prayers were said in line with Christianity, the Bible was taught, and such questions were asked in exams as could create a faith in Christianity.[66]

The missionaries' activities were not confined to educational institutions only. They began teaching Christianity in jails, too, to induce the prisoners to convert. Therefore, when there was a rumour at Banaras in 1852 that prisoners in the jail were going to be converted, people believed it to be true and rioted. The government had to use force to quell the disturbance.[67]

The Company Government too helped the missionaries to facilitate the process of conversion. It passed Act 21 in 1850 which gave a convert the right to inherit the paternal property.[68] Earlier, a Hindu or a Muslim was automatically deprived of his share in paternal property if s(he) converted to Christianity. The missionaries' allurements could not equal this loss, and more so for the upper caste people. This law was not going to benefit the Hindus or Muslims in any way. In this atmosphere of mistrust, the conservative Indian society viewed even the positive reformative steps of the government, like the ban on sati (1829) and recognition of a widow's right to remarry (1856), as an interference in religious matters. It was now gripped with the idea that various laws were part of the government's policy to facilitate conversion. From time to time the Company Government attempted to pass new laws in the name of modernisation of the army, like a ban on having a mark on one's forehead, keeping beards, wearing a turban, etc; instead, the government ordered the soldiers to wear a leather cap. It also required them to go abroad for a war. All this was linked to religion and the soldiers protested these moves, but they were suppressed by force. Despite the protests and injuring the soldiers' feelings, Lord Canning passed the General Army Enlistment Act in July 1856, which said that a person enlisting in the army could be sent anywhere for duty. If necessary, he could even be sent abroad by sea-route, and this posed a threat to the soldiers' religion. In sum, whether the Hindus or the Muslims, the entire Indian society now felt concerned about protecting their religion. In order to avoid conversion and to protect their religions, Hindus and Muslims united against the Company Government and took the path of rebellion.

The fear of proselytism remained even after the rebellion was crushed. In his narrative sent to W. Muir, Secretary to the Government of the North Western Provinces, for the week ending 22 January 1859, C. Wingfield, the Commissioner of Gorakhpur, wrote, "He (Khyrooddeen) thinks many more will come in and says, the fear of being made Christians, which, as I before mentioned, their leaders, with the view of keeping them together, have laboured to instill into them, alone deserve then. Strange to say, this impression is not entirely confined to the lower rank of the rebels, for several natives of respectability and intelligence have, in the course of conversation, let expressions, showing they thought it quite possible over government might make converts in this way."[69] In a letter sent during the revolt to Maharaja Jang Bahadur Rana, the Prime Minister of Nepal, Raja Debi Bakhsh Singh of Gonda had urged him to help Begum Hazrat Mahal against the English, in order to safeguard the religion.[70] Various other rebel leaders too had said that they were taking up arms to protect the religion.[71]

Soldiers of the Bengal Army had many grievances against the Company Government regarding salaries, allowances, promotions, maltreatment by the English officials, etc. But when they clearly perceived an attempt to defile their religion and proselytise them, in other words, to make them Christians, they felt shaken and took up arms in order to protect their religions. In 1856, Indian soldiers were given new Enfield rifles for use, in place of the earlier Brown Bess rifles, and the greased cartridges used in the former also came from England. Soon these cartridges were being manufactured in Calcutta, Dumdum and Meerut, Indian soldiers learnt at Dumdum that cows and pigs marrow was being used in these cartridges. For this reason, they were considered unfit for Hindus and Muslims, both. Before being loaded in a rifle, one had to bite these cartridges by teeth. The animal marrow defiled the religion of Hindus as well as Muslims.[72] Therefore, the suppressed discontent of the soldiers now flared up as a revolt.[73] On 29 March 1857, Mangal Pandey, a soldier of the 34th Native Infantry (NI) which was stationed at Barrackpore, and a resident of Ballia in Eastern Uttar Pradesh, staged a revolt and killed a European army officer. He was taken prisoner and tried. He was hanged to death on 8 April 1857 and the 34th NI was disbanded.[74] Earlier, on 26 February 1857, the 19th NI stationed at Behrampur was also disbanded for refusing to use the greased cartridges.[75] Most of the soldiers in these regiments hailed from Eastern Uttar Pradesh. It was thus natural that they returned home after these regiments were disbanded. The 17th NI was stationed in Gorakhpur and Azamgarh. Azamgarh was made its headquarters also. The recruitment and training of the 17th, 19th and 34th NI regiments were conducted together at Lucknow. Therefore, the soldiers of these regiments already had cordial relations. Hence, when dismissed soldiers of the 19th regiment came to the barracks of the 17th regiment, they were warmly welcomed. Because of the fear of unrest in the army there, the District Collector of Gorakhpur issued a proclamation that any 19th NI soldier found in the district would be arrested.[76] In brief, a revolt had already started in the Bengal Army on the greased cartridges issue and it had even started impacting the far-off Gorakhpur and Azamgarh districts.

Beginning of Rebellion in Eastern Uttar Pradesh

The 17th NI regiment was stationed in Gorakhpur and Azamgarh on 12 February 1857. Earlier, it was stationed in Delhi during 1853-54 and its Indian officials used to visit the Mughal court and make presentations to the Emperor. It was later shifted to Lucknow in 1854-55. At the time of the annexation of Awadh, the 17th, 19th and 34th NI regiments, stationed there, had offered their services to the Emperor of Awadh. The 17th NI was shifted to Kanpur in July 1856 and it remained there till October 1856. Subsequently, it was taken to Allahabad, Banaras and Azamgarh, and then brought to Gorakhpur. However, when most of the soldiers fell ill because of adverse climate, the regiment was sent back to Azamgarh. The responsibility of construction of new lines there, for its stationing, was entrusted to Subedar Bhondu Singh Yadav to be supervised by a committee. But in April 1857, when another Subedar, Bhola Upadhyaya, announced that he would publicly use the greased cartridges, he was promoted to Subedar Major. Moreover, Bhondu Singh was also divested of responsibility of the construction job. Most of the regiment's soldiers had already refused to use the greased cartridges. Such discriminatory acts of the Company Government motivated the 17th NI soldiers to revolt, and they did revolt under the leadership of Bhondu Singh Yadav on 3 June 1857.[77] In this way, in Eastern Uttar Pradesh, the 17th Regiment, stationed in Azamgarh, began the revolt under Subedar Bhondu Singh Yadav. Apart from Bhondu Singh Yadav, his son Ram Tahal and son-in-law Madho Ram too participated in the revolt.[78] When the news of army's revolt in Azamgarh reached the two companies of the 17th NI stationed in Gorakhpur, they too revolted.[79] However, before them, the zamindars of Paina village in Deoria tehsil of Gorakhpur district had already begun the rebellion on 31 May 1857, by looting the British boats laden with grains.[80]

Notes and References

1. Aitchison, C. U. (ed): *A Collection of Treaties, Engagements and Sanads Relating to India and the Neighbouring Countries*, Vol. 2 (Foreign and Political Department, Calcutta, 1863), p. 87; Mishra, Kamla Prasad, *Banaras in Transition, 1738-1795* (Munshi Ram Manohar Lal Publishers P. Ltd, New Delhi, 1975), p. 92; Rizvi, Syed Najmul Raza, *Atharahvin Sadi ke Zamindar* (Hindi, People's Publishing House, New Delhi, 1988), p. 24.
2. Mishra, Kamla Prasad, *op cit*, pp. 13, 15, 17.
3. Cohn, Bernard S., "Structural Change in Indian Rural Society (1595-1885)," in Robert Eric Frykenberg (ed.), *Land Control and Social Structure in Indian History* (first Indian edition: Manohar Publications, New Delhi, 1979), Table of p. 74.
4. *Ibid*, Tables, pp. 72-73.
5. Oldham, Wilton, *Tenant Rights and Auction Sales in Ghazeepoor and the Province of Benares* (printed for the author by John Falconer, 53, Upper Sackville Street, Dublin, (1873), p. 5.
6. *Ibid*, p. 6. By 1851-52, the number of buyers who got 280 estates in Ghazipur-Ballia through outright purchase or in auction was 280, of which 139 lived in cities, See, Robert Eric Frykenberg (ed.), *op. cit.* pp. 76-77.
7. *Ibid*, p. 6.
8. Taylor, Robert, *The Rebellion of 1857 in The Province of Benares, (Jaunpur, 15th October, 1858),* (printed at the Government Press, Allahabad), p. 12, para 27.
9. Aitchison, C. U, *op cit*, p. 61; Om Prakash (ed), *Gazetteer of India, Uttar Pradesh, District Gorakhpur* (printed at the Government Press, Allahabad), Lucknow, 1987, p. 32.
10. Husain, Imtiaz, *Land Revenue Policy in North India* (New Age Pvt. Publishers, Delhi), 1967, pp. 16, 60 and Conclusion; Rizvi, Syed Athar Abbas (ed), *Freedom*

Struggle in Uttar Pradesh (Publication Bureau, Information Department, Uttar Pradesh), Lucknow, 1957, Vol 1, pp. 150, 55.

11. Habib, Irfan, "Commemorating 1857: The role of the Bengal Army in the first war of independence", outlookindia.com; also see, Anderson Clare, "*The Indian uprising of 1857-58; Prisons, Prisoners & Rebellion*" (Anthem Press, London 2007) pp. 7-8.
12. Husain, Imtiaz, *op cit*, pp. 13-14; Bhargava, Meena, *State, Society and Ecology: Gorakhpur in Transition, 1750-1830* (Manohar Publishers and Distributors, New Delhi), 1999, pp. 28-29.
13. Rizvi, Syed Najmul Raza, *Zamindars and Revenue Farmers of Eastern Uttar Pradesh* (Anamika Publishers and Distributors, New Delhi), 2004, p. 161.
14. *Supplementary Notes and Statistics to Volume XXXI of the District Gazetteers of the United Provinces of Agra and Ouadh* (printed at the Government Press, Allahabad), 1909, District Gorakhpur, Appendix, Table IX, p. x.
15. Reid, J. R., *Report on the District of Azamgarh Compiled in Connection with the Completion of the Sixth Settlement* (NWP and Oudh Government Press, Allahabad), 1877, p. 175.
16. *Ibid*, p. 184.
17. Singh, Rejendra, *Land, Power and Peoples* (Sage Publications India P Ltd, New Delhi), 1988, p. 110.
18. Letter from Commissioner, Bihar and Benares, to Collector, Gorakhpur, 5 November 1819; Commissioner's Office Gorakhpur, *Revenue Records*, Vol. 7, File 9, Part I, Serial No. 12, pp. 63-64, preserved in Regional Archives, Allahabad. According to the description, a contract for gradual increase in land revenue over five years was made with a total of 1,284 estates, of which 1,029 were *taufir*, 99 were *nankar* and 156 were *panjsala* estates. They had to pay 33,393 rupees for Fasli 1229 (AD 1821).
19. Reid, J. R., *op cit,* pp. 197-98.
20. Letter from Gorakhpur Collectorate, 20 July 1836, Government of India, Home Proceedings, Revenue Department, Consultation, 14 October 1836, Consultation No. 6, 1836 (National Archives of India, New Delhi).
21. Husain, Imtiaz, *op cit*, p. 52; Bhargava, Meena, *op cit*, p. 197.
22. Bhargava, Meena, *op cit*, pp. 67-69.
23. *Ibid*, pp. 70-71.
24. *Ibid*, p. 71.
25. *Ibid*, pp. 72, 75, 85.
26. *Ibid*, p. 72.
27. *Ibid*.
28. *Ibid*, pp. 84-85; Nevill, H. R., *District Gazetteer Gorakhpur*, Vol. XXXI (Government Press, Allahabad), 1909, p. 19.
29. Bhargava, Meena, *op cit*, p. 148.
30. *Ibid*, p. 203.
31. *Pre-Mutiny Records*, Gorakhpur Collectorate, Bag No. 7, Revenue Letters Received, Series 1, Civil Court, Gorakhpur. Meer Riyasat Ali son of Raja

Zulfiqar Ali, Zamindar of Taluqa Shahpur in the Pargana of Dhuriyapar, 10 July 1807 (Regional Archives, Allahabad), pp. 170-74.

32. Nevill, H. R., *District Gazetteer Gorakhpur*, Vol. XXXI, 1909, p. 114; Pandey, Rajbali, *Gorakhpur Janpad aur Uski Kshatriya Jatiyon ka Itihas* (Thakur Mahatam Rao Publisher and Bookseller, Gorakhpur), V.S. 2003 (AD 1946), p. 280.
33. Pandey, Rajbali, *op cit*, p. 280.
34. Bhargava, Meena, *op cit*, pp. 181-82.
35. Reid, J. R., *op cit*, p. 193.
36. Bhargava, Meena, *op cit*, pp. 182-83.
37. Reid, J. R., *op cit*, p. 194. In Azamgarh district, only 81 *maafi* grants, with an area of 11,779 acres, were found legitimate, and of these, 56 were meant for the livelihood of one or two persons.
38. Bhargava, Meena, *op cit*, pp. 179-80.
39. The Company Government did not enact any act about the rights of ryots in the ceded districts (Gorakhpur and Azamgarh). The first law for the benefit of the ryots was promulgated in 1859. See Singh, Rajendra, *op cit*, pp. 112-13. In the Banaras Province which had Permanent Settlement, the self-cultivating ryots were given the occupancy right through Regulation 51 of 1795. But they could not get its benefits because of ignorance. Mishra, Kamala Prasad, *op cit*, pp. 91-97.
40. *Pre-Mutiny Records*, Commissioner's Office Gorakhpur, Vol. XVI, File No. 17, Serial No. 28, Enclosure in a Letter from the Collector of Gorakhpur to Revenue Department, 23 November 1822; Nevill, H. R., Gorakhpur *op cit*, p. 134; Singh, Rajendra, *op cit.*, pp. 102-03.
41. Thomson, J., *Report of the Ceded Portion of the District Commonly Called Chakla Azimgarh*, 16 December 1837 (printed at Government Press, Agra), para 93-96, p. 12; Stokes, Eric, "The Peasant and the Raj," in *Cambridge Economic History* (Cambridge University Press, New Delhi), 1978, pp. 195-96; Sen, Surendra Nath, Eighteen Fifty Seven (English) pp. 34-35.
42. Swinton, Alan, Officiating Commissioner of Gorakhpur, *Manual of the Statistics of the District of Goruckpore* (Dr J P Walker, Superintendent, Government Press, Allahabad), p. 7.
43. Sen, Surendra Nath, *Eighteen Fifty-Seven* (Publication Division, Ministry of Broadcasting and Information, Government of India, New Delhi), 1957, p. 36; Habib, Irfan, *op cit*, p. 41; Husain, Iqbal, The world of the Rebels of 1857, (Primus Books, Delhi) 2019, p. 57.
44. Husain, Iqbal, *Ibid,* p. 60.
45. Husain, Iqbal, *Ibid,* pp. 57-58.
46. *Ibid*, p. 56, J. Thomson too regarded the British laws as the biggest cause of the zamindars' resentment against the government. See Thomson, J., *op cit*, para 94, p. 12.
47. Nevill, H. R., (Gorakhpur-1909) *op cit*, p. 59.
48. Prakash, Om, (Gorakhpur-1909) *op cit*, p. 36.

49. Taylor, Robert, Officiating Joint Magistrate of Jaunpur, wrote in *The Rebellion of 1857 in the Province of Benares*, para 4, p. 7: "The city, always the most turbulent in India, was now more dangerous from the severity with which the high price of corn pressed on the poorer classes; the Poorbeah Sepoys now publicly called on their Gods to deliver them from the Feringhees". (Jounpoor, 15th October, 1858, Printed at the Government Press, Allahabad)
50. Datta, K. K., *Reflections of the Mutiny 1857-59* (University Press, Calcutta), 1967, p. 5.
51. Shah, Syed Ahmed Ali, *Kashful-Baghaavat, Gorakhpur*, [Urdu, Arifeen Press, Mirzapur, 1860], English transliteration and translation by Farhat Nasreen [Rupa Publications India P Ltd, New Delhi, 2010], Stanza No. 2226-2238, pp. 342-43.
52. Khan, Syed Ahmed, *Causes of the Indian Revolt* (Oxford University Press), 2006, p. 5.
53. Nash, J. T., *Volunteering in India* (George Philipp & Sons, London), 1893, p. 112.
54. Rizvi, Syed Athar Abbas, *op cit*, Vol. IV (Letter from Mohammed Hasan to Khyrooddeen, 24 October 1858), Lucknow, 1959, pp. 371-73, 390; Sen, Surendra Nath, *op cit*, pp. 388 (app II).
55. Rizvi, Syed Najmul Raza, "Some Little Known and Unknown Freedom Fighters of the War of Independence, 1857-58," *Proceedings of the Indian History Congress*, Kannur session, 2008-09, pp. 493-97.
56. On her escape, the Rani of Amorha had taken shelter in Faizabad. See, Home Department, Public Consultation, No. 91, 30 April 1858.
57. Singh, Phoolbadan, *Azamgarh ka Swadhinata Sangram* (Zila Swadhinata Sangram Sainik Sangh, Azamgarh), Part 1, 1974, p. 109.
58. Foreign Department, Political, 11 March 1859, No. 44-45; From C. Wingfield, Commissioner of Gorakhpur, to W Muir, Secretary to Government of North Western Provinces, p. 7.
59. *Ibid*, para 8, p. 3; Abul Kalam Azad, 9 February 1957; c.f. Sen, Surendra Nath, *op cit*, Preface, section 5 p. XIII.
60. *Ibid.*
61. Khan, Farha, *Christian-Muslim Encounters and Debates in Northern India, 1579-1857* (unpublished PhD thesis, University of Delhi, Delhi, 2014).
63. Nevill, H. R., *District Gazetter,* Gorakhpur 1909, pp. 104, 124; Swinton, Alan, *op cit*, p. 13. Anvil A Powell has given a description of the spread of London, Missionary Society's activities. See Powell, Anvil, A. Ann, *Muslims and Missionaries in Pre-Mutiny India* (Curzon Press Ltd, Richmond Surrey), 1993, p. 66.
63. Chick, Noah Alfred, *Annals of the Indian Rebellion, 1857-58*, Part IV, Aug 1859, (Saunders, Cones & Company, No. 23, Loll Bazar, Calcutta), 1859, pp. 368-69, Timothy Luther was school superintendent of Azamgarh in 1857.
64. Chandra, Moti, *Kashi ka Itihas* (Vishwavidyalaya Prakashan, Varanasi), 2003, p. 322.
65. Jaunpuri, Syed Iqbal Ahmed, *Sharqi Rajya Jaunpur ka Itihas* (Shiraz-e-Hind Prakashan Bhavan, Jaunpur), 1968, p. 799.

66. Khan, Syed Ahmed, *op cit*, p. 19.
67. Chandra, Moti, *op cit*, p. 289.
68. Sen, Surendra Nath, *op cit,* p. 12.
69. Foreign Department, Political, 11 March 1859, No. 46-48; From C. Wingfield, Commissioner of Goruckpore, to W Muir, Secretary to Government of North Western Provinces, para 5, p. 3 (preserved in National Archives of India, New Delhi). Regular sepoys too were afraid about conversion. See Rizvi, Syed Athar Abbas, *op cit*, Vol. IV, p. 321.
70. Foreign Department, Political, Consultation No. 75-77, 19 November, Abstract translation of a Letter from Raja Devi Bakhsh Singh Jabarjang to Maharaja Jang Bahadur Rana Ji, 19 September 1858 (National Archives of India, New Delhi).
71. The letters sent by Birjis Qadr, the Crown Prince of Awadh, to Maharaja Jang Bahadur Rana, the Prime Minister of Nepal, are examples. See Rana, Padma Jang Bahadur, *Life of Maharaja Sir Jang Bahadur* (Ratna Pustak Bhandar, Bibliothica, Himalayan Series, Kathmandu), second reprint, pp. 217-18; Rizvi, Syed Athar Abbas, *op cit*, Vol. IV, p. 302.
72. Sen, Surendra Nath, *op cit*, pp. 41-42, 44-45; Malleson, col. G B, *The Indian Mutiny of 1857* (Seeley and Co. Limited, Essex Street Strand, London, 1891) pp. 18-20; Ball, Charles, The History of Indian Mutiny, Vol. I, [The London Printing and publishing company Limited, London 1858], p.37; Holmes T.R.E, A History of Indian Mutiny, pp. 78-81, [W.H Allen & Co., Waterloo Place, London, 1883] Chick N.A, *op cit*. Part – I, May 1859, p. 30;

    The poem composed in Nepali language, "Lakhno ko Sawai" says:

    > "Gaee soogurko boswa haali kartos banayo
    > Daant le kartos chyaapi bandook bharayo,
    > Chaare varan chhattis jaat sab yakai garaayo,
    > Chhatri ra brahman tesai bela jaagyaa,
    > Jaati ko kura jhiki gul garn lagayaa"

    Translation—

    Cartridges were made with the animals (Cow and Pigs)' marrow; they forced the biting of cartridges by teeth to fill up the rifles. They mixed up the four varnas and thirty-six castes together. That was the time when the Kshatriyas and the Brahmins woke up. They raised the issue of caste and religion to create a hullabaloo.

    The poem was composed in V 1938, i.e. AD 1881, and was published in *Dhadingma Phela Pareka*, edited by Dinesh Raj Pant and published from Kathmandu in V 2061 (AD 2004). See p. 49 of the facsimile, publisher: Khilsharm-Rjiv Lochan Pratishthan, Raktkali, Kathmandu, Nepal.
73. "The greased cartridge was so powerful factor that it destroyed the loyalty of Sepoys." See Nash, J. T, *op cit*, pp. 101-103, 112.
74. Sen, Surendra Nath, *op cit*, pp. 49-50; Malleson, G B, *op cit*, pp. 53-56, 67; Ball, Charles, The History of Indian Mutiny *op cit*, pp. 45-47-50; Chick, N. A, *op cit*, pp. 63-67; Kaye's and Malleson's History of Indian Mutiny 1857 (edited by Malleson G.B.) Vol. I, Sir John Kaye, New Impression (Longmans Green and Co. 39, paternoster Row, London, 1898) Book III, chapter IV &V pp. 395-98, 402, 404; Holmes, T.R.E *op cit* pp. 84-86.

75. Sen, Surendra Nath, *op cit*, pp. 51; Moinuddin Hasan, *Khadang-e-Ghadar*, (Hindi translation: as 'Gadar' by Abdul Haq, Directorate of Hindi Medium Implementation, University of Delhi, Delhi), second edition, 2006, pp. 25-26; Malleson, G. B., *op cit pp. 55-57;* Ball, Charles, *op cit.* Vol. I, pp. 47-48*;* Chick, N. A, *op cit*, pp. 51, 52-53; According to G.W Forrest, 400 Brahmins and 150 Rajput soldiers of this regiment were sent back home, see, A History of Indian Mutiny, Vol. I. [William Blackwood and sons, London, MC MIV] p. 24; Also see, Kaye's and Malleson's History of Indian Mutiny 1857-58, Vol. I pp. 399-401; Holmes, T.R.E, *op cit*, pp. 85-86.
76. Volume 177, Bag No. 27, List No. 14, Letter Sent by Gorakhpur District Magistrate Paterson to officiating Commissioner Wynyard on 2 July 1857 (preserved in Regional Archives, Allahabad).
77. Rizvi, Syed Athar Abbas, *op cit*, Vol. IV, pp. 85-89; Letter from: F. W. Burroughs, Lt. Colonel Commanding 17th Regiment NI, 30th January, 1857, also see, Taylor, Robert, the Joint Magistrate of Jounpoor, dated 15 October 1858, *The Rebellion of 1857 in the Province of Benares*, para 19-23, pp. 10-11.
78. Rizvi, Syed Athar Abbas, o*p cit,* Vol. IV, p. 89.
79. Syed Ahmed Ali Shah wrote in *Kashful-Baghaavat, Gorakhpur*,

    "Yahaan ki bhi afwaaj baaghi huei I
    Shararat se apni woh daaghi hui II (Stanza-163)
    Azamgarh ka ahwaal usne suna; I (Stanza No. 165)
    Ke haakim se sab ne Baghaavat kiya II
    Luta maal-o-asbaad hukkam ka,
    Baghaavat ki dil mein samayee hawa II (Stanza No. 166)"
    [The armies here also rebelled.
    Due to their mischief they became spoiled. (Stanza No. 163)
    They heard of the condition of Azamgarh,
    Where all had rebelled against the rulers. (Stanza No. 165)
    Wealth and belongings of the rulers were looted.
    The idea of rebellion entered their hearts. (Stanza No. 166)]

    — (English Transliteration and Translation by Farhat Nasreen, stanza 163-66, p. 25)
80. Rizvi, Syed Athar Abbas, *op cit*, Vol. IV, p. 144; C. Wingfield (Commissioner of Goruckpore), Narrative of Events Attending the Outbreak of Disturbances and the Restoration of Authority in the District of Goruckpore, 5 July 1858, para 7, p. 2. (Printed at the Government Press, Allahabad).

Chapter - 2

Nature of the Revolt

The protracted debate among historians, writers, thinkers and politicians regarding the nature of the revolt of 1857 has now virtually come to the conclusion that it was a "popular revolt" and that it had a national character.[1] In other words, the "revolt of 1857" was a "national revolt of the people." Those who do not subscribe to this view say that it was not spread over the country, that all the sepoys did not stage a revolt, that all the social classes did not join it, etc.[2] Even today, to raise one's voice against an alien and autocratic power is not an easy task. Those benefitting from the regime endeavour to maintain the status quo, and use all their might for the purpose, while those seeking change lack enthusiasm. Various classes of society join a rebellion in view of the possibility of its success or failure, instead of the sanctity of its aims. Only a limited section of society is motivated by a strong sense of dedication and sacrifice. An analysis of the nature of the revolt ought to be made with such facts of human nature in view.

This regional level study endeavours to find out whether the people of only a particular religion or community staged the revolt in Eastern Uttar Pradesh. Whether all the classes and castes took part in it, more or less, or only a particular class or caste did so? What thinking motivated the participants of the revolt? Did they took up arms for personal interests, to get some problems or difficulties redressed, or did they want to achieve some higher aim? A study of the events that took place in Eastern Uttar Pradesh and of those who played an active role in it, makes the nature of the revolt in this region clear.

There is evidence to show that people from the lower to the higher classes of society, from the rank and file to the high-ups, took an active part in the revolt. When Hargovind Singh of Shahabad in Bihar, who belonged to the Rajput caste and had been a Hawaldar in the English Army, was arrested, he deposed before the Magistrate of Saran that "In Gorakhpur a fakir too has joined the rebels and makes wooden guns for them."[3] According to a report by C. Wingfield, the Commissioner of Gorakhpur, "While going to Nepal to arrange help for the rebels, the government there had arrested Damman Khan, along with two Gosain disciples (those who beg for alms) of Jaikishanpuri."[4] Those who guided the rebellion in Gorakhpur also included some pundits, as has been written by Shah Syed Ahmed Ali:

> *Musharraf-o-Pundit rahe Peshwa,*
> *Khataawaar yeh log hain barmala II (Stanza, 556)*
> *(Musharraf and Pandits were the guides,*
> *These people are conspicuously guilty).*[5]

Elsewhere, while taunting those who rebelled at the instigation of Maulvis and Pandits, he says:

> *Jo Mulla-o-Pundit ke dam mein Pade.*
> *Aql aur faham kya na rakhte rahe. (Stanza, 312)*
> *(Those who were duped by the boastfulness of Hindu and Muslim priests,*
> *Did they not possess any intellect and perception?)*[6]

The rebel sepoys who had run away from various regiments were scattered but were prepared to fight under anyone's leadership as they had a common aim. When Kunwar Singh reached Ayodhya in order to capture Azamgarh, he had with him 2,000 persons, of which 800 were soldiers. They too had come from different regiments.[7] But the strength of the rebel army soon swelled to ten thousand.[8] The Raja of Narharpur too accompanied him.

Nazim Mohammed Hasan, who was appointed chakladar of Gorakhpur district by the Awadh Government, was an outsider. He had no link with Gorakhpur. He had been the Nazim of Khairabad (in Sitapur district) and was managing some villages of his near Tanda (Faizabad) at the time of the revolt. However, when he came to Gorakhpur as the Nazim, all the rajas, zamindars and common people welcomed him.[9] With cooperation from the people, he recruited 25,000 soldiers and raised a big army. People of all castes, and particularly of the lower castes, joined his army in large numbers. In his work *Khadang-e-Ghadar* (*Arrow of the Rebellion*), Moinuddin Hasan wrote that "In his army he recruited the people of all the seven castes, e.g. cotton-carders, weavers, oil-pressers, betel-sellers."[10] There is evidence that Madho Ram, who was a potter by caste and a sepoy of Mohammed Hasan's army, was apprehended and given capital punishment. Earlier, he was a sepoy in the 18th NI which had revolted in Bareilly.[11] Similarly, we learn about Shiv Gulam Pandey, a soldier of Mohammed Hasan's army, who was apprehended and given 16 years of rigorous imprisonment (RI) while his belongings were attached.[12] In short, Mohammed Hasan's army was an army of the people.

On 31 May 1857, the zamindars of Paina village, located on the northern bank of Ghaghra River in Barhaj tehsil of district Deoria of today, looted the English boats laden with grains and plying in Ghaghra, and obstructed the river traffic, thus beginning a rebellion.[13] Next, on 6 June 1857, followers of the Raja of Narharpur (Chillupar) occupied Barhalganj, beat the policemen stationed there into fleeing, and released about 50 prisoners who were lodged in the jail there. They also captured the boats and blocked the Azamgarh Road.[14] It was the raja and his supporters who perpetrated these happenings. Similarly, villagers of Bansgaon too created chaos and disturbances.[15]

The most important event of revolt in Gorakhpur district (which included the Basti district of today) took place on 10 June1857 and witnessed full participation of the rural people. Mahua Dabar was a Muslim village in Nagar pargana of the present Basti district; cloths were printed here and were exported to Nepal. But the large-scale import of foreign textiles had pushed the indigenous textile industry into a crisis. People of this village were seething with anger against the Company Government because of the continuing fall in textile industry and trade. When a revolt took place in the Faizabad cantonment on 8 June 1857, this scared the English officers and on 9 June 1857, 22 of them boarded in three boats and proceeded through the river route for Danapur (Bihar) in order to save their lives. Some Indian sepoys were helping them. But they had not gone very far when some rebel soldiers spotted them, and they rained bullets upon the boats. The English then had to abandon the boats and run away. Seven of somehow reached Amorha and then went to Captainganj. But the Tehsildar of Captainganj expressed apprehension about their safety and did not send them to Basti; instead, he arranged their exit to Gaighat on the Ghaghra bank so that they could proceed to Danapur through the river route. He also deputed three musketeers for their safety. Also, he provided five mules for the journey and fifty rupees for expenses. But a musketeer called Ruda Khan misled and brought them to his village, Mahua Dabar, telling the villagers about those Englishmen. Incensed against the English rule, Muslim villagers of Mahua Dabar attacked the English officers and did six of them to death. Only one Sergeant Busher somehow escaped. On getting the news, the Company government appointed one Mr. Peppe (the grantee of a forest) as the Honorary Magistrate and sent him along with some soldiers to punish the culprits. Mr. Peppe got the village torched and began a drive to apprehend the culprits.[16] Nabba Khan, Saeed Khan, Umur Khan, Wazeer Khan, Jumman Khan, Sheikh Durab, Kullu Bheastee (water-carrier), Gurdar Khan, Jummoo Rungrez (dyer), Bhola Dafali (tambourine player), Sanaw Khan, Sheikh Kallan, Jafir Allee, Wafatee and Raja Khan were listed as the perpetrator of the event, while Nabba Khan and Saeed Khan were dubbed as the ring leaders.[17] Moreover, Gulab Khan, Gulzar Khan, Nihal Khan, Badlu Khan and Gheesa Khan were also tried for treason. On 9 February 1858, these five persons were sentenced to death and their properties too were attached.[18] The Mahua Dabar event was the biggest event of popular revolt in Eastern Uttar Pradesh. Ruda Khan who was a government musketeer to Bhola Dafali, Jummu Rangrez and Kallu Bhishti participated in this revolt and also most of the Sheikhs and Pathans of the village, participated in the revolt. People of many other villages too rose up publicly against the English. We learn from a letter of Mohammed Hasan that Colonel Lennox and his family too were under the siege of the rebels. Mohammed Hasan had himself saved their life by sending some persons for the purpose.[19] Common people who did not actively join the rebellion, stood against the English and were in favour of the rebels. The English realised this fact on various occasions. If some rajas and zamindars supported the English, their ryots heartily sided with the rebels. A proof came from Basti. When a troop of Bengal Yeomanry Cavalry reached Basti, the people feigned happiness over its arrival and displayed pseudo-sycophancy, but yet they could not conceal their sense of enmity, though Digambar Kunwari, the Rani of Basti, was siding with the Company Government. J.T. Nash wrote: "Our next halting ground was in the town of Buste, where the inhabitants—though with disguised sycophancy they pretended to be pleased with our arrival— could not hide from us their hostile looks, which seemed to express the truth that we were not welcome."[20]

The people of Bansi were indifferent to the English. C. Wingfield, the Commissioner of Gorakhpur, wrote in his narrative: "The Bansee Rajah does his best to make head against them, but half his people are cowed and the rest lukewarm in our quarrel."[21] The rajas of Gorakhpur who sided with the Company Government were in no good position. The Raja of Gopalpur was unable to defend himself and had to run away to take shelter in Azamgarh.[22] Similarly, the Raja of Bansi had to face pressures.[23] The Raja of Tamkuhi was in covert collusion with the rebels while the Raja of Majhauli did not have courage to take action against the rebels beyond protecting his own estate.[24] On the contrary, common people were involved in an armed struggle against these rajas. In village Tilji that fell in thana Bakhira under pargana Hasanpur-Maghar, a person called Wali Mohammed acted as the commander of 500 sepoys in the army of the Nazim of Gorakhpur, while Talib and Sultan acted as *jamadars* when they joined a raid against the Raja of Gopalpur. Joining hands with Wali, Talib and Sultan, Fazal and Badal rained bullets against Mr Peppe, the Honorary Magistrate, who had to run away to save his life. For this attack, these five were hanged to death.[25] Similarly, at Biskohar on the eastern border of Bansi estate, a group of common people led by Mendhu Khan was conducting rebellious activities against the raja. Along with 100 of his men, Mendhu Khan was killed in an encounter with the Company Government's army. He was also in touch with Mohammed Hasan, the Nazim of Gorakhpur. He was appointed Tehsildar of Bansi East and was asked to put to death the infidel *firangis* including Mr. Peppe.[26]

In the same way, along with his brother Lal Khan and two to three hundred supporters, Damman Khan, the jagirdar of Jhandanagar (present-day Krishnanagar in Nepal) was conducting rebel activities on the north-eastern border of Bansi. Begum Hazrat Mahal had appointed him the chakladar of Bansi. He too was in touch with Mohammed Hasan and was creating a lot of trouble in Bansi. He was along with the rebel army when it laid siege on Bansi. Eventually, he was taken prisoner by the Nepal Government's officials.[27] The area of Bansi was teeming with rebels as well as refugees who had come there for shelter. They were also in league with the local officials of Nepal. Thus, they would come out of the *terai* of Nepal, conduct subversive activities, and run back there when pressure was mounted against them. They were divided into several groups or factions, and numbered about 1,500.[28] Important rajas of Gorakhpur district, including the rajas of Satasi, Narharpur, Barhyapar, Shahpur, Nagar and Nichlaul, etc, and the Rani of Amorha openly participated in the rebellion. Similarly, the *babus* (younger brothers of a raja and their successors) of Pandeypar, Dumri, Tighra, Bhowapar, Rudhauli and Pipra enthusiastically participated in the rebellion.[29] The zamindars of Amorha openly declared allegiance to the Kingdom of Awadh and ended the Company rule there.[30] Those deprived of their *maafi* grants also rose against the Company rule. Their ryots too sided with them. On this basis, S B Chaudhuri wrote about the Gorakhpur division: "The character of the risings in this part of the country was the same as in Oudh, the chiefs and talukdars hoisting the flag of revolt."[31]

Like their rural counterparts, the urban people of Gorakhpur also played an active role in the rebellion. When Mohammed Hasan reached Gorakhpur (out of the city, on the other side of Rapti river) as the Nazim, the rich Muslim residents of the city welcomed him. On his part, he chose his officials from among the Muslim families of the city.[32] However, Shah Syed Ahmed Ali, caretaker of the Gorakhpur Imambada, who was a contemporary observer, was troubled by the rebels and was a supporter of the English, said the aristocrats of the city did not support the rebels. He wrote:

Kiya agarche afwaaz ne inhiraaf,
Rausa Magar yahaan ke the paak-o-saaf
(Though the armies did deviate,
The aristocrats of this place were clean and innocent).[33]

But this was not the truth. Shah Syed Ahmed Ali, who wanted to fight against the rebels on behalf of the English, did not find even a handful to support him, which he deeply rued. He wrote:

Agar thode se log hoowen shareek.
Abhi kardoon zalim ki haalat rakeek.
(If only a few people participate,
At this instance I would bring the brute to his knees).[34]

Kisi ne diya saath mera na Jab.
Saha dil hi par maine ranj-o-taab. II
(When no one accompanied me,
My heart was inflicted with pain and debility).[35]

According to Shah Syed Ahmed Ali, only the foolish and mean people joined the Nazim. He wrote:

Humare shahar ke jo naadaan the,
Woh masnui nazim se ja kar mile II
(Those who were the fools of my town
They joined hands with the fake Nazim).[36]

Bahut log kamzarf naukar rahe,
Kahan tak sharah uski raavi likhe.
(Many malicious people were servants,
How far of their details can the narrator write?)[37]

He has mentioned Sardar Ali Khan, the sons of Mirza Hasan Ali, and several other rebels.

Nay more, a number of employees of the Company Government also joined the rebels.[38]

When the rebellion broke out, only two companies of the 17th NI regiment were stationed in Gorakhpur district. They too rebelled when they heard about their regiment's rebellion in Azamgarh. Shah Syed Ahmed Ali has written:

> *Yahaan ki bhi afwaaj baaghi hui*
> *Shararat se apni woh daaghi hui. II*
> *(The armies here also rebelled.*
> *Dare to their-mischief they became soiled)*[39]
> *Yahaan par jo do company fauj thee,*
> *Bahut bhid se mauj dar mauj thee*
> *[The two company armies which were here,*
> *Were swarming in layers].*[40]

In other words, there were not many rebel soldiers in Gorakhpur district. Those coming from outside had taken shelter at various places according to their safety requirement and convenience and had joined the armies of different rebel leaders. Yet the number of rebels was not such that it could look like a "sepoy mutiny" in any part of the district. Everywhere, the rebel army had a large number of untrained and unarmed persons, devoid of guns or cannons. The rebel army could be called, at the best, a courageous crowd of people who were carrying their old, traditional weapons. As an example, on 29 October 1858, 2,500 rebels moved to launch an attack against Bansi but they did not have a single gun.[41] The army of the rebels, who were like an enthusiastic and courageous crowd, faced for a long time the trained and well-armed troops of the English and Gorkha armies through their tactics of guerrilla warfare. Government records do corroborate that the rebels had fewer soldiers and more of the common people. According to C. Wingfield, the Commissioner of Gorakhpur, the rebels numbered 2,500 in Bansi but they included only 200 soldiers.[42] Of the 2,000 rebels who had gathered in Domariaganj, only 600 were soldiers.[43] In May 1858, Mohammed Hasan had three to four thousand souls, of which, 1,000 were soldiers.[44] The rebel army, which faced the troops of Colonel Rowcroft, had about 15,000 rebels but the regular soldiers numbered only 4,000.[45] During the battle of Sohanpur village which lay between Majhauli and Mairwa (Bihar), the rebel army numbered four to five thousand, but only 1,000 or 1,200 of them were soldiers.[46] Gorakhpur Commissioner, C. Wingfield, tells us that after the rebellion, many of the rebels would settle in the Nepal *terai* after getting land from the government thereof or would come back. According to him, by 4 January 1859, 430 rebels had surrendered before various magistrates while a number of people had returned to their villages without informing anyone.[47] People of the Muslim villages in Bansi pargana, particularly those situated on the border of Utraula, who had worked as sepoys in large numbers, had returned to their villages. According to the tehsildar's estimate, they numbered somewhat less than 1,000.[48] They hailed from the same common mass. Territories to the north of Ghaghra, which adjoined the border of Nepal, were covered with thick forests. A number of common rebels had made this area their shelter, and even the government of that time, did not know about them. Therefore, in the report of C. Wingfield, also very few people were mentioned.

The western borders of Azamgarh and Jaunpur districts, situated to the south of the Ghaghra river, not only adjoined the territories of Awadh; a number of persons of these areas had their zamindaris in one another's territory. Moreover, residents of Azamgarh and Jaunpur had also been employees of the Awadh Government. It was therefore natural that the revolt of Awadh influenced them and, hence, they too joined the rebellion. In Azamgarh, however, it was the soldiers of the 17th NI regiment, stationed there, who started the rebellion under the leadership of Subedar Bhondu Singh Yadav. They looted the government treasury, containing seven lakh rupees that were being set to Banaras, near Rani ki Sarai. They returned to Azamgarh but then moved towards Faizabad with great pomp.[49] According to Shah Syed Ahmed Ali, the rebel soldiers moved towards Delhi after having looted eight lakh rupees. He wrote:

Azamgarh ka ahwaal aage suno,
Zara baaghiyon pe taassuf karo,
(Hear the news of Azamgarh now;
Pity the rebels a little).
Mukhaalif yahaan ka bhi lashkar hua,
Misaal-e-shutar woh bhi Dehli chala II
Woh jab aath lakh naqad-o-zar le chuke
Toh Seedhe woh Dehli ko raahi hue II
(The army of this place also became an adversary;
That too like a camel left for Delhi.
When they had taken eight lakhs (rupees) of cash and gold,
Then they straight away fled to Delhi).[50]

Inspired by the soldiers' rebellion, jail guards of Azamgarh also freed the prisoners and went to join the rebels. One of the writers has compared this event with the "Fall of Bastille" during the French Revolution.[51] As soon as the rebels had left and the English had run away to Ghazipur, incidents of loot increased in the villages close to Azamgarh. People of Sagri, Muhammadabad-Gohna, etc, began committing loot under the leadership of their zamindars.[52] At Sikandarpur, people stoned the tehsil office and jail.[53] Beni Madho, the Kurmi raja of Atraulia, and Madho Prasad Singh, a Palwar leader, jointly fought against the English.[54] When the English re-occupied Azamgarh city for some time, the people could not tolerate it. On 23 July 1857, under the leadership of Rajab Ali, some 400 persons of the city and its vicinity launched a daylight attack on Kotwali and captured it.[55] This too was a kind of popular revolt. Similarly, the zamindar of Pasipur village under Maharajganj thana, looted the *kothi* and warehouse of Goods Saheb, a *nilha* (indigo planter) Englishman. With the help from the people of Laharpar village, they also captured the carts which carried the things of military use, along with the bullocks.[56] Elsewhere, the people of Kokunda village destroyed the *nilha kothi*. A person called Phooli Singh, who worked there, took an active part in the loot and destruction.[57] This was a revolt of the rural masses.

As soon as the sepoy rebellion broke out in Azamgarh, people of the Rajput, Pathan and Nehran communities assumed leadership of the vandals and looters everywhere.[58] However, Palwar Rajputs played the most active role in the rebellious activities and became famous for it far and wide. About them, Shah Syed Ahmed Ali wrote:

Jo Palwaar ki qaum bigdi thi sab,
Uthani padi unko ranj-o-taab, II
(All those people of Palwar who had gone astray,
They had to bear sorrow and fatigue).[59]

Palwar Rajputs also braved the Gorkha troops. In Azamgarh district, according to the official data, 2,000 Rajkumars of Chandipur, 7,000 or 8,000 Palwars of Lohra, 1,200 soldiers of the Ghaghra area, and 1,200 irregular soldiers of Singramau joined the rebellion against the Company Government.[60] This rebellion burried the generations old enmity between the Rajkumars and Palwars, and they fought together against the English.[61] If we look upon the structure of the rebel army during some of the important battles, the common people always outnumbered the soldiers. On 16 July 1858, the rebels who captured the Koilsa tehsil office included 1,300 soldiers and 1,500 rural people. Subedar Kanhaiya Singh was leading this army.

Two maulvis, belonging to Tanda (Faizabad) and Belwa (Basti), accompanied them.[62] In Ghosi tehsil, the rebel army included 800 sepoys, 400 *sawars* (mounted soldiers) and 800 commoners. Seedha Singh was their commander.[63] Koilsa and Atraulia tehsils of Azamgarh district were teeming with rebels.[64] The district had four or five groups of rebels, each with 50 or 60 soldiers while the rest were the common people. Of these, Pargan Singh's group had the maximum strength — 200 soldiers and a large crowd of common people.[65] One of the groups was led by Ali Kareem of Patna, and its soldiers hailed mostly from Bhojpur.[66] At Mahul, a popular revolt took place under Raja Muzaffar Jehan.[67] Kunwar Singh received phenomenal mass support in Azamgarh. He stayed in Azamgarh for 35 days. Here, the people provided to his army everything of necessity.[68]

In Ghazipur, which lay to the east of Azamgarh and which included the Ballia district of today, attacks on the British supporters had begun on 6 June 1857. Here the most active role was of the zamindars whose estates had been auctioned during the Company rule. These displaced zamindars had their intimate contacts with their ryots intact, and the ryots valued their old masters more than the new zamindars. Therefore, the revolt of the displaced zamindars assumed the shape of a mass revolt, though this was not spread over the district. The revolt by Kunwar Singh of Jagdishpur (Arrah) all the more affected the eastern parts of the district. Ghazipur too had a centre for recruitments to the Bengal Army and a large number of the people in the district were in the army. Activities of rebel soldiers were witnessed here when the rebellion broke out. Moreover, the Indians working in the British-owned indigo and opium factories were also dissatisfied with their masters. Thus, most of the participants of rebel activities included displaced zamindars, peasants, sepoys, artisans and labourers, which made it a mass rebellion. Wilton Oldham has described in detail the displaced zamindars who joined the rebellion in Ghazipur, and his description was based on the official information. He wrote, "The ex-Zamindars of Chowra burned down an indigo factory, and sought to kill the manager, who narrowly escaped with his life. Oosea was long the headquarter of the rebels. The villagers of Barah procured cannon and fired on the steamers passing up and down the Ganges. The ex-Zamindars of Chit-Ferozpoor were so formidable that the military were with difficulty persuaded to advance on the villiage without a siege train. The ex-proprietors of Reotee were among the chief leaders of the rebellion in the district."[69] About the eastern part of Ghazipur, he said that even after the rebellion had been crushed, 20 declared rebels were living openly in just one village till a few years ago.[70] In a letter sent to J. Base, the Magistrate of Ghazipur, on 29 September 1858,

W. Brown, commander of St Mister Gunboat, Banaras, informed that a crowd of armed Muslims had taken shelter in the house of Nishan Khan in village Bara, and that they were chased away and some of their arms were captured.[71] This was a crowd of rebels. Earlier, on 22 September, Mr. Brown had informed Base that the zamindar of Bara had captured all the boats in his area and would not allow them to go to the other side of the river. He also said that Bara village was then packed with ruffians (rebels).[72] The Village of Chit Baragaon too had openly rebelled,[73] as the surrounding area had done.[74] Gahmar, a renowned village of Ghazipur district, had also rebelled. People of this village, which was situated to the west of Buxar, by a railway line, heartily supported the rebels. They committed plunder in the company of about 300 rebels and arsoned all the movable and immovable properties.[75] In his Oath on 3 July 1858, Robert Smith Coombs wrote that, at Gahmar, on 4 June 1858, the rebels had burnt his residence and indigo factory to ashes. On 5 June, the rebels reached Sewari village, four miles to the west of Gahmar, and from there sent a team which put afire his factory in Bhadaura, though it suffered only partial destruction. Numberdars and zamindars, whose numbers were not known, joined the rebel soldiers in this matter. On the same date, rebels put afire Roniwan's factory in pargana Chausa.[76] According to Robert Taylor's narrative, rebels attacked Mr Matthew in Chaura village on 21 June. Though he managed to escape to safety, his factory and other properties were plundered and arsoned.[77] Mengar Singh or Maghar Singh of Gahmar village played an important role in rebel activities. He collaborated with Amar Singh, a brother of Kunwar Singh, and remained with him in Nepal as well. The Company Government had declared an award for his capture. When he was arrested, he accepted his role before the English rulers.[78]

In Ballia too, rural people joined hands with the soldiers for the rebellion. About four to five hundred sepoys and villagers of nearby areas joined the rebellion in Ballia and Rasra, as did more than 150 soldiers, discontented zamindars and villagers in Zamania.[79] In Ballia, when a rebel soldier was captured in a village, the villagers rushed forward to his help and got him forcibly rescued.[80] People of Maniar village in Bansdih tehsil provided much help to Kunwar Singh. Robert Davis, the Acting Magistrate of Azamgarh, wrote to Mr Gubbins, the Commissioner of Banaras, that "At Maniar, Kunwar Singh found himself amongst friends, and the wants of his troops were voluntarily supplied by the villagers who were almost universally in his favour. Through their collusion, our spies were seized and detained, and our information delayed."[81] Similarly, in Ghazipur, the

Babus of Shivpur not only organised a feast in honour of Kunwar Singh but also made 20 boats available to take his army across the Ganges.[82]

Sikh soldiers of the Ludhiana Regiment, stationed in Jaunpur district, revolted by default on 5 June 1857, on the basis of some rumour. But they moved towards Lucknow after they had looted the treasury and weapons and played no further role in the revolt in the district. Even then, the British fled to Banaras and left the city vulnerable to plunder. Thus, the people's feelings against the Company Government came to the fore. From the statement of Mr Matthew, an indigo planter, we come to know that the Hindu and Muslim servants in his employment not only looted him but even joined the rebels. For example, a servant called Harnandan Singh joined the army of Raja Iradat Jehan of Mubarakpur, while Jatan Singh joined the group of famous Amar Singh.[83] During the revolt, Amar Singh, who was a commander in the army of Raja Iradat Jehan, was killed by the English along with 50 of his men.[84] Amar Singh's son, Janki Singh, too attacked Mr Matthew, the indigo plantation owner, along with 400 of his men.[85] Raghuvanshi Rajputs of Dobhi taluka raised the banner of revolt against the English and fought against them with arms. Their leaders and prominent supporters were killed in this fight.[86] Many of the rajas and taluqadars of Jaunpur district forged contacts with the people of Awadh and gave momentum to their rebellious activities. According to the telegraphic information of November 1857, the number of rebels at the border of Jaunpur had swelled up to 20,000.[87] Raja Iradat Jehan of Mubarakpur declared Raja Beni Madho Singh the Nazim and himself the Naib (Deputy) Nazim of Jaunpur and Azamgarh. He was accorded this position by the Awadh government,[88] which was an open challenge to the Company Government. After Iradat Jehan, his son, Muzaffar Jehan, too took the path of revolt.[89] He recruited the Rajkumar Rajputs and Sheikhzadas in his army in large numbers.[90] The armies of both these leaders had large number of Hindus and Muslims who belonged to various classes of the society. Thus, the armies which they led were a people's army for rebellion. Besides, with cooperation from their collaborators and the rural people, Zamindar Jogeshwar Bakhsh of Badlapur, his brother Arjun Singh,[91] Sangram Singh of Mariahu[92] and Drigpal Singh of Badshahpur[93] gave a tough fight to the Company Government. In this territory, untrained common people were preponderant in the army of the Awadh people as well. Ghulam Husain, the son of Mohammed Hasan, the Nazim of Gorakhpur, came to Badlapur (Jaunpur) with four to five thousand persons, but soldiers numbered less than one-fourth of it.[94] Similarly, Khudabakhsh, the chakladar of Jaunpur, had about 2,000 persons but these included only 200 soldiers 40 Sawars.[95]

The rest were the common people who were moved by the feeling of fighting against the British. Moreover, Bhairo Prasad and Ishwari Prasad, two *mahajans* (bankers) who were active in Banaras and Jaunpur, were caught using their couriers to clandestinely send information to the rebels and were punished.[96] This shows the increasing role of various sections of society in the rebellion.

Symptoms of mass rebellion were visible in Mirzapur district after the news of revolt reached there on 6 June. Rajputs of Akodi village announced an attack on the Mirzapur city.[97] Gaura village on the right bank of the Ganges became the centre of the rebels.[98] Village Ramnagar Sikri became another similar centre of the rebels.[99] At Bhadohi on the left bank of the Ganges, Udwant Singh, leader of the Mona Rajputs, assumed the title of 'Raja' and began to run a parallel government. He appointed two Diwans and began to collect the revenue. His force took the Grand Trunk Road in control and closed the traffic. British Government sent an army against him. A representative of the Raja of Banaras arrested him by deceit and handed him over to the British who hanged him to death. Joint Magistrate Mr. Moore was given the credit for it. But the wife (Rani) of Udwant Singh announced an award of 300 rupees on Mr. Moore's head. A more than 300 strong group of Mona Rajputs, led by Jhuri Singh, killed Moore and thus avenged the execution of their "raja."[100] Munai, a scheduled castes person of Palipur village, had taken the severed head of Mr. Moore to the Rani.[101] Jhuri Singh's group conducted its rebellious activities not in Mirzapur alone but in Jaunpur as well.[102] The Company Government had announced a reward for whoever assisted in Jhuri Singh's arrest, but he was not apprehended till the end and died a natural death.[103] Jhuri Singh was the most active and popular hero of his area, and the popular memory and folksongs of the region are full of unmixed praise for him.

At Banaras, the British officials were well aware of the mass discontent against the Company Government.[104] Hence, on 4 June, they decided to ask the sepoys of the 37th NI to lay down their arms, which revealed the sepoy's opposition. Because of confusion, Sikh soldiers of Ludhiana took up arms against the British at Banaras, but the government managed to pacify them soon.[105] The revolt spread all over the district even though it had been crushed in the cantt and the sepoys had run away. The Company Government took harsh measures to crush the rebels.[106] Though no mention worthy event took place in Banaras because of the constant presence of British soldiers,[107] the British endeavour to divide the Hindus and Muslims failed. By clandestinely helping the rebels, both the communities showed that the rebellion was against the British rule.

What was the aim of the rebels? To find an answer to it is difficult as no rebel's diary, memoir or statement from this area is available. Yet their intentions can well be gauged. On 11 May 1857, the rebel soldiers of Meerut reached Delhi, declared Bahadur Shah Zafar to be the country's ruler, and formed a national government there. In other words, they ended the rule of the Company Government and formed a national government under the Emperor's leadership. Thus, they offered an alternative to the Bengal Army's soldiers, which all the sepoys accepted. In Awadh also, the rebel officers said that they would accept Birjis Qadr, (the son of Begum Hazrat Mahal), as the "wali" (heir apparent) only if he declared allegiance to the Mughal Emperor.[108] Rebellious soldiers at various places were moving towards Delhi only to fight for the national government formed there. In Eastern Uttar Pradesh, the 17th NI regiment of Azamgarh was the first to revolt. After looting the government treasury, these soldiers did not go home but moved towards Delhi; as Shah Syed Ahmed Ali too has written, "Toh Seedhe woh Dehli ko raahi hue I (Stanza 114) (they left directly for Delhi)."[109] Maulvi Sarfaraz Ali of Gorakhpur too motivated Bakht Khan to go to Delhi.

Mazzini, the great patriot and revolutionary of Italy says, "Wherever our flag flies, that is our capital. The capital must follow the Revolution and not vice-versa."[110] All the rebel leaders followed this maxim of Mazzini. Hence, when Kunwar Singh left Jagdishpur (Arrah), Delhi was his destination, as he knew the final settlement of the struggle would take place in North India only. He, however, received the news of Delhi's fall when he reached Banda. Hence the only aim of the rebels now was to defend Lucknow, the capital of Awadh, which was now their strongest post. Bakht Khan and Maulvi Sarfaraz Ali of Gorakhpur, etc, came from Delhi to Lucknow along with their soldiers and followers. Kunwar Singh too came to Lucknow via Kalpi and Kanpur. There, Birjis Qadr, the heir apparent of Awadh, honoured them and entrusted the task of recapturing Azamgarh. If Kunwar Singh received the support and cooperation of Raja Devi Bakhsh Singh of Gonda and Raja Har Prasad Mall of Narharpur (Gorakhpur), it was only because he had joined the war from the Awadh side. These people did not support any of their kins but those fighting for the independence of Awadh. If Mehdi Hasan Khan or Ghulam Husain Khan of Awadh or Prithvi Pal Singh, the Palwar leader of Tighra, attacked Jaunpur or Azamgarh, it was actually aimed to strengthen the rebellion in Awadh. If Raja Iradat Khan of Mahul accepted the post of Naib Nazim and if Beni Madhav, the Kurmi leader of Atraulia, accepted the post of Nazim, and if they declared allegiance to the Government of Awadh, this too was for fighting for Awadh. Palwar leader Madho Prasad and Pargan Singh too fought to defend this last outpost of independence. In a letter, Mohammed Hasan, the Nazim of Gorakhpur, talked till the end about returning the kingdom of Awadh to its legitimate ruler.

From the very beginning, Maulvi Sarfaraz Ali[111] of Gorakhpur intended to end the British rule. He also knew that this aim was impossible to achieve without an armed struggle, and that this needed soldiers. Hence, he preferred to deliver his *wa'iz* (religious sermons) in army cantonments. He delivered *wa'iz* to the soldiers of the Sagauli Cantt on the Nepal border and began to take influential Muslims of *terai* region on the Indo-Nepal border as his *murids* (disciples). Damman Khan, the jagirdar of Jhandanagar, was the most prominent among them. In the Sagauli Cantt. Ghulam Mohammed Khan and Ghulam Imam Khan of Shahjehanpur were among his disciples. With them he went to Shahjehanpur[112] and continued to deliver his sermons there for the Rohilla Pathans. He was a quite influential orator. A number of soldiers used to listen his sermons. He was in fact mobilising public opinion against the British. Both Hindus and Muslims came to the gatherings which he addressed. Historians have mentioned the secret meeting which took place at the house of Maulvi Mazhar Kareem in Shahjehanpur on 1 May 1857. Nizam Ali Khan, Qudrat Ali Khan, Abdul Rauf Khan, Sheetal Singh, Daulat Rai, Kalka Prasad, Ghanshyam Singh etc. joined this meeting.[113] While addressing the gathering, Maulvi Sarfaraz Ali asked the people, "Should these Britishers continue to be our Lords? Swear by Rasul Allah (Prophet), they should not be allowed to defile our country any more. I have come here to devise a strategy for this....Just think what tools they used to capture this country? They were Indian soldiers who won this country for them, and now, by swear of the sword of Ali (Ali ki Talwar ki Kasam), this very group will ensure their destruction....How can you forget that our brave countrymen repeatedly defeated them in Malabar and Hind, Kabul and Punjab and Insha-Allah, this will happen again here also. O Brothers… Our religion is in danger. After loosing our country and self-respect, are we going to loose our religion also? At the end he asked them that, "The century of the battle of Plassy is coming. Do, I declare, with the consent of all of you, that on the very day, Kaafirs will be sent out of this country?" To this, peoples responded, "Even before that"."[114]

It was after listening to Maulvi Sarfaraz Ali's sermons in a mosque that Bakht Khan turned into a rebel[115] and, in company with Maulvi Sarfaraz Ali, he took an army to Delhi. Along with prominent maulvis of Delhi, Maulvi Sarfaraz Ali too signed the edict which was issued against the English from Delhi. After the fall of Delhi, he returned to Lucknow along with Bakht Khan. Here he continued to organise the rebels. Even after the fall of Lucknow, he remained active along with rebel leaders on the Nepal border. He continued his efforts to solicit help for the rebels from the Nepal Government,[116] and, finally, along with Begum Hazrat Mahal, he went to Kathmandu where he died.[117]

Activities of Maulvi Sarfaraz Ali show that the people of Eastern Uttar Pradesh did have a wide horizon. Maulvi Sarfaraz Ali was working for a nationwide revolt and endeavoured for it till the end. It is not possible to accept Dr R.C. Mazumdar's opinion about Maulvi Sarfaraz Ali.[118] One may well concede that there is no proof about what he used to say in his sermons. But it was not without reason that the British Government continued to search out Maulvi Sarfaraz Ali in Nepal; Indeed, it had taken him to be a dangerous figure because of his rebellious activities.[119] Maulvi Sarfaraz Ali was definitely working in a national perspective.

Maulvi Sarfaraz Ali of Gorakhpur, the Purabiya soldiers of the Bengal Army, many persons of Awadh and Eastern Uttar Pradesh who were working in administrative positions, the rajas, taluqdars, zamindars, workers, peasants, artisans, mendicants, people of all castes, viz, the Brahmins, Kshatriyas, Vaishyas, Shudras, Syeds, Pathans, weavers, dyers, etc. and even women — all were striving to end the Company Government. After the fall of Delhi, they fought till the end to defend Awadh which was the last bastion of the rebellion. They welcomed all sorts of punishment including life imprisonment and execution or led the life of self-exiles. Even the life of those who had escaped to Nepal for safety was not happy either. They did all this to achieve a larger goal. Thus, it was indeed a mass revolt. To Lord Canning, recapturing Delhi and Lucknow was an urgent necessity. After the fall of Delhi, conquering Awadh became top priority for the British Government. But the rebel world of Eastern Uttar Pradesh remained the biggest obstacle to this goal.

Notes and References

1. Many of the British officials, writers and historians like Sir John William Kaye, Colonel G.B. Malleson, Lawrence, Charles Raikes, G.W. Forrest, T.R.E. Holmes, Charles Ball, N.A. Chick etc as well as Indian authors described the revolt of 1857 as a 'sepoy mutiny'; Sir John Seeley even described the revolt as 'Wholly unpatriotic and selfish ... with no native leadership and no popular support." He further maintains, that it was a rebellion of the Indian sepoy. See the article by Talmeez Khaldun in Joshi P.C. (ed.), "Rebellion; 1857" New Delhi; National Book Trust, Reprint: 2013, p. 3; Sir Syed Ahmed Khan and many Bengali historians like Rajni Kant Gupta, Shambhu Chandra Mukherjee and Kishori Chand Mitra etc too described it as a 'Sepoy Mutiny'; R.C. Majumdar expressed a radically different view. He wrote that the so called first national war of

independence in 1857 is neither first, nor national, nor a war of independence; see "History of freedom Movement in India" Second revised edition, Calcutta - 1971, p. 225. But Benjamin Disraeli, a statesman, had said in the British parliament during the revolt itself, "A mere military mutiny may be met by mere military effort, but if, on the contrary, what we have to deal with an insurrection favoured by the great mass of the population, our measures must, as I think, be both in nature and degree different from those of which we have had an intention from Her Majesty's Government. He further said that, "Looking upon this as a national revolt.....I cannot arrive at a belief that the measures announced by the Government merely military, are adequate to the occasion." See, Rizvi, Syed Athar Abbas, *Freedom Struggle in Uttar Pradesh*, Vol. I, Lucknow: Information Department, Uttar Pradesh, 1957, pp. 486-88. Drawing attention to the number of armed people (rebels) and spread of the rebellion over a wide area, Disraeli had in those very days described it as a nationwide struggle in a sense. See *Ibid*, pp. 487-88 (now onward referred to as *FSUP*). Karl Marx too described it as a national revolt. On July 1857 he quoted with approval Disraeli's remark on the previous day, "the Indian disturbance is not a military mutiny, but a national revolt. On July 31, 1857, Marx asserted that 'what John Bull considers to be military mutiny is, in truth, a national revolt.' See, "Marx and Engels on 1857 Revolt", by Sushodhan Sarkar, Monday 14th May 2007, Mainstream Weekly, Vol XIV, No 21; New York Daily Tribune August 1857. (transcribed by Tony Brown); Marx Engels, "The First Indian War of Independence, 1857-59" (Progress Publishers, Moscow) p. 47, Newyork Daily Tribune No. 5091 of August 14, 1857; Husain, Iqbal, "Karl Marx on India," New Delhi: Tulika Books, for Aligarh Historians Society, p. 70 Aligarh, 2006. In 1909, Vinayak Damodar Savarkar was the first Indian who described it as the "War of Independence." He wrote in his introduction, that "I found to my great surprise the brilliance of a war of independence shinning in 'the mutiny of 1857'. See, Savarkar, Vinayak Damodar, *The Indian War of Independence of 1857,* (London, 1909, Introduction p. VII, Columbia University Libraries Digital Collections); National Leaders like Jawahar Lal Nehru and Asoka Mehta also called it a War of Independence. Jawahar Lal Nehru wrote that "It was much more than a military mutiny and it spread rapidly and assumed the character of a popular rebellion and a war of Indian independence." [The Discovery of India, Sixth Impression Oxford University Press, Oxford Delhi, 1994] p. 323; According to Asoka Mehta, "1857 was therefore no sepoy mutiny. It was a grim war of independence, worthy of our best traditions and deserving of our homage". See, Asoka Mehta, "1857: The Great Rebellion", (Hind Kitabs, 1946); pp. 37-38. In his conclusion he wrote that ".... The rebellion of 1857 was more than a mere sepoy mutiny, was an eruption of the social volcano where in many pent-up forces found vent." (See, p. 67); Not only Indians but some British writers also accepted the revolt of 1857 as a people rebellion. John Bruce Norton regarded the uprising as a rebellion of the people rather than a merely a mutiny of the soldier, see, John Bruce Norton, "The Rebellion in India" [Richardson Brothers, 23 Cornhill, E.C. London, 1857]. Surendra Nath Sen (*Eighteen Fifty Seven*, New Delhi: Government of India), and Tarachand (*History of Freedom Movement in India*, Vol. I, Government of India, New Delhi, 1961) describe it as a war of independence. Pakistani historian Syed Moinul Haq (*The Great Revolution of*

1857, Karachi: Pakistan Historical Society, 1968) described it as a "great revolution; Sashi Bhusan Chaudhuri, *Civil Rebellion in Indian Mutinies, 1857-59*, (The World Press Private Ltd. Calcutta 1957) and, Theories of Indian Mutiny (1857-59), (The World Press Private Ltd. Calcutta 1965) described it as a 'freedom struggle'. Rudrangshu Mukherjee, in his book '*Awadh in Revolt*' (Oxford University Press, New Delhi, 1984), studied the revolt in Awadh only. He considered it as a "Popular resistance" i.e. 'People's Revolt'. Arguments about a conspiracy to restore the Mughal rule, a feudal revolt or a "peasant revolt," have all been thoroughly rejected by now. In October 2006, the speaker of the Lok Sabha, Somnath Chatterjee said, "what the British sought to describe as a mere sepoy mutiny was a India's First War of Independence in a very true sense, when people from all walks of life, irrespective of their caste, creed, religion and language rose against the British rule". See, ICHR News Letter. "The glorious example of the heroes of 1857, By D.N. Tripathi, (May 09, 2007, Rediff.com); The events that took place in the limited region of Uttar Pradesh fully corroborate Somnath Chatterjee's contention.

2. *Anbhai Sancha*, (Joint number. July – December, 2007; Guest Editor; Singh, Murali Manohar Prasad; Published by Madhu Prasad, Delhi), pp. 51-52.
3. Home Department (Public), Fort William, 11 June 1858, Deposition of Sepoy Hargovind Singh (preserved in National Archives of India, New Delhi), pp. 55-56.
4. Rizvi, Syed Athar Abbas, *FSUP*, Vol. IV, p. 350. (Hereafter, mentioned as *FSUP*, Vol. IV); The Gosain of Tolia was honoured by Mohammed Hasan. See *Kashful Baghaavat, Gorakhpur*; (transliteration and translation by Farhat Nasreen) Stanza no. 1248, p. 191. (Hereafter mentioned as to *Kashful Baghaavat, Gorakhpur)*
5. *Kashful Baghaavat, Gorakhpur,* Stanza No. 556, p. 88.
6. *Ibid,* Stanza no. 312, p. 50.
7. Home Department, Public Proceedings, Fort William, 11 June 1858, pp. 53-56; Rizvi, Syed Athar Abbas, *FSUP*, Vol. IV, p. 436.
8. *FSUP*, Vol. IV, *op cit*, p. 436.
9. Haider, Kamaluddin, *Qaiser-ut-Tawarikh*, Vol. 2, (Lucknow: Nawal Kishore Press, 1896), p. 304; Hasan, Moinuddin, *Khadang-e-Ghadar*, (Hindi translation: Abdul Haq, University of Delhi, reprint 2006), pp. 73-74; *FSUP*, Vol. IV, *op cit*, pp. 371-73, 157.
10. Hasan, Moinuddin, *op cit*, (English translation by H. A. Qureshi, Lucknow, 2007), p. 90. Defeated by the Nepalese army, the lower caste people of Mohammed Hasan's army ran away. The author of *Khadang-e-Ghadar* (p. 137) wrote:

    "Julahe, Dhuniye the, kahin the Chamar, Unhe bhagne mein hain kis tarah zor"

    (Here were weavers, carders, there were cobblers; what strength they have got to run away) (Hindi translation: p. 74; English translation: p. 90). The statement shows the high-low feelings prevalent in those days, though people of other castes too had run away from the battlefield. Lack of training was the basic cause of this army's defeat. The truth is that Mohammed Hasan's army was a people's army, but it was not more than five to six thousand. See *FSUP*, Vol. IV, p. 385; Haq, Syed Moinul, *op cit*, p. 454, FN 3.

11. *Pre-Mutiny Records*, Gorakhpur Collectorate, List No. 14, Vol. 177, Bag No. 27, Letters Issued to the Magistrate (January 1855 to 1858), p. 58; Weekly Report of the Proceedings of the Special Commissioner under Act XIV of 1857, for Zilla Gorakhpur, ending with 31 July, Mr. Burton, Special Commissioner; preserved in Regional Archives, Allahabad.
12. *Pre-Mutiny Records*, Gorakhpur Collectorate, List No. 14, Vol. 177, Bag No. 27, p. 26.58; Weekly Report of the Proceedings of the Special Commissioner under Acts XIV and XXI of 1857, for Zilla Gorakhpur, ending with 27 February 1858, Camp: Basti, C. Wingfield, Commissioner, preserved in Regional Archives, Allahabad.
13. Wingfield, C, Commissioner of Goruckpore, to William Muir, Secretary to Government, North West Provinces, 5 July 1858; *Narrative of Events Attending the Outbreak of Disturbances and Restoration of Authority in the District of Goruckpore in 1857-58*, No. 196 of 1858, para 7, p. 2 (now onward, *Narrative of Events*); *FSUP*, Vol. IV, p. 150. There were 600 warriors in village Paina and they continued their rebellion for two months. See *Ibid.,* p. 342.
14. Wingfield, C, *Narrative of Events*, 5 July 1858, para 7, p. 2.
15. *FSUP*, Vol. IV, *op cit,* pp. 160-62.
16. Foreign Department, Secret Consultation No. 199, 26 March 1858; from C. Wingfield to Lt Colonel Strachey, Secretary to the Government of Central Provinces, Allahabad, pp. 7-9; Foreign Department Political 1859, Consultation No. 60-62, KW, 27 May; Copy of the Statement of Sergeant Busher, 29 June 1857, Ghazipur, preserved in Regional Archives, Allahabad, pp. 27-41; Savarkar, V D, *op cit*, 2011 reprint, pp. 206-07; *FSUP*, Vol. IV, p. 146; Wingfield, C, *Narrative of Events*, para 13, p. 2; Ball, Charles, *op cit*, Vol. 1, pp. 398-401, Chick N.A, *op.cit,* pp. 471-77.
17. *Mutiny Records*, Gorakhpur, Vol. 192, 1857 and 1858, preserved in Regional Archives, Allahabad, p. 5.
18. *Pre-Mutiny Records*, Gorakhpur Collectorate, List No. 14, Vol. 177, Bag No. 27, Letters Issued to the Magistrate (January 1855 to April 1858); Weekly Report of the Proceedings of the Special Commissioner under Acts XI, XIV and XVI of 1857, for Zilla Gorakhpur, ending with 19 February 1857, Camp: Basti, 19 February 1858; preserved in Regional Archives, Allahabad.
19. Rizvi, Syed Athar Abbas, *FSUP*, Vol. IV, p. 371. (I immediately sent 10 of my sepoys to protect the boat from the country people who were all in rebellion.) Ball, Charles, *op cit,* Vol. I, p. 393.
20. Nash, J. T, *Volunteering in India*, London, 1893, p. 42.
21. Rizvi, Syed Athar Abbas, *FSUP*, Vol. IV, p. 343.
22. Wingfield, C, *Narrative of Events*, 5 July 1858, para 32 and 41, pp. 4-5. One of the many letters captured from the palanquin of Mohammed Hasan was of Krishna Kishore Chandra, the Raja of Gopalpur, in which he had expressed his willingness to obey the rebel Nazim. See *FSUP*, Vol. IV, Letter No. 19, p. 380.
23. Wingfield, C, *Narrative of Events*, 5 July 1858, para 42, pp. 5-6. The Raja of Bansi was, personally, a coward and had no courage to revolt or to face the rebels. See *FSUP*, Vol. IV, p. 356. Though Digambar Kunwari, the Rani of Basti,

sided with the British, she did not want to fight against the rebel Nazim. See *ibid*, p. 381.

24. Wingfield, C, *Narrative of Events*, 5 July 1858, para 49-50, p. 6.
25. *Pre-Mutiny Records*, Gorakhpur Collectorate, List No. 14, Vol. 177, Bag No. 27, p. 58; Weekly Report of the Proceedings of the Special Commissioner under Act XIV, for Zilla Gorakhpur, Ending with 22 January 1858.
26. *FSUP*, Vol. IV, pp. 359, 397.
27. *Ibid*, pp. 345, 347, 350-51; Foreign Department, 1858-59, No.13 of 1858 from C. Wingfield, Commissioner of Goruckpore, to G.P. Edmunston, Secretary to the government of India, dated 27 November 1858, para no. 5, pp. 6-7; Foreign Department, 1858-59, No.1 in a letter from Assistant and the in-charge of Nepal Residency, dated 11 December, 1858, copy of the resume in the case of Damman Khan forwarded by Mr. Wingfield C, Commissioner of Goruckpore, pp. 10-18 (preserved in National Archives of India, New Delhi).
28. *FSUP*, Vol. IV, p. 343.
29. Wingfield, C, *Narrative of Events*, 5 July 1858, para 38, p. 5; *FSUP*, Vol. IV, p. 157.
30. *FSUP*, Vol. IV, p. 152.
31. Chaudhuri, Sashi Bhusan, *Civil Rebellion in Indian Mutinies*, 1857-59, pp. 143-44.
32. *FSUP*, Vol. IV, p. 156; Wingfield, C, *Narrative of Events*, 5 July 1858, para 38, p. 5. Wingfield wrote that "The wealthy Muhammaden families of the town naturally were among the first to welcome him, and from them his officials were mostly selected."
33. *Kashful Baghaavat, Gorakhpur*; stanza 170, p. 26.
34. *Ibid*, stanza 610, p. 95.
35. *Ibid*, stanza 620, p. 96.
36. *Ibid*, stanza 1465, p. 222.
37. *Ibid*, stanza 591, p. 92.
38. According to C. Wingfield, the Commissioner of Goruckpore, "only a tehsildar but several police thanedars offered their services to the rebel government. See *Narrative of Events*, 5 July 1858, para 36, p. 5. Shah Syed Ahmed Ali has mentioned a tehsildar called Haider Husain: He wrote that;

    Aur Haider Husain, ek Tahsildaar,
    Raha Woh bhi Dajjaal ka yaar-e-ghaar
    (And Haider Husain, a Tehsildar,
    He too was an intimate friend of Dajjaal).

    See stanza 1481, p. 224. In *Vishvenvansh Vatika*, Lal Khang Bahadul Malla, has mentioned Tehsildar Zamin Ali who was with the rebels during the siege of Majhauli. See p. 81; There is a record preserved in Regional Archives, Allahabad, which gives a list of those who were related to the Magistrate Office of Gorakhpur but were serving the rebel government. See *Pre-Mutiny Records*, Gorakhpur Collectorate, List No. 14, Vol. 177. Also, return Showing the Conduct during the Late Interaction of the Native Officials of Magistrate office. See, pre-mutiny records, Gorakhpur collectorate, List no. 14, Vol. 177 (page no. not mentioned).

39. *Kashful Baghaavat, Gorakhpur*, stanza 163, p. 25.
40. *Ibid*, stanza 164, p. 25.
41. *FSUP*, Vol. IV, p. 354.
42. Foreign Department, Secret Consultation, No. 30, Dated 29 October 1858, Preserved in National Archives, New Delhi.
43. Foreign Department, Secret Consultation, No. 05, Dated 24 September 1858, Preserved in National Archives, New Delhi.
44. *FSUP*, Vol. IV, p. 339.
45. *Ibid*, p. 316.
46. *Ibid*, p. 299. The rebels, according to the Raja of Majhauli, numbered more than six or seven thousand.
47. Foreign Department, Political, 1859, 11 March, Secret Consultation No. 46-48; from C. Wingfield, Commissioner of Gorakhpur, to William Muir, Secretary to the Government of North Western Provinces, 24 January 1859, para 9, p. 3.
48. Foreign Department, Political, 1859, 11 March, Secret Consultation No. 44-45; from C. Wingfield, Commissioner of Gorakhpur, 6 January 1859, p. 7.
49. Taylor, Robert, The Rebellion of 1857 in the Province of Benares, 15 October 1858, par 21-23, pp. 10-11.
50. *Kashful Baghaavat, Gorakhpur*, stanza 111, 113, 114, p. 18. Syed Ahmed Ali Shah knew about the loot of 70,000 rupees which were kept in the Azamgarh treasury. That was why he mentioned the loot of eight lakh rupees by the sepoys. Moreover, some of these sepoys took part in the battle of Kanpur also, which shows that Delhi was their destination.
51. Chatterjee, Nandlal, "New Light on the Revolt of 1857 at Azamgarh," *The Journal of Indian History*, Trivandrum, Vol. XXXIV, Part III, December 1956, cf: Haq, Syed Moinul, *op cit*, p. 451, FN 1.
52. *FSUP*, Vol. IV, pp. 102-06.
53. *Ibid*, pp. 106-07.
54. Taylor, Robert, *op cit*, para 43-45, pp. 14-15; Chaudhuri, Sashi Bhusan, *op cit*, p. 156, FN 1.
55. Taylor, Robert, *op cit*, para 41, p. 14.
56. Singh, Phoolbadan, *op cit*, Vol. 1, p. 138.
57. Chaudhuri, Sashi Bhusan, *op cit*, p. 154.
58. *FSUP*, Vol. IV, p. 101.
59. *Kashful Baghaavat, Gorakhpur*, *op cit*, stanza 142, p. 22.
60. Chaudhury, Sashi Bhusan, *op cit*, p. 156.
61. *Ibid*, p. 153; *FSUP*, Vol. IV, p. 174.
62. *FSUP*, Vol. IV, pp. 205-07.
63. *Ibid*, p. 207.
64. Chaudhuri, Sashi Bhusan, *op cit*, p. 154.
65. *FSUP*, Vol. IV, p. 205.
66. *Ibid*.

67. Haq, Syed Moinul, *op cit*, p. 452.
68. *FSUP*, Vol. IV, pp. 109, 111, 447-450.
69. Oldham, Wilton, *Tenant Rights and Auction Sales in Ghazeepoor and the Province of Benares*, Dublin, 1873, para 4, p. 6.
70. *Ibid.*
71. *FSUP*, Vol. IV, p. 122. Mr. Brown had used the word "Badmashes" for rebels.
72. *Ibid*, p. 121.
73. *Ibid*, p. 269.
74. *Ibid*, p. 269.
75. *Ibid*, p. 271.
76. *Ibid*, pp. 117-19.
77. Taylor, Robert, *op cit*, 15 October 1858, para 58, p. 18.
78. *FSUP*, Vol. IV, pp. 280-89.
79. *FSUP*, p. 272.
80. *Ibid*, p. 268.
81. Foreign Department, Secret Consultations No. 59, 28 May 1858; *FSUP*, Vol. IV, p. 467.
82. Home Department, Public Consultations No. 50, 30 April 1858; *FSUP*, Vol. IV, p. 467.
83. *FSUP*, Vol. IV, pp. 123-25.
84. *Ibid*, pp. 473-74.
85. *Ibid*, pp. 125, 136.
86. Taylor, Robert, *op cit*, para 25, p. 11 and para 35, p. 13; P. N. Chopra (Ed), *Who is Who of Indian Martyrs of 1857*, Vol III, New Delhi: Government of India, New Delhi, 1973, pp. 2-3.
87. *FSUP*, Vol. IV, p. 136.
88. *Ibid*, pp. 242-43, 244-45.
89. *Ibid*, p. 247; Taylor, Robert, *op cit*, para 68, p. 20.
90. *Ibid*, p. 247.
91. *FSUP,* Vol. IV, pp. 210-14-239-42.
92. *FSUP,* Vol. IV, pp. 229-30, 235-36, R. Taylor, 19th Nov. 1858, p. 4.
93. Foreign Dept. Secret consultation No. 81, dated 28 May 1858; Taylor, Robert, officiating Magistrate of Jounpoor, 19th, Nov. 1858, Supplement to the Narrative of Events in the Benares Division, p. 4; (Preserved in National Archives, New Delhi.)
94. *FSUP,* Vol. IV, p. 230.
95. *Ibid,* pp. 226-27.
96. *Ibid,* pp. 236-239.
97. Drake-Brockman, D. L., *Mirzapur: A Gazetteer Being Volume XXVII*, Allahabad: Government Press, 1911, p. 240.

98. *Ibid*, 241; Taylor, Robert, *The Rebellion of 1857 in the Province of Benares, 15th October 1858, Para, 54.* p. 17.

99. *FSUP*, Vol. IV, p. 57; Drake-Brockman, D L, *op cit*, p. 241.

100. *FSUP*, Vol. IV, pp. 74-75, 78-82; Taylor, Robert, *The Rebellion of 1857...15 Oct. 1858,* Para 55-56, pp. 17-18.

101. *FSUP*, Vol. IV, p. 83.

102. *Ibid,* pp. 231-34, 248-49.

103. *Ibid,* p. 235.

104. Taylor, Robert, *op cit*, para 5, p. 7; According to Sir John William Kaye "there had always been something more than the average amount of discontent and dissatisfaction among the citizens and now in summer of 1857, this was increased by the high price of provisions always believed to be one of the curses of British rule". See, Kaye's and Malleson's History of the Indian Mutiny of 1857-58, Vol. II, p. 150 (W.H. Allen & Co. Waterloo place London, 1889).

105. Taylor, Robert, *op cit*, para 12, 13 and 14, pp. 9-10; *FSUP*, Vol. IV, pp. 17-20; Kaye's and Malleson's History of the Indian Mutiny of 1857-58, Vol. II, p. 167-69, p. 172-74, (Hereafter mentioned as to Kaye's and Malleson's Vol. II).

106. Taylor, Robert, *op cit*, para 34, p. 13; Kaye's and Malleson's Vol. II, pp. 175-77; Chandra, Moti, *Kashi ka Itihas*, Varanasi: Vishwavidyalaya Prakashan, 2003, p. 291; Fisher and Hewett, *Statistical, Descriptive and Historical Account of North Western Provinces*, Vol. IV, Part I, Banaras, Allahabad: North Western Provinces and Awadh Government Press, p. 117; Ball, Charles, *The History of the Indian Mutiny*, Vol. I (London Printing & Publishing Company, 1858), pp. 242-44; Savarkar, *op cit*, p. 163; *FSUP*, Vol. IV, p. 44.

107. "The town is quite quiet." Wrote Commissioner Tucker to Lord Canning, See, Kaye's and Malleson's Vol. II, p. 175; There is an event which can be mentioned 'On 8 February 1858, 26 prisoners who had been sentenced to life imprisonment, made an abortive attempt to escape.'

108. Haider, Kamaluddin, *op cit*, Vol. 2, pp. 224-26; Pemble, John, *The Raj, The Indian Mutiny and the Kingdom of Awadh, 1801-1859*, first Indian reprint, New Delhi: Oxford University Press, 1979, p. 210.

109. *Kashful-Baghaavat, Gorakhpur*, p. 18.

110. Quoted in Savarkar, *op cit*, p. 152.

111. For his biography, see Hasan, Mujahidul, *Mecca Muazzama se Muazzamabad tak*, Urdu, Lucknow: Kakori Offset Press, 2010, pp. 106-07 for details, see the chapter III.

112. Haq, Syed Moinul, *op cit*, p. 63.

113. Rizvi, Syed Khursheed Mustafa, *Tarikh-e-Jang-e-Azadi-e-Hind: 1857*, Urdu, Rampur: Raza Library, 2000, p. 575.

114. *Ibid*, pp. 46-47; Chaudhuri, Sashi Bhusan, *Theories of Indian Mutiny (1857-58)*, Calcutta: The World Press Private Ltd 1965, pp. 26-32; In his unpublished thesis titled "Madrasas Scholars and Saints: Muslim Response to the British Province of Delhi and Upper Doab, 1803-1857 (Oxford 1983)," Farhan Ahmed Nizami too has given in his own words a portion of the sermon delivered by Maulvi Sarfaraz Ali at Shahjehanpur on 1 May 1857: "Our religion is now in

danger, having lost the sovereignty of the land, having bowed in subjection to the impure kafir; shall we surrender the inalienable privileges which we received from the prophet, upon whom be peace?" Quoted by Dalrymple, William, *The Last Mughal: The Fall of a Dynasty, Delhi, 1857*, New Delhi: Penguin Books India P. Ltd, 2006, p. 285 and reference number 80 on p. 529.

115. Dalrymple, William, *op cit*, p. 285.
116. Foreign Department, Secret Consultation No. 3, 24 September 1857; Letter from Commissioner of Gorakhpur to Secretary to Government, 27 July 1858, p. 7; *FSUP*, Vol. IV, p. 347.
117. The tomb is still there in the Muslim Jami Masjid at Kathmandu.
118. Mazumdar, R C, *The Sepoy Mutiny and the Revolt of 1857*, Calcutta: Firma K L Mukhopadhyaya, second edition, 1963, pp. 102-04.
119. Foreign Department, Political Branch A, No. 375-378, July 1868, Proceedings, May 1868, No. 153/155, (Preserved in National Archives, New Delhi).

Chapter - 3

Architect of the Rebellion: Maulvi Sarfaraz Ali

Despite the presence of various causes of discontent, the revolt of 1857 did not flare up all of a sudden; various factors for it were already active in different parts of the country. Though there is disagreement about whether a well-planned scheme had been prepared for the revolt,[1] there is no denying the fact that propaganda against the Company Government was already going on among the people as well as the sepoys. Secretly, the process of motivating the people for revolt was already on. Hence the Company Government did not have precise information about the motivators of the revolt. Among the Muslim masses and soldiers, a number of maulvis were propagating for revolt in the name of *wa'iz*. Mentionable among them were Maulvi Ahmedullah Shah[2] who hailed from Chinapattan near Madras in South India, Maulvi Liyaqat Ali[3] of Allahabad, Fazl-e-Haque Khairabadi,[4] and Maulvi Sarfaraz Ali of Gorakhpur. These maulvis motivated the people for a *jihad* against the British, but their *jihad* was not against any particular religion or community, as they well knew that the cooperation of all, of majority Hindus in particular, was necessary to liberate the country from the British. Hence, they also tried to remove the impediments to Hindu-Muslim unity. They gave the biggest proof to it by supporting the ban on cow-slaughter imposed by Emperor Bahadur Shah Zafar on Eid in Delhi.[5]

Actively propagating for a revolt, Maulvi Sarfaraz Ali of Gorakhpur worked so silently that the British Government did not have precise information about him for ten years even after the rebellion had been crushed. His field of activity included a large area — from Gorakhpur and its vicinity to Shahjehanpur and then to Delhi via Bareilly and Moradabad, after the fall of Delhi, to Lucknow, the capital of Awadh, to Bahraich and Jhandanagar (Butwal) in the *terai* and to Kathmandu, the capital of Nepal. In this wide area of action, British officials came across several persons called Sarfaraz Ali, but nothing specific they got against Maulvi Sarfaraz Ali of Gorakhpur.

From the Secretary's letter to the Chief Commissioner of Awadh, numbered 1627, dated 24 April 1868, we learn that when the Resident at Nepal sent the information in September 1867 about the presence of Maulvi Sarfaraz Ali, the rebel of 1857-58, in Nepal, all the documents about this person were scanned. But this yielded nothing except a letter sent by Lieutenant Roome to the Governor General's Agent to Central India. The letter talked about the capture and execution of some Sarfaraz Ali.[6] Nor could the British Resident in Nepal provide any specific information that could help in tracing this man. Sarfaraz Ali Khan was known as a rebel in Awadh. Hence when the Chief Commissioner of Awadh was contacted about him, he said, "It appears that there were two leaders of rebellion by the name of Surfaraz Ally. One of them was Kazee Surfaraz Ally, who was transported to the Andamans. The other was the rebel tehsildar of Bansgaon in Goruckpore, who accompanied the mutineers to Bareilly and subsequently marched with them to Delhi, where was appointed Chief of Ghazees. On the fall of Delhi, he is said to have returned to Goruckpore, whence he fled to Nepal. He is described as one of the chief instigator, both of mutiny and the murderer of the European residents of Shahjehanpore. Moreover, his name appears in the register of proclaimed offenders of the Goruckpore district."[7] The Chief Commissioner also said that the Maulvi was in Lucknow along with the rebel army and accompanied the Begum (Hazrat Mahal) to Nepal. His name is not included in the list of proclaimed offenders of Oudh.[8]

The official documents of the North West Provinces included a letter from Ganesh Prasad Chaube who was a translator (*munsarim*) in the court of the Moradabad judge. After excessively describing the cruelty of Sarfaraz Ali, he did concede that producing against him a proof of any particular cruelty or murder was difficult.[9] Moreover, it is highly doubtful whether the man whom the Resident intimated to be present in Kathmandu in 1867 was the same Sarfaraz Ali who was talked about by Ganesh Prasad Chaube or was he the rebel tehsildar of Bansgaon in Gorakhpur.[10] British officials said the person indicated by Ganesh Chaube was most probably the rebel tehsildar of Bansgaon in Gorakhpur.[11]

From Letter Number 31 sent by R. H. Clifford, the Officiating Magistrate of Gorakhpur, to the Under Secretary to the government of North Western Provinces on 1 February 1868, we learn that Sarfaraz Ali, who was appointed the tehsildar of Bansgaon by Mohammed Hasan, the rebel Nazim of Gorakhpur, belonged to Awadh while Maulvi Sarfaraz Ali was a quite different person.[12] According to Mr Bird's memorandum, "Maulvi Sarfaraz Ali" was a resident of Delhi and had come to Gorakhpur for the renovation of a mosque with the help from the Muslims. During the disturbances (rebellion) of June, he had issued a directive, through another maulvi called Abdul Rafi, to the Muslims to hoist the green flag, i.e. to start a *jihad*. When the enemies (rebels) occupied the district (Gorakhpur), Sarfaraz Ali was in Delhi. In that period, several residents of Gorakhpur left the city for Delhi, and said that he (Sarfaraz Ali) had become a vizier (minister) of the Emperor (Bahadur Shah Zafar) and that he had called them to fill up many of the positions in offices.[13]

According to Mr. Bird, he had purchased a house in Gorakhpur city and when this house was searched after the British recaptured it, they got some apparel of irregular cavaliers; these were confiscated and sold out.[14] Maulvi Sarfaraz Ali had left Gorakhpur in March or April 1857 and had run away to Nepal after the rebellion was crushed.[15] There is also evidence suggesting that the note prepared by Mr Ousley, referring to Sarfaraz Ali, the rebel tehsildar, as Maulvi Sarfaraz Ali was a mistake.[16]

The British Government was striving to collect such evidence as could prove Maulvi Sarfaraz Ali as guilty of heinous crimes and thus demand his extradition from the Nepal Government on the basis of the 1855 treaty. But it failed in this endeavour.[17] In sum, the Company Government had no concrete and authentic information about Maulvi Sarfaraz Ali of Gorakhpur.

Not much is known about Maulvi Sarfaraz Ali's early life and education. A person called Mujahidul Hasan, who was related to his descendants, has written a book in Urdu, under the title *Mecca Muazzama se Muazzamabad tak* (*From the Holy Mecca to Gorakhpur*). It gives a genealogy of Maulvi Sarfaraz Ali and writes, "He was the youngest son of Hussein Bakhsh alias Rajab Ali Saheb. Elder to him were Ikram Ali Saheb and some sisters whose names we could not find. He was a great scholar. He helped his elder brother, Ikram Ali Saheb, in the family occupation of trade. But he spent most of his time in looking after the arable lands of his father's share which, after the division, were situated in the north-western part of the undivided original district of Gorakhpur. Despite the decline, the family had maintained its ties with the Mughal Sultanate. He remained attached to Bahadur Shah Zafar's court for nine months."[18] A perusal of the work reveals that the writer did not have much about Maulvi Sarfaraz Ali; it only tells us his father's name.

On the basis of the details provided by the author of *Tarikh-e-Shahjehanpur* (*History of Shahjehanpur*), Mohammed Ayub Qadri has written in the section of 'Waqiyaat wa Shaqsiyaat' (Events and Personalities) of his book, "*1857: Jang-e-Azadi*", under the title: "Maulvi Sarfaraz Ali, Imamul Mujahideen", that, "Maulvi Sarfaraz Ali was a scholar and sweet-speaking preacher. He was a disciple of Shah Abul Lais, successor (*khalifa*) to Shah Subhan Ali, successor to Shah Fakharuddin Dehlavi in the Chishti-Nizami order. He ignited in the army a feeling of hatred against the British rule. Several persons from Shahjehanpur were employed in the Sagauli cantonment near Gorakhpur; among them, Ghulam Mohammed Khan *risaladar* and Shah Ghulam Imam Khan, residents of Shahjehanpur, were particularly mentionworthy. People of Shahjehanpur often came to listen the sermons delivered by Maulvi Sarfaraz Ali. Thus, the sepoys of Sagauli were influenced by Maulvi Saheb's ideas. Ghulam Imam Khan became a disciple of Maulvi Sarfaraz Ali and the latter came to Shahjehanpur during 1857. His meetings were organised at various places in the city. Muslim sepoys organised a sermon in the cantonment itself, and thus he came in direct contact with the sepoys of Shahjehanpur. Maulvi Sarfaraz Ali was present in Shahjehanpur when the troops threw away the yoke of British slavery there. In company with the troops of the city, Maulvi Saheb reached Bareilly and then, following Bakht Khan's advice, left for Delhi. Maulvi Sarfaraz Ali already had ties with the group of revolutionaries at Delhi. As we learn from a letter of Maulvi Sarfaraz Ali, he was in Delhi in February 1857, when the *urs* of Hazrat Shah Baqibillah was held there, and had met Risaladar Sardar Khan there.

When Maulvi Sarfaraz Ali reached Delhi, his and Bakht Khan's efforts gave a new energy to the freedom movement in Delhi. He remained a colleague of Bakht Khan till the last moment. Maulvi Sarfaraz Ali too had signed the well-known Delhi edict for a *jihad*. After the fall of Delhi, he came to Lucknow along with Bakht Khan and finally, along with other leaders of the movement, he went to Nepal where he breathed his last.[19] The author of *Tarikh-e-Shahjehanpur* wrote, "He went to Nepal after the Ghadar. The King welcomed him with great honour and respect and fixed an allowance for him. He breathed his last and was burried in Nepal. The Maulana was a great scholar, magical orator and ethically perfect *dervish*. He also used to listen sama (psalms)."[20] On the other hand, in *Tarikh-e-Salatin-e-Awadh* (*History of the Sultans of Awadh*), Volume 2, Kamaluddin Haider described Maulvi Sarfaraz Ali as a disciple of Maulvi Karamat Ali of Jaunpur, who was a leading figure of the Wahabi movement and a renowned successor of Syed Ahmed of Raebareli.[21]

Maulvi Sarfaraz Ali has thus been described as a Sufi on the one hand and as a Wahabi on the other. Describing a Muslim as a Wahabi was a way to alienate him from the orthodox Sunni Muslims and make the Shia Muslims his enemies. Thus, Kamaluddin Haider, a supporter of the Company Government, helped in the British design to alienate Maulvi Sarfaraz Ali from the Muslim community by dubbing him as a Wahabi. Later writers took Kamaluddin Haider's statement at its face value, without corroboration.

In regard to the edict for *jihad*, which Maulvi Sarfaraz Ali too had signed, Mohammed Ayub Qadri has thrown much light on the attitude of other maulvis as well.[22] On 27 July 1857, newspaper *Sadiqul-Akhbar* also published the said edict of the maulvis against the British.[23] But nowhere we get detailed information about Maulvi Sarfaraz Ali's activities.

We may say on the basis of the available evidence that Maulvi Sarfaraz Ali was a resident of Gorakhpur. He took his education in Delhi. Mufti Sadruddin 'Azurda' had been one of his teachers. From this, it is clear that he got educated in Madrasa "Darul-Baqa," situated to the south of Jama Masjid in Delhi. He also taught in this madrasa for some time. He had a command over algebra and geometry. He was reckoned among the leading scholars of Delhi.[24] While praising him, Syed Ahmed Khan described as the most shining gem in the crown of intellectuality in Delhi.[25] Maulvi Sarfaraz Ali's family had relations with the Mughal Empire. Therefore, he was unhappy with the Company Government's control over Delhi and had been thinking of putting the foreign rule to an end. He thus decided to rouse the people of India against the foreign rule and made a plan for it. He came back to his ancestral home in Gorakhpur and began to enlist disciples through his sermons. His sermons did contain things that could incite feelings against the English. He was an influential orator and easily attracted people. Mr. Bird's memorandum also mentions that many people had gone to Delhi at his call.[26] The fact shows that he had got several followers and supporters, and that he exercised a deep influence upon them. He wanted to preach revolt among the sepoys, along with the common people. From the angle of a battle and security, he also understood the importance of the northern parts of Gorakhpur which was forest covered and adjoined the southern border of Nepal. Therefore, he began to visit this area to deliver sermons. He also delivered sermons in the vicinity of the Sagauli cantonment near the Nepal border. He had got, as his disciple, Diwan Damman Khan, the influential jagirdar of Jhandanagar (at present Krishnanagar in Nepal) who was in the Nepal Government's service.[27] Apart from him, the Maulana had also enlisted a large number of faithful there. Several persons from Shahjehanpur were then working in the Sagauli Cantt, and they were much influenced by his sermons. Sepoys of the army were also influenced by him. Among them, Risaledar Ghulam Mohammed Khan and Shah Ghulam Imam Khan were particularly mentionworthy. Shah Ghulam Imam Khan was not only a faithful but also his Khalifa (successor) in Shahjehanpur.[28] It was at his invitation that Maulvi Sarfaraz Ali went to Shahjehanpur where he delivered sermons at numerous places and thus a large number of people became his followers. For example, Qudrat Ali, the Naib Sarishtadar of the criminal court, and his brother Niyaz Ali also became his followers.[29] At Shahjehanpur too, sepoys attended his sermons in good numbers and were influenced by him. It seems that Maulvi Sarfaraz Ali had already been visiting Shahjehanpur.[30] Sa'adat Ali Khan, the spiritual teacher (*pir*) of Nawab Ghulam Qadir Khan of Shahjehanpur, was a resident of Bansi tehsil of Gorakhpur district,[31] which shows that the people of Shahjehanpur too had close relations with Gorakhpur. Maulvi Sarfaraz Ali too had widespread influence in Bansi. Maulvi Sarfaraz Ali was present in Shahjehanpur for 20 days before the revolt started there. On 1 May 1857, he had held a secret meeting of Hindus and Muslims at Maulvi Mazhar Karim Khan's house and had urged them to start a 'jihad' in order to liberate the country from the *firangis*. In fact, Maulvi Sarfaraz Ali is credited with the outbreak of the rebellion in Shahjehanpur.[32] From Shahjehanpur, he went to Bareilly along with the rebel sepoys and his followers. Influenced by his sermon there, Subedar Bakht Khan of the Neemuch army's artillery, became his disciple and a rebel.[33] At the bidding of Khan Bahadur Khan, Bakht Khan and Maulvi Sarfaraz Ali started for Delhi. According to Kamaluddin Haider, Bakht Khan had left for Delhi along with 14,000 sepoys, three cavalry regiments, an artillery and a few lakh rupees in cash.[34] He was accompanied by the '*jihadi*' followers of his spiritual teacher (*pir*) Maulvi Sarfaraz Ali. The Nawab of Rampur, a supporter of the British, had occupied Moradabad. Therefore, Bakht Khan launched a raid upon Moradabad. As Bakht Khan's representative, Maulvi Sarfaraz Ali made an attempt to enlist Nawab Yousuf Khan of Rampur for the rebellion. Though the Nawab talked sycophantically, gave some monetary help and an assurance, he kept himself apart.[35]

Along with his *mujahids* (warriors) who numbered about four thousand and with Bakht Khan's army, Maulvi Sarfaraz Ali reached Delhi on 1 July 1857. He was well in touch with the Delhi court and the city dwellers,[36] and was already planning a rebellion with the people. A letter written by him corroborates this point.[37] On 2 July, and in company with Bakht Khan, Maulvi Sarfaraz Ali met Emperor Bahadur Shah. The Mughal Emperor drafted him into his council.[38] But after the emperor appointed Bakht Khan his commander-in-chief, Maulvi Sarfaraz Ali again met the emperor and urged that he should be made the vizier. Syed Mubarak Shah writes that "He told the emperor: 'I cannot think of any other person who could have your trust and of the council. Therefore, if you think it proper, you should nominate me as the vizier. After that, you won't have any anxiety or trouble.' "[39] In view of Maulvi Sarfaraz Ali's prestige and influence, the emperor did not reject the proposal outright and just said: "We will consider it."[40] But Bakht Khan did appoint his *pir* as Amir-ul-Mujahideen and Imam-ul-Mujahideen (leader of warriors).[41] Though Maulvi Sarfaraz Ali was not appointed as vizier, he did remain one of the emperor's chief advisor.[42] At Delhi, large numbers of people joined the rebellion because of Bakht Khan and Maulvi Sarfaraz Ali, and also informed the latter about it. A sepoy called Faiz Ahmed informed Maulvi Sarfaraz Ali that he had deserted the British and joined the Neemuch army.[43] This shows Maulvi Sarfaraz Ali was indeed so important and influential that people thought it necessary to inform him after joining the rebellion.

Though Maulvi Sarfaraz Ali preached *jihad* against the British, he was above religious bigotry and communalism. He proved it during the rebellion in Delhi. On the occasion of Eid-ul-Azha, in order to maintain the Hindu-Muslim unity, Emperor Bahadur Shah Zafar banned cow slaughter through an edict, but the opponents of the rebellion didn't want it implemented, in the hope that Hindus and Muslims would fight and the British would be in advantage. Mufti Sadruddin Azurda was sent to talk to the rebels on the issue and he had a talk with Maulvi Sarfaraz Ali. The latter persuaded the warriors to obey the emperor's command.[44] This shows Maulvi Sarfaraz Ali's influence and command over the rebels. The number of the rebels was then estimated to be thirty to forty thousand.[45]

In July 1857, Bakht Khan got an edict issued with the maulvis' signatures. A number of maulvis, including Maulvi Sarfaraz Ali, signed it. Later, however, a number of them, including Mufti Sadruddin Azurda who was a friend of Mirza Ghalib, declared that they had been compelled to sign the said edict and were threatened that their families would be killed and destroyed in case they did not sign it.[46] Maulvi Sarfaraz Ali was not included in them. He had willingly signed the edict that had a wide impact on the Muslim psyche.[47] Maulvi Sarfaraz Ali remained active in the rebellion in Delhi, along with other warriors, till 17 September.[48] Eventually, in view of the imminent fall of Delhi, and after Bahadur Shah Zafar refused Bakht Khan's advice to leave Delhi, Maulvi Sarfaraz Ali left Delhi with Bakht Khan and his followers. They proceeded towards Awadh which was, the stronghold of the rebellion and still fighting.

We don't have anything about Maulvi Sarfaraz Ali's activities in Lucknow; yet he was actively involved with Begum Hazrat Mahal and her supporters. His murid (disciples), Bakht Khan and his forces fought gallantry against the British in the battle of Alambagh, the gallantry was praised by the Malleson though he failed to recognize the real person behind the tough resistance. In the battle, Bakht Khan lost his guns and a number of men. Bakht Khan was commended by Hazrat Mahal for his gallant fight and assured that the loss of guns would be made good. After the fall of Lucknow, he moved to Shahjehanpur and from there crossed over Nepal via Mohammadi."[49] British records do have evidence that Maulvi Sarfaraz Ali was in contact with Begum Hazrat Mahal at Bondi, after she had left Lucknow.

We may see his influence in Gorakhpur district as well. Damman Khan was his faithful disciple. Begum Hazrat Mahal had appointed him the chakladar of Bansi tehsil.[50] Along with Maulvi Sarfaraz Ali, he also went to Bondi to meet Begum Hazrat Mahal, and both stayed there for twelve days. It was at Bondi that Begum Hazrat Mahal honoured Damman Khan with a *khil'at* (robe of honour).[51] Damman Khan also provided shelter to Fazal Khan who had shot upon Boileau C S in the *terai* of Nepal.[52] Bolwur (Mr. Boileau) was shot upon at the Arra Brook which made the border of British India and Nepal. The place was called Muchmunia and Maulvi Sarfaraz Ali was then living there. The English did not know about it.[53] Maulvi Sarfaraz Ali may also be regarded as motivator of the rebellion in Sagauli Cantonment where Major Holmes was killed.[54] Maulvi Sarfaraz Ali was sent to Nepal as the representative of Birjis Qadr, the son of Begum Hazrat Mahal.[55] Her trusted employee, Darogha Mammu Khan, remained with Maulvi Sarfaraz Ali in Nepal.[56] These details show that Maulvi Sarfaraz Ali was highly active from Bahraich to Jhandanagar (Nepal) even after the fall of Lucknow. Along with Begum Hazrat Mahal, Maulvi Sarfaraz Ali too went to Kathmandu, the capital of Nepal, but the British Government did not have any real information about him.

Nothing is known about Maulvi Sarfaraz Ali's activities in Nepal, nor do we know how long he remained alive. But British records make it clear that he honourably died only after 1868 AD.

On 29 May 1868, C. U. Aitcheson, Secretary to the Government of India in the Foreign Department with Governor General, wrote a letter, No. 543, to Colonel R. C. Lawrence, the Resident in Nepal. He asked the Resident to probe the rumour that the Nepal Government of Sir Jang Bahadur had allotted two villages to the rebellious Maulvi Sarfaraz Ali as jagir, and that the latter was then living in Nepal.[57] In this regard, Colonel G. Ramsay, the Resident in Nepal, had earlier informed the Secretary to the Government of India in the Foreign Department with Governor General, at Simla, through letter number 28 on 10 September 1867, that a few days ago a letter had been thrown at the Residency gate in the night by a person in a fakir's garb. After throwing the letter, that fellow had run away saying that he was an Irakee. The Resident then said that he was forwarding the letter's translation to the Secretary. The letter mentioned the presence of Maulvi Sarfaraz Ali in Kathmandu, the killing of Bolwur (Mr. Boileu), and the allotment of a jagir of two villages to Maulvi Sarfaraz Ali by Damman Khan.[58] On his part, Colonel Lawrence confidentially deputed a Muslim in order to unravel the reality. His Muslim spy told him that the Nepal Court had exiled a fakir, who had been living in Kathmandu for years together, just on the doubt that he had sent the unsigned petition informing the Resident about Sarfaraz Ali Khan living in Kathmandu. This meant that the Nepal Darbar did not want to reveal the facts regarding the Maulvi Sarfaraz Ali. However, the informer told that in previous year Maulvi Sarfaraz Ali was living in Kathmandu by the name of Maulvi Abdul Aziz. In the *terai* area to the north of Gorakhpur, the Nepal Darbar had allotted him three small villages as jagir. These villages were in the name of his son Monitaj Ali (Mumtaz Ali) who worked as a Munshi in Butwal tehsil. Sarfaraz Ali Khan was highly respected among the Muslims of capital Kathmandu and had taken many of them as disciples.[59] The Resident also learned that "The Maulvi lived in Jhandanagar which is one of the three villages the Nepal Durbar had assigned him as a jagir. This village was located in the jagir of Diwan Damman Khan, a rich zamindar, who secured the refuge for Sarfaraz Ali Khan in the *terai*."[60] The reason of this extraordinary generosity of the court for Sarfaraz Ali was that, according to the Muslim informant (or spy!), he as a great learned man, was highly influential among the Muslims from the west, and he was the *pir* of Prince Feroz Khan.[61] In fact he was a person who could be highly useful (for the Nepal Court) as an emissary. Through him, the Nepal Durbar could confidentially contact whomsoever it wanted to contact.[62] But when Colonel Lawrence (Resident in Nepal) categorically asked the Maharaja (Jang Bahadur Rana) about it, the latter flatly denied grant of land or any other help to Sarfaraz Ali. Sir Jang Bahadur said the rebel's family had taken refuge in the *terai* in the beginning of 1858 and the Maulvi had joined them there. Since then, the family had got some land from the zamindars of Butwal on rent. The Maharaja further said the Muslims of the area too had given Sarfaraz Ali Khan some land on their own and had made him their Maulvi.[63] He also said, "When the family first reached Nepal, his son

Monitaj (Mumtaz) Ali, was only six or seven. Soon he was appointed a Munshi in Butwal tehsil at 200 rupees a year."[64] The Maharaja admitted that Maulvi Sarfaraz Ali had come to Kathmandu the previous year (in 1867) and had requested help, but it was denied.[65] The Maharaja also pleaded ignorance about his earlier deeds.[66]

Two of Maulvi Sarfaraz Ali's friends, Haider Khan and Izzat Ali, were among the bodyguards of Maharaja Jang Bahadur. Both were earlier in the employ of the British but had turned rebels along with Maulvi Sarfaraz Ali and were living with him in the *terai*. They had joined the Nepal Durbar's service. They were with the Maharaja during his last hunting expedition in the *terai*. With them, they had brought Maulvi Sarfaraz Ali to the city (Kathmandu) where he was then living (in September 1867) and had taken many Muslims as disciples.[67] But Maharaja Jang Bahadur did not provide correct information to the Resident about Maulvi Sarfaraz Ali. However, Resident Colonel G Ramsay wrote to the Foreign Secretary of the Government of India at Fort William on 13 November 1867 that

1. I have not yet been able to obtain the reliable information respecting the part taken by Sarfaraz Ali Khan during the rebellion calculated to enable the Government to trace his identity in the records.
2. Of his presence at Khatmandoo there can be no doubt, but just now no one is willing to come forward and to state the particular circumstances which obliged his seeking an asylum in Nepal.
3. He receives subsistence from the Begum Hazrat Mahal of Lucknow and also from certain Irakee merchants of Khatmandoo some of whom have appointed him to be their Maulvee."[68]

In Nepal, after meticulous investigations, spies Ram Singh and Lal Singh, could only find that "A Maulvi lived with the Begum."[69]

These details make it clear that, after the suppression of the revolt, Maulvi Sarfaraz Ali had taken refuge in Nepal along with his family and was alive even after 1868. His tomb still exists in the compound of Jami Masjid in Kathmandu and is close to Begum Hazrat Mahal's tomb.[70] This proves that, along with Begum Hazrat Mahal, Maulvi Sarfaraz Ali passed a hard life till the end but never begged pardon from the English for his deeds.

Maulvi Sarfaraz Ali was one of the great men of the 1857 rebellion who aimed to liberate India from the foreign rule, had a broad horizon, and had most of North India as the field of his activity. He kindled the fire of a rebellion from Gorakhpur, his home town in Eastern Uttar Pradesh, to

Rohilkhand, Delhi and Awadh, and also tried to bring the neighbouring Nepal to the anti-British revolt, though unsuccessfully. There is no evidence to show who had collaborated in taking to the masses Begum Hazrat Mahal's reply to Queen Victoria's proclamation, and how they had propagated it. But in view of Maulvi Sarfaraz Ali's erudition, his style of clandestine work, the number of his disciples all over the country and his capacity to face the odds, one cannot write off the possibility that he could well have used his intellect and his pen to play his part in turning people against the English though to date no concrete proof of this fact has come to light.

The contribution made by Maulvi Sarfaraz Ali of Gorakhpur is unforgettable and was an inspiration behind the revolt of 1857. He was indeed one of the architects of the rebellion.

Notes and References

1. In his book, Syed Moinul Haq has a chapter titled "The Patriots Organise a Movement" in which he mentions Syed Ahmadullah Shah, Maulvi Sarfaraz Ali, Maulvi Liyaqat Ali, Azimullah Khan and Nana Saheb, the emissaries, the chapattis, the lotus flower, fixation of 31 May as the date for revolt, the premature beginning of the revolution, etc. See, *The Great Revolution of 1857*, Karachi, 1968, pp. 55-73. Also see Kaye, Sir John William, *op cit*, Vol. 1, pp. 416-21; Rizvi, Syed Athar Abbas, *FSUP*, Vol. 1, pp. 351-416. According to R. C. Majumdar, there was no planned conspiracy behind it. See *The Sepoy Mutiny and the Revolt of 1857*, Book IV, Chapter I and II. Most of the authors have refused to take it as a planned conspiracy.
2. See, "The Profile of a Saintly Rebel: Maulvi Ahmadullah Shah" in Moosvi, Shirin (Ed), *Facets of the Great Revolt, 1857*, New Delhi: Tulika Books for Sahmat, 2008, pp. 39-50, Haq, Syed Moinul, *op cit*, pp. 55-63.
3. Haq, Syed Moinul, *op cit*, pp. 64-65; Husain, Iqbal, *Religion and Ideology of the Rebels of 1857*, New Delhi: Primus Books, 2013, pp. 167-68.
4. Husain, Iqbal, *op cit*, pp. 178-87.
5. Dalrymple, William, *The Last Mughal: The Fall of a Dynasty, Delhi, 1857*, New Delhi: Penguin Books, 2006, pp. 296-97.
6. Foreign Department, Political – A, December 1867, No. 52/53, "From Lieutinent Roome, to Col. Sir R. Shakespear, G.G.," agent Central India, pp. 1-3.
7. Foreign Department, Political – A, May 1868, K. W. Proceedings, May, No. 153-155, pp. 1-2, preserved in the National Archives, New Delhi. Qazi Sarfaraz Ali son of Amanat Ali belonged to a respectable family of Shahjehanpur. He received his initial education in Amroha and then moved to Delhi. After completing higher education there, he got appointed Munsif in the Government of Bahadur Shah Zafar. After the revolt was suppressed, the British gave him life sentence and sent to the Andamans. He returned to Shahjehanpur after completing his sentence and died there in 1876. See Qadri, Mohammed Ayub, *1857: Jang-e-Azadi, Waqiyat-o-Shakhsiyat* (Urdu, *The 1857 War of*

Independence: Events and Personalities), Karachi: Pak Academy, 1975, pp. 459-60. Mohammed Hasan, the rebel Nazim of Gorakhpur, had appointed Sheikh Sarfaraz Ali, as the tehsildar of Bansgaon. He belonged to Awadh. See, Foreign Department, Political – A, May 1868, No. 31, 1 February 1868, p. 2. Both these persons were not Maulvi Sarfaraz Ali.

8. Foreign Department, Political – A, May 1868 KW, Proceedings, May, No. 153-155, p. 2.
9. *Ibid*, 22 May 1868, pp. 2-3.
10. *Ibid*, p. 3.
11. *Ibid*, 23 May 1868.
12. *Ibid.* From Mr R. H. Clifford, Officiating Magistrate of Goruckpore, 1 February 1868, Letter No. 31.
13. *Ibid*, para 1.
14. *Ibid.*
15. *Ibid*, para 2.
16. *Ibid*, para 3.
17. Foreign Department, Political – A, May 1868 K.W. Proceedings, May, No. 153-155, p. 2. From Ganesh Prasad Chaube to Officiating Court Judge, Lucknow.
18. Hasan, Mujahidul, *Mecca Muazzama se Muazzamabad tak* (Urdu, *From Holy Mecca to Gorakhpur*), Lucknow: Kakori Press, 2010, 106.
19. Qadri, Mohammed Ayub, *op cit*, pp. 541-42.
20. *Ibid*, p. 542.
21. See, Ashraf, K M, "Muslim Revivalists and the Revolt of 1857" in Joshi, P. C. (Ed), *Rebellion 1857*, New Delhi: National Book Trust, 2007, p. 107, FN 59. See Yadav, K. C. (Ed), *Delhi in 1857*, Vol. 1: *The Trial of Bahadur Shah*, Gurgaon: The Academic Press, 1980, p. 141.
22. Qadri, Mohammed Ayub, *op cit*, pp. 406-16.
23. *Sadiqul-Akhbar*, Vol. 4, No. 4, Hijri 1273 (6 Bhado, V.S. 1914), p. 191; 27 July 1857, p. 4. It was an Urdu paper and was being published during the revolt.
24. Dalrymple, William, *op cit*, pp. 285, 296.
25. *Ibid,* p. 285.
26. Foreign Department, Political – A, May 1868, K W Proceedings, May, No. 153-54, Letter No. 31, 1 February 1868, para 1, p. 12.
27. Rizvi, Syed Athar Abbas, *FSUP*, Vol. IV, pp. 347.
28. Qadri, Mohammed Ayub, *op cit*, pp. 541-42; Haq, Syed Moinul, *op cit*, p. 63.
29. Haq, Syed Moinul, *ibid,* p. 512.
30. *Ibid*, pp. 512-13.
31. *Ibid*, p. 512.
32. Rizvi, Syed Khurshid Mustafa, *Tarikh-e-Jang-e-Azadi-e-Hind 1857* (Urdu, *History of Indian War of Independence 1857*), pp. 46-47, 575, Rampur, 2000; Mian, Hazrat Maulana Mohammed, *Ulema-e-Hind ka Shandar Mazi* (Urdu, *Glorious Past of Indian Ulema*), Vol. IV, 1857; *Jan-b-Jan-e-Hurriyat* (Urdu, *Staking Life for Independence*), Lahore: Maktaba Mehmoodiya, p. 406; Chaudhuri Sashi Bhusan, Theories of the Indian Mutiny (1857-59), pp. 26-31.

33. Haider, Kamaluddin, *Sawanihat-i-Salatin-i-Awadh* (Urdu, *History of the Sultans of Awadh*), Lucknow,1889, Vol. 2, p. 425; Shahabi, Intezamullah, *East India Company aur Baghi Ulema* (Urdu, *East India Company and the Rebel Ulema*), Lahore: Maktaba Rizwan, Delhi reprint: p. 73; Mehar, Ghulam Rasool, *1857 ke Mujahid* (Urdu, *The Warriors of 1857*), Lahore: Kitab Manzil, p. 106; Husain, Iqbal, *op cit*, p. 156; Bhargava, M L, *Saga of 1857: Successes and Failures*, New Delhi: Reliance Publishing House, 1992, p. 82; Dalrymple, William, *op cit*, p. 285.
34. Haider, Kamaluddin, *op cit*; Joshi, P. C., *op cit*, p. 107, FN 58.
35. Haq, Syed Moinul, *op cit*, pp. 539-40; Mian, Hazrat Maulana Mohammed, *op cit*, pp. 331-32.
36. Dalrymple, William, *op cit*, p. 285.
37. *Ibid*, p. 64; the letter's copy is printed; Qadri, Mohammed Ayub, *op cit*, p. 466.
38. Haq, Syed Moinul, *op cit*, p. 182.
39. *Ibid*, p. 181.
40. *Ibid*, p. 182.
41. *Ibid*, p. 179.
42. *Ibid*, p. 189.
43. Press List of Mutiny Papers 1857, August 1857, Bundle No. 151, Document No. 12 and 13, p. 376, folio 2, preserved in National Archives of India, New Delhi.
44. Dalrymple, William, *op cit*, pp. 296-97.
45. *Ibid*, FN on p. 338.
46. *Ibid*, p. 294.
47. According to a description, the number of *jihadis* had swelled to 90,000. According to Dalrymple, the number of sepoys as on 10 September 1857 was 60,000, while the warriors numbered half of it, about 25,000. See, *The Last Mughal*, p. 338.
48. The Wahabis, even when empty-stomached, fought against the British. See, Rizvi, Syed Athar Abbas, *Swatantra Dilli* (*Independent Delhi*), Lucknow: Hindi Samiti, p. 1968, p. 105.
49. Husain Iqbal, "Bakht Khan: A leading Sepoy General of 1857" in Saiyid Zaheer Hussain Jafri (ed.) Delhi and Awadh during 1857, Studies, Images and Documents, p. 230 (Gyan Publishing House, New Delhi, 2020).
50. Rizvi, Syed Athar Abbas, *FSUP*, Vol. IV, pp. 345, 347.
51. Foreign Department, Foreign Consultation from Captain G. H. Byers, Officiating Resident in Nepal, In-charge of the Residency, to G.P. Edmonston esq. Secretary to the Government of India in the Foreign Department with the Governor General, Allahabad, 11 December 1858, pp. 7, enclosure copy of resume in the case of Dummana Khan forwarded by C. Wingfield, Commissioner of Goruckpore, 27 November 1858, pp. 17-18, preserved in National Archives of India, New Delhi.
52. Foreign Department, Political A, Proceedings, October, Letter No. 21, 10 September 1867, para 3, preserved in National Archives of India, New Delhi.

53. *Ibid,* Letter No. 22. Fuzul Ali was living incognito in the *terai* forests, in a mud fortress near Jarva. Colonel Boileau, the newly appointed First District Collector of Gonda, laid a siege on him. During the encounter, Fazal Ali shot Colonel Boileau dead, beheaded him and went into hiding in the thick forests in the north. Lieutenant Clark surrounded him after a few months and killed him in the encounter. See, Carnegy. P, Commissioner, *A Gazetteer of the Province of Awadh (A to Z)*, Delhi: Low Price Publications, reprint, 2006, p. 546. The place in Jarva where Fazal Ali had beheaded Colonel Boileau is now famous as Mudkatwa Bagh. Anup Giri Gosain son of Kewal Giri Gosain, of village Gugauli, was sentenced to one year of imprisonment for instigating Fuzul Ali to kill Boileau. See, Singh, Bhagwati Prasad (Ed), *Rashtriya Swatantrata Sangram aur Gonda Janpad* (Hindi, *War of National Independence and Gonda District*), Varanasi: Shivam Printers, pp. 74-76. Jaykishan Puri and Damman Khan had provided a hideout to Fuzul Ali.
54. Wingfield, C, Narrative of Events: 5 July 1858, para 19, p. 3.
55. Rizvi, Syed Athar Abbas, *FSUP*, Vol. IV, p. 347; Haq, Syed Moinul, *op cit*, p. 494.
56. Foreign Department, 1858, Secret, 24 September, No. 3, From Commissioner of Gorakhpur to the Secretary of Government, North Western Provinces, Gorakhpur, 27 July 1858, para 7, p. 2, preserved in National Archives of India, New Delhi.
57. Foreign Department, Political – A, Proceedings, July 1868, No. 375, para 1, p. 1, preserved in National Archives of India, New Delhi.
58. Foreign Department, Political – A, Proceedings – October, No. 21, 10 September 1867.
59. Foreign Department, Political – A, Proceedings, July 1868, No. 375, From Colonel R.C. Lawrence No. 14 dated 10th July 1868 (confidential), para 2 and 4. p. 1.
60. *Ibid*, para 3, p. 1.
61. *Ibid*, para 5, p. 1.
62. *Ibid.*
63. *Ibid*, para 7, pp. 1-2
64. *Ibid*, para 7, pp. 1-2
65. *Ibid*, para 8, p. 2
66. *Ibid.*
67. Foreign Department, Political – A, Proceedings, October 1867, Letter No. 22.
68. Foreign Department, Political – A, Proceedings, December 1867, No. 52, preserved in National Archives of India, New Delhi.
69. Bhargava, M L, *Architects of Indian Freedom Struggle*, New Delhi: Deep and Deep Publications, p. 86.
70. In November 2014, the author visited the tombs of both in Kathmandu. Shamima Siddika wrote that "Maulana Sarfaraz Ali of Delhi, a *mufti* of Mughal Emperor, Bahadur Shah Zafar, came to Kathmandu and, living here, got the Jami Masjid of Nepal renovated. Here he died and was buried in the courtyard of the Masjid.

After her death, Begum Hazrat Mahal too was buried about a hundred yards to the south of the Jami Masjid of Nepal." See, *Muslims of Nepal*, Kathmandu, 1993, p. 132. (Xerox copy of this page was provided to me, by Triratna Manandhar, an eminent historian of Nepal. I am thankful to him).

Chapter - 4

Main Events of Rebellion in Eastern Uttar Pradesh

The sepoys' revolt at Meerut, the arrival of rebel sepoys in Delhi and the declaration of Bahadur Shah Zafar as the Emperor of India, stunned the British rulers all over the country. They now put their complete efforts to strengthening their security and crushing the rebellious elements. However, despite all their efforts, they could not prevent the mass discontent from turning into a mass revolt. Eastern Uttar Pradesh did not remain untouched either. Below we describe the major events of this mass revolt according to the then existing British districts.

Major Events of Revolt in Gorakhpur District

Gorakhpur district spanned from the north of Ghaghra river to the *terai* of Nepal and from the border of Awadh in the west to the border of Bihar in the east. Strategically, it was very important because of its geographical and climatic characteristics. Despite the Company Government's heavy security preparations in Gorakhpur district, the Rajput zamindars of Paina village to the north of Ghaghra declared an open revolt on 31 May 1857, by capturing the grain-laden boats of the English, plying through the waterway.[1] Then the district had two and a half companies of the 17th Native Infantry (NI) under Captain Steel and one and a half companies (Risala) of the 12th Irregular cavalry.[2] Further, a small troop of the 17th NI was stationed in the military cantonment at Sagauli. The 17th NI had its headquarter in Azamgarh district where the rest of the regiment stayed. Several sepoys had refused there to use the greased cartridges.[3] Apart from this fact, however, there was nothing that could make the English officials anxious. Soldiers of the 19th NI could be a conduit of discontent; at Behrampore they had refused to use the greased cartridges on 26 February 1857. That regiment had been disbanded and its soldiers had scattered all over in North India. Some of its soldiers were also accorded a welcome in Azamgarh as both the regiments had been formed and trained at Lucknow together.[4] Hence, Mr. Paterson, the District Magistrate of Gorakhpur, had announced on 25th May 1857 that, "any soldier of 19th NI should be arrested if found anywhere in the district."[5] Nay more, at Gorakhpur, English officials were ready to release (dismiss) the soldiers who did not want to use the greased cartridges.[6] Taking precautions, they sent the surplus treasury from Gorakhpur to Azamgarh in the custody of 125 soldiers of 17th NI, and it did reach there safe on 29 May.[7]

The news of 17th NI's revolt at Azamgarh reached Gorakhpur on 5 June 1857. The news spread like a forest fire. Enthused by it, men of the Raja of Narharpur beat up the policemen at Barhal Ghat police post on 6 June and made them run away. They also freed the 50 prisoners working there. They captured the *ghat* to control the ferry traffic, and also disrupted the postal service for Azamgarh.[8] Attempts were made on 8th June to break the jail at Gorakhpur and free the prisoners, and to capture the treasury on 9th June, but in vain.[9]

10 June 1857 was the most memorable day in the history of popular revolt in Gorakhpur; this was when the first and most notable event of the Mahua Dabar village took place. Following a revolt in the Faizabad Cantonment on 9 June, some British military officials boarded three boats and left for Danapur (Bihar) through the waterway. Some native soldiers accompanied them for security. En route, they came across some rebel soldiers of the 17th NI who were then going from Azamgarh to Faizabad. When the rebel soldiers rained bullets, the British had to abandon the boats and seek shelter. Next day they reached Captainganj tehsil (at present in Basti district) where the tehsildar hesitated to send them to Basti and suggested that they should go to Danapur via waterway. He provided them fifty rupees, some mules and two Muslim musketeers as security personnel and guide and sent them to Gaighat. On the way, at the Muslim preponderant village of Mahua Dabar in pargana Nagar, a crowd killed six of the English officials, while Sergeant Busher alone managed to escape. The Muslim musketeer had taken these officials to that village by deceit.[10] The event of Mahua Dabar village was the first major expression of mass discontent against the English Government in the district, and also showed the people's fearlessness. Therefore, in order to generate fear among the people anew, Mr. Peppe, a Deputy Magistrate, was sent to the district to punish the culprits. Mr. Peppe got the whole Mahua Dabar village torched to ashes. People had already deserted the village before he arrived there. However, the police filed cases against 13 persons and held two to be the ring leaders.

We have no information about what happened to them, but five Pathans of the village were indeed executed on the charge of sedition.[11]

The Mahua Dabar event is important also because on the same date, 10 June, the government had issued a proclaimation that "those zamindars who may be guilty of any act or of aiding any act to subvert the government will forfeit their estates and those estates will be made over to such zamindars as may exert themselves for the cause of order and the powers that be."[12] But the event demonstrated that the announcement had no impact upon the people. On 11 June, a troop of the 17th NI looted 7,800 rupees from the chest of the opium factory in Basti and thus demonstrated its rebelliousness.[13] The Englishmen were scared to death in this district. Hence, when Gountier, the owner of an indigo factory, was told to go to Basti as the Deputy Magistrate and restore peace and order there, he fled from home for Danapur.[14]

The popular revolt had now engulfed Gorakhpur district. The Gorakhpur-Barhalganj Road was virtually closed and Mr. Bird, the Joint Magistrate, was striving to get it opened.[15] Moreover, the government appealed to the pensioners, prominent rajas and taluqdars for help.[16]

On 15 June 1857, in order to scare the people, an announcement was made that those rebelling or helping the rebels would be punished under Act XIV of 1857. Two new police battalions were also formed. But the people were getting fearless. Hence, on 20 June 1857, Martial Law was promulgated in the entire Commissionerate and a number of English traders and forest grantees were made deputy magistrates.[17] On 30 June, at the request of the Company Government, 200 Gorkha soldiers from Palpa, in the Nepal terai, too arrived at Gorakhpur to help the district administration.[18] But rebellious activities continued to spread despite all this. In taluka Ganeshpur under pargana Nagar, rebels shot upon Mr. Peppe who then ran away to save himself.[19]

Zamindars of pargana Amorha openly declared allegiance to the Nawab of Awadh. Similarly, rajas of Narharpur, Nagar and Satasi Raj as well as the babus of Pandeypar and other places held secret meetings. Then they publicly declared that they would abide by Awadh Government's orders and extend help to it.[20]

Moved by rebellious thoughts, soldiers at Sagauli killed Major Holmes on 26 July 1857 and then left for Salempur where they plundered the house of an opium agent and set it afire. They also tried to loot the treasury there, but in vain.[21]

The revolt in the Sagauli Cantt compelled Lord Canning, the Governor General, to seek military help from Nepal, which he had refused a few days back. At the request of Major Ramsay, British Resident at Kathmandu, an army of 3,000 strong Gorkhas led by Colonel Pahalwan Singh Basnet and, simultaneously, a small troop under Lieutenant Heera Singh left for Gorakhpur. Of these, two Gorkha regiments were sent to Champaran which, along with Brigadier Rowcroft, faced several encounters and scored successes against the rebels. The Gorkha army that came from Sagauli to Gorakhpur was dead tired, cholera had gripped it, and it had lost about 150 soldiers. Moreover, most of its soldiers had fever. Its commander publicly admitted that its military power had dwindled to that of only four regiments. They were not prepared to do any military expedition in separate groups. Rebels of Gorakhpur and those from Awadh were well aware of all these circumstances.[22]

In these circumstances, on 10 August 1857, a rebel contingent led by Mohammed Hasan came from Tanda after crossing the Ghaghra. Along with the local rebels, this contingent raided and looted tehsil Khalilabad. On the same day, the Babu of Bakhira beat the policemen of his thana and chased them away. Rebels captured tehsil Captainganj too on 12 August. From the troop of the 12th Irregular Cavalry which was sent to protect the tehsil, 40 mounted sepoys deserted the government and joined the rebels.[23] The Gorkha troop, which had come to help the British, looked incapable of containing the rebellion. As such, the British found themselves scared and helpless. They decided to leave Gorakhpur district for Azamgarh.

The English civilian officers in the district said they would stay back only if at least four regiments were there. Finally, through a proposal, they decided to leave Gorakhpur after handing over the administration to five of the rajas — those of Satasi, Bansi, Gopalpur, Majhauli and Tamkuhi.[24] Then all the European families collected at the district headquarter. All these Europeans, and some pro-British Indians, left for Azamgarh, along with the treasure containing five lakh rupees, under the protection of Gorkha soldiers.[25]

The helplessness, fear and weakness of the British as well as the sad plight of Gorkha army only added to the rebels' enthusiasm and ardour. Hence, they decided to capture the treasure being taken to Azamgarh. They attacked the group at a place called Gagaha, 10 miles before Barhalganj, on 18 August. But the Gorkhas killed 200 rebels and forced others to flee. The British captured Mohammed Hasan's palanquin[26] which had number of letters from rebels.

Mr. Bird, the English Joint Magistrate of Gorakhpur, was staying there in the vain hope of keeping the district under British control with the zamindars' help. But he found only 17 out of 150 prison guards loyal to the government. Nor was any raja, except that of Gopalpur, loyal to the British.[27] Thus, the British policy of running the government with the help of rajas (zamindars) failed. On 15 August he released the prisoners,[28] including Musharraf Khan.[29] While the Gorkha troop safely reached Azamgarh along with the treasure and the European civilians and officials, Mohammed Hasan reached the outskirt of Gorakhpur city, on the western bank of the Rapti, on 20 August. The rebel government of Awadh had appointed him the Nazim of Gorakhpur. As the British had fled away, Musharraf Khan, representative of the Raja of Satasi, other rebellious rajas, the babus and respectable residents of the city fearlessly welcomed him as the Nazim and brought him to the city next day, on 21 August.[30]

As the Nazim, Mohammed Hasan declared a reward of five thousand rupees on the head of Mr. Bird, the Company Government's sole officer staying in the city. Hearing about it, Mr. Bird remained incognito whole day on 22 August and then left for Motihari where he did reach safe.[31]

Establishing his independent government in Gorakhpur, Mohammed Hasan appointed Musharraf Khan his deputy (Naib Nazim). He also appointed a judge and a collector. Soon he appointed respectable persons on other important positions. But he also knew that a new system of administration could not be created overnight, as it required experienced persons. Hence, he issued the order that all government servants should come back to their posts; otherwise they will be punished. In his narrative, C. Wingfield, the Commissioner of Gorakhpur, wrote with satisfaction that not a single Deputy Collector joined his employ, that only a tehsildar and some *thanedars* offered their services. Despite this, Mohammed Hasan saved properties from destruction, got the *kachahari* documents preserved, and got them bound. From these documents and from the *qanungos*, he learnt about the amount every zamindar owed to the government. Most of the *qanungos* accepted his employment and continued in their positions as earlier. Hence his government easily learnt about the pending land revenues and other arrears. He honoured the big landlords (rajas and babus), who had accepted his rule, with robes of honour and gun salutes. He gave them the right to use their civil and criminal powers in their zamindaris and restored the former rights which they demanded. In response to all this, the rajas and babus put their military troops at his disposal. The rajas of Satasi, Nagar, Narharpur, Badhyapar, Nichlaul and Shahpur and the babus of

Tighra, Pandeypar and Rudhauli were prominent among those who accepted his suzerainty, rights and obligations.[32]

The rebel government left most of the *pucca* buildings intact; it got only Mr. Bird's house destroyed by a special order. About this, the Commissioner wrote, "Mahomed Hussun seems to have at first thought his power permanently established: at least he never imagined it would be disturbed by us."[33] That was why he did not undertake destruction. This was a wrong thinking of the English officer. Besides, he also wrote paradoxically that "Large sums of money were extorted by the violence or threats of it from the Merchants and Bankers of the city, and the female members of many families were dishonoured by his lawless and licentious soldiery."[34] According to C. Wingfield, "In the district those who had lost their estates through the Agency of the Civil Courts, now ousted the purchasers and re-entered in possession: great search was also made for deeds and decrees. The strong preyed everywhere on the weak."[35]

According to Moinuddin Hasan who was pro-British, "Mohammed Hasan recruited an army of 25,000, which included people of seven castes like the weavers, carders, oilmen and betel-sellers."[36] This shows that Mohammed Hasan formed not only a national government but also a national army which comprised people from all the classes and castes.

The next task before Mohammed Hasan's government was to subdue, by force, such rajas (zamindars) of the district as had refused to accept his rule and sided with the British, and to collect revenue from them. Most important from this viewpoint were the Raja of Gopalpur on the Ghaghra bank, the Raja of Bansi in the north-western part of the district, and the Rajas of Majhauli and Tamkuhi in the east. Mohammed Hasan, first of all, despatched an army to collect revenue from the Raja of Gopalpur, which the Raja defeated and drove away. Then he sent another, bigger army which the Raja was unable to face. So, he fled to Azamgarh and returned only after the British rule was restored in the district.[37] Similarly, the Raja of Bansi too had refused to obey Mohammed Hasan's orders and hand him over the tehsil's treasure. Therefore, Naib Nazim Musharraf Khan went to Bansi with a big army. The Raja of Bansi readily accepted Mohammed Hasan's lordship and welcomed the tehsildar appointed by him, as he had seen the Raja of Gopalpur's fate.[38] Begum Hazrat Mahal had appointed Damman Khan, a jagirdar in the Nepal *terai*, the chakladar of Bansi and Mohammed Hasan had appointed Mendhu Khan the tehsildar of Bansi East.[39] This shows that rebels wanted to have a full control over Bansi, due to its strategic importance. The Raja of Basti was a minor and his mother,

Rani Digambar Kunwari, used to manage the Basti Estate. She was Babu Kunwar Singh's niece while the Raja of Satasi was her son-in-law. She was on the side of the British and did not allow the thanedar of Basti to enter the city. But no harsh step was ever taken against her in view of her links.[40] The Raja of Tamkuhi covertly and the Raja of Majhauli, situated in the south-east of the district, openly helped the British, and did not stand by Mohammed Hasan's government.[41]

In Gorakhpur, Mohammed Hasan's rebel government continued from 22 August 1857 to 5 January 1858. The rebels dominated their adversaries. This situation was intolerable for the British Government. Its plight was pitiable in Lucknow as well. Therefore, at Governor General Lord Canning's request, Maharaja Jang Bahadur Rana, the Prime Minister of Nepal, moved out to help the British, with an army of ten thousand trained Gorkhas. As their way to Lucknow passed through Gorakhpur, they reached Sagauli on 21 December and came to Pipra, after crossing the Chhoti Gandak, on 30 December.[42]

On the other hand, rebels of Gorakhpur decided to attack and capture the Majhauli Raj in order to spread the rebellion in the east. With 500 sepoys, Harkishan Singh, nephew of Babu Kunwar Singh, left Gorakhpur for Majhauli. With a contingent of 5,000 people who included 1,100 to 1,200 sepoys, Naib Nazim Musharraf Khan too started for Majhauli. Finding Majhauli in trouble, the British Government ordered Colonel Rowcroft, the Commander of Saran Field Force, to bring his army to defend Majhauli. Colonel Rowcroft demanded more soldiers in order to face the rebels. Therefore, 500 Gorkha soldiers were sent to him on 25 December. Now he had 1,600 soldiers who included 160 of the Naval Brigade and 160 European soldiers. Along with his strong army, he moved towards Majhauli. Getting the news, the rebels decided to move forward from Majhauli and fight Colonel Rowcroft en route. They created a front in Sohanpur village on the Chhoti Gandak's bank, between Mairwa (in Bihar) and Majhauli. They fought against Colonel Rowcroft's trained army on 26 December 1857, and the rebels had to retreat after a few hours of battle. About 120 rebels sacrificed their lives in this battle. The rest went to Gorakhpur and some went to fight the Gorkhas.[43] Majhauli was vacated by the rebels. The Raja of Majhauli welcomed Colonel Rowcroft when he reached there. Next day, on 27 December, Colonel Rowcroft got the houses of Qanungo Narayan Dayal and his nephew Sangram Lal Tumandar, who were pro-rebels, burnt down. These houses were in Salempur, two miles to the east. He also took some people prisoners in order to create fear among the rebels' supporters.

Then he moved ahead and stationed himself at Barhal Ghat, waiting for the next instruction.[44]

While the defeat of the rebels at Sohanpur village was yet to be reparationed, Mohammed Hasan got the news of arrival of Maharaja Jang Bahadur's Gorkha army at Pipra. The Gorkha army moved towards Gorakhpur along the right bank of Chhoti Gandak and reached Pipraich town, about 15 miles from the city, on 6 January 1858. The rebels were no match to this army. Hence, they adopted the tactic of surprise attacks. However, nothing took place except some minor skirmishes. Led by Mohammed Hasan, the rebels fought against the Gorkha army when it reached Gorakhpur, and three to four hundred people were killed. The rebels were defeated. On the same day, along with his men, Mohammed Hasan crossed the Ghaghra and escaped to Tanda. On 11 January, the British recaptured Gorakhpur.[45] Syed Ahmed Ali Shah has presented an exaggerated description of the British officers' arrival along with the Nepalese army, their battle with the rebels, the retreat and destruction of the rebels, and the British re-occupation of Gorakhpur. He writes:

"Satrahween ko afwaj Nepaliyaan
Do-Shambah raha rooz, aiye doostaan".
[On the seventeenth arrived the Nepalese armies,
O friends! The day was Monday]
"Sidhawa mein afwaj aakar rahi
Ke har kas-o-naakas pe shaadi hui".
[The armies came and stayed at Sidhawa, (Jobna)
Happiness descended upon all and sundry]
"Hain Sahib collector bhi humraah-e fauj
Zahe shaan -o shaukat zahe faar-o-auj".
[Collector sahib also came along with the army
Excellent glory and splendour, wonderful zenith of humility]
"Aur sahib Bird unke humraah hain
Jo khursheed hain woh to ye maah hain".
[And Bird Sahib is along with him
If that one is the Sun, then this one is the Moon]
"Aur Sahib Commissioner bhi lashkar ke saath
Nishan e zafar sab ke hain haathon haath".
[And Commissioner Sahib is also accompanying the army

Everyone flaunts signs of a speedy victory]

"Siwa unke paltan ke sab sahibaan

Chale aate hain yahan ke hamla kunaan".

[Besides them all the officers of the platoon

Are arriving here for making attacks]

"Do-sham'bah se sham'bah ko sab sahibaan

Maa fauj -e-Gorkhai ba-izz-o shan".

[on Monday and Tuesday, all the officers

Escorted by the Gorkha army, with dignity and grandeur]

xxxxxx xxxxxxxxx xxxxxxxx xxxxxxx

Sidhawa mein aakar hue khaimazan

Hua wan ka maidaan rashq-e-chaman

[Arrived at Sidhawa and encamped, the fields there became envy of gardens]

xxxxxx xxxxxxxxx xxxxxxxx xxxxxxx

"Sada toop ki phir nikalne lagi

Banadeeq ki baadh chalne lagi".

[Then the sounds of cannons started coming, Floods of muskets started flowing]

"Chali toop-e-Nepaliyaan dhayeen dhayeen

Aur banduq karne lagi thayeen thayeen".

[The cannons of the Nepalese boomed with a great din 'dhayeen dhayeen' and the fired shot guns made the sounds 'thayeen thayeen']

Toh afwaaj-e-adu mein khalbal machi,

Kamar bhagne par har ek ne kasi

[Thus, chaos and confusion reigned in the armies of the enemy,

Everyone was prepared to flee]

xxxxxxxx xxxxxxxxxx xxxxxxxx xxxxxxxx

Talaatum mein masnui Nazim pade

Sitam kya karen khud faraari hue

[The fraudulent Nazim was buffeted by the dash of events, what could he oppress? He himself became a fugitive.]

Jo aawaz toopon ki aane lagi
Hui tab to zaalim ko ek bekali
[when the sounds of cannons started coming, then the ruthless becomes the restless]

Misaal-e-nazar fauj pahunchi yahaan
Chali aayi kahti ke baaghi kahaan
[Instantenously, like a momentary glance the army reached here, came bellowing, where are the rebels]

Toh dariya pe jaa ke hue sab baham,
Faramosh sab dil se raah-e-sitam
[So, they all collected near the river, all violent ways discarded by their hearts]

Bahut log kishti pe hokar sawaar,
Lage hone jaldi se dariya ke paar
[many people boarded the boat, started crossing the river in haste]

Ke yakbargi fauz English ki wahaan,
Jo pahunchi toh sab ko kiya benishaan
[However, the English army came there, and on reaching wiped out everyone].

Diya taak ke ek gola wahin
Ke lehra ke kashti hui tahnashin
[Then and there they aimed and fired a shot from the cannon, swinging and out of balance the boat sunk]

Jo hone lage pher-e-toop-o-tufang
Hue shaad dariya ke saare nahang
[when the exchange of cannons and guns begun
All the crocodiles were pleased]

Bahut baaghi dariya pe maare gaye
Bahut khud ba khud duub kar ke muye
[Many rebels were killed on the rivers, many drowned themselves to their death]

Mohammad Hasan tha jo ek bad khisaal
Woh bhaaga hai yahaan se ba misl-e- shaghaal
[Mohamed Hasan who was an evil man, fled from there like a jackal]

Sitam aur jaur uska sab ho gaya

Raaya ko aaraam bus ho gaya

[All his tyranny and oppression was over, finally the subjects were at rest.]

xxxxxx xxxxxxxxx xxxxxxxx xxxxxxx

Gorakhpur mein aaye sab sahibaan

Chahaar sham'bah tha rooz aiye doostaan

[all these persons came to Gorakhpur,

O friends! that day was Thursday.]."[46]

However, the rebellion did not subside with the British re-occupation of Gorakhpur. Instead, the next phase of a guerrilla war commenced and it continued for about a year in 1858.

After Mohammed Hasan left for Tanda, the British concentrated on Naib Nazim Musharraf Khan and his master, Raja Udit Narayan Singh of Satasi. The Rudrapur fortress of this Raja had become the shelter for the rebels. The Raja got this stronghold fortified. So, with an army, Colonel Rowcroft reached Rudrapur on 11 January 1858. However, the rebels had already got the news and vacated Rudrapur. Yet, Rowcroft got the fortification destroyed, seized the weapons found there, and got the grains despatched to the Gorakhpur Cantt.[47] The Raja of Satasi was compelled to hide in a jungle and conduct a guerrilla war.

Musharraf Khan ran away and took shelter with the Rani of Mahson at Mahuli. She was the mother-in-law of Satasi raja Udit Narayan Singh. The Rani of Mahson sent Musharraf Khan as his envoy to the English to negotiate peace, but the English arrested him. He was tried in a military court and sentenced to death. Then he was put in a cage, displayed in Alinagar, the main market of Gorakhpur where he regularly held his durbar and moved about in a kingly style, and publicly executed.[48]

Mohammed Hasan did not lie idle even after escaping to Tanda and chalked out strategies to defeat the British. Pargana Amorha on the northern bank of Ghaghra became his next target. Amorha had become a military base of the British, and he wanted to capture it in order to turn the tide in his favour. Most of the rebels too had congregated here. They began to prepare for a showdown by digging a ditch in Belwa village near Amorha. Here, soldiers of the Raja of Gonda, Raja of Nanpara and Raja of Charda as well as soldiers of several taluqdars of Awadh were prepared to fight under Mehdi Hasan, the Nazim of Sultanpur. On 2 March 1858, this army had a face down with Colonel Rowcroft's army, forcing Rowcroft to retreat. This boosted the rebel army's morale. But the two sides again collided on

5 March 1858 and the rebel army had to retreat, with heavy losses, though Rowcroft could not muster courage to chase the rebels. From Belwa, he returned to Amorha.[49]

After this collision, the rebels adopted the guerrilla tactic. They used to cross the river, Ghaghra from Tanda side, burn the police stations down, and returned back after plundering.[50]

Mohammed Hasan started from Belwa to occupy Amorha and had a battle with Rowcroft's army on 17 April 1858. Mohammed Hasan was defeated and had to escape to Domariaganj in the northern part of the district. He had lost some 100 soldiers in this battle while four officers and 17 soldiers of the British army had been killed.[51] This shows the severity of the fight between rebels and Rowcroft's armies.

When the rebels found the British in a strong position on the Ghaghra bank, they increased their activities in the north of Basti and also planned to capture Basti. Along with some rebels from Awadh, Babu Shiv Ghulam Singh of Rudhauli plundered Bakhira and killed the government's receiver (representative) stationed there. Dividing themselves into several groups, the rebels began their plunder and also made an abortive attempt to plunder Menhdawal Bazaar, a famous market place of Bansi pargana.

Along with 300 followers, Babu Shiv Ghulam Singh reached Pauda (Paura) village, six miles to the north-east of Basti, and began his fortification. His plan was to attack Basti, in league with the Raja of Nagar. The latter was already camping in the jungles of Babhni, along with his followers. As soon as, Mr. Wilson, the Assistant Magistrate of Basti got to know about the rebels' planning, he, despatched an army troop with Captain Clark to Poorwa village. Babu Shiv Ghulam Singh was killed in the battle there, along with 30 companions.[52]

Mohammed Hasan was in Domariaganj at the time, wanting to attack Bansi. But differences developed between him and his soldiers. So, he gave up the plan to attack Bansi and went to Tulsipur.[53]

In April 1858, the Raja of Nagar (situated to the north of Ghaghra), and his employees and followers intensified their rebellious activities. On 26 April, the raja's bailiff and a number of sepoys tried to re-occupy his estate that had been confiscated. On 27 April, they occupied the house of the Pindari zamindar of Ganeshpur. The Pindaris were pro-British. Hence an army troop was sent against them. In the meantime, the rebels moved out to occupy the Raja of Nagar's hereditary fortress. En route, they plundered Major Richardson's camp, laying hands upon Major Richardson's pretty horse and some valuables. On 29 April, therefore, Colonel Rowcroft was sent against them, with a troop. This army had a showdown with the rebels. The latter could not hold ground, crossed the Ghaghra and moved into the Awadh territory.[54]

Dividing themselves into small groups, the rebels also tried to obstruct the way of the Gorkha army that was returning from Lucknow and excessively frightened Captain Plowden who was in-charge of the Gorkha army. Eventually, the Gorkha army managed to cross the river some distance away, with the help from Mansingh, the taluqdar of Shahganj (Jaunpur).[55]

During the phase of guerrilla warfare, those who terrorised and oppressed the British most were Babu Bandhu Singh of Dumri and his followers. There were very secret and aggressive activities. On 29 April 1858, along with 300 supporters, this rebellious Babu of Dumri raided the government post and killed 11 policemen. On 4 May, they attacked the Dumri thana. On 5 May, under Mr. Bird, a troop of Gorkha soldiers was sent to capture them, but they could not apprehend the rebels. On 14 May, the Babus of Dumri looted 40 carts laden with grains, which were being taken to a government godown.[56] On 16 May, the same party chased the Gorkha troop returning from Lucknow for Nepal and looted some of its belongings. Next day, they attacked the Pipraich thana and killed the thanedar and some policemen. On 17 May they killed a postal employee. On 21 May, the party sent under Mr. Bird to capture them, returned empty-handed once again.[57]

In this period, the rebels crossed the Ghaghra river and committed some plunder in Gorakhpur, in order to try divert the attention of the British from the babus of Dumri. On 10 May 1858, about 150 armed rebels crossed the Ghaghra river at Salona Ghat, to the west of Tanda, did some plunder and, while returning, took a pro-British zamindar as hostage.[58] Further, on 14 May, the Raja of Narharpur, who was staying in Jahangirganj area along with his followers, crossed the Ghaghra river near the Chandipur Ghat along with a large number of Palwar Rajputs, and looted Hainser Bazaar and three nearby villages. On the same day, he also took four persons hostage while returning.[59] On 16 May, the Raja of Nagar crossed the river near Tanda, looted several villages, and also took some rich zamindars as hostages in order to raise money.[60] Simultaneously, a troop of rebels looted the Gaighat market and killed the tehsildar of Khalilabad who was collecting land revenue. Government employees under him ran away. They were so afraid of the rebels that they agreed to work only in the British army's protection.[61]

On 21 May, along with other rebels, Ranjit Singh, uncle of the Raja of Nagar, looted a village in pargana Nagar.[62]

While the rebels' aggressive activities were still continuing on the southern border of the district, an event drew attention of the British towards the northern parts. Along with about a hundred persons, Raja Randul Sen of Nichlaul attacked Mr. Peppe's house in Birdpur (on the north-east border of Bansi) and compelled him to run away to Gorakhpur for life. Five of Mr. Peppe's men were killed.[63]

Rebels had not yet abandoned the plan to capture Amorha. There were six to seven hundred rebels, along with four cannons, at Belwa, in the south-western part of the district. They took advantage of the situation, moved to Amorha, and made the Rani of Amorha's house their post.[64] Along with two cannons of the Nasirabad Brigade's artillery and the survivors of the Nasirabad regiment, comprising seven to eight hundred sepoys, the Raja of Gonda occupied Belwa. Now they wanted to proceed via Captainganj in order to capture Basti. In this situation, Commissioner C. Wingfield feared that "In such case Mohamed Hussun from the north and the Menhdee Hussun from Tanda would also probably advance in concert and their united force would be most formidable." Therefore, he decided to send the Yeomanry Cavalry, along with two cannons, to stop the rebels' advance.[65]

At the time, pargana Amorha and Domariaganj were fully in the rebels' control. At the same time, at Begum Hazrat Mahal's order, an expedition was launched against Mansingh, the taluqdar of Shahganj, in which 1,500 of Mohammed Hasan's men and the Nasirabad regiment also participated.[66] Simultaneously, rebels from Awadh looted and destroyed the pargana, thana and town of Bansi. Along with 4,000 rebels, Mohammed Hasan proceeded for Bansi, which compelled the British officers and the Raja of Bansi to run away and take shelter in a strong jungle fortress. Rebels occupied the Bansi town and the raja's palace. Therefore, along with 250 soldiers and cannons, Wingfield came to the Raja of Bansi's rescue, while Colonel Rowcroft proceeded to capture Amorha.[67] The rebels continued their guerrilla war. Mr. Bird's attempt to apprehend the Babu of Dumri failed.[68] Overall, the situation was still in favour of the rebels. But soon the rebels had to vacate Bansi. Mohammed Hasan's army then had three to four thousand persons, including 1,000 sepoys, and six small cannons. Rebels were still in control of Captainganj. But they had to vacate it when Rowcroft reached there.[69]

At Colonel Rowcroft's bidding, an army under Major Cox attacked Domariaganj. The rebels faced defeat and retreated. With his 4,000 men,

Mohammed Hasan had left Domariaganj for Amorha. Hence Major Cox invaded Amorha on 9 June. Rebels could not withstand his armed strength and had to retreat. Aiming to fully crush Mohammed Hasan, the British army attacked his party at Haraiya, five miles from Amorha. Mohammed Hasan was defeated and moved towards Gonda district for safety. Rebels activities had come to a standstill in Amorha by the end of June.[70]

But the terror of the Babus of Dumri still haunted the district, and the British Government was unable to do anything. They continued their activities from their hideout in the dense forests of Gorakhpur. In the middle of June, they attacked the Hatwa thana between the Gandak and Gorakhpur, killed two policemen and razed the thana to the ground. A day before, they had disfigured the limbs of a Revenue Department peon.[71]

On the northern border of the district, several rebel troops were coming from the Awadh border to the *terai* of Nepal, and in a sense, they had finished the Domariaganj, Itwa and Tharauli police stations. Mendhu Khan, the appointed tehsildar of Bansi East, was forcibly collecting revenue there. Similarly, in Badhni area, Damman Khan, the jagirdar of Jhandanagar, was doing the same job of forcibly collecting revenue for the rebel government.[72]

On the same day, when the British had compelled the rebels to retreat from Haraiya village, a troop of Sikh army men under Lieutinent Pullan, accompanied by Mr. Bird, the Acting Magistrate, attacked the famed village of Paina which was in rebellion for the preceding two months. About 600 inhabitants of the village were in revolt. As the village was situated on the Ghaghra bank, the government army received help from the steamer "Horangotta" also. Some of the rebels faced the attack while others deserted. The rebels had to pay a heavy price; their village was torched and women were molested. The steamer also put afire the river side jungle where the rebels were sheltered.[73]

After the defeat in Haraiya, differences developed between Mohammed Hasan and his soldiers. And after a quibble, the soldiers went towards Shahganj. In these circumstances, the Raja of Gonda sent 200 sepoys to help Mohammed Hasan. With those soldiers, he took shelter at Bair in Bilwa jungle.[74] Rebels had already vacated Amorha. However, in the second week of June, a party under Balli Singh and Balikaran did invade a village from the Awadh side. The village was situated close to Captainganj on the other side.[75]

Rebels had trampled pargana Bansi in the month of June. There, divided into groups, 1,500 rebels were continuing their activities and were receiving the patronage of local officials in the *terai* of Nepal. The people of Bansi remained aloof in this struggle, with no sympathy for the British.[76]

In the first week of July 1858, the Babus of Dumri had spread their terror in the eastern part of Gorakhpur. They had made a fortress near Gorakhpur their stronghold. Taking advantage of the dense forests, they were fast running their rebellious activities. During the week ending 3 July, they killed a zamindar who had informed the government about them.[77] Attempts to apprehend them failed. But when a troop of the Sikhs was deployed, the Babus of Dumri moved to the north of Bansi and continued the effort to run the rebellious activities in cooperation with the Raja of Nichlaul. Therefore, the government sent against them a Sikh troop under Lieutenant Pullan, along with Mr. Peppe. They knew the territory well.[78]

A group of the rebels was present in pargana Amorha in the month of July and another troop was plundering Bansi. On 23 July, the troop under Lieutenant Pullan attacked the Amorha rebels and then the second rebel troop, and not only caused it harm but also compelled it to run away. The same troop also tried to attack the stronghold of Raja of Nichlaul and a stronghold of the Babus of Dumri. But they had deserted the place before this troop could reach there.[79]

In the middle of July 1858, the group of Awadh rebels under Ashraf Bakhsh Khan, (the Raja of Utraula), and Jawahar Bakhsh Khan captured several posts which controlled the border of Domariaganj, and thus created a crisis for the government. Along with the Raja of Bansi, a Sikh troop captured a chowki in Domariaganj. But as soon as they moved away, 500 rebels recaptured it. At the time, Mohammed Hasan was fortifying his position at Bangaon in Babhni forests, and the rebels were expecting help from him as well.[80]

The possibility of attack on Bansi tahsil by the rebels, camping at Dumariaganj, was not over. They had crossed the river Rapti at Itwa, which was near Bansi. They were planning to attack. Lieutenant Pullan was deployed at Bansi along with his Sikh soldiers, but he was not in good position. He demanded military help from Brigadier Rowcroft. The British Government was concentrating all attention on this area in order to retain the hold of Bansi.[81] Taking advantage of it, a group of 200 rebels torched the police post at Rudrapur, capital of the Satasi Raj on 31 August and occupied Chauri Chaura on 1 September. Commissioner C. Wingfield proceeded against them, but the rebels moved into the forest without any harm.[82]

Taking advantage of the situation, the rebels attacked the outer posts of Amorha and Haraiya in the south-western part of the district. Most of them were the Raja of Gonda's followers. The rebels then had the upper hand. But under Major Cox, a big army arrived from Basti, and it forced the rebels to retreat. The escaping rebels joined Mohammed Hasan's army.[83]

The rebel group, collected at Itwa, moved through Dumariaganj and attacked Bansi. But the Sikh army, led by Lieutenant Pullan, forced them to retreat. On 9 September 1858, rebels and the British army had another encounter at Bansi, when 30 to 40 rebels sacrificed their lives.[84] Demoralised by it, the rebels postponed their campaign. But they again attacked the Bansi palace on 22 September. However, they had to face yet another setback.[85] Now they scattered in the nearby villages and began preparing for the next attack. In order to liberate Bansi from the rebels, Mr. Bird proceeded via the north of Bansi and Captain Hallett proceeded via the northwest. Through this campaign, they forced the rebels to run away to the Nepal *terai* and Awadh. Yet rebels could not be completely cleared from Dumriaganj.[86]

The rebels posed yet another challenge for the British Government in the last week of October 1858. They occupied a house (residence) at village Jagdishpur, nine miles to the northwest of Amorha. The British army sent against them failed to push them out, and more troops were then sent from Haraiya. But the arrival of military help from the Raja of Gonda and Mohammed Hasan further enthused the rebels and they chased the British army away. The latter reached their cantonment with difficulty.[87]

The rebels' enthusiasm grew excessively in November 1858 as their ranks were continually growing. Raja Lal Singh of Faizabad and Raja Ramdutt Singh of Charda had sent their soldiers to help the rebels. With his army, Bala Rao, the brother of Nana Saheb, had also entered Gorakhpur. Mehdi Hasan too had come with his army. Along with 600 to 700 men, Balli Singh and Balikaran too were ready for an attack between Dumariaganj and Bangaon. This scared the British.[88]

At the same time, led by Ashraf Bakhsh Khan, the taluqdar of Utraula, Mohammed Nawaz, former thanedar of Captainganj, and some babus of Rudhauli, about 1,100 rebels occupied Bhanpur, some 25 kilometres southwest of Dumariyaganj. But the British army attacked the rebels at Bhanpur on 11 November 1858. The rebels moved far away after a small skirmish.[89]

Taking advantage of the small strength of British army in Gorakhpur city, Babu Bandhu Singh of Dumri, along with three to four hundred followers, looted the carts carrying goods for the British on 8 November.[90]

Moreover, along with the Babu of Pandeypar, he was planning to attack Gorakhpur. But the British army launched a surprise attack and forced them to escape to Nepal.[91]

Bala Rao too joined the rebel activities in this area. On 20 November 1858, he attacked the British army at Bhanpur but was defeated and went back to Awadh. He re-entered Bansi in November end, looted village Kamsar, nine miles before Tulsipur, and collected money from zamindars.[92] Mohammed Hasan, who was in Bangaon, reached a village nine miles to the west of Domariaganj, along with 1,200 to 1,500 persons. A combination of Mohammed Hasan and Bala Rao could prove dangerous. Therefore, Rowcroft attacked Mohammed Hasan on 3 December 1858. A defeated Mohammed Hasan moved to Utraula.[93] In view of the imminent English attack, Bala Rao also moved to Tulsipur and then into the jungles.[94]

In December end, Mohammed Hasan and Bala Rao jointly launched another attack at British army near Tulsipur. But they were defeated by a British force and fled to the hills.[95] The Rebellion had virtually come to an end now. The despondent rebels began to surrender or, else, take shelter in Nepal *terai*. Raja Udit Narayan Singh of Satasi and others surrendered themselves. Many of the rebels and sepoys began to return home.[96] In the first week of January 1859, Bala Rao, Raja Devi Bakhsh Singh of Gonda and some other rebels left for Nepal along with Begum Hazrat Mahal.[97] Mohammed Hasan too left for Nepal in company with the Begum. But on 31 March 1859, along with 150 of his soldiers, he surrendered to the British at the British camp near Butwal.[98] He was not given capital punishment because he had saved the life of Colonel Lennox and family.[99] The popular revolt in Gorakhpur came to an end with Mohammed Hasan's surrender.

Major Events of Revolt in Azamgarh District

In Azamgarh district, the revolt was started by sepoys of the 17th NI on 3 June 1957. Azamgarh was the headquarter of this regiment but did not have more than 500 sepoys. This regiment was formed and trained along with the 19th and 34th NI regiments. In May, this regiment demonstrated its rebellious propensity by welcoming in its barracks the sepoys of 19th NI, which was disbanded. On 24 May 1857, some of its sepoys also refused to use the new cartridges. By pleading inability to punish these sepoys or persuade them, Major Burroughs displayed the weak position of the government.[100] But they did make wide-ranging security arrangements to protect the Collector's *kutcherry*.[101] On the other hand, sepoys of the 17th NI held a secret meeting on 1 June 1857, and decided to prevent the treasure, which had come from Gorakhpur, from reaching Banaras. On the morning of 3 June 1857, seven lakh rupees of the treasure of Gorakhpur and Azamgarh were to be sent to Banaras in the custody of Lieutenant Palliser who was accompanied by sepoys of the 17th NI and 80 mounted soldiers of the 12th and 13th Irregular Cavalry. At about 8 in the evening, when they had already covered some distance, sepoys of the 17th NI, under Subedar Bhondu Singh, revolted and captured seventy thousand rupees from the Azamgarh treasury. A sepoy called Madho Singh sought dead Lieutenant Hutchinson who had opposed the attempt. Breaking the jail gate open, they freed the prisoners.[102] Then they moved forward and, at a place called Rani ki Sarai, they also looted the treasury being sent to Banaras. They returned to the city as the victors. [103] In the meantime, British officials handed the city over to Kotwal and fled to Ghazipur. But the Kotwal could not discharge his responsibility.[104]

The rebel sepoys had no immediate plan. After capturing the city, they did not make any arrangements there; rather they proceeded for Faizabad as victors.[105] Immediately after their departure, non-sepoy rebels captured the city and began to plunder. Anti-government rebellious activities began in various parts of the district.[106] On 4 June 1857, a mass began to plunder Chiraiya Kot. They also chased the Britishers leaving for Ghazipur. On 5 June, zamindars declared an open revolt there. They looted the bazaar at Jehanganj.[107]

At Belha Bans, in cooperation with the people, zamindars attempted to loot the tehsil and thana. But the government employees resisted and foiled their attempt. Then they attacked and looted the Barhalganj market. Next, they looted and destroyed village Bhagatpur near Bilariaganj.[108]

On June 3, people of pargana Sikandarpur stoned the tehsil and jail, thus displaying their rebellious attitude. On 4 June, Nawabganj Bazaar in pargana Deogaon was thoroughly plundered. On the same day, rebel sepoys looted the treasury at Koilsa.[109]

In order to protect the remaining Christians and English indigo planters in the district, Mr. Venables, an English indigo planter, came from Ghazipur to Dohrighat, raised an army there and captured Azamgarh town on 20 June 1857. Mr. Venables tried to maintain law and order in the district even in adverse circumstances.[110] His enthusiasm grew after troops reached from Gorakhpur and Ghazipur. In the last week of June, he succeeded in restoring the British rule in eastern and the larger half of the district.[111] On the other hand, on 26 June 1857, Muzaffar Jehan captured pargana Mahul in the south-western part of the district and declared himself the raja. He had the support and cooperation of Palwar leader Prithvipal Singh and of Rajkumar Rajputs. With an army, Lieutenant Havelock proceeded against him but returned without success after three days.[112] Mr. Venables had meanwhile made a little dour on his own account and with a little more success and on the 30th June, he attacked Mohabbatpur, a rebel village, captured many rebels and incarcerated them in Kotwali.[113]

Koilsa and Atraulia in the western part of the district were teeming with rebels. Hence, on 12 July, Mr. Venables proceeded to invade Koilsa. Here Madho Prasad, the Palwar taluqdar of Birhur (in Faizabad district), was ready to help the Kurmi Raja of Atraulia. Muzaffar Jahan and Prithvipal Singh were present there with their troops. The rebels proved stronger and Mr. Venables's army had to face defeat and retreat. Rebels gave it a chase. On 18 July, near village Sahda, three miles to the west of Azamgarh, both the armies again collided. The British suffered heavy losses and Mr. Venables had to run away for life. In such circumstances, the British again quit Azamgarh on 18 June.

Enthused by it, on 23 July, about 400 rebels led by Rajab Ali attacked the Kotwali in broad daylight and freed the prisoners by force. The police could not match them.[114] This shows that the rebels still had a firmer grip on Azamgarh.

On 9 August, after the British had departed, Palwar leader Prithvipal Singh occupied Azamgarh town. Here he collected ten thousand rupees from the people. Prithvipal Singh held sway in Azamgarh from 9 to 25 August.[115]

On 25 August, accompanied by Colonel Wroughton and Gorakhpur officials, the Gorkha army reached the eastern end of Azamgarh city. The Palwars thought it better to leave the city and vacated it.[116] The Gorkha army entered the city on 26 August. Getting the news, the Judge and Magistrate of Azamgarh came back with Mr. Venables and Legge and assumed the administration on 3 September. The British quickly restored order in the southern and eastern parts of the district, though the northern and western parts remained in rebel control. Thinking it impudent to fight the Gorkha army, Muzaffar Jahan and his Rajkumar Rajput associates kept low in Mahul. But Palwars did not hesitate to fight the Gorkhas. Along with Palwars, Raja Beni Madho put his tents in Mandoni, nine miles from the city. Therefore, with a big Gorkha contingent under Captain Boileau, Mr. Venables proceeded against them. Mandoni witnessed a severe fight between the two sides on 20 September. Three hundred of the rebel army lost life; the British also captured three cannons.[117] The rebels had to retreat.

Raja Beni Madho ran to take shelter in the Atraulia fortress. After a few days, he got the news that the Gorkha army was moving towards Atraulia. Then he went to the Awadh area and his fortress remained the government officials' residence for two months.[118]

Led by Mr. Bird, the Gorkha army soon launched a second campaign against the rebels. This time the aim was to punish Raja Muzaffar Jahan and Palwar leader Prithvipal Singh in Mahul. The army moved towards Mahul and, en route, burnt the Shamsabad and Baramadpur fortresses to ashes. Rebel leaders had got the news of Gorkhas' arrival and had already vacated Mahul. Therefore, the Gorkhas found Mahul deserted when they reached there. Bird returned after establishing a Police post there.[119]

In fact, it was the Gorkha army that caused heavy losses to the rebels in Azamgarh district and forced their important leaders to quit the district, thus making an important contribution to strengthening the British position there. But the rebels did not lie low. From two sides, they posed a challenge to the newly restored British rule in the district. Acting Magistrate, Mr. Pollock met the Palwars to pacify them, while Ross led a campaign against the rebels who had gathered at Barhalganj, (Gorakhpur), in the north, and were preparing to attack Azamgarh. Mr. Ross drove them away. He also destroyed their fleet of boats which were used to cross the river. Pollock toured through the Palwars' area and succeeded to pacify them, to an extent, by promising them decent behaviour. He punished the Rajkumar Rajputs and destroyed their fortresses while he had a cordial meeting with the Palwars at Koilsa.[120] All this had a visible impact on the rebel activities. However, in the beginning of November, rebels came from the Awadh side and recaptured the Atraulia fortress. From Jaunpur, Colonel Longden was sent against them. He attacked the rebels on 9 November night and forced them to vacate the fortress. Longden returned to Jaunpur after destroying Atraulia.[121] But, immediately after his return, Rajkumar Rajputs of Awadh and Jaunpur trampled Atraulia, while Palwars again became active under Madho Prasad Singh. They intensified their attack on the eastern and northern borders of the district. Acting Magistrate Pollock described the situation as too gloomy.[122] Therefore, in order to defend the district, the British administration recruited 2,325 men of the Raja of Gopalpur (district Gorakhpur) at higher wages and appointed them as policemen at strategic sites. This proved quite useful and beneficial for them.[123]

It appeared that the rebellion had been crushed in Azamgarh district. In reality, it was only the first phase of the rebellion. The second phase began after Babu Kunwar Singh reached Azamgarh.

Babu Kunwar Singh had left for Lucknow after he had suffered defeat, along with Nana Saheb, in the battle of Kandhpur. There, Birjis Qadr, the Crown Prince of Awadh, received him with a robe of honour and issued a *farman* telling him to capture Azamgarh. He also gave him 12,000 rupees in cash as war expenses and a draft for 16,000 rupees.[124] The situation at Azamgarh was then favourable for the rebels. In February 1858, Kunwar Singh reached Ayodhya with 2,000 men of whom, 800 were rebel soldiers.[125] The British and Gorkha armies were then striving to capture Lucknow. The eastern districts were virtually sans army. Hence Kunwar Singh occupied Atraulia on 17 March.[126] Local rebels too joined him in large numbers. Against them, Colonel Milman came to Atraulia along with his men but defeated and ran away, to Koilsa on 22 March. Kunwar Singh's army defeated him in Koilsa too, forcing him to run to Azamgarh.[127] After reaching Azamgarh, Milman apprised the officials of Banaras, Allahabad and Lucknow of the details of the battle, and asked for immediate military help.[128]

At the request of Colonel Milman, a troop led by Colonel Dames arrived for his help from Banaras and Ghazipur. Under Colonel Dames' leadership, the entire British army attacked Babu Kunwar Singh, but he too had to run away. He took refuge within the fortification of the city (Azamgarh).[129] On 26 March 1858, Babu Kunwar Singh captured Azamgarh without any resistance. At the time, he had four thousand men and four cannons.[130]

Simultaneously, the rumour spread that Babu Kunwar Singh was about to attack Banaras. In that case, the English could have lost contact with Calcutta, Lucknow and Delhi. Governor General Lord Canning was then camping at Allahabad. In view of two successive defeats of the English and of the possibility that contacts with Calcutta could get snapped, he realised the seriousness of the situation. Therefore, the Governor General instructed Mark Kerr, who had earned renown in the Crimean war, to attack Azamgarh immediately. Besides, on 29 March, a big and well-armed force, led by Edward Lugard, was sent from Lucknow against Azamgarh. This was a proof of the Britishers' fear of Babu Kunwar Singh.

With his army, Lord Mark Kerr reached from Allahabad to Banaras on 31 March. There he included in his army the royal cannonry and some soldiers of the Second Dragon Guard and then, at 10 in the night on 5 April, reached a place called Sarsena which was only eight miles from Azamgarh. There he waited for the morning, thinking that a night attack was impudent. But Babu Kunwar Singh had got the news of his arrival. As his tactic, he had got ditches dug on both sides of the road and decided to face the British army. There was a fierce battle between the two sides, killing several soldiers including 8 English army officers, and seriously injuring 34. Babu Kunwar Singh could not score victory because of the royal cannonry and returned to Azamgarh. Mark Kerr too reached Azamgarh but could not muster courage for an attack.[131] He waited for Lugard's army coming from Lucknow. Babu Kunwar Singh too kept low and there was no battle between the two sides for a week. The British Government tried to capture Kunwar Singh through enticement. It declared a reward of 25,000 rupees for Kunwar Singh. But in vain.[132]

Kunwar Singh soon got the news of arrival of Edward Lugard's army. Now it was beyond his capacity to face the joint forces of Mark Kerr and Edward Lugard. Therefore, he decided to leave Azamgarh for Jagdishpur, his hereditary estate. But this too was not easy. Yet he demonstrated his strategic expertise and courage. He deployed his selected and reliable soldiers at the ferry bridge on Tamsa (Tons) river and entrusted them the job of preventing the British army from entering the city, so that he could safely leave Azamgarh with his remaining army. On 13 April 1858 he left Azamgarh along with his troops. The few remaining there left next day.

When General Lugard reached the Tons bank, Babu Kunwar Singh's soldiers, lying in ambush, faced it determinedly and retreated in order.[133] Babu Kunwar Singh had gone a long way by now. Malleson too has admired the rebels.[134] In this battle, 25 of the British army were badly injured.

Reaching Azamgarh, General Lugard instructed Brigadier Douglas to chase Kunwar Singh, which he did with his army. Employing the guerrilla tactics, Kunwar Singh divided his army into two parts. He moved ahead with one part and turned towards Bagahi Dand from near Shahgarh. The other part remained in hiding. When Douglas passed by with his army, this group followed him. When Douglas reached Bagahi Dand, he was encircled from two sides and attacked. A fierce battle followed, causing much damage to Douglas' army. He ran away to Azamgarh. Douglas' failure highly irritated General Lugard. He gave Douglas an extra troop and told him to chase Kunwar Singh again.

On 17 April, Douglas attacked Babu Kunwar Singh in an orchard at village Naghai which was close to Azmatgarh. After a bit of fighting, Kunwar Singh adopted a new tactic. He divided his troops into three parts. Two of them moved via Ghosi while the third guarded the route. By now, Kunwar Singh had gone some 17 miles ahead. When Douglas learnt about it, he began the chase on 18 April. In the night, the British army camped three or four miles behind the rebel army. Taking advantage of it, Kunwar

Singh quickly entered Ghazipur district via Sikandarpur. Douglas continued the chase. With his troops divided into small groups, Kunwar Singh reached Shivpur Ghat where the babus (zamindars) welcomed him and helped him to cross the Ganges.[135]

Babu Kunwar Singh's departure from Azamgarh ended the second phase of the rebellion in the district. But the rebellion did not subside. Now began its third and final phase.

After Kunwar Singh's departure, Pargan Singh continued the anti-British struggle in the district. On 23 April, he invaded and looted the Maharajganj Bazaar. Later he attacked the Maharajganj thana and injured some government musketeers.[136] On 10 May 1858, Pargan Singh attacked Koilsa tehsil but Mamnoon Khan, the tehsildar, faced him and foiled the attack.[137] In the first week of June, on his behalf, advertisements in Persian and Hindi were printed, informing that there would be a big revolt on 21 June, the Dussehra Day.[138] When pressure intensified in the middle of June, he crossed the Ganges and moved into Ballia where he captured a government employee and got his limbs dismembered.[139] Pargan Singh's attacks continued on the northern border of the district. But eventually he had to leave Azamgarh.[140] The rebels thus became passive in Azamgarh district. Towards the end of October, Colonel Kelly got the district free from rebels and the governmental process of reward and punishment began.

Events of Revolt in Banaras District

District Banaras in Eastern Uttar Pradesh was highly important for the British from strategic and other angles. It was an important military centre on the Calcutta-Allahabad route. At the time of the rebellion, a company of European artillery under Brigadier George Ponsonby, a company of the Ludhiana Sikh regiment and a regiment of the 37th NI were stationed here. Yet the English officials were afraid of a revolt here. They had already an inkling of discontent among the 37th regiment's soldiers, while the common people were not happy because of rising prices. Gradually, they lost confidence in the 37th regiment. Therefore, for security sake, they summoned the 13th Irregular Cavalry, which was known for their loyalty towards the British, from Sultanpur to Banaras. Even then, the English began to think to leave Banaras and even mooted the proposal to go to Chunar, which was not accepted. They even talked of all Christians taking shelter in the Mint House in case of a crisis. In fact, English officials were highly scared of the possibility of revolt. However, Magistrate Lynd and Judge Gubbins put up the show of everything being okay.[141]

At about 1.30 on 31 May night, flames were seen in the barracks which had recently been vacated by the 37th NI; next day some persons were seen gathering there and confabulating. This was enough to further scare the British officials who were already shaken to the core. On 3 June, they decided that, at the time of a crisis, all Christians would gather in the Collector's court and stay there until the European soldiers took them to the Mint House.[142]

On 3 June, with Madras Fusilier, Colonel Neill too reached Banaras, which gave the English some confidence. On 4 June, English officials called a meeting to decide about asking the 37th NI soldiers to lay down arms. During the meeting itself, they got the news of 17th NI's revolt at Azamgarh. Hence, they decided to ask the 37th NI to lay down arms on 5 June.[143] Colonel Neil was not present in that crucial meeting; he was then preparing to leave for Kanpur. After the meeting, Brigadier Ponsonby went to meet him and to tell about the decision. Colonel Neill wanted to supervise the surrender of arms and hence he insisted that this should be done on the same day. Accepting his point, Brigadier Ponsonby decided to get it done on 4 June evening and, to avoid anything untoward, urged Colonel Neill to be there with his army.

At the parade held at 5 pm on 4th June, 37th NI soldiers began to lay down arms at Ponsonby's order. But then they saw armed European soldiers coming their way. Just as the English officers had lost confidence in Indian soldiers, the latter too had no trust in the English. The Indians thought that once they were disarmed, European soldiers would kill them. Hence, they picked up arms again and began firing upon European soldiers. The latter too returned the fire. Captain Olphert began firing cannon balls. Ponsonby gave the command to Colonel Neill and left the Parade Ground. At the same time, Sikh soldiers felt enraged when cannon balls landed nearby. They thought the European army was out to kill them too, and they too began firing upon the English. The 13th Irregular Cavalry also sided with the Indian soldiers. The battle continued for some time, but eventually the Indians could not withstand the cannon firing and ran helter-skelter. Thus, a revolt broke out at Banaras on 4 June 1857, even if due to a misunderstanding.[144] The revolt at Banaras was crushed within three hours, but its impact on the city continued for several days.

The Sikh soldiers deployed to protect the Collector's court were also enraged by the attack on their regiment. But Sardar Surat Singh and Pt. Gokul Chand, the Nazir of the Judge, reached there soon and managed to pacify them.[145] On 6 June, the British spread the rumour that Muslims had hoisted a flag on the celebrated Vishwanath Temple, in order to break the Hindu-Muslim unity, and also punished a few in the name of suppressing the mischief.[146] But they failed to incite a riot. However, this communal harmony was of no avail for the rebellion. Running into the rural areas, the rebel soldiers did incite the people but failed to create any mentionworthy episode of mass rebellion. On the contrary, the British oppression targeted these rural people on a large scale. On 9 June, the British Government promulgated Martial Law and thus intensified their cycle of repression.[147]

In Banaras district, one more episode of rebellion took place in 1858. On 8 February 1858, 26 soldiers lodged in Banaras Jail, who were sentenced to life imprisonment and were about to be sent to the Andaman, snatched arms from the prison guards and tried to run away. But they were hauled and then executed.[148] It had no impact on the public psyche which only felt sorry, and the district remained calm.

Earlier, the Rajputs of Dobhi had posed a threat to the security of Banaras but the British had crushed them. On the whole, British rule in Banaras district continued without any hitch.

Events of Revolt in Jaunpur District

In Jaunpur district, the rebellion was started by a contingent of the Ludhiana Sikh regiment, under Lieutenant Mara, which was deployed to safeguard the treasury. When, on 5 June, the news of British army's firing on the Sikh regiment of Banaras reached Jaunpur, Sikh soldiers at Jaunpur felt enraged. They shot Joint Magistrate Cuppage dead, fired upon the commanding officers, looted the treasure and after taking the weapons kept in the armoury, left for Awadh.[149]

Enthused by the soldiers' revolt, rebels in the district also became active. On 6 June, they killed Deputy Magistrate Thomas Tripland and got the court vacated from the British. When the British took shelter in Rai Hingan Lal's house, Rajputs of Dobhi got the news, came there and chased them away. The British then took shelter in the indigo factory at Pussewah. From there, they safely escaped to Banaras on 9 June.[150] The rebels also destroyed the European officers' bungalows in the district. Afraid of the rebels, Mr. Fane, the District Magistrate, gave the district into the charge of Raja Shiv Ghulam Dubey of Jaunpur, who was pro-British, and himself left for Banaras.[151] Thus, Jaunpur remained free from British rule for some time.

Zamindars, who had been divested of their zamindaris, found the time favourable to them. They began to drive the new zamindars away and reoccupy their estates. Raghuvanshi Rajputs of taluqa Dobhi attacked the nearby territories and obstructed the Banaras-Azamgarh Road, for which an army under Chapman came from Banaras and punished them.[152]

The situation in Jaunpur improved only after a Gorkha army, led by Colonel Wroughton, reached there on 8 September 1857. The administrative system was then restored in the district. But rebels still held the sway in the northern and western parts of the district. Mubarakpur, the fortress of Raja Iradat Jehan, was their main centre. The Adampur fortress of their commander, Amar Singh, and the territories held by other supporters of Raja Iradat Jehan were still mocking the British. Hence the British military officers moved against them with the Gorkha army. The rebels lost the battle that ensued. Raja Iradat Jehan and Fasahat Jehan were taken prisoners and executed while Amar Singh died fighting. With this battle, rebels were virtually finished in that area. But they were still active in the western parts that adjoined Awadh.[153]

Meanwhile, a rebel called Malik Mehdi Bakhsh drove the police away from Katghar thana. The British magistrate offered him pardon on certain conditions. But still he did not surrender. Hence his property was confiscated.[154]

On 15 October 1857, the British army had to go to the western parts of the district, as rebels had intensified their activities in this area adjoining Awadh. At Chanda near the Jaunpur border, Mehdi Hasan, the Nazim of Sultanpur, was planning to attack the district with 5,000 soldiers. Colonel Wroughton reached Singra Mau on 19 October to foil the rebel attack. Mehdi Hasan appointed Hasan Yar Khan the chakladar of Jaunpur and instructed him to attack the British. With 1,500 men, Hasan Yar Khan then proceeded towards Singra Mau. He camped about four miles before village Kuduwa. Against Hasan Yar Khan's expectations, Diwan Randhir Singh of Singra Mau sided with the British. But he lost in the battle with the British and came back running to Hasan Yar Khan. The British army was sensing itself weak vis-a-vis Hasan Yar Khan's army and therefore returned to Jaunpur. Staying in Chanda, the rebels began preparing to attack Jaunpur. On the other hand, on 30 October 1857, Colonel Wroughton proceeded towards Chanda with 1,100 Gorkha soldiers and two cannons. The rebels too moved ahead. A fierce battle followed in village Koeripoor. The rebel army suffered heavy losses and had to lie low for some time.[155] The rebels began to reorganise in November 1857. Therefore, Colonel Longden had to move towards Singra Mau. The rebels were in strength now. Their number was said to be 10,000 on 22 November, which swelled to 16,000 on

28 November. These included trained soldiers of Mehdi Hasan and Muzaffar Jehan. Hence Colonel Longden had to go back defeated.[156] This enthused the rebels. They attacked the police posts on the district's borders, drove the policemen away, and obstructed the revenue collection.

Makhdoom Bakhsh, a representative of Raja Iradat Jehan, attacked Tighra in tehsil Khuthan on 24 December, drove the pro-British Kisan Narayan away and plundered the tehsil.[157] On 4 January, rebels attacked Badlapur and tried to destroy the police thana there.[158]

In view of the growing rebel strength, General Franks was sent against them with 3,200 Gorkhas, 2,300 Britishers and 20 cannons. The rebels could not face it and ran away to Chanda. General Frank defeated them there. After wiping out the rebels, General Frank left Jaunpur for Lucknow on 19 February 1858.[159] The rebels of Jaunpur felt renewed enthusiasm after Babu Kunwar Singh came to Azamgarh. Mobilising under Ghulam Husain, the son of Mohammed Hasan, the Nazim of Gorakhpur, 3,000 rebels planned to attack Jaunpur. But Lugard attacked them on 11 April 1858 and forced them to run away.[160]

In May 1858, some other people too challenged the law and order in Jaunpur. Jhuri Singh, the rebel leader of Mona Rajputs in Bhadohi area, attacked Machhalishahar. But he failed. In the same month, Sangram Singh tried to create disturbance in Madiahu area and Drigpal Singh in Badshahpur by their attacks. But Robert Taylor, the Joint Magistrate of Jaunpur, did not consider them rebellious as they had not faced even a thanedar.[161] In June 1858, Jaunpur was completely free from rebel activities.

Events of Revolt in Mirzapur District

On 6 June 1857, when the news of rebellion in Banaras and Jaunpur reached Mirzapur, the British administrators, military officials and European civilians felt dead scared. Their activities and moves betrayed their fear. For example, Colonel Pott, commander of the 47th NI, sent all soldiers on leave except the reliable ones. Similarly, hearing the gunshot in a marriage procession, European civilians ran and hid themselves in the *kachahari*. On 8 June, the Sikh soldiers went to Allahabad after laying down their arms, Colonel Pott got those arms destroyed. Hearing the rumour of a rebel attack on 9 June, all the European civilians ran to take shelter in the Chunar Fort. District Magistrate Tucker arrested some persons on the suspicion that they were rebels.[162]

In Mirzapur district, the first collision with the rebels took place when Colonel Pott and his soldiers attacked village Gaura on the right bank of the Ganges; which was considered a rebel stronghold. The rebels resisted hard but withdrew as they could not stand the two-pronged attack from the river side and the land route. Some of the rebels were taken prisoner. Deputy Magistrate P. Walker then attacked the rebels in Ramnagar Sikri village and freed the areas on right bank of the Ganges from rebels.[163]

The most serious rebel activity in Mirzapur district was that by Raja Udwant Singh, Mona Rajput chief in Bhadohi. Pargana Bhadohi was once the zamindari of Mona Rajputs. But Raja Balwant Singh of Banaras had captured it in 1749, and pargana Bhadohi remained since then in the zamindari of the Raja of Banaras. Mona Rajputs and their chief thus became inimical to the Raja of Banaras. The Raja of Banaras was pro-British. Therefore, when the rebellion broke out, Udwant Singh of Bhadohi assumed the title of Raja, appointed two Diwans and began collecting revenue in Bhadohi. One of his troops captured the Grand Trunk Road and closed it down. The Company's rule in Bhadohi thus came to an end. This territory was in the estate of Raja of Banaras. Therefore, under Lieutenant Pulser and Chapman, a contingent was immediately sent against the rebels. Munshi Darshan Lal, representative of the Raja of Banaras, was also striving to get Raja Udwant Singh captured. He succeeded, got Raja Udwant Singh captured by deceit and handed him over to the British who executed him after a summary trial. Joint Magistrate Moore was held responsible for it, and the wife of Raja Udwant Singh announced a reward of 300 rupees for Moore's head.[164]

On 4 July 1857, Mr. Moore took some rebels prisoner at Gopiganj and brought them to the indigo factory of Pali. Some men of Mona Rajputs learnt about it. Led by Jhuri Singh, they surrounded the factory, beheaded Moore and sent his severed head to the Rani. Next day, Mr. Tucker came with an army to capture the rebels but failed.[165] The government declared a reward of 1,000 rupees for Mr. Moore's killers — Jhuri Singh, Mata Bheekh Singh, Mata Bakhsh Singh and Sarnam Singh — but they could not be apprehended. Along with his party, Jhuri Singh engaged till his end in rebellious activities in Bhadohi-Allahabad, Jaunpur and Awadh areas. He died of cholera in the Awadh area.[166]

Too much fear gripped Mirzapur when, on 3 August 1857, rebel soldiers of Dinapur proceeded towards it. On 4 August they looted the Ahraura Bazaar. Moving ahead, they also looted the markets at Robertsganj and Shahganj. They were intending to attack Mirzapur but they were defeated when the British suddenly reached a place called Amoi. Then they went towards Allahabad.[167]

On 14 August, rebel soldiers of Ramgarh battalion in Hazaribagh also entered the southern part of Mirzapur but could not cross the river. Then they went to Singrauli and, with cooperation from the raja there, their rebellious activities influenced the Rihand areas.[168] On the 24th in the same month (August), Kunwar Singh came to Mirzapur along with his party and stayed in Ramgarh. The British fear was natural. But Kunwar Singh went to Rewa and Mirzapur was spared.[169]

On 16 September, soldiers of the 50th NI created a crisis by rebelling at Naugarh. But the British officials managed to disarm and send them on leave.[170] Despite remaining calm, Mirzapur was not entirely free from rebellious activities. Stray incidents occurred here and there. Eliot's campaign proves this point.

Symptoms of revolt were visible also from the crisis in the Bijaygarh royal family. After the death of the raja there, his relative Lakshman Singh declared himself the raja, joined hands with rebels and began collecting revenue. This created a crisis in pargana Bijaygarh. An army, led by Magistrate Tucker, was sent against them. But the rebels moved into the Rohtasgarh forests before the army reached there. However, during the attack made on 9 January 1858, several rebels lost life while some were taken prisoner, brought to Banaras and executed.[171] The British managed to drive the rest out of the district. No more incident of rebellion took place in the district.

Events of Revolt in Ghazipur District

Ghazipur was the only district of Eastern Uttar Pradesh where the British sat assured in the beginning, though it was Mangal Pandey's home district and large number of people joined the army here. The district also had an army recruitment centre. When the rebellion broke out in Azamgarh, on 3 June, English officers and European civilians rushed to Ghazipur and Banaras for safety. But this changed the environment at Ghazipur all at once. Local civilians rose against them. The police turned helpless and civil war like conditions developed in the district by 6 June. In view of the civilian resistance, the district's treasure, having five lakh rupees, was sent to Banaras for safety. Till 16 June, English officials used severe punishments and martial law to restore the normalcy in the district.[172]

At Chaura village in Ghazipur district, villagers committed the first big act of revolt by burning Matthews' indigo factory to ashes. Matthews had to run away for life. Villagers vandalised all his property. In revenge,

Bax, Joint Magistrate of the district, torched the whole Chaura village to ashes on 7 July. Peace then prevailed for a few days.[173]

On 14 July, the news of revolt by Kunwar Singh of Jagdishpur estate in Arrah reached Ghazipur and then came the news of sepoy revolt in Dinapur on 27 July. Sepoys of the 65th NI, stationed in Ghazipur, had already made it clear that they would join whenever a revolt took place in Dinapur. Most of the soldiers there hailed from Ghazipur. Hence their revolt would also have got the local people's support. But the 65th NI did not revolt. Yet, for security sake, they were later disarmed on 10 August. European soldiers were given the responsibility to protect the opium factory.[174]

Returning from Azamgarh to Jagdishpur, when Babu Kunwar Singh entered Ghazipur district, people extended him all cooperation and thus demonstrated their participation in the rebellion. On 18 April 1858, he reached a place called Nagra in the district. From there, via Sikandarpur, he reached Maniyar in Bansdih tehsil. The people of Maniyar gave him full cooperation. Mr. Davis, Acting Magistrate of Azamgarh, had written to Mr. Gubbins, the Commissioner of Banaras, that "At Muneeahur, Kunwar Singh found himself amongst friends and the wants of his troops were voluntarily supplied by the villagers who are almost universally in his favour. Through their collusion, our spies were seized and detained, and our information suspended."[175] In a sense, this was an open anti-British mass revolt by the people of Maniar.

From Maniar, despite his defeat at the hands of Douglas, Kunwar Singh reached a place called Sahatwar on 20 April and, through a deliberate rumour and deceit, he reached Shivpur Ghat, 10 miles to the south of Ballia. There the Babus not only organised a feast for Kunwar Singh but also provided him boats to help him cross the Ganges with his army.[176] Helping an anti-government rebel is also an act of rebellion. But the babus of Shivpur behaved like anti-government rebels.

Even after Kunwar Singh had left Ghazipur, people continued their rebellious activities there.[177] Village Gahmar became the main centre of rebellion. According to Robert Smith Coomb, an English indigo planter of Gahmar, some people of the village came to him at midnight on 30 May 1858 and told him that rebel soldiers had killed two persons of Rajpur village in pargana Chausa on the day and were intending to come to Gahmar. Later it was learnt that they had left for Deval. The rebels numbered about 300. They stayed in Deval on 31 May and 1 June. They left for Gahmar on

2 June. People of Gahmar advised him to quit. A powerful faction of the village supported the rebels. Coomb took a boat and escaped to Buxar.

On 3 June, the Bengali clerk of his factory also escaped to Buxar. Joining hands with influential zamindars of the village, the rebel soldiers torched Coomb's factory and house, and looted his belongings. On 5 June, they went to village Sewari, four miles to the west of Gahmar, and sent some people who torched his factory at Bhadaura. On the same day, they burnt another factory of his and looted all his property at Rohnivan in pargana Chausa.[178]

Government records tell us that, at the invitation of Megar Singh, Amar Singh of Jagdishpur came to Gahmar on 3 June 1858, but ran back when the British army arrived there. Yet Megar Singh continued his rebellious activities.[179] Rebels damaged the railway bridge on Karmanasa river. On 4 June, a group of 500 rebels torched all the railway bungalows and indigo factories in Ghazipur district.[180] On 7 June, another group of rebel soldiers, plundered tehsil Mohammedabad.[181] Rebel attacks on Saidpur took place towards the end of June.

Rebellious activities were in full swing in pargana Ballia. Some four to five hundred rebels and the local people were engaged in rebellious activities in Ballia and Rasra tehsils. They had teamed with about 150 persons, including some mounted soldiers, of pargana Zamania. When necessary, this group got cooperation from a large number of rebel minded persons and discontented zamindars. They had created terror in the eastern part of Ghazipur district.[182] Hence the government felt it necessary to deploy military contingents in Ballia, Bairia, Rasra and Zamania.[183] When a military campaign was launched against the rebels, they destroyed a road bridge to obstruct the campaign. They continued to punish the government officials. They killed a thanedar by trick. According to a government narrative of July 1858, the rebels were continuing their cruel policy to check and terrorise the government officials.[184]

In the middle of July 1858, about 1,200 rebels of Ballia encircled the military troop of Probyen at Reotee but were compelled to retreat. Rebels were putting up strong resistance at Bairia too. On 13 June, rebels displayed the courage to attack Captain MacMillan's military contingent that was returning to Ballia.[185] Eventually, the rebels had to run away in different directions after Brigadier Douglas' campaign. The activities of Megar Singh, Jyodhar Singh and Sada Singh or Seedha Singh continued the rebel activities in the Ghazipur territories which adjoined Bihar, particularly in pargana Zamania and Rath.

The 22 September 1858 letter from W Brown, Commander of the Saint Mister Gunboat, Banaras, informs about the rebellious activities in Baragaon. From the 29 September 1858 letter, we learn about the repressive activities, which corroborates the mass revolt in Bara area.[186] In Ghazipur district, rebellious activities came to a halt only after Brigadier Douglas' successful campaign in October 1858. In this way, rebellious events received a comprehensive character in all the districts of Eastern Uttar Pradesh. Common people made special contributions to this process.

Notes and References

1. Wingfield, C, *Narrative of Events: Gorakhpur in 1857-58*, 5 July 1858, para 7, p. 2.
2. *Ibid*, para 3, p. 1.
3. *Ibid*, para 5, p. 2.
4. Taylor, Robert, *The Rebellion of 1857 in the Province of Benaras*, 15 October 1858, para 19, p. 10.
5. Pre-Mutiny Records, Gorakhpur Collectorate, List 14, Vol. 177, Bag No. 27, Letter sent by W. Paterson, District Magistrate of Gorakhpur, to Wynyard, the Officiating Commissioner, on 2 July 1857, preserved in Regional Archives, Allahabad.
6. Wingfield C., *op cit*, para 5, p. 2.
7. *Ibid.*
8. *Ibid*, para 7, p. 2.
9. *Ibid*, para 10, 11, 12, p. 2.
10. *Ibid*, para 13, p. 2; Foreign Department, Secret Consultation No. 199, 26 March 1858, pp. 7-9; Foreign Department, Political, 1859, Consultation No. 60-62 KW, 27 May, pp. 27-41, preserved in National Archives of India, New Delhi; Pre-Mutiny Records, Gorakhpur Collectorate, Vol. 192, 1857-58, p. 5, (preserved in Regional Archives, Allahabad); Ball, Charles, *The History of the Indian Mutiny*, Volume I, London: 1858, pp. 400-401 (The London Printing and Publishing Company Ltd. London); Chick N.A, Annals of the Indian Mutiny, Part 5, September 1859, pp. 471-78 (Statement of Farrrier Sergent Busher of no. 13, Light field Battery, regarding the mutinous outbreak at Faizabad); Rizvi Syed Ather Abbas, Freedom Struggles in Uttar Pradesh, Vol. IV, pp. 146-151. (Hereafter referred as to FSUP, Vol. IV)
11. *Ibid*; Pre-Mutiny Records, Gorakhpur Collectorate, List 14, Vol. 177, Bag No. 27, Letters Issued by the Magistrate, January 1855 – April 1858.
12. *FSUP*, Vol. IV, p. 146.
13. *Ibid*, p. 146.
14. *Ibid.*
15. Pre-Mutiny Records, Gorakhpur Collectorate, List 14, Vol. 177, Bag No. 27, Letter No. 147, preserved in Regional Archives, Allahabad; *FSUP*, Vol. IV, pp. 160-62.

16. *FSUP*, Vol. IV, p. 147, 14 June 1857.
17. Wingfield C., *op cit*, para 17, p. 3; FSUP Vol. IV p. 152.
18. *Ibid.*
19. Home Department (Public), Consultation No. B 17/20, 17 September 1858, (preserved in National Archives of India, New Delhi).
20. Wingfield C., *op cit*, para 18, p. 3.
21. Wingfield C., *op cit,* para 21, p. 3.; FSUP Vol. IV, pp. 152-53; In his narrative dated 13 October 1861, Major G Ramsay, Resident at Kathmandu, said that at Sagauli, "rebels of the 12th Irregular Cavalry had killed Major Holmes, his wife, regiment's surgeon Dr Gardner and the small European community living there". See, V.S. Foreign Department, Political, V, No. 145-164, March 1875 (1), quoted by Hasrat, Bikramjit, *History of Nepal as Told by Its Own Contemporary Chroniclers*, Hoshiarpur (Punjab): B. B. Research Institute, 1970, p. 335; *Kashful-Baghaavat, Gorakhpur*, stanza 342-348, pp. 55-56.
22. Hasrat, Bikramjit, *op cit*, pp. 334-35; Wingfield C., *op cit*, para 20, 23-24; pp. 3-4; Sen, Surendra Nath, *Eighteen Fifty- Seven*, pp. 237-38. Gorkha poem "Lakhnau ko Sawai" gives the details of the Gorkha army, its officers, Colonel Pahalwan Singh, Colonel Madan Man Singh, instructions issued by Shri Teen Maharaj, including those about the difficulties en route, useful food, salaries given by the English government, etc. Moreover, it also mentioned the outbreak of cholera in the troops, English Captain Wroughton and his brave contingent. See Pant, Dinesh Raj (ed), *op cit*, *Dhading ma Phela Pareka Nepali Kavita*, Kathmandu, V 2061 (AD 2004) pp. 52-55.
23. Wingfield, C, *Narrative of Events:* 5 July 1858, para 22, p. 3; FSUP, Vol. IV p. 153.
24. Wingfield, C, *Narrative of Events:* 5 July 1858 para 23-27, pp. 3-4; *Kashful-Baghaavat, Gorakhpur*, stanza 410-16, pp. 66-68.
25. Wingfield, C, *op.cit*, para 26, p. 4.
26. *Ibid*, para 29, p. 4; *Kashful-Baghaavat, Gorakhpur*, stanza 488-491, 494, pp. 77,78, 79; The said Nepali poem describes in detail the battle fought by the Gorkha army against the rebel army at Kaudiram and Gagaha, and then its victory and march towards Azamgarh. See, Pant, Dinesh Raj (ed), *op.cit*, pp. 55-57.
27. Wingfield, C, *op.cit,* para 27, 31, 32, p. 4.
28. *Ibid*, para 28, p. 4.
29. Ball, Charles, *op cit*, Vol. II, p. 228, Footnote; FSUP, Vol. IV p. 384.
30. Wingfield C., *op cit,* para 34, p. 5; *Kashful-Baghaavat*, *op cit*, stanza 540-556, pp. 86-88.
31. Wingfield C., *op cit*, para 34-35 p. 5; FSUP, Vol. IV, p. 384; Writing about Bird's flight to Padrauna and then his movement towards Betiah, Syed Ahmed Ali Shah wrote:

    "Gaye shahar se Jab ke Sahib Bird
    Tha Hitti Bahadur bahut zeekhirad
    [When the Sahib Bird left the City
    Hitti Bahadur was very Wise]

Rahe ek shab unke dehaat par
Rifaqat mein haazir raha woh bashar
[Stayed for a night in his village (farm house)
That man was present in Comradeship]
Wahaan se Padrona mein Sahib gaye
Ataat mein Hafiz Tehsildaar the
[From there sahib went to Padrona
Where with reverence, Hafiz Tehsildar was present]
Taman le ke wahaan pahuncha Fazle Ali
Khabar uski Sahib ki unse mili
[Fazle Ali reached there with an army
Sahib received his information from him]
Bahut Khair-o-khubi se Sahib gaye
Ataat se Hafiz ke khurram hue
[Sahib left with lot of ease and pleasantness
Was delighted with the obedience of Hafiz]
Hai ek mauza Mathiya nihaayat basa
Ilaaqah woh hai yaaron Padrona ka
[One village Mathiya is very well populated
Friends, that is the region of Padraona]
Qadam wahaan pe Sahib ka jis dam gaya
Gosain Bandhal aake haazir hua
[the moment sahib reached that place
Gosain Bandhal came to present himself]
Ataat mein bandhi kamar usne chust
Qadam rakha raah-e-wafaa mein durust
[He made a brisk and firm resolve for the obedience
He promised to remain steadfast in the path of loyalty]
Gaya sath Sahib ke woh chand kos
Phira raah se woh pas az paaye bos
[He went with sahib for few miles
Returned from that route only after making obeisance]
See *Kashful-Baghaavat*, *op cit*, stanza 2059-67, pp. 319-20.

32. Wingfield C., *op cit*, para 36-38, p. 5.
33. *Ibid*, para 39, p. 5.
34. *Ibid*, para 40, p. 5.
35. *Ibid*.
36. Hasan, Moinuddin, *Khadang-e-Ghadar*, Hindi translation as '*Gadar*', Delhi, p. 74.
37. Wingfield C., *op cit*, para 41, p. 5.

38. *Ibid*, para 42, pp. 5-6; FSUP Vol. IV, p. 158.
39. *FSUP*, Vol. IV, pp. 345, 347, 350-51, 359, 397.
40. *Ibid*, p. 158; Wingfield C., *op cit*, para 42, p. 6; Letter from Rani Digambar Kunwari, See FSUP, Vol. IV, p. 381.
41. Wingfield C., *op cit*, para 43, p. 6; FSUP, Vol. IV, pp. 158-59.
42. Wingfield C., *op cit*, para 44, p. 6; Rana, Padma Jang Bahadur, *Life of Maharaja Sir Jang Bahadur*, pp. 198, 200, 206.
43. Rana, Padma Jang Bahadur, *op cit*, pp. 202-03; Wingfield C., *op cit*, para 43-44, p. 6; Ball, Charles, *op cit*, Vol. II, p. 229; *FSUP*, Vol. IV, pp. 296-300.
44. Rana, Padma Jang Bahadur, *op cit*, pp. 203; *FSUP*, Vol. IV, pp. 300-301; *Kashful-Baghaavat*, *op cit*, stanza 1388-91, p. 211; Ball, Charles, *op cit*, Vol. II, pp. 228-30; Ramsay, Major G., Narrative (1852-1861), 13 October 1861: c.f; Hasrat, Bikramjit, *op cit*, p. 335.
45. Wingfield C., *op cit*, para 44-45, p. 6; Ball, Charles, *op cit*, Vol. II, pp. 226-27; Rana Padma Jang Bahadur, *op cit*, p. 206. According to the Rana Padma Jang Bahadur, "when the Gorkha army, led by Jang Bahadur Rana, attacked Gorakhpur on 5 January 1858, with the aim of capturing it, they killed 211 men of the rebel army and injured a large number while it lost only 2 men and 9 injured. The Gorkha army snatched seven cannons and many guns from the rebels." See, Life of Maharaja Sir Jung Bahadur, p. 206.
46. *Kashful-Baghaavat*, *op cit*, stanza 1357-63, 1368, 1383-85, 1405-15, 1429, pp. 207-216.
47. Foreign Department, Consultation No. 82-83, 26 March 1858, (preserved in National Archives of India, New Delhi); *FSUP*, Vol. IV, p. 304; Chaudhuri Sashi Bhusan, Civil Rebellion in Indian Mutinies (1857-1859), p. 148.
48. *FSUP*, Vol. IV, pp. 305-06; Ball, Charles, *op cit*, Vol. II, p. 228; Ramsay, Major G, *op cit*, p. 335. Records of proceedings of Musharraf Khan's regular *kachahari* are not available. These could have shed much light on the *modus operandi* of the rebel government.
49. *FSUP*, Vol. IV, pp. 315-16; Nevill, H R, Nevill, H R, District Gazetteer, Basti (1907), Allahabad: Government Press, p. 161.
50. Home Department (Public), Consultation No. 91, 30 April 1858, preserved in National Archives of India, New Delhi.
51. *FSUP*, Vol. IV, p. 322.
52. Home Department (Public), Consultation No. 116, Governor General's Proceedings of May 1858, (preserved in National Archives of India, New Delhi); *FSUP*, Vol. IV, pp. 324, 330-331. It has been said that the village was called Purwa, which appears correct.
53. *Ibid*. *FSUP*, Vol. IV, p. 328
54. *Ibid*; *FSUP*, Vol. IV, pp. 326-37, 331-32.
55. *FSUP*, Vol. IV, pp. 329-30, 332.
56. *Ibid*, pp. 333-34, Home Department (Public), Consultation No. 116, Governor General's Proceedings of May 1858, preserved in National Archives of India, New Delhi.

57. Foreign Department, Consultation No. 139-140, 25 June 1858, preserved in National Archives of India, New Delhi; *FSUP*, Vol. IV, p. 336.
58. *FSUP*, Vol. IV, p. 334.
59. Foreign Department, Secret Proceedings, 25 June 1858, Vol. 1413, from the Commissioner of Gorakhpur, 22 May 1858, para 2, p. 3877 (preserved in National Archives of India, New Delhi).
60. *Ibid*, para 7, p. 3877, (preserved in National Archives of India, New Delhi).
61. *FSUP*, Vol. IV, p. 334, Home Department (Public), Consultation No. 116, Governor General's Proceedings of May 1858, preserved in National Archives of India, New Delhi.
62. Foreign Department, Secret Proceedings, 25 June 1858, Vol. 1413, from the Commissioner of Gorakhpur, 22 May 1858, para 12, p. 3878, preserved in National Archives of India, New Delhi.
63. *Ibid*, para 13, p. 3878; *FSUP*, Vol. IV, pp. 336.
64. *FSUP*, Vol. IV, pp. 336-37.
65. *Ibid*, p. 337.
66. *Ibid*, pp. 337, 345.
67. *Ibid*, p. 338; The Story of Indian Mutiny (1857-58), pp. 193-94 (W. P. Nimmo, Hay and Mitchell, Edinburgh 1885).
68. *Ibid*, p. 338.
69. *Ibid*, p. 339.
70. Foreign Department, Secret Consultation No. 145; 27 August 1858, (preserved in National Archives of India, New Delhi), Nevill H. R., District Gazetteer, Basti (1907), p. 162, Printed at Government Press, Allahabad.
71. *FSUP*, Vol. IV, p. 341.
72. *Ibid*, pp. 345, 397; Foreign Department, Political Consultation, 18 March 1859, No. 15: Foreign Department 1858-59, No. 13 of 1858, from C. Wingfield, Commissioner of Gorakhpur to G.P. Edmunston, Secretary to the government of India, 27 Nov 1858, para 15, pp. 6-7. preserved in National Archives of India, New Delhi.
73. *FSUP*, Vol. IV, p. 342.
74. *Ibid*, p. 343.
75. *Ibid*, p. 357.
76. *Ibid*, p. 343.
77. *Ibid*, p. 343-44.
78. *Ibid*, p. 346.
79. *Ibid*, p. 347.
80. *Ibid*, pp. 348, 352.
81. Foreign Department, Secret Consultation No. 5, 24 September 1858, preserved in National Archives of India, New Delhi.
82. Foreign Department, Secret Consultation No. 6, 24 September 1858, preserved in National Archives of India, New Delhi; *FSUP*, Vol. IV, p. 354.
83. *Ibid*.

84. Foreign Department, Secret Consultation No. 27, 29 October 1858, preserved in National Archives of India, New Delhi.
85. *FSUP*, Vol. IV, pp. 356-57; Foreign Department, Secret Consultation No. 30, 29 October 1858, (preserved in National Archives of India, New Delhi).
86. Foreign Department, Secret Consultation No. 47, 26 November 1858, preserved in National Archives of India, New Delhi; *FSUP*, Vol. IV, p. 358.
87. Foreign Department, Secret Consultation No. 49, 26 November 1858, preserved in National Archives of India, New Delhi; Foreign Department, Secret Consultation No. 13, 31 December 1858, preserved in National Archives of India, New Delhi; *FSUP*, Vol. IV, p. 359.
88. Foreign Department, Secret Consultation No. 6, 26 November 1858, preserved in National Archives of India, New Delhi.
89. Foreign Department, Secret Consultation No. 14, 31 December 1858, preserved in National Archives of India, New Delhi.
90. *Ibid.*
91. Foreign Department, Secret Consultation No. 15, 31 December 1858, preserved in National Archives of India, New Delhi; *FSUP*, Vol. IV, pp. 362-65.
92. *FSUP*, Vol. IV, pp. 367-68.
93. Foreign Department, Secret Consultation No. 16, 31 December 1858, preserved in National Archives of India, New Delhi; *FSUP*, Vol. IV, p. 368.
94. *FSUP*, Vol. IV, pp. 368, 370.
95. *FSUP*, Vol. IV, pp. 373-74, 396; *Kashful-Baghaavat*, stanza 1883-86, p. 290.
96. Foreign Department, Political 1859, 11 March 1859, No. 44-45; Wingfield C., *op cit*, 6 January 1859, para 7 and 8, pp. 6-7; Foreign Department, Political 1859, 11 March 1859, No. 46-48; From: Wingfield C., *op cit*, 24 January 1859, para 7 and 9, p. 3, preserved in National Archives of India, New Delhi.
97. Foreign Department, Political 1859, 11 March 1859, No. 46-48, para 4, p. 2; From Assistant Secretary to Government, Abstract, para 2 and 3: From the Weekly Narrative of the Gorakhpur Ending ....., para 3, p. 7; *FSUP*, Vol. IV, pp. 373-74.
98. Badayuni, Maulvi Mohammed Suleman, *op cit*, pp. 126-27; Sen, Surendra Nath, *Eighteen Fifty-Seven*, pp. 363-67; Chaudhuri, Sashi Buhusan, *op cit*, pp. 143.
99. *FSUP*, Vol. IV, pp. 377, 385-86.
100. Taylor, Robert, *The Rebellion of 1857 in the Province of Benares*, 15 October 1858, para 19, p. 10. (Henceforward it will be quoted as Taylor, Narrative). A printed copy of it is preserved in State Archives, Lucknow; Kaye, Sir John William, *A History of the Sepoy War in India*, Vol. II, London: (W. H. Allen & Company, London), pp. 213-14.
101. Taylor, Narrative, para 20, p. 10.
102. *Ibid*, para 21 & 23, pp. 10-11; Foreign Department, Secret Consultation No. 355-62, 30 April 1858, (preserved in National Archives of India, New Delhi); *FSUP*, Vol. IV, pp. 94-95, 97; Chick, Noah Alfred, *Annals of the Indian Rebellion, 1857-58* (Saunders, Cones & Company, Calcutta), 1858, p. 365.
103. Taylor, Narrative, para 23, p. 11; FSUP Vol. IV, p. 106.
104. *Ibid*, para 22, p. 11.

105. *Ibid*, para 23, p. 11; Kaye, *op cit*, Vol. II, pp. 213-14, 216.
106. *FSUP*, Vol. IV, pp. 101-06.
107. *Ibid*, pp. 103-04.
108. *Ibid*, p. 104.
109. *Ibid*, pp. 106, 110.
110. Taylor, Narrative, para 37, pp. 13-14.
111. *Ibid*, para 39, p. 14.
112. *Ibid*, para 41, p. 14.
113. *Ibid*.
114. *Ibid*, para 41, 46, pp. 15-16; Haq, Syed Moinul, op cit, p. 462.
115. *Ibid*, para 62, p. 19.
116. *Ibid*.
117. *Ibid*, para 63, p. 19.
118. *Ibid*, para 64, pp. 19-20; Rana, Padma Jang Bahadur *op cit*, p. 201. Syed Ahmed Ali Shah has described the battle between Raja Jay Lal Singh's party and the / Gorakhpur army in Azamgarh and of the rebels' defeat. He wrote:

    "Hua Rajaji lal aamaadah jung,

    Kiya kaafiya uska Gorkha ne tang

    [Raja Jai Lal was in preparedness for war;

    He was pushed in desperate straits by the Gorkhas.]

    Gira unpe chaapaa liya toop do

    Bas ab se zawaal uske aafaal ka

    [Raid was conducted on them and Two cannons were seized.

    From this instant began the warning of his ascendant acts.]; See, Stanza no. 504-505, pp. 79.
119. Taylor, Narrative, para 65, p. 20.
120. *Ibid*, para 78-79, p. 22.
121. *Ibid*, para 80, p. 22.
122. Home Department, Judicial, Consultation No. 20-25, 9 April 1858, preserved in National Archives of India, New Delhi.
123. *Ibid*.
124. Sen, S N, *op cit*, p. 262; Haq, Syed Moinul, *op cit*, p. 315; Taqi, Roshan, *The Two Wars at Lucknow: The Dusk of an Era*, (Lucknow: New Royal Book Company Publishers, 2001), p. 233.
125. *FSUP*, Vol. IV, p. 436. S N Sen says that Kunwar Singh was somewhere between Lucknow and Daryabad in February 1858. See Sen, *op.cit*, p. 262.
126. *FSUP*, Vol. IV, pp. 109, 437; Taylor, Robert, Supplement to the Narrative of Events & C. in the Benaras Division, 19 November 1858, p. 2, (henceforward referred to as Taylor, Supplement).; Chaudhuri Sashi Bhusan, *op.cit*, p. 325, Footnote no. 2 (Appendix E).
127. Taylor, Supplement, p. 2; Chaudhuri Sashi Bhusan, *op.cit*, p. 325; Savarkar, V.D, The Indian War of Independence, (London 1909), pp. 340-42; Sen, S N, *op.cit*, p. 262. Malleson, G B, *op.cit*, Vol. IV, pp. 319-20.

128. Savarkar, V.D, *op.cit,* p. 342. Malleson, G B, *History of the Indian Mutiny*, Vol. IV, p. 320.

129. Foreign Department, Secret Consultation No. 337, KW, 30 April 1858, preserved in National Archives of India, New Delhi; Savarkar, V.D, *op.cit* p. 343; Ball Charles, *op.cit,* Vol. II, p. 285; Chaudhuri Sashi Bhusan, *op.cit*, p. 326 Appendix E.

130. Taylor, Supplement, p. 2; Ball, Charles, *op.cit*, Vol. II, p. 285; Malleson, G B, *op.cit*, Vol. IV, pp. 320-21; Savarkar, V.D, *op.cit* pp. 342-43.

131. Foreign Department, Secret Consultation No. 337, KW, 30 April 1858; Ball, Charles, *op.cit*, Vol. II, p. 286, Savarkar, V.D, *op.cit,* pp. 343-45; Chaudhuri Sashi Bhusan, *op.cit*, pp. 326-27 (Appendix E); Malleson, G B, *op.cit*, Vol. IV, pp. 321-26.

132. FSUP, Vol. IV, p. 458; Chaudhuri, Sashi Bhusan, *op.cit*, pp. 156, 312 (Appendix D); Ball Charles *op.cit,* Vol. II, p. 287.

133. Ball Charles, *op.cit*, Vol. II, p. 287; Savarkar V.D., *op.cit*, pp. 345-47; FSUP, Vol. IV, p. 444; Chaudhuri, Sashi Bhusan, *op.cit,* p. 329; Malleson, G B, *op.cit*, Vol. IV, pp. 330-31.

134. Colonel G.B. Malleson wrote that "That leader had showed himself greater as strategist than as a tactician. His plan of campaign was admirable". At another place he wrote "But the Wily chieftain had matured plans far deeper than even those about him could fathom", See, Malleson, G B, *op.cit*, Vol. IV, p. 326-27, 330; Savarkar V.D, *op.cit*, pp. 344-46; Sen, Surendra Nath, *op.cit*, p. 263.

135. Taylor, Supplement, p. 2; *FSUP*, Vol. IV, pp. 453-57, 458-63; Savarkar V.D, *op.cit*, pp. 347-50; Malleson, G B, *op.cit*, Vol. IV, pp. 331-34.

136. *FSUP*, Vol. IV, pp. 202-03.

137. Foreign Department, Secret Consultation No. 81, 28 May 1858, preserved in National Archives of India, New Delhi.

138. Foreign Department, Secret Consultation No. 143, 25 June 1858, 1858, preserved in National Archives of India, New Delhi; *FSUP*, Vol. IV, p. 203.

139. Foreign Department, Secret Consultation No. 139, 27 August 1858, preserved in National Archives of India, New Delhi.

140. Taylor, Supplement, p. 3; *FSUP*, Vol. IV, p. 205.

141. Taylor, Narrative, para 4-8, pp. 7-8; Chandra, Moti, *Kashi ka Itihas*, *op.cit*, p. 290; Sen S.N, *op.cit*, p. 152; Kaye's & Malleson's, *History of the Indian Mutiny*, 1857-58, edited by Colonel Malleson, Vol. II, by Sir John Kay (London 1892), pp. 151-53, 162. (Hence forward mention as Kaye Vol. II).

142. Taylor, Narrative, para 6 and 9, pp. 7-8; Haq, Syed Moinul, *op.cit*, p. 448; Chandra, Moti, *op.cit*, p. 291.

143. Taylor, Narrative, para 11, pp. 8-9; Kaye Vol. II, *op.cit*, pp. 162-64.

144. Taylor, Narrative, para 12-13, p. 9; Sen, Surendra Nath *op.cit*, p. 153; Chick, N.A. *op.cit*, pp. 142-43; Kashful Baghawat Gorakhpur, stanza No. 249-55, pp. 40; FSUP Vol. IV, pp. 38-39; Kaye, Vol. II, pp. 165-69.

145. Taylor, Narrative, para 14, pp. 9-10; FSUP Vol. IV, p. 44; Kaye, Vol. II, pp. 173-74.

146. Taylor, Narrative, para 16, p. 10; Haq, Syed Moinul, *op.cit*, p. 449; Chandra, Moti, *op.cit*, p. 291.
147. Taylor, Narrative, para 34, pp. 13; Chandra, Moti, *op.cit*, p. 291; Haq, Syed Moinul, *op.cit*, pp. 449-50; FSUP Vol. IV, p. 44; Kaye, Vol. II, pp. 175-78.
148. Taylor, Narrative, para 84, p. 23.
149. *Ibid*, para 25, p. 11; Kaye, *op.cit,* Vol. II, pp. 178-79.
150. *Ibid.*
151. *Ibid*, para 26-27, pp. 11-12.
152. *Ibid*, para 35, p. 13.
153. *Ibid*, para 27, 68-69, 71, pp. 12, 20; Rana, Padma Jang Bahadur, *op.cit*, p. 201.
154. Taylor, Narrative, para 70, p. 20.
155. *Ibid*, para 71-73, pp. 20-21; Rana, Padma Jang Bahadur, *op.cit*, pp. 202-03. The Nepali poem makes a mention of the killing of Colonel Madan Singh of Gorkha army and injury to Gambhir Singh in the battle of Chanda. See Pant, Dinesh Raj (ed), *op.cit*, pp. 58-59.
156. Taylor, Narrative, para 82, p. 23.
157. *Ibid.*
158. *Ibid*, para 83, p. 23; Pant, Dinesh Raj (ed), *op.cit*, p. 59.
159. *Ibid;* In the description of the battle of Chanda, Padma Jang Bahadur Rana mentions the self-declared Nazim of Chanda and Banda Hasan. See, Rana, Padma Jang Bahadur, *op.cit*, p. 204; Nevill, H R, District Gazetteer, Jaunpur (1909), p. 194.
160. Foreign Department, Secret Consultation No. 65, 29 May 1858, preserved in National Archives of India, New Delhi.
161. Taylor, Supplement, p. 4.
162. Taylor, Narrative, para 29-32, p. 12.
163. *Ibid*, para 54, p. 17; *FSUP*, Vol. IV, pp. 54-55, 57-58.
164. *Ibid*, para 55-56, pp. 17-18; *FSUP*, Vol. IV, pp. 78-79.
165. Taylor, Narrative, para 56, p. 18; *FSUP*, Vol. IV, pp. 79-81.
166. *FSUP*, Vol. IV, pp. 232-35. The case following the murder of Moore led to the execution of eight persons, eight got life imprisonment, one was sentenced for 14 years, three were sentenced for 7 years each, and one was to be lashed. See *FSUP*, Vol. IV, p. 81.
167. Brockman, Drake, District Gazetteer, Mirzapur, 1911, pp. 242-43, Allahabad: Government Press.
168. *Ibid* p. 243; Taylor, Narrative, para 60, p. 19.
169. Taylor, Narrative, para 60, p. 19.
170. Brockman, *op.cit*, p. 244.
171. Taylor, Narrative, para 87, p. 24.
172. *Ibid*, para 28, p. 12.
173. *Ibid*, para 58, p. 18.
174. *Ibid.*

175. Foreign Department, Secret Consultation No. 49, 28 May 1858, preserved in National Archives of India, New Delhi.
176. *FSUP*, Vol. IV, pp. 446, 449-50, 459, 463.
177. Taylor, Supplement, p. 2.
178. *FSUP*, Vol. IV, pp. 117-119.
179. *Ibid*, pp. 285-86.
180. Foreign Department, Secret Consultation No. 147, 27 August 1858, (preserved in National Archives of India, New Delhi).
181. Foreign Department, Consultation No. 149, 27 August 1858 (preserved in National Archives of India, New Delhi).
182. *FSUP*, Vol. IV, p. 272.
183. *Ibid*, p. 273.
184. *Ibid*, pp. 273-275.
185. *Ibid*. p. 276.
186. *Ibid*, pp. 120-23.

Chapter - 5

The Rebel World and Its Prominent Leaders

The rebel world of 1857 comprised, more or less, the people of all classes and castes among the Hindus and Muslims. The region of Eastern Uttar Pradesh was no exception. The rebels of the region willingly accepted the government of Birjis Qadr, the son of Begum Hazrat Mahal of Awadh,[1] and widened the reach of the revolt under the leadership of his officials. They thus made themselves a part of the rebel world in India. The people of Gorakhpur willingly accepted Mohammed Hasan whom the rebel government had appointed the Nazim of Gorakhpur, though he belonged to Sahaswan in Budaun district, and the government formed under him ruled for about four months and a half.[2] Raja Iradat Jehan declared himself Naib Nazim of Jaunpur, appointed by the Government of Awadh,[3] while Raja Beni Madho declared himself Naib Nazim of Azamgarh.[4] When Babu Kunwar Singh of Arrah got the instruction to capture Azamgarh district, rebels of this region extended him full support and cooperation.[5] Kunwar Singh's brother Amar Singh,[6] nephew Harkishan Singh,[7] Shiva Prasanna Singh, Nishan Singh,[8] Maulvi Ali Kareem of Patna,[9] Nana Saheb's brother Bala Rao,[10] etc, fought against the British and their supporters in this region. Damman Khan, the jagirdar of Jhandanagar in the *terai* of Nepal, joined the rebellion as the chakladar of Bansi.[11] In the areas adjoining the eastern parts of Awadh, the taluqdar of Utraula,[12] Raja Devi Bakhsh Singh of Gonda,[13] Mehdi Hasan, the Nazim of Sultanpur,[14] Hasan Yar Khan, the chakladar of Jaunpur,[15] and also the rebels of areas adjoining the western borders of Bihar joined the rebellious activities in Eastern Uttar Pradesh. A large number of rebel soldiers of the Bengal Army took this region as conducive from the viewpoint of security and struggle, and made it their field of action.[16] People of this area also went out and played a role in rebellion elsewhere.[17] In short, the rebel's world of Eastern Uttar Pradesh included the people not only of this region but of other regions as well. It is obvious that their field of action was not narrow but quite wide.

(A) Structure of the Rebel World

Syed Ahmed Ali Shah, the caretaker of the Gorakhpur Imambada, who had specific knowledge of the rebels of Eastern Uttar Pradesh, particularly of Gorakhpur district, divided the rebels of 1857 into four categories. In his work *Kashful-Baghaavat, Gorakhpur*, he wrote:[18]

Qism chaar dekha hai hum baaghiyaan
Ke aage main likhta hun uska bayaan,
Woh hai asl baaghi jo tha peshwa
Duuwam baaghi woh jo ke naukar hua
Sawaaron mein jo log naukar hue
Woh sarkaar ke khaas baaghi bane
Sivuum Raja, Babu jo haazir rahe
Maa log apne madadgaar the
Bad amli ka aaghaaz jisne kiya
Kalan baaghiyon mein woh baaghi hua.

[I have witnessed four kinds of mutineers,
In the following Verses, I write their description. (1)
The real rebel is the one who was a leader,
Second is the rebel who accepted his service, (2)
Among the cavalry who became servants,
They became notable rebels against the Government, (3)
Thirdly, Rajas and Babus who were present for service
Together with their people, were helpful. (4)
Whoever initiated the bad operations,
Among rebels, he was the greatest rebel. (5)]

According to the above classification, Mohammed Hasan, the Nazim of Gorakhpur, was the real rebel of the first category. He ran an independent government in Gorakhpur for about four and a half months (from 21 August 1857 to December 1857). People in his employ comprised the second category. These included the civilians running the administration and the military officials. Among those under Mohammed Hasan, the most important and most influential was Musharraf Khan who according to the official records, had assumed the title of Naib (Deputy) Nazim. It has even been said that, compared to Mohammed Hasan, he had more and real powers.[19] Apart from him, Syed Ahmed Ali Shah has also mentioned Sardar

Ali Khan and his relatives, Ali Hasan, Navanda Rai, Mirza Fatah Ali, sons of Mirza Hasan Ali, Ulfat Ali, Amir Ali, Mohammed Saeed, Kaman Khan, Imdad Ali, Abid Ali, Mazhar Ali, Wajid Ali, Ahmed Khan, Ibrahim Beg, Kallu Beg, Brij Mohan, Mansoor Ali, Makhdum Bakhsh, Faiz Bakhsh, Najaf Ali, Nusrat Beg Hawaldar, Mirza Humayun, Ramzan Khan, Abd-e-Khaliq, Alahdad Khan, Fazle-Haq, Mohammed Fakir, Aali Hasan and Bihari, etc, as those joining the service of Mohammed Hasan. Shah has separately mentioned the cavaliers, taking them as most important during the rebellion.[20] In this category, he has mentioned Sardar Ali Khan as the leader of the cavaliers. Besides, he has mentioned Nawab, Gauhar, Shamsher Ali, Ehsan Ali, Khursheed Ali Khan, Kallu Beg, Dildar Khan, Hasan Khan, Ram Bahaal, Ghazi-ud-Din Khan and his sons, Walidad Khan, Rahimdad Khan, Abid Ali, etc, as the cavaliers.[21]

The description makes it clear that the aforementioned persons had played an important role in the rebellion, or were involved in key activities, because Shah Saheb knew them by name, while those in the Nazim's or Naib Nazim's service numbered in thousands. Moinuddin Hasan has talked of the recruitment of 25,000 soldiers and Kamaluddin Haider talked of 25,000 gunners.[22]

Admitting that a large number were recruited in the army, Syed Ahmed Ali Shah himself wrote that

Taman ka sipahi bhi humraah tha
Mulazim yeh azlam ka sab ho gaya
Aur the chand kash aur bhi bad sheaar
Mulazim the sarkaar-e-aali tabaar
Yehi log badraah gumraah the
Badil Company ke woh badkhah the
Soldiers of the army were also accompanying,
They all became servants of the tyrant.[23]
And there were some more ill-mannered individuals,
Were servants of the government of noble descent.[24]
These very persons were wicked and apostate,
From the core of their hearts they wished ill of the Company.[25]

Some persons were sentenced to death or imprisonment, after the rebellion was crushed, but were not mentioned earlier in the list of employees or sepoys or cavaliers. These included, according to *Kashful-Baghaavat, Gorakhpur*, Rasool Ali, Aulad Ali, Wahid Ali who was close to Musharraf Khan, Trilok's brother Pashupati Nath, Lal Khan, a sepoy of Tuman, Sheikh Faizu, Haider Hussein tehsildar as those who were hanged, and Khairat Ali as sentenced to ten years of imprisonment.[26] Besides, it has been said that ten unknown persons including Inayat Ali, Ramzan Ali Khan and Haider Khan, a follower of Umar Khan, were hanged to death.[27]

In the third category of rebels, Syed Ahmed Ali Shah mentions the rajas and babus (other brothers of rajas or zamindars, who were allotted separate estates or villages), who had joined Mohammed Hasan's employment with their men and soldiers. In this regard, rajas of Narharpur, Tilpur (Nichlaul),[28] Satasi,[29] Badhyapar[30] and Nagar are mentioned.[31] The British records also mention the Raja of Shahpur and Rani of Amorha among the supporters and cooperators of the Nazim.[32] Similarly, the Babu of Pandeypur,[33] Babu of Rajpur Pania,[34] Babu of Madanpur Belwa,[35] Babu of Bhowapar,[36] Babu of Dumri[37] and Babu of Rudhauli[38] were also mentioned in *Kashful-Baghaavat, Gorakhpur*. Besides them, British records also mention the Babu of Tighra,[39] Babu of Bakhira,[40] Babu of Chillupar[41] and Babus of Pipra[42] as the rebelling babus. Syed Ahmed Ali Shah also mentions the Gosain of Tolia in the *terai* of Nepal (today known as Taulihwa), whom Mohammed Hasan had presented a robe of honour. He wrote —

> Phansa Toliya ka Gosain bhi aa
> Pahanne mein khilat ke shamil hua
> [The Gosian of Toliya was also entangled
> He was involved in donning the robe of honour].[43]

He did not quote the Gosain's name but the British records mention him as Jaikishan Puri Gosain whose two disciples were taken as prisoners by Nepali authorities when, along with Damman Khan, they were going to Maharaja Jang Bahadur Rana to solicit military help for the rebels.[44] Moreover, Jaikishan Puri also gave shelter to the group of Fazal Ali in 1856-57 after they fired upon Boileau, CS, in the Nepalese territory.[45] This shows that the Gorakhpur rebels' field of action was extended to the Nepal *terai*. In the fourth category of rebels, Syed Ahmed Ali Shah included all those who started the rebellious activities. He regarded them as the "greatest" rebels. In this category, we may include the rebel soldiers who negated the British rule and began the plunder;[46] the Rajputs of Paina and nearby villages who began the rebellion by capturing the British boats in Ghaghra river and obstructing the waterway;[47] the villagers of Mahua Dabar who killed six English officers;[48] Mendhu Khan and his followers who challenged the British rule in Bansi tehsil;[49] the groups of those like Balli Singh, Balikaran

Singh, Rajivan Singh and Wali Mohammed whom the British Government described as dacoits and vandals;[50] and the zamindars[51] who revolted.

Syed Ahmed Ali Shah described the Palwar Rajputs of Azamgarh as rebels.[52] Robert Taylor too has mentioned the Palwar Rajputs who joined the most rebellious activities in this district.[53] Similarly, Shah Saheb also mentioned Zamindar Sada Singh of Ballia[54] and Makar Singh of Gahmar in Ghazipur district.[55] From British records too, we get the names of the rebels who played an active role in the rebellion in Azamgarh, Ghazipur, Banaras, Jaunpur and Mirzapur districts. The narrative which Robert Taylor sent to the government on 15 October 1858 under the title "The Rebellion of 1857 in the Province of Benares," mentioned Palwar leader Madho Prasad Singh, Prithvipal Singh, Pargan Singh, Kurmi Raja Beni Madho and Rajab Ali of Azamgarh, Raja Iradat Jehan of Mubarakpur and his commander Amar Singh in Jaunpur, Raja Muzaffar Jahan of Mahul, Raghuvanshi Rajputs of Dobhi, Malik Mehdi Bakhsh of Katghar, Jhuri Singh of Bhadohi, Raja Udwant Singh, etc.[56] Wilton Oldham did mention the names of rebellious villages in Ghazipur district, but did not name the rebel leaders.[57] In the British records edited by Syed Athar Abbas Rizvi, we find the names of Udresh Singh, leader of Rajkumar Rajputs, and Chandresh Singh on the border of Jaunpur district,[58] Jageshwar Singh (taluqdar of Badlapur),[59] Arjun Singh,[60] Raja Jai Lal Singh (Nazim of Jaunpur),[61] Khudabakhsh,[62] Sangram Singh (Madiahu),[63] Bhairon Prasad Banker[64] and Sarvajit Singh.[65] It is not possible to classify the rebels of districts in Banaras zamindari, like we can do in case of the Gorakhpur rebels. We may only say, in brief, that the world of rebels in Eastern Uttar Pradesh was not confined to a few people but was quite wide, with a big mass base.

To present a full description of main leaders of the rebel world in Eastern Uttar Pradesh is not possible either. Records are lacking about the leaders who came from the common mass. We have the names of only a few prominent ones. Among the main rebels of this region, only piecemeal information is available about the hereditary rajas and babus. For example, about the Rajputs of Paina village who began the revolt, we only know that the zamindars of the village captured the grain-laden boats. From the narrative of 20 June 1858, we learn that the village had continued the revolt and had 600 fighters. Some of the rebels fought when the British army arrived and were killed, while others ran away. The village had been burnt to ashes.[66] Similarly, we know only the names of villages of so many babus. Even then, we present here a brief description of the main leaders of the rebel world in Eastern Uttar Pradesh in 1857.

(B) Main Leaders in Gorakhpur District

Muhammad Hasan (Nazim, Gorakhpur)

Appointed as the Nazim of Gorakhpur by the Government of Birjis Qadr, son of Begum Hazrat Mahal of Awadh, Muhammad Hasan was the most important leader of rebel world in Eastern Uttar Pradesh. During the rebellion, he not only led the rebels but also ran an independent government in Gorakhpur for about four and a half months — (from 21 August 1857 to 4 January 1858). He remained active against the British till the last phase of the rebellion.

Urdu writers have written the name of this rebel leader as "Muhammad Hasan" or "Meer Muhammad Hasan Khan" while British records mention him as "Mohammad Husain" or "Muhammed Hasan." In *Khadang-e-Ghadar*, Moinuddin Hasan wrote that Meer Muhammad Hasan Khan was a Syed by caste and belonged to village Bahra. During the Nawab's rule, Meer Mohammed Hasan was a Sardar and had been the administrator of Gonda-Bahraich.[67] In *Qaisar-ut-Tawarikh*, (Volume Two, Zikr – 116, Lucknow, November 1879), Kamaluddin Haidar wrote that Meer Mohammed Hasan Khan, Nazim of Gonda and Bahraich during the Nawab's rule, was made in-charge of Gorakhpur by the grace of the king.[68] According to Syed Athar Abbas Rizvi, "Meer Mohummud Hussein" and occasionally "Meer Muhammad Hussun," mentioned by the British records, were one and the same person.[69] Maulvi Mohammed Suleiman Badayuni said his real name was Meer Mohammed Hussein Khan and his father's name was Meer Mohammed Hasan Khan. Before the outbreak of the 1857 rebellion, Meer Mohammed Hussein Khan was the Nazim of Khairabad.[70] According to this writer, Mohammed Hasan belonged to Sahaswan in Budaun district.[71] Thus, this leader of the rebellion did not belong to Gorakhpur or any other part of Eastern Uttar Pradesh. He had captured Gorakhpur and declared himself the Nazim appointed by the Awadh government.[72] Birjis Qadr honoured him with the title of "Mokarrab-ud-Daulah" and also gave him a *sanad* (certificate) of appointment as the Nazim or chakladar of Gorakhpur.[73] Descriptions by pro-British writers seem to insinuate that he had declared himself "Nazim" on behalf of the government.[74] In the letter written at the time of surrender, Mohammed Hasan tried to show that fear had made him accept the position. This was natural on his part. Mohammed Hasan wrote that he was in his villages (zamindari) at Tanda (Faizabad) for ten days at the time of revolt. Meanwhile there was an outbreak in Lucknow, and he came to know about it after a fortnight when he returned home. Ten days after it, he got the news of a revolt in Faizabad. So, from his house, he went to village Digdowur which was close to Dalpatpore Ghat on Ghagra river. Same day, running away from Faizabad, Colonel Lennox's family disembarked at the same ghat. When rebellious villagers encircled these Englishmen and he got the news, he sent ten soldiers to save them and later he himself went there with 150 persons. When he was helping the Englishmen disembark, a group of rebel sepoys of 17th NI opened fire, but his men faced them, and he brought the Englishmen to his house safe and they stayed there for 15 days. Then he sent them to Gorakhpur in safety.[75] He received a parwannah from the Begum about 15 days after this incident, calling him to Lucknow. He was afraid of going to Lucknow as he had saved some Englishmen. Hence, he pleaded inability to come to Lucknow. But he received the *sanad* of appointment as chakladar of Gorakhpur and was told to assume duty immediately. In case of non-compliance, he was threatened that his family, then in Lucknow, would be arrested. Nay more, Narpat Regiment was dispatched against him and it reached there in ten days. Hence, he felt helpless. While all this was going on, the Naib Risaladar of the 12th Irregular Cavalry at Sagauli and other people, Musharraf Khan, bailiff (karindah) of the Raja of Narharpur, the Raja of Barhyapar and the Rani of Amorha, etc, were writing letters to the Begum, telling her that Gorakhpur was free from the British army, that they are old faithfuls of Awadh, and would make all arrangement for that part of country. As a result, two regiments, called Mirza Oomrao Jan and Jehangir Khan, were also sent to him from Lucknow. He joined them and left for Gorakhpur.[76] Mohammed Hasan also contended that he had sent a letter to Mr Bird after reaching Basti but Ram Prasad, the taluqdar of Bichhiya, arrested the messenger and the letter did not reach to Mr. Bird.[77] Mohammed Hasan said all this at the time of surrender.

The fact was that Mohammed Hasan was the Nazim of Khairabad (now in the district of Sitapur) during the reign of Wajid Ali Shah, the last Emperor of Awadh. He became jobless when the British annexed Awadh. When the revolt broke out, he was in Tanda which was a rebel's stronghold. He raised a rebel army in Tanda and decided to capture Gorakhpur. Raja Abbas Ali of Tanda also helped him. With his soldiers, he invaded Khalilabad tehsil, about ten *kos* to the north of Tanda. Mr. Bird, the Collector of Gorakhpur, resisted him, but failed and fled away. Mohammed Hasan distributed the booty, collected here, among his soldiers. But he could not fortify his position. When the English army launched the second attack, he was badly defeated and was in the British siege. But he could not be recognised and managed to escape safe.[78]

On 13 August 1857, in view of the multiplying events of rebellion, Mr. Wynyard, the Judge and Collector of Gorakhpur, decided to leave Gorakhpur. He collected all the European citizens in the district and left for Azamgarh, along with the government treasury and English officials, in the Gorkha army's protection. Mohammed Hasan learnt about it. With his soldiers, he left for Gorakhpur and attacked the Gorkha army at a place called Gagaha, ten miles to the north of Ghagra river. But he was defeated and at least 200 of his men were killed. Gorkhas also took his palanquin in custody and continued to move towards Azamgarh.[79] Returning from Gagaha on 20 August, Mohammed Hasan reached the Rapti banks on the outskirts of Gorakhpur; Musharraf Khan, representative of the Raja of Satasi, and leading Muslim dignitaries of Gorakhpur city welcomed him here jail guards also joined him.[80] On 21 August, he captured Gorakhpur and formed a national government there, taking necessary steps to run the administration. According to C. Wingfield, the first step Mohammed Hasan took was issue an order that all government servants should rejoin duty or, else, they would be punished. But no deputy collector obeyed the order; only a tehsildar did it. However, several thanedars accepted him as the master. He continued the revenue and judicial systems, while several landlords opposed the idea of thanedar as this position did not exist in the Nawab's regime. The Civil Court decisions were implemented on the condition of payment of half the dues. He preserved the records, and, from *qanungos*, he elicited complete information about the revenue demands every landlord owed. To the big landlords who expressed allegiance, he provided a robe of honour and gun salute as guard of honour, and to exercise the civil and criminal powers within their estates (zamindaris). They were also allowed the titles which they demanded. In return, they had to provide their military troops to his army. These included the rajas of Satasi, Nagar, Narharpur, Barhyapar, Nichlaul and Shahpur as well as the babus of Tighra, Pandeypur and Rudhauli. Rich Muslims of the city got most of the official positions. Besides, a Judge and a Collector were appointed while Musharraf Khan was made the Naib Nazim.[81]

To fight the enemies, Mohammed Hasan recruited a large number of soldiers. According to Moinuddin Hasan, his army comprised 25,000 persons from all the seven castes.[82] In other words, he formed a national army. About his management, Kamaluddin Haider wrote that "He made his own arrangements. He released the prisoners and got their shackles removed. They said to him (Mohammed Hasan), We would shed our blood for your sweat." Most of them were *kasbis*. Hundreds of them weaved carpets, rough carpets, cotton and woollen textiles. Every person was appointed for whatever trade he knew. He kept magzines in the jail; there were in all eight or ten cannons, and he employed 25 thousand gunmen and several hundred *sowars*. Every day, 26 thousand rupees were spent on the army, charity, etc."[83] Syed Moinul Haq believes that Kamaluddin Haider's account was exaggerated.[84]

As the chakladar of the rebel government of Awadh, Mohammed Hasan ruled Gorakhpur for four and a half months.[85] In his time, most of the Englishmen's bungalows were put afire. But except Mr. Bird's residence, no masonry house was damaged. He did not brook for rebels' atrocities against the people and kept the public property and offices safe. Yet British officials and pro-government writers have condemned his reign as full of atrocities. In his narrative, C. Wingfield, Commissioner of Goruckpore, has described atrocities of Muhammad Hasan.[86] Other accounts also purported that law and order constantly declined during his chakladari and anarchy prevailed everywhere.[87] Moinuddin Hasan,[88] Kamaluddin Haider[89] and Syed Ahmad Ali Shah[90] have also described his administration as atrocious. But this is far from the truth.[91]

Mohammed Hasan was fighting for his emperor, to snatch his rule back from the British. He had accepted fighting for his ruler as his duty. He was not only determined to achieve his goal but also made all possible efforts for it. Displaying his foresightedness, he wrote a letter to Maharaja Jang Bahadur Rana, the Prime Minister of Nepal, to desist him from helping the British. The letter expressed surprise that "the Maharaja was helping those who were the killers of Brahmins and cows."[92] However, he did not succeed to achieve his aim of preventing Nepal from helping the British. Kamaluddin Haider wrote that "In this period he constantly wished to have a favourable response from Maharaja Jang Bahadur, the Prime Minister, and the commander-in-chief of Nepal, but in vain."[93] It was Mohammed Hasan who had to fight against Nepal first. Mentioning his army's battle against the Nepalese army and his defeat, Kamaluddin Haider and Moinuddin Hasan have also written about his flight to Tanda.[94] Padma Jang Bahadur Rana, the son of Maharaja Jang Bahadur Rana, says that "The combined army of Jang Bahadur and the English officials reached near Gorakhpur on 5 January 1858. When the Nepalese attacked the rebel army, they fled to the other side of the Rapti. The winners got seven cannons and a number of guns. Two of the Gorkha army died and nine were injured, while 211 of the other side were killed and so many were injured. British administration was restored in Gorakhpur."[95]

We learn from British documents that Mohammed Hasan did not accept defeat even after losing Gorakhpur and continued the fight. He had also to face penury after vacating Gorakhpur. He had three regiments of rebel soldiers. They pressed him for salary arrears and, after extracting a lakh of rupees, they crossed the Ghaghra and joined the Raja of Gonda's army.[96] Yet he did not lose heart. On 17 April 1858, his army faced Colonel Rowcroft as he had left Belwa in order to capture Amorha. In this battle, he lost 100 of his men.[97] A defeated Mohammed Hasan left for Domariaganj but again came to Amorha. He then had about 4,000 men. He had to retreat after the 9 June battle.[98] On 18 June 1858, Mohammed Hasan's troop had to face the English attack at Harraiya and had to run to Gonda district after defeat. He was camping in the forests of Babhni on 29 July. In October 1858, along with his army, Mohammed Hasan was in Bangaon. In November 1858, he left Bangaon and reached a village to the east of Domariaganj where, on 3 December 1858, Colonel Rowcroft's army administered him another defeat and forced him to flee to Utraula.[99] Finally, getting the news that Begum Hazrat Mahal had gone into the hills for survival, he presented himself before the Begum at Bara. Unfortunately, there too, rebels were defeated and ran into the hills.[100] Thus, Mohammed Hasan remained continually involved in the fight.

When the British rule was reinstalled and law and order, and peace, were restored, Mohammed Khairuddin, the Magistrate of Gorakhpur, wrote him a letter under Queen Victoria's proclamation, asking him to surrender. The correspondence between the two gives an idea about the high ideals of this rebel hero. In his letter, he dubbed the British as unreliable, with inhuman conduct, and the appropriator of Awadh. He did not give any importance to his own life and death.[101] Even Governor General Canning appreciated his letter.[102] Eventually, he surrendered and was tried. Despite all efforts by Wingfield C., he was found not guilty and was released.[103] But his properties were confiscated and his haveli was cannoned. He spent the rest of his life incognito and in penury. He died in 1888.[104] Thus, this great hero's life ended in anonymity.

Musharraf Khan (Naib Nazim, Gorakhpur)

Musharraf Khan, bailiff of the Raja of Satasi, was the prime mover of the rebellion in Gorakhpur district. He was the most courageous and active among the rebels.[105] According to Syed Ahmad Ali Shah, he hailed from village Belwa. He wrote —

> "Musharraf Khan tha ek qaidi yahaan
> Ke muddat se tha qaid -e – bekhaanumaan.
> [Mushaaraf Khan was a prisoner here,
> For long time, he had been a captive of Vagabondness]

Makaan uska Belwa ke mauza mein tha
Nihaayat safi abla-o-behaya
[His house was in the village of Belwa
He was extremely daft, unreasonable and shameless][106]

In Fasli 1207 (1799 AD), Raja Pahalwan Singh of the Satasi Estate had given the village of Belwa as the *maafi* (revenue free) Birt to his confidant Diwan Safdar Khan.[107] This Diwan had played an important role in the history of the zamindar family of Satasi, and remained highly influential till 1818.[108] Musharraf Khan perhaps belonged to this very family and was therefore also known as the Diwan of Raja Udit Narayan Singh. As the attorney or bailiff (agent) of the Raja, he had, along with his men, welcomed Mohammed Hasan the Nazim at the Rapti bank outside the city on 20 August 1857, and had installed him in Gorakhpur city the next day.[109] Mohammed Hasan appointed him as his Naib (Nazim) mainly because he was the representative of the Raja of Satasi who was also known as the Raja of Gorakhpur.[110]

Musharraf Khan was of a rebellious disposition from the beginning. That was why he was an eyesore to the government even before the rebellion had started. Mr. Bird, the Joint Magistrate of Gorakhpur, had therefore got him arrested and thrown behind the bars on the charge of vagabondage. However, on 13 August, when the Englishmen left Gorakhpur for Azamgarh, along with the treasury and leaving Bird behind, prisoners too were released as per a government order, on 15 August 1857.[111] Musharraf Khan was one of them. After his release, along with some friends, he went straight to Mr. Bird's house and got the message conveyed that he had come to settle the account. In his footnote, Mr. Charles Ball wrote about Musharraf Khan that "This individual had formerly been sentenced to imprisonment for 'badmashee', by Mr. Bird, the joint magistrate of Goruckpore. When the station was abandoned by the British, Mr. Bird alone remained at his post, but his efforts to maintain order were fruitless; the gaol was thrown open, and the prisoners liberated; and the first visitor Mr. Bird was honoured with from that undesirable locality, was Musharraf Khan, who coolly walked into his house, and, sitting down upon a sofa, informed the magistrate that he had come to settle the little account they had between them. Musharraf Khan was armed and accompanied by a number of his gaol companions. Mr. Bird was alone, all police, goal-guard and rajah followers having deserted him. After a tolerably long stay, the worthy Naib Nazim left the house with a promise that he would repeat, his visit before long: in the interim, however Mr. Bird escaped from the place on an elephant and got safely through the jungle to Chupra."[112]

This demonstrated his fearlessness and courage.

Musharraf Khan demonstrated his administrative and military abilities during his four months stint as the Naib Nazim. In his narrative for the week ending 23 January 1858, C. Wingfield, an English official, wrote that "This man had held his court in regular form, and its records which have fallen complete into our hands, are likely to prove of great value."[113] This is the best proof of Musharraf Khan's administrative abilities. According to C. Wingfield, Musharraf Khan commanded more influence than even Nazim Mohammed Hasan.[114] Inspired by him, a number of employees and sepoys joined the rebellion. When the rebellion started, according to C. Wingfield's narrative, Gorakhpur's Joint Magistrate Mr. Bird wanted to prevent the rebels from crossing the Rapti river and therefore told the most disciplined "*taman*" (or jail guards) to come and destroy the river bridge two miles from the city, but only 17 out of the 150 guards accompanied him.[115] Syed Ahmad Ali Shah told the reason —

> "Taman ne Musharraf se saazish kiya
> Bird ke na humraah koi gaya"
> [The troops conspired with Musharraf
> No one proceeded with (Mr.) Bird].[116]

This statement shows that Musharraf Khan had succeeded in winning over the *taman* guards. Elsewhere, Shah has narrated that government employees had joined the rebellion at Musharraf Khan's bidding —

> "Mulazim yeh ho kar ke baaghi hue
> Musharraf ke kehne se daaghi hue"
> [Despite being employees, they became mutineers,
> On Musharraf's incitement they became tarnished].[117]

Musharraf Khan himself had several employees who were loyal to him. Shah wrote:

> "Koi jaa ke azlam ka chakkar hua,
> Musharraf ka bhi koi naukar hua"
> [Some went and became servants of the most, cruel one,
> Some became servants of Musharraf also].[118]

During the revolt, the biggest problem faced by the rebels, was economic. Rebel leaders had to give something as salary for their soldiers' and men's livelihood, and money was needed for it. Mobilising resources was a big problem for the rebel government of Gorakhpur as well.

Musharraf Khan attended to this problem. He collected money from zamindars, rajas, moneylenders, traders and other rich people, which has been deplored by British officers and their supporters.[119] Syed Ahmad Ali Shah has made a detailed description of the plunder of Imambada where he had sheltered some Englishmen, and also mentioned the prices of the things which the rebel soldiers had looted.[120] However, there is no description of the loot of any *tazia* or *alam* (religious banner) made of gold and silver, which shows the rebels' respect for all religions. The properties of the Shah and the British were specifically marked during this plunder.[121] Musharraf Khan took special note of the pro-British. He was particularly annoyed with Syed Ahmad Ali Shah as the latter supplied information to the British. Through a person called Sanaullah, Musharraf Khan had sent the message that "the Shah should give some dinars (gold coins) and gold to the rebel government, or else the Nazim would send him to Lucknow."[122]

Musharraf Khan conducted a military expedition against the pro-British Raja of Bansi and forced him to submit,[123] though his success proved momentary. *Kashful-Baghaavat, Gorakhpur* makes a mention of this expedition:

> "Sifat Raja Bansi ki mashoor hai
> Shujaat ka ab unke mazkoor hai
> Musharraf gaya yan se lekar sipah
> Na jana ki aayaa kidhar rusiyah"
> [Qualities of Raja of Bansi are famous
> Now his bravery is being related
> Musharraf went from here with soldiers
> Did not care to know where the criminal had come].[124]

Musharraf Khan sent an army against the Raja of Gopalpur also and forced him to flee to Azamgarh.[125] At Sohanpur village between Mairwa and Majhauli, Musharraf Khan faced the army of Colonel Rowcroft and the regiment of 500 Gorkhas who were coming to protect the Majhauli Raj. In this battle, Harkishan Singh, the nephew of Kunwar Singh, and Maulvi Ali Kareem of Patna had also taken positions along with Musharraf Khan. But they faced defeat in this battle.[126] Around this time, the Gorkha army of Maharaja Jang Bahadur Rana of Nepal reached Gorakhpur along with British officers. In the battle at Pipraich, Mohammed Hasan's army faced defeat and fled away. Along with this army, Mr. Bird also reached Gorakhpur as the Joint Magistrate.[127]

After the British reoccupied Gorakhpur on 6 January 1858, Musharraf Khan somehow reached Mahson, situated to the south-east of Basti town, and strove to continue the revolt with the help from the zamindar family there. The Rani of Mahson posed as if she was involved in rebellious activities and sent him to British officials to negotiate peace on her behalf. But he was taken prisoner there.[128] He was tried in a special military court and given the death sentence. However, before he was executed, he was put in a cart, as a prisoner, and taken around in Ali Nagar, the main market of Gorakhpur. This was the seat of the Nazim's *kachahari* where, till only a few days ago, he used to move around with princely pomp and grandeur. Thousands of civilians came to see the spectacle of his execution. He was publicly hanged to death in the main market at Alinagar.[129] Syed Ahmad Ali Shah wrote —

> "Musharraf Ali dekho khaati raha
> Ali Nagar mein usko phaansi diya"
> [Look, Musharraf Ali was a guilty
> He was hanged in Ali Nagar][130]

Following him, his close aides like Rasool Ali, Aulaad Ali, Navandah Rai and Wahid Ali were also executed.

> "Rasool Ali or Aulaad Ali
> Unhe jaa ke Maqtal mein phaansi hue
> Tha Navandah Rai unke darbaar mein
> Ghanimat ke rehta tha wo kaar mein
> Nahi naukri uski usne kiya
> Badaulat mohabbat ke woh bhi gaya
> Musharraf ka dildaar Wahid Ali
> Yeh chaaron ko, ek rooz phaansi hui"
> [Rasool Ali and Aulaad Ali, they were taken to the land of execution and hanged.
> Navandah Rai was in their court, it was blessing that he remained on duty
> He did not ever serve him, because of affection he too was gone
> Musharraf's beloved Wahid Ali, these four were hanged one day].[131]
> Shah wrote in the end: Musharraf Khan thus came to an end, as did his collaborators.
> "Wohi log duniya se ghaaib hue

Musharraf ke jo log naib hue."
[Those very people disappeared from the world
Who had become assistants of Musharraf] [132]

Raja Udit Narayan Singh of Satasi

Satasi, Bansi and Unwal were the three most powerful estates of Srinet Rajputs in Gorakhpur district. They all trace their common origin from the single family. In due course of time, the family divided and according to family traditions they got their respective shares and started ruling separately. Of these, Rudrapur (at present in Deoria district) was the main centre of Satasi Raj. The babus of this princely family were also very powerful in Gorakhpur district. Udit Narayan Singh was the Raja of Satasi at the time of the revolt and lived in the Rudrapur fortress. He was the grandson of Maharaja Kawalwan Singh of Bhowapar and son of Lal Awadhoot Singh. He was nominated Raja after the death of Rani Haniwant Kunwari in 1838.[133] According to Reade, he was about 40 in May 1843, and had an extensive zamindari with an annual income of 70,000 rupees. He was the chief of Srinet Kshatriyas.[134] During the 1857 revolt, he had pleaded allegiance to Nazim Mohammed Hasan and presented him 500 rupees.[135] In his letter sent on 17 August 1857, he addressed Mohammed Hasan as the Nazim and pleaded that he would follow his commands; he also informed that he would welcome the Nazim through his *mukhtar* (attorney).[136] This makes clear that he was in touch with Mohammed Hasan even before the latter came to Gorakhpur. Moreover, he sent his *mukhtar (representative)*, Musharraf Khan, to welcome Mohammed Hasan, as he had promised. On the other hand, when British officials formed a committee of five rajas to run the administration of Gorakhpur, Udit Narayan Singh did not join it even though he was nominated for it.[137] Mohammed Hasan took the raja's *mukhtar* as his *naib*. He invited Raja Udit Narayan Singh to Gorakhpur. When the latter reached there, he was given a salute of guns and a robe of honour. He was put up in Mr. Bird's residence.[138] Syed Ahmad Ali Shah wrote —

Tama mein Satasi ka Raja phansa
Kiya raat bhar jashn usne bada
[The Raja of Satasi was lured by greed celebrated pompously the entire night].[139]

Raja Udit Narayan Singh had organised the vandalism of the police post near his house, even when British officials were still there.[140] Describing his activities, Syed Ahmad Ali Shah wrote —

Ke Raja Satasi jo badraah hain
Woh masnui Nazim ke dilkhaah hai
Yurish hai jo Raja ki es dam kamaal
Hifazat kar aiye Khaliq-e Zuljalaal
Kisi ahad mein jisko dekha nahin
Nazar mein kisi ke na ayaa kahin
Woh Belwa ka babu ma ek tuman
Har ek mauza us se hua pur mehan
Jahan pahucha laya ek aafat nayee
Kiye usne veeran mauze kayee
Jahan haathi ghode ko lekar pade
Woh daakuon ki manind ja kar ade
Nazar bhent dus bees lete rahe
Aur dehaat ko khaam karte rahe
Bhowapara ka Babu tehsil kar
Rawaana woh karta tha Raja ke ghar
Yahi log patra ke maalik bane
Unhi ke sabab tabaah ghaarat hue
Himayat se Raja ke sab loot te
Aur qaryah ba qaryah yeh bakte phire
Ke sab milk Raja Satasi ka hai
Kisi ki nahin milk koi kahe
Mangaate hain patwari ke kaghazaat
Yeh taqreer sab unki thi besabaat
Aur patwariyon par bhi yurish hui
Jo the ahle mulk unpe shorish hui

[The Raja of Satasi who is wicked, is covetous of the fake Nazim.
At the moment, aggression of the Raja is excessive.
O, Glorious Creator, protect us.
Who was not seen at any time, who was not noticed by anyone, anywhere,
That Babu of Belwa, with an army, caused every village to be engulfed in suffering,
Brought untold miseries to the places he reached.

He reduced many villages to desolation.
Wherever they arrived with elephants and horses,
They acted wayward and obstinate like dacoits,
Collected ten or twenty (rupees) as an offering-oblation,
And reduced the villages to crudity.
The Babu of Bhowapar after collection, used to dispatch it to the Raja's place (palace).
These very people became the proprietors of destruction.
Because of them there was ruinousness.
They looted under the patronage of the Raja (Satasi),
And from village to village they kept babbling
That all properties belong to the Raja of Satasi,
No one should claim the properties to be of anyone.
Have summoned papers of the revenue official, Patwari.
All this oration of theirs was transitory.
And the Patwaris were also oppressed.
Those who were residents of the region were disturbed].[141]

Thus, the process of forced collections and eviction from land was going on under the Raja of Satasi's patronage. He had well-fortified his palace and collected arms and ammunition, supplies (grains), etc, so that rebellious activities could be conducted for long. When the rebels faced defeat in the battle of Sohanpur, some of them ran away and took refuge in the fortress at Rudrapur. Their intention was to attack Gorakhpur. Chasing them, therefore, Colonel Rowcroft too started for Rudrapur along with his army. When Raja Udit Narayan Singh knew of it, he left Rudrapur with his weapons, supplies and followers. Colonel Rowcroft still got many valuables and grains in the Rudrapur fortress. A letter sent by him tells us about the situation of the Rudrapur fortress and the things kept there.[142] Rowcroft destroyed the fortification and sent the grains, particularly rice, to Gorakhpur for the Nepalese army's use.[143] British records do not mention the activities of this important hero after the British re-established their rule in Gorakhpur. But he was certainly not lying low. Of the babus associated with him, Srinet babus of Pandeypar and Dumri were quite active. The Commissioner's narrative for the week ending 16 October 1858 mentioned the capture of the Raja of Satasi's elephant and expressed the possibility that, for revenue collection, he was returning to his house from his estate that had been confiscated.[144] This showed his activity.

The pro-British Rani Digambar Kunwari of Basti and the Raja of Bansi had sympathy for Raja Udit Narayan Singh. He was Rani Digambar Kunwari's son-in-law while Bansi and Satasi estates were two independent, sprawling and influential zamindaris of a single family of Srinets. This too must have helped him in hiding, though no proof of it is available. He surrendered when the rebellion was crushed in a sense by December 1858, and amnesty with certain conditions was promised by Queen Victoria's proclamation. In his narrative for the week ending 6 January 1859, C. Wingfield, the Commissioner of Gorakhpur, informed that Raja Udit Narayan Singh of Satasi and some less important rebels had surrendered before the government.[145]

Raja Udit Narayan Singh was tried for sedition in the special court of the Commissioner. His zamindari and properties were confiscated and he was divested of the title of "Raja," though there was no charge of murder against Raja Udit Narayan Singh and he should have been granted pardon. Yet, on 12 March 1859, in the case foisted against him in the special court of the Commissioner under Act XIV of 1857, he was tried for rebellion and plunder. He was sentenced to ten years of imprisonment. When he was ordered to be transported to Port Blair, it was said that "The defendant is the representative of the highest Hindoo family in the district." All charges against him were taken to be true and he was punished for them, though Raja Udit Narayan Singh rebutted every such charge. In his appeal too, he advanced arguments in defence. The Rani of Basti too made an appeal for pardon. But this did not have any impact. Maintaining his punishment, he was sent to Port Blair on 14 July 1859.[146] On 28 July 1864, he sent an application to Major B. Ford, Officiating Superintendent of Port Blair, and requested the repeal of his sentence. He also requested that his family members be allowed to come from India to visit him at Port Blair.[147]

In his letter sent to E. C. Bailey, Secretary, Home Department, at Fort William, on 25 October 1864, J. D. Sandford, Junior Secretary to the Government of the North Western Provinces, made it clear that the Raja's sentence could not be scrapped.[148] On the basis of his illness, the Raja requested that his five wives, nine sons, five daughters, a daughter-in-law and six other persons including four gents and two ladies be allowed to come to Port Blair. It was also said that two of the servants would go back. The Raja also submitted a list of 27 names. From the government's side, it was said that the number of visitors should be reduced from 24 to 19. A letter on 9 November 1864 expressed the possibility that his family could be allowed to visit Port Blair; later it was indeed allowed.[149] But we have no information if his family went to meet him or not. Raja Udit Narayan Singh died at Port Blair while serving his sentence.

Raja Har Prasad Mall of Narharpur

Among the rajas of Gorakhpur district, Raja Har Prasad Mall of Narharpur was the first to begin rebel activities. Narharpur was once a part of Dhuriyapar. About 200 years ago, Babu Barnath Singh, who was a relative of the Raja of Majhauli, and the babu of Semra in Bansgaon, had conquered Chillupar and made Narharpur near Barhalganj his capital. He had also assumed the title of "Raja."[150] In 1843, Raja Har Prasad Mall became the owner of Narharpur. He lived in Barhalganj where the British had established their police post. This place was situated to the north of Ghaghra river and midway on the Gorakhpur to Azamgarh road. Raja Har Prasad Mall had an annual income of about 6,000 rupees. He had some very fertile villages. He was a quite wise person and free from any debt. He was about 32 in 1843.[151]

Raja Har Prasad Mall of Narharpur was much enthused after receiving the news of revolt by the soldiers of the 17th NI regiment at Azamgarh on 3 June 1857 and at Gorakhpur on 5 June and the earlier revolt by the zamindars of Paina village on 31 May. Hence, he too decided to get freed from the British rule. On 6 June 1857, he sent his men to capture the police post at Barhalganj. Policemen were beaten and forced to run away, and 50 prisoners were set free. Besides, the Gorakhpur-Azamgarh water route and communication were disrupted. One musketeer was kept prisoner in the Raja's house.[152] They also obstructed the waterway. A letter written by Babu Shiv Ghulam Singh of Rudhauli to Mohammed Hasan tells us that, along with the Babu of Pandeypar and the Raja of Narharpur, he had planned to attack and snatch the government treasury going to Azamgarh.[153] In this way the Raja was clandestinely involved in rebellious activities. After getting the Gorakhpur-Azamgarh route reopened, on 16th June, 1857, Joint Magistrate Bird asked Raja Har Prasad Mall to come to his camp in Barhalganj. In view of the possibility that he could be taken prisoner by deceit, the Raja went there along with some 250 of his armed men, and entered the camp of Mr. Bird along with his well-armed brothers and three or four other armed men. Bird told him to follow the orders of Gorakhpur's Magistrate who had earlier called him to Gorakhpur, but he had not gone there despite repeated orders. The Raja too gave his assurance to Bird but did not fulfil it. However, the waterway, police post, post office and the things looted by the Raja's soldiers were restored as they were. But the Raja did not return the grain that was looted, as that grain had already been sent to the zamindars of Dhanauli village on the other side of the Ghaghra river, as per a secret agreement with them.[154]

In order to end the British rule, Raja Har Prasad Mall had been regularly holding secret meetings with the Rajas of Satasi and Nagar and with the Babus of Pandeypar and other places. In the end, they decided to solicit help from Awadh against the British.[155] Along with these people, the Raja of Narharpur too welcomed Mohammed Hasan as the Nazim and promised him military assistance.[156] Along the Ghaghra bank, they had virtually ended the British rule, as the lone pro-British raja, the Raja of Gopalpur, had fled and taken refuge in Azamgarh, while others, the rajas of Barhyapar, Shahpur and Nagar as well as the zamindars and the Rani of Amorha, were supporting Mohammed Hasan. In order to deal with any crisis, Raja Har Prasad Mall had also created a strong base in Azamgarh. That was why he remained active even after the British had reoccupied Gorakhpur. C. Wingfield was sure that he was hiding in the jungles of Gorakhpur.[157] But his rebeleous activities appear as his arrival in Gorakhpur from Azamgarh and then his return. On 12 February 1858, along with his soldiers, the Raja of Narharpur was with Babu Kunwar Singh at Ayodhya.[158] In his narrative for the week ending 10 July 1858, C. Wingfield wrote: "On 8th July 1858, rajah of Barhyapar and Narharpur had led the huge amount of rebel soldiers into the district through the Chandipur ghat of river Ghagra and looted the market area and went away to other side."[159] Earlier, in his narrative for the week ending 20 May 1858, C. Wingfield had mentioned the Raja of Narharpur's arrival at Chandipur along with the Palwars, when he plundered Hainser Bazaar and three other villages, taken four persons prisoner and, with them, gone back the same day.[160] This description demonstrates his imaginative wisdom. He had already enlisted the support of Palwar Rajputs of Azamgarh.

Thus, Raja Har Prasad Mall of Narharpur did not lie low during the rebellion and constantly challenged the British. His crime did not deserve clemency under the conditions of Queen Victoria's proclamation. It was sure that he would be punished. Therefore, Raja Har Prasad Mall remained rebellious even after the raja of Satasi and other important rebels had surrendered.[161] His properties and zamindari were confiscated; it was handed over to the Raja of Gopalpur.[162] We did not come across any official evidence about his end. But, according to Dr Rajbali Pandey, he was apprehended and sentenced to death.[163] As the Raja of Narharpur was a rebel, Syed Ahmad Ali Shah did not concede that he was wise and predicted his end in a few days. He wrote:

"Narharpur ka Raja hai bekhirad
Nihaayat safih abla-o-pur hasad"
[The Raja of Narharpur is unwise
Very mean, gullible and full of jealous]

xx xx xx

Abhi toh bahut khurram -o-shaad hain,
Vale thode hi din mein barbaad hain
[currently they (Raja of Narharpur and Tilpur) are very euphoric and cheerful
But in few days, they will be ruined].[164]

Raja Randul Sen of Nichlaul

Raja Randul Sen of Tilpur, adjoining the *terai* of Nepal, played an important role in the rebellion. Earlier, the area was under the Raja of Butwal who used to get his revenue dues waved by gifting something to Nawab Asafuddaulah. In 1801, the Company Government entered a three-year arrangement of Tilpur and Binayakpur with the Raja of Butwal, for an annual revenue of 4,500 rupees.[165] In 1806, the King of Nepal arrested Prithvi Pal Sen of Butwal and put him to death. His son, Ratan Sen, fled and took shelter in Gorakhpur. The Company Government gave him protection and fixed a monthly pension for his livelihood.[166] After Raja Ratan Sen's demise in 1826, Bijay Sen, his lone survivor, became the raja.[167] Raja Bijay Sen's zamindari constantly dwindled in his lifetime. He made Nichlaul in Pargana Tilpur his residence. Hence, he came to be known as the Raja of Nichlaul. He had a constant quibbling with the Bansi Raj, situated to the west, about the zamindari. Moreover, a very big part of his zamindari had been subsumed in Nepal. Raja Bijay Sen of Nichlaul had an annual income of about 18,000 rupees in 1843.[168] After Raja Bijay Sen, Randul Sen became the Raja of Nichlaul. He began to lose his zamindari very fast because of his indulgences, extravagances and litigations. Very little of zamindari had been left in his time.[169] He was not satisfied with his situation. Therefore, during the revolt of 1857, he decided to take up arms against the British Government. He accepted Mohammed Hasan as the Nazim and promised him cooperation.[170] Mohammed Hasan gave him a robe of honour. Taunting about it, Syed Ahmad Ali Shah wrote —

Na samjha tilismaat hai zoor ka
Mukhil hua Raja Tilpur ka.
[Did not understand that this is a magical spell of power
The Raja of Tilpur became an inter-meddler] [171]

Equating the Raja of Tilpur with the Raja of Narharpur, the Shah said elsewhere —

Hai Tilpur ka Raja bhi waisa hi
Hamesha hai shaitaan ka dil se rahi.
[The Raja of Tilpur is also the same
His heart has always pledged loyalty to satan.][172]

The Raja of Nichlaul had two aims. First, he wanted to chase Mr. Peppe away from Birdpur and expand his zamindari by creating disturbances in the Raja of Bansi's territory. Secondly, he wanted to help other rebels of the district, and to fight against the British in collaboration with them. After the British reoccupied Gorakhpur district, Raja Randul Sen got anxious about his safety. Hence, he fortified his residence and mobilised men. Learning about it, British officials dispatched two regiments of army to arrest him and to raze his house to the ground.[173] The Raja had to desert his house. The British army failed to apprehend him and returned after destroying his house. This soon had its reaction. On 21 May 1858, along with the Muslim taluqdar of Utraula and with 1,000 of his armed men, the Raja entered and attacked the Honorary Deputy Magistrate Mr. Peppe's factory at Birdpur, 13 miles to the north-east of Bansi. After an iota of resistance, Mr. Peppe's men deserted him, and Mr. Peppe had to run to Gorakhpur along with two other Europeans.[174] The Raja of Nichlaul continued a guerrilla war in cooperation with Bandhu Singh, the rebellious babu of Dumri. Jointly, they had got ditches dug for safety purpose, apart from taking shelter in jungles. Learning about it, the British Government sent an army troop on 24 July 1858, but they came to know about it. Therefore, they quitted the place before the British troop could reach there.[175] Randul Sen extended great cooperation to the Babu of Dumri in his conduct of the guerrilla war, hence, the British Government sent a troop of Sikhs under Lieutenant Pullan to apprehend Randul Sen, but it failed.[176] On 5 October 1858, Joint Magistrate Mr. Bird too made an attempt to apprehend Randul Sen, but he too failed.[177] The Raja remained unapprehended till the end, but the British Government stopped his pension.[178] Raja Randul Sen of Nichlaul was the most fearsome hero for the British during the revolt.

Raja Tej Pratap Bahadur Chand of Barhyapar

Most of the territory of pargana Dhuriyapar, situated in the southern part of Gorakhpur district, was in the zamindari of Kaushik Rajputs. The royal family (zamindar family) here was split into two in the eighteenth century, with Barhyapar and Gopalpur as their seats. Descendants of Raja Todar

Chand held Barhyapar. At the outset of the Company Government, Raja Fateh Chand was receiving 2,922 rupees and 12 annas as *nankar* and he was paying 12,404 rupees a year as revenue.[179] Due to some arrear of revenue, the government confiscated a part of his zamindari and gave it in jagir to Kareem Khan Pindari in 1818. Making Sikriganj his seat, the Pindaris began to call themselves nawabs.[180] Later, the zamindari of Barhyapar was divided between Ram Bahadur Chand and Tej Pratap Bahadur Chand. In 1843, Raja Ram Bahadur Chand had an annual income of 5,000 rupees. As the division of the zamindari was affected by a Special Commissioner,[181] Raja Tej Pratap Bahadur Chand had a grudge against the Company rule. He was in touch with the Bisen raja of Narharpur and the Muslim raja of Shahpur. They too harboured discontent against the Company rule and were the former's neighbours. Hence, they too decided to join the rebellion. Doubting their loyalty to the Company Government, British officers did not include the Raja of Barhyapar in the five rajas' committee formed to run the administration of Gorakhpur; rather they inducted in it his competitor and enemy, Raja Krishna Kishore Chand of Gopalpur. The latter's annual income was 9,000 rupees but he was neck-deep in debt. He was indebted for about a lakh rupee and had a craze for chess.[182] This too might have been a reason of the Raja of Barhyapar's personal anguish.

Raja Tej Pratap Bahadur Chand too recognised and supported Mohammed Hasan's government in Gorakhpur, for which he was honoured by the Nazim. He was given a robe of honour.[183] Syed Ahmad Ali Shah wrote —

> Badhyyapaar ka Raja bhi hai kharaab
> Pahan kar woh khillat phansa dar azaab
> [The raja of Badhyyapar is also bad
> For donning the robe of honour, he was in trouble].[184]

British records do not provide much information about the rebellious activities of the Raja of Barhyapar. He too had adopted the tactic of guerrilla warfare after carving out a safe hideout in Azamgarh district across the Ghaghra. In his narrative for the week ending 10 July 1858, Gorakhpur Commissioner C. Wingfield wrote: "On 8th July 1858, Rajah of Barhyapar and Narharpur had led the huge amount of rebel soldiers into the districts through the Chandipur ghat of river Ghagra and looted the market area and went away to other side."[185] This makes clear that joining hands with other rebel rajas, he conducted the struggle in a very secretive manner, about which the British Government could not know much. An evidence of his style of clandestine work was that the British Government could not know about his whereabouts for fourteen long years even after the rebellion was crushed.[186] As punishment, the British Government confiscated Raja Tej Pratap Bahadur Chand's zamindari and his title of Raja.[187] However, when he came out, he was granted pardon and not punished for his crime of rebellion.

Raja Inayat Ali Shah of Shahpur

The Muslim estate (zamindari) of Shahpur was situated in pargana Dhuriyapar of Gorakhpur district, on the northern bank of Ghaghra.[188] As the Company Government had stopped the *nankar* of its Raja Meer Zulfiqar Ali, his son, Meer Riyasat Ali, had moved the Civil Court of Gorakhpur on 10 July 1807, praying for restoration of the *nankar*.[189] Thus, from the very beginning, the Company Government had an uneasy relationship with the Raja of Shahpur. During the revolt of 1857, Inayat Ali Shah was the Raja of Shahpur. He recognised Mohammed Hasan as the Nazim of Gorakhpur and thus joined the rebellion.[190] After the suppression of the revolt, the British Government confiscated the Shahpur estate.[191] The British gazetteers of Gorakhpur (1909 and 1987) have no mention of the rebel Raja of Shahpur. But the local sources say Inayat Ali was the Raja of Shahpur at the time of the revolt and, through a plot, he got sunk the boat carrying 11 Europeans coming to Gorakhpur from Azamgarh by crossing the river Ghaghra, and they all died by drowning.[192] For this criminal plot, he was tried and sentenced to death. He was hanged in January 1875. His body was brought to his ancestral graveyard in village Belwa, on river Ghaghra bank, and burried there. His tomb is still there.[193]

Raja Udai Pratap Singh of Nagar

Raja Udai Pratap Singh, the Gautam Rajput, raja of pargana Nagar (situated on the Ghaghra bank in the south-west part of the present-day district of Basti), was the person who caused maximum trouble to the British by his rebellious activities during the revolt of 1857. Raja Udai Pratap was a close relative of Raja Krishna Kishore Chand of Gopalpur, who was an ardent supporter and collaborator of the British. Raja Krishna Kishore Chand was also confident that he would persuade the Raja of Nagar to give up the path of rebellion, but he failed in his mission.[194] Raja Udai Pratap Singh remained an eyesore to the British throughout the rebellion.

In Nagar, the Gautam Rajput zamindari started with Jagdev Singh Gautam and Raja Gajpati Rao made Ganeshpur his main centre. Ram Prakash Singh was the Raja of Nagar in 1801. His zamindari comprised 114 revenue villages and he received the *malikana* (ownership dues) from 62 revenue villages. According to a government record of 1805, he was getting the *nankar* of 3,000 rupees.[195] In 1843, Raja Lal Jai Pratap Singh was the Raja of Nagar and had an annual income of 18,000 rupees, but his zamindari was declining fast. He made Nagar his residence, as the Company Government had given taluqa Ganeshpur to Qadir Bakhsh Khan Pindari for a pittance as revenue.[196]

"Gorakhpur mein ek Ganeshpur hai
Yeh mauza bahut dur mashhoor hai"
[In Gorakhpur, there is one Ganeshpur,
This village is famous far and wide]

"Qadarbaksh Jamadaar ko de diya
Toh qabze se Gautam ke khaali kiya"
[Gave it to Qadarbakhsh Jamadar
So, it was relieved of the occupation of Gautam]

As a result, the Raja of Nagar was seething with anger.

Udai Pratap Singh was the Raja of Nagar at the outbreak of the 1857 rebellion. He prepared the Gautam Rajputs for a revolt under his leadership. Gautam Rajputs then began to recapture their lost zamindari.[197] They attacked and recaptured Ganeshpur, the seat of the Nagar estate which was then under Pindaris and plundered it. Syed Ahmed Ali Shah wrote;

"Yakayak nazar aaya jab inqalaab,
Liya loot bar Gautamon ne shitaab
Liya cheen mauza basad zoor -o shoor
Jataya har ek gaun wale ko zoor
Sab asbaab aur maal ghaarat kiya
Khas-o khaar tak le gaye behaya"

[When an unexpected revolution came in sight
The followers of Gautam looted him
They seized the village very forcefully
Every villager was intimidated with Violence
All property and wealth were destroyed
The shameless took away even hay and thorns][198]

At the same time, Raja Udai Pratap Singh began to hold secret meetings with the rajas of Narharpur and Satasi as well as the babus of Pandeypar and of other places, and they unanimously decided to cooperate with Awadh.[199] There was Tanda to the south of Nagar, across the Ghaghra. Raja Udai Pratap Singh also had ties with its raja, Abbas Ali. When they were preparing to attack Khalilabad, the Raja of Nagar wrote a letter to the Raja of Tanda on 6 August 1857, informing him that he, with 2,000 of his men, would help Mohammed Hasan and also win over the Raja of Gopalpur and the Rani of Basti. In return, he wanted a "consent letter" from Mohammed Hasan that he could hold Nagar, his ancestral estate.[200] Besides, he had written on separate piece of paper that Mr. Cook had left one lakh rupees with his bailiff and also that one lakh rupees were there in Khalilabad tehsil, and he wanted to know about his share after these moneys were captured.[201] In another letter, Raja Abbas Ali had assured Mohammed Hasan that "he and the Raja of Nagar would ensure him the supplies."[202] It is thus clear that Raja Udai Pratap Singh had a big role in Mohammed Hasan's invasion of Khalilabad tehsil on 10 August 1857. Nay more, he also made the Gautam Rajputs of taluqa Pipra capture Cook's boats: They also made an attempt to capture the treasury which was going from Gorakhpur to Azamgarh.[203] Raja Udai Pratap Singh also extended recognition and cooperation to the government which Mohammed Hasan had formed in Gorakhpur on 22 August 1857. In response, Mohammed Hasan offered him a robe of honour, organised a gun salute for him and recognised his right to his ancestral zamindari as well as his *diwani* and judicial authority in the territory under his jurisdiction.[204] Raja Udai Pratap Singh's uncle had appointed a bodyguard at Mr. Bird's house in Gorakhpur, and ridiculed and humiliated the later.[205]

The authority of the Raja of Nagar remained intact during the four months and twenty days of Mohammed Hasan's government. Though he had to hide in the jungles of Gorakhpur for safety, after the British army captured Rudrapur.[206] But he was not deterred and kept the flame of rebellion burning through the tactic of guerrilla warfare. With the Babu of Rudhauli, he made a plan to capture Basti, but could not implement it as Babu Shiv Ghulam Singh was killed.[207] In the night of 26 April 1858, the bailiff (karinda) of Udai Pratap Singh proceeded towards Captainganj, along with a number of rebels, to recapture the confiscated estate (zamindari) of his master and his residence in Nagar. He occupied the house of pro-British Pindari zamindar Amanullah Khan in taluqa Ganeshpur, eight miles to the north-west from Captainganj. Then he moved towards Nagar. While moving towards the Raja's fortress in Nagar, he plundered the camp of Major Richardson, who was already posted there, and got the major's pretty horse along with other valuables.

Hence, on 28 April, Colonel Rowcroft proceeded towards Nagar with a troop of infantry and cavalry, and with cannons and guns. Nagar was six miles to the south-east from Captainganj. The rebels could not face this well armed troop. Hence, they divided themselves into groups, crossed the Ghaghra from separate *ghats* and went back to Tanda.[208] The English army could cause them no loss. On 16 May 1858, some agents of Raja Udai Pratap Singh again crossed the Ghaghra, looted some villages, and also took some rich zamindars as hostages for ransom.[209] On 21 May 1858, some agents again crossed the river along with Ranjit Singh, the Raja's uncle, and looted a village.[210] Also, there was a rumour about Raja Udai Pratap Singh that he was out to capture Basti in league with Mohammed Hasan.[211] In this way, through the rumour and the guerrilla tactic, Raja Udai Pratap Singh remained a headache for the British.

After the amnesty announced by Queen Victoria in January 1859, Raja Udai Pratap also surrendered along with the Raja of Satasi and many other rebels. They were tried in the Commissioner's special court. But he died on 3rd April, 1859 AD, while the trial was still on.[212] Syed Ahmad Ali Shah wrote —

"Nagar ka jo Raja raha pur ghuroor
[Raja of nagar, who was full of conceit]
Rahi teeswin maah-e-Shaabaan ki
Pachattar sun Hijri barah rahi
[It was the thirtieth of the month of Shaabaan
The Hijri year was twelve hundred seventy-five]
Ke mahbas mein Raja Nagar mar gaya.
[That, the raja of Nagar died in prison.] [213] His estate too was confiscated.[214]

Rani Jagatraj Kunwari of Amorha

Women too played a very important role in the revolt of 1857. Rebels of Eastern Uttar Pradesh were, in a way, fighting under the leadership of Begum Hazrat Mahal. Besides her, Rani Ishwari Devi of Tulsipur, on the north western border of Gorakhpur district, and the widow of Raja Udwant Singh, a Mona Rajput, at Bhadohi in Mirzapur district, made important contributions. But the role of Rani Jagatraj Kunwari of Amorha in Gorakhpur district was especially noteworthy. The borders of pargana

Amorha in Gorakhpur district adjoined the borders of Awadh in the south and west. River Ghaghra separates it from Awadh while pargana Nagar and Basti are in North and East, respectively. Hence the revolt in Awadh had the utmost impact here. Amorha, Belwa and Dubaulia were the important markets in this pargana.[215]

Pargana Amorha was in the zamindari of Surajvanshi Rajputs. Here the last raja (zamindar) was Raja Jang Bahadur, who died heirless in 1855. Besides his widow, Rani Jagatraj Kunwari, his family consisted of his step mother Dulhin Shivraj Kunwari and step sister Manraj Kunwari only. For managing her estate, Rani Jagatraj Kunwari depended on the help of the Raja of Bansi who was also a distant relative.[216]

However, she was inclined towards Begum Hazrat Mahal. Hence most of the zamindars of Amorha recognised the Nawab's rule and supported the rebellion. They received tacit support and cooperation from the Rani. She was also in touch with the main rebels in the district and was clandestinely corresponding with them. She was tacitly helping the rebels. But the Company Government came to know about the role of Rani Jagat Kunwari in the rebellion, about her help to the rebels, and they began to think of arresting her. The Rani got an inkling of the British intentions. Hence, in order to escape arrest, she ran away to Faizabad, where she spent the rest of her life incognito.[217] In her absence, her army commander, Awdhoot Singh, who belonged to Haraiya, fought many battles against the British. When he was captured, he was hanged to death from a peepal tree in Haraiya only.[218] Rani Jagat Kunwari died heirless, and her estate was forfeited by the British Government.[219] But she became a legend in Amorha and was eulogised for her rebellion and her valiance. Rural people still sing folk songs about her qualities and her resistance to the British.[220]

Govind Bali Singh, the Babu of Pandeypar

Govind Bali Singh, the Babu of Pandeypar in pargana Bhowapar of Gorakhpur district, played a very important role in the rebellion of 1857. The Babuai of Pandeypar was a very old one. Raja Gaj Singh of Satasi had given Pandeypar as a Babuai to his son, Niranjan Singh.[221] Since then, his family held the zamindari here. The zamindari existed in the British period as well, and he was counted among the important persons. The name of Babu Govind Bali Singh of Pandeypar also figured in the list of the dignitaries of Gorakhpur district, which was prepared by E. A. Reade in 1843. It was written about him that: "Baboo of Pandepur, Gobind Bali Singh, aged 35 years, annual income about 4000 rupees (He) is intelligent and influential native gentleman."[222] But he was not happy with the foreign rule. He was in close contact with the Raja of Narharpur and the Babus of Rudhauli and Dumri. Strategically, his residence was very important as it was situated by the Rapti river, near Barhalganj or, in other words, close to the Gorakhpur-Azamgarh road. When the rebellion broke out, Babu Govind Bali Singh decided to play an important role in it. This Babu of Pandeypar took part in the secret anti-government meetings with the Rajas and Babus of Narharpur, Nagar, Satasi and others. These important people finally decided to oust the British, with the help from Awadh.[223]

Joining hands with the Raja of Narharpur and the Babu of Dumri, Babu Govind Bali Singh planned to capture the government treasury that was being sent to Azamgarh, in the protection of the Gorkha army, somewhere between Gagaha and Barhalganj.[224] But the rebels faced defeat in the battle of Gagaha, fought under Mohammad Hasan, and about 200 of them died.[225] Babu Govind Bali Singh was among the figures who supported and cooperated with the independent government formed by Mohammad Hasan on 21 August in Gorakhpur. For this he was offered a robe of honour and he was told to use his civil and judicial authorities as they were exercised during the Nawab's rule.[226] Babu Govind Bali Singh also promised military help to the independent government during a crisis.

Syed Ahmad Ali Shah, an eye witness of the rebellion, accused Babu Govind Bali Singh of Pandeypar of looting the Englishmen's belongings and also harassing the pro-British Raja of Betia. He wrote:

> "Pandeypaar ka Babu azbas hai bad
> Kiya loot par Usne bhi jadd-o-kad
> [The Babu of Paṇdeypaar is quite notorious,
> He also made serious attempts to loot.]
> Vinet Sahib ka maal kashti pe tha,
> Use usne bekhauf ghaarat kiya.
> [Vinet sahib's belonging were on the boat,
> Which he fearlessly plundered]
> Aur Buran ka bhi maal sab le liya
> Khataawaar hukkaam -e aali hua
> [And by taking the goods of Buran also
> He became a culprit of lofty rulers]
> Kiya tang Raja -e-Betiyah ko bhi
> Raaya ko us se azeeyat hui

[He troubled the Raja of Betiyah too
Subjects were tormented by him]".[227]

Babu Govind Bali Singh too had to go in hiding after the British recaptured Gorakhpur. But he persisted with his rebellious activities. He joined hands with the Babu of Dumri and continued the struggle. As for the British documents, C. Wingfield, the Commissioner of Gorakhpur, has made a mention of their going underground together to escape the campaign launched by the British army. In his narrative sent by Mr. Bird on 20 November 1858, we find a mention of the army campaign against the Babus of Dumri and Pandeypar in the forests of Gorakhpur, and their escape from their stronghold while leaving their belongings and the war booties behind.[228] Mr. Bird also said these babus were such a terror to the people that no one was prepared to give any information against the two. One night they attacked and killed a neighbouring zamindar as they suspected that he had provided information against them.[229] The narrative of 27 November 1858 also mentioned the escape of the two babus.[230]

Yet another narrative mentions the great influence which Babu Govind Bali Singh had on Mohammad Hasan and the Raja of Narharpur. This narrative of 17 May 1858 says:

> "Bulee Singh, the Pandeypar Baboo, a man said to have great influence over Mahommud Hasan and the other disturbers of Goruckpore, came across in person and persuaded the Nurhurpore Rajah to take his force near the Gogra. He accordingly crossed about the 2nd or 3rd instant and it was reported that the plan was to march in two days via Bansgaon and in concert with Mohemud Hussun to Goruckpore. Something unknown occurred to frustrate this plan and the Nurhurpur Rajah recrossed at Munsoorganj on the 5th. Since then he has lost most of his men and is now said to have only 50 sepoys with him, the others having joined Mohemud Hussun."[231]

The narrative also makes it clear that despite the British reoccupation of Gorakhpur, the Babu of Pandeypar was not just hiding for life in the forests but was also active. After the suppression of the rebellion, the zamindari of Babu Govind Bali Singh was forfeited.[232] We could not get any information about the end of this hero of the rebellion.

Babu Bandhu Singh of Dumri

The name of Babu Bandhu Singh of Dumri, situated in pargana Haveli of Gorakhpur district, figures among the important leaders of the 1857 rebellion. The zamindari of Dumri was handed over, as Babuai, to Babu Ram Singh, son of Raja Roop Narayan Singh of Satasi, in 1720.[233] Since then, this very family held the zamindari of Dumri. Babu Bandhu Singh belonged to this very family. His father's name was Babu Shiv Prasad Singh.[234] Babu Bandhu Singh harboured deep resentment against the atrocities of the British rule. Hence, he joined the revolt when it broke out, and cooperated with the government of Mohammad Hasan. Even before the revolt broke out, he was involved in a case of murder in the Nizamat court.[235] He began to attack the British supporters and accomplishes when the rebellion started. In this task, all his pattidars openly sided with him. In Gorakhpur, Syed Ahmad Ali Shah was proving protection and security to the British and their belongings. Therefore, Bandhu Singh attacked the Shah's kothi in Kusamhi and looted his belongings. Syed Ahmad Ali Shah wrote the following about it:

> "Woh Dumri ke Babu jo the naabkaar
> Bandhu Singh maa apne sab pattidaar"
> [That Babu of Domri, who was wicked
> Bandhu Singh with all his supporters (Pattidars)]
> "Batarghib-e-shaitaan baaghi hue
> Shararat se apni woh daaghi hue"
> [Became rebels by inducement of the Satan, Due to their roguery, they became satanic]
> "Unhi sab ne Kosamhi ko ghaarat kiya
> Jo asbaab tha mera, sab le liya"
> [They all ravaged Kosamhi, whatever provisions I had, they looted][236]

Babu Bandhu Singh also raided Pipraich, about which the Shah wrote:

> "Ke Gadhwa wa Gaya ka asbaab sab
> Hai Pipraich mein sab se ziyaadah ghazab"
> [That all the assets of Gadhwa and Gaya
> In Pipraich, there was a greatest tumult]
> "Bandhu Singh ne luta -o ghaarat kiya
> Sab asbaab taaraaj unka hua"
> [Bandhu Singh looted and ravaged
> All their goods were plundered].[237]

When the Gorkha army, led by Jang Bahadur Rana, captured Gorakhpur and handed it over to British officials, the rebels had to take refuge in forests and elsewhere and take to guerrilla warfare in order to continue the struggle. Forfeiting the properties of Babu Bandhu Singh, the British Government appointed a Receiver (Incharge) there. On 29 April 1858, Babu Bandhu Singh came out of his hiding, along with about 300 persons, and launched a sudden attack on the Receiver (Incharge), killing 11 policemen and some other persons and injuring a number of others. In this process, the police had captured a Babu (Bhai) whom he freed by attacking the Dumri thana on 4 May. When Mr. Bird, Joint Magistrate, got the news on reaching Gorakhpur, he immediately left with a Gorkha troop in order to arrest him. However, a few hours even before he reached the spot, Babu Bandhu Singh had sneaked into the dense Dumri forests and Mr. Bird had to return empty-handed.[238]

Along with his men, Babu Bandhu Singh remained in the jungles for about ten days. Meanwhile, he got the news that grain-laden carts were going to Gorakhpur for the British and that guards of a pro-government zamindar were protecting these carts. So, he came out of his refuge on 14 May, attacked the convoy, killed seven of the zamindar's men and captured 40 grain-laden carts. Mr. Bird again went to capture him but again returned empty-handed.[239]

On 17 May, the babus of Dumri set afire a Dak Chowki (Mail Station) which was on the Sagauli Road, close to Gorakhpur. They killed a runner who was carrying the mail and got the nose of another cut off as punishment. The same group looted the carts that were carrying the Gorkha army's provisions along the same route.[240] Then they attacked the Pipraich thana, about 15 miles from Gorakhpur, and killed the thanedar and several policemen while the Gorkha army had been there only a day before.[241] Along with his group, Babu Bandhu Singh was hiding in the dense Dumri forests in the middle of Gorakhpur district, and was greatly harassing the government. He attacked the Hathua thana, situated between Gandak river and Gorakhpur, and killed two policemen.[242] Despite living in forests, Babu Bandhu Singh had maintained his power of offence and had earned reputation for his indomitable courage. Mr. Muir, Secretary of the North Western Provinces, too had to write that the Babu of Dumri was great and extremely courageous.[243] When he came to know that a zamindar had complained to the government against him, he came out of his refuge and killed him.[244] According to the British officials, he was such a terror to the people that nobody was willing to give any information about him,[245] and that this was the main reason for Babu Bandhu Singh's successes. But the reality was to the contrary. The masses abhorred the British rule and were not willing to say anything against their hero.

Babu Bandhu Singh conducted his activities so discreetly that the government's spies failed to collect correct information about him in time. He constantly changed his hideout. He had close contacts with Raja Randul Sen of Nichlaul and Babu Govind Bali Singh of Pandeypar, and they jointly conducted rebellious activities. Mr. Bird's campaigns against them were repeatedly proving unsuccessful. When the spies brought the news that Babu Bandhu Singh and Raja Randul Sen were fortifying the place where they had taken refuge, Lieutenant Pullan was sent to capture them. But Babu Bandhu Singh got prior information about the coming of troops. Both of them deserted the place and Lieutenant Pullan found the camp empty when he reached there.[246] As a response to it, in the beginning of November 1858, Babu Bandhu Singh and 200 of his men, mostly rebel soldiers, reached close to Gorakhpur in order to ravage it, as there was no army in Gorakhpur to chase them away.[247] Then they returned to the Dumri forests. The group of the Babu of Pandeypar also accompanied them. After discreetly gathering information about them, and under Mr. Bird's direction, 350 soldiers of the 13th NI and the police force of Gorakhpur, led by Colonel Kin, suddenly attacked their refuge in order to capture the two babus (Bandhu Singh and Govind Bali Singh). Though their arrest was almost a certainty, they did not lose their patience, fought for a while, and safely escaped through a clandestine route which the British army did not know about. However, they had to leave behind, their clothes, utensils and all the war booty, including the things captured from the Gorkha army.[248] Earlier, the English troop had attacked the babus of Dumri and Pandeypar in a dense forest near Gorakhpur, and had successfully chased them away from their stronghold, and recovered some of the things looted from the Gorkhas.[249]

Babu Bandhu Singh remained a rebel even when a number of rebels, including the Raja of Satasi, surrendered in the beginning of January 1859. Another name of terror for the British, Babu Bandhu Singh well knew that the British Government would not allow him to live. Therefore, in November 1858, he had disappeared from the forests of Dumri. It was then believed that he had sneaked into Nepal and that the rebel soldiers who had left Ghazipur for Nepal must have surely joined hands with him.[250]

While the rebellion had been crushed, most of the rebels had surrendered, and the rebel soldiers and people had begun to return home, the government could consider only capture and execution of Babu Bandhu Singh as the end of the rebellion. The same feeling gripped the British supporters. *Kashful-Baghaavat, Gorakhpur* writes:

"Bandhu Singh baaghi ka sar jab kate
To yahaan se bhi gard-e-Baghaavat mite"
[When the rebel Bandhu Singh's head is severed,
Then the dust of mutiny shall be expunged from here too][251]

Eventually, the British Government was able to apprehend and execute him. According to a brochure, printed on 1st May, 2010 by Vinay Kumar Singh "Binnu" (a descendent of Bandhu Singh family and secretary of Bandhu Singh Smarak Committee, Gorakhpur), "Babu Bandhu Singh was arrested from Shatrughanpur forest, with the help of a man named, Nirmal, who was associated with Sardar Surat Singh. On 12th August 1858, Babu Bandhu Singh, was hanged to death in Alinagar, the main market of Gorakhpur".

Half of the Dumri estate was given, as a reward, to Sardar Surat Singh who had helped the British in Banaras.[252] The other half of Dumri remained in the hands of Babu Ram Prakash Singh who was a descendant of Raja Roop Narayan Singh of Satasi.[253] Thus the rebellion in Gorakhpur district ended with the end of this rebel hero, Babu Bandhu Singh.

The Babu of Tighra

Taluqa Tighra, which emanated from the Satasi Estate, was situated in tappa Pachwara. Babu Raghunath Singh, the second son of Raja Digvijay Singh of Satasi, had received tappa Pachwara as babuai in 1381.[254] His descendants later became the babus of Pachwara, Barhya Chowk and Tighra.[255] A son of Maharaja Kawalwan Singh of Bhowapar also had his zamindari in Tighra mahal.

The Babu of Tighra was among the dignitaries who had supported and cooperated with the government of Mohammed Hasan in the beginning of the rebellion and had been rewarded with honours and authority. The then British Commissioner, C. Wingfield, also mentioned him in his narrative.[256] Though his activities find no mention in the British documents, the British Government viewed him as an unpardonable criminal. Hence the government decided to forfeit the zamindari of Tighra and hand it over to Mr. Peppe.[257] Other pattidars fought a number of court cases in order to save their shares in the zamindari of Tighra but, except the share of Rani Subhash Kunwari,[258] all other parts were forfeited and handed over to Mr. Peppe who had, as Honorary Magistrate, played an important role in crushing the rebellion.[259]

The Babus of Rajpur-Pania and Bhowapar

Syed Ahmad Ali Shah, an eye witness of the rebellion, has mentioned the activities of the Babus of Rajpur-Pania and Bhowapar. About the Babu of Rajpur-Pania, he wrote:

"Hain Rajpur paniya ke Babu kharaab
Zaroor unpe howega naazil azaab"
[The Babu of Rajpur-Paniya is bad,
Definitely divine wrath will be descend upon him]
"Bahut shorish un sab ne ki ja-ba-ja,
Sitam or balwa nihaayat kiya"
[They all created a lot of disturbances everywhere
Committed extreme atrocities and rioting]
"Baghaavat ke uski bhi azbas hai dhoom,
Kharaabi ka baais hai Jun boom shum"
[His rebellion is quite a popular talk of time
The reasons for this calamity are cycles of vicissitude, land and niggardliness]
"Badi par hua mustaid es qadar
Ke har ek ne us se kiya al-hazar"
[He was so very prompt in evil,
That everyone become cautious and asked for God's protection]
"Baghaavat pe tha apni usko ghuroor
Woh jaayega ab kale pani zaroor."
[He was arrogant about his rebellion
He shall definitely go to Kala Paani, now]
"Ajab tarha ka zulm us ne kiya
Ke ban kal ke jaane ke laaiq hua"
[He committed bizarre kind of brutalities
And easily deserves exile in darkness][260]

Similarly, the Shah said about the Babu of Bhowapar who he made collections of money and sent it to the Raja of Satasi:

"Bhowapara ka babu tehsil kar
Rawaana woh karta tha Raja ke ghar"
[The Babu of Bhowapar after collection,
Used to dispatch it to the Raja (Satasi)'s house].[261]

Bhowapar was situated in pargana Bansgaon. It stretched up to the Rapti river in the north-east, and this border separated it from the parganas Silhat and Haveli of Gorakhpur, and from the parganas Magahar, Anaula and Dhuriyapar in the south-west. It comprised seven tappas.[262] Raja Gaj Singh of Satasi had Bhowapar as the seat of his estate.[263] Thus, the Babu of Bhowapar was a close relative and collaborator of Raja Udit Narayan Singh of Satasi.

Babu Ram Pratap Singh of Bakhira

Situated in pargana Hasanpur-Magahar, Bakhira was the zamindari of Srinet Rajputs.[264] When an important event like the plunder of Khalilabad tehsil took place under the leadership of Mohammad Hasan on 10 August 1857, Babu Ram Pratap Singh[265] of Bakhira thrashed and drove away the policemen of Bakhira thana,[266] and thus sounded the bugle of revolt. British raj came to an end in Bakhira and its vicinity. After the recapture of Gorakhpur, the British took Babu Ram Pratap Singh as prisoner, tried him and gave him death sentence, and also confiscated his zamindari.[267] His supporters too were awarded death sentences.[268]

The Babu of Mehdawal

Thakur Jaggi Singh was the zamindar of Mehdawal at the time of the revolt of 1857.[269] He sided with the rebels and was hanged to death in Khalilabad, along with his followers, when they were captured.[270] Another Srinet Rajput zamindar of Mehdawal, called Har Govind Singh, too, had to lose his zamindari at the time.[271]

Babu Shiv Ghulam Singh of Rudhauli

Rudhauli too is situated in pargana Hasanpur-Magahar. The zamindar of this place was linked with the family of Srinet Raja of Bansi and was also addressed as "Bhaiya."[272] Babu Shiv Ghulam Singh was the zamindar of Rudhauli at the time of the revolt. He joined hands with the rebels when the revolt began. The rebels started guerrilla warfare when Mohammad Hasan government came to an end. Babu Shiv Ghulam Singh had close ties with the rebel Raja of Nagar and other rebels. When the British army and the rebels had a trial of strength for capturing Amorha, Babu Shiv Ghulam Singh embarked on a new strategy to give strength to the rebels and divert the British army's attention. He along with his own followers and with the zamindars who had run away from Awadh and had taken refuge there, he attacked and ravaged Bakhira and drove away the government controller appointed there. Next, they divided themselves into groups and made attempts to ravage the renowned market of Mehdawal so that it could divert the British attention. In order to protect the traders of Mehdawal, the neighbouring zamindars set up a front against the rebels, and the latter had to vacate the area. After it, with 300 of his men, Babu Shiv Ghulam Singh reached village Paura, about six miles to the north of Basti, began to fortify with a view to attacking Basti. At the time, Raja Udai Pratap Singh, whom rebels had deputed to attack Basti, was in the jungles of Babhni along with his rebel troop. Babu Shiv Ghulam Singh wanted to invade Basti, along with him. But Mr. Wilson, the Assistant Magistrate camping in Basti, got an inkling of the plan. He ordered Captain Clark to attack Paura. The British army invaded Paura on 25 April 1858. Both sides fought a fierce battle, and Babu Shiv Ghulam Singh lost his life along with 30 followers.[273] Songs are still sung eulogising him. A folk song of Indian peasants starts like this:

> "Dipty bhaye khepti, tehsildaar bhaye payeea, Khed-khed maarat hain Shiv Ghulam Bhaiya"
>
> *[The brave Sheo Ghulam Singh has reduced the Deputy Collector to a chip and the tehsildar to chaff and is constantly chasing and killing the army.]*[274]

Babu Shiv Ghulam Singh's sacrifice served to further ignite the flame of the rebellion.

Rawat of Haiti

An eye witness and sufferer of the rebellion, Syed Ahmad Ali Shah has mentioned how the Rawat of Haiti turned a rebel and played an important role in Mohammed Hasan's government. His sepoys were deployed at the tolls on the city's outskirts and used to collect the toll tax. They were appointed on the chowkies of Mehra Ghat (Deoria) and Shahbazganj, and also had a chowki in Nakaha. The chowkies in Shahbazganj and Nakaha were on the north-east and north-west routes of Gorakhpur city. Shah wrote:

> Hain Haiti ke Rawat ki sarkash sipah,
> Woh karte hain raahi ko aksar tabaah
> [The sipahis of the Rawat of Haiti are rebels
> They often devastate the travellers].
> Taiyyun Mehra ke hain ghaat par
> Aur Shahbaaz Ganj ki bhi hain chauki par
> [They are deputed at the wharf of Mehra
> And are also appointed at the check post of Shahbazganj]

Aur Nakaha mein bhi unki chounki hui
Unhi sab ki rasta mein sakhti hui
[And their outpost was fixed at Nakaha as well
Along the routes they subjected others to violence]
Aur danku ke bhi log rahte rahe
Jafa saath un sab ke karte rahe
[Accomplices of dacoits were also present
Together with them, they too oppressed]
Doon Singh taman leke rahta raha
Giraftaar raahi ko karta raha
[Doon Singh used to stay with armed forces
Travellers were captivated by him] [275]

Syed Ahmad Ali Shah provides no information about their end and the punishments involved.

Sardar Ali Khan

Mounted soldiers had much importance in Mohammed Hasan employ. Shah put them in the second important category of rebels and regarded them as special rebels.[276] Sardar Ali Khan was a risaladar in the Awadh army and the zamindar of Muftipur and Begpur muhallas of Gorakhpur city. His father's name was Muazzam Ali Khan. When the revolt began, he joined it with his brother, Ramzan Ali Khan, and other relatives and was among the people close to Mohammed Hasan, the Nazim. Sardar Ali Khan complained to the Nazim about Syed Ahmad Ali Shah, telling him about his reality, about the wealth hidden in the Imambada and the Shah's kothis, and helped in its capture. Therefore, he became the special target of attack. In his *Kashful-Baghaavat, Gorakhpur*, he wrote in particular about Sardar Ali Khan:

"Maa aqriba apne Sardar Ali
Aur Aali Hasan bhi basad khush dili."
[Sardar Ali with all his allies
And Aali Hasan also with an extremely euphoric heart]
"Hain Sardar Ali khan toh baaghi kamaal
Maa aqriba apne daaghi kamaal"
[Sardar Ali Khan is an utmost rebel
Together with his allies, he is exceedingly spoiled] [277]

"Sawaaron ke maalik the Sardar Ali
Buri baat ko usne jaani bhali"
[Sardar Ali was the master of the cavalry men
He considered the malevolent thing as benevolent][278]

About Sardar Ali Khan's unjustified complaint against him, the Shah wrote:

"Bada zulm Sardar Ali ne kiya
Muhammad Hasan baaghi se ye kaha"
[Sardar Ali did great injustice
He said this to Muhammad Hasan, the rebel]

"Kiya fitna barpa zireh keejiye
Ke tarik hain salaat ke Shah ji"
[Raised the devilment that manacle him
Because Shahji is relinquisher of salaat]
"Nahin mutlaqa paye bandhe salaat
Kisi ko nahin dete Khams-o-Zakaat"
[The has never ever been found offering salaat
Does not gives khams or zakat to anyone]
"Juma ko bhi masjid mein jaate nahin
Raah-e-rasti par woh aate nahin"
[Does not go to mosque even on Friday
He never treads the path of good conduct]
"Kisi ke nahin saath woh ham taam
Hain hukkaam-e-English ke pairau mudaam"
[He does not have meals together with anyone
Has always been a disciple (fellow) of the English rulers]
"Na Sunni na Shia se hai raghbat unhe
Umoorat-e-Din se hai nafrat unhe"
[He is inclined neither towards the Sunnis nor Shias,
He hates the matters of religion] [279]

Sardar Ali Khan and his relatives helped in the loot of things in the Shah's Imambada. He writes:

"Woh Sardar Ali Khan aur Fazle Ali
Diya un sabhon ne bahut bekali"

[The Sardar Ali Khan and Fazle Ali
They gave a lot of discomfort][280]

* * *

"Aur Sardar ali Khan ke sab aqriba
Mere maal ka dete the sab pata"
[And all the allies of Sardar Ali Khan, used to give
all the information about my assets].[281]

Sardar Ali Khan and his relatives were highly active during the rebellion. After Queen Victoria's proclamation, his relatives appeared before the Magistrate of Gorakhpur, and the Magistrate granted them clemency, but Sardar Ali Khan refused to surrender. In *Kashful-Baghaavat, Gorakhpur,* Syed Ahmed Ali Shah wrote:

"Woh Sardar Ali Khan ke sab aqriba
Bane the jo baaghi hue who reha"
[All the relative of Sardar Ali Khan
Who had become the mutineers were released]
"Baghaavat na Sardar Ali ki chhuti
Shararat na ab tak unki miti"
[Sardar Ali never forshook rebelliousness
His mischief had not been eradicated yet]
"Siwa unke sab log haazir hue
Khataa maaaf haakim ne sabki kiye"
[Except him, everybody reported in attendance
The rulers forgave everyone's offences].[282]

But the British Government finally got hold of Sardar Ali Khan. His properties were confiscated and he was executed.[283] The British handed over the Muftipur mohalla to Syed Ahmad Ali Shah as a reward.[284] Even today, Sardar Ali Khan's descendants and other people say a grave in the Police Kotwali as Sardar Ali Khan's grave and are demanding the construction of a memorial there.[285]

The Mirza Family of Gorakhpur

Members of the Mirza family of Gorakhpur also played an important role in the rebellion. They had got employment in the government of Mohammed Hasan, the Nazim and were among his confidants. Syed Ahmad Ali Shah wrote:

"Faqat Mirza ke ghar ke naukar hue
Jo ham jins the log sab jaa mile."
[Only from Mirza's house became servants
Those people who were genetically same, united] [286]

The Mirzas were the zamindars of Kaptanganj (Captainganj) situated to the north-east of the city. During the reign of Nawab Shuja-ud-Daulah, Mirza Ahmad Ali Beg came to Gorakhpur as an army officer (Kaptan or Captain), established a big zamindari by taking advantage of the prevailing anarchy.[287] His son, Mirza Hasan Ali Beg, was regarded among the respected figures of Gorakhpur district. His name figured in the list of dignitaries of Gorakhpur, which E. A. Reade had prepared in May 1843. About Mirza Hasan Ali Beg, it was said that "Mirza Husun Alee Beyg, age 72, is a wealthy man and parsimonious. Has two rent free and several zamindari villages. He is reputed to be worth about three lakhs rupees."[288] Syed Ahmad Ali Shah noted this fact in a different way. He wrote:

"Khush Iqbaal the Mirza Hasan Ali
Vaz aur tabiyat thi unki bhali"
[Mirza Hasan Ali was very fortunate
His behaviour and temperament, was good]
"Ba juz ranj-e-Hasnain tha kuch na ranj
Ilaaqah bahut aur kasrat se ganj"
[There was no other sorrow, except for the sorrow of Hasnain,
Had lots of estates and many markets].[289]

Mirza Fateh Ali Beg and Mirza Mohammed Ali Beg, born of one of the wives of Mirza Hasan Ali Beg, joined the rebellion and cooperated with the Nazim. Khuda Bakhsh Khan's petition dated 29 September 1857 corroborated this fact.[290] It is clear from a letter recovered from Mohammed Hasan's palanquin, that Mirza Fateh Ali Beg was already active in the revolt and had gained prominence even before the Nazim reached Gorakhpur. The commander of the rebel army had informed him that "when he reached Rajghat (the ghat on Rapti river by the city), he came to know that the Nepalese army was in Bhowapar along with the treasure, and when he reached there, they had gone to Belipar."[291] Then Mohammed Hasan attacked the Gorkhas at Gagaha to snatch the treasure. It was through the Mirza family that Mohammed Hasan sent money from Gorakhpur to Lucknow which shows the confidence they enjoyed, though there is no information about where this money finally reached.[292]

Mirza brothers took an active part in the revolt and it was natural that they were punished after the revolt had been crushed. Both brothers were apprehended after the restoration of British rule in Gorakhpur. Mirza Fateh Ali Beg was executed on the charge of sedition, while Mirza Mohammed Ali Beg was sentenced to life imprisonment. Their properties were confiscated. Later, half of the property was handed over to their step brother, Mirza Nawazish Ali.[293] About this fateful end, Syed Ahmad Ali Shah wrote:

"Magar betoon ne kar diya ghar tabaah
Nawaazish Ali par thi Haq ki nigaah'
[But his sons destroyed the house,
Nevertheless, God was kind to Nawaazish Ali][294]

In this way, the sons of late Mirza Hasan Ali lost the zamindari of Captainganj, received death sentence and life imprisonment, but made a contribution to the struggle to liberate the country from the British by playing an important role in the revolt of 1857.

Raghupati Rai and Dubri Rai

The zamindari of Padrauna was situated in the north-east of Gorakhpur district. It was formed by Gahnu Rai. After his demise, this zamindar family was split into two branches. In 1310 Fasli (1802 AD), Ram Narayan Rai and Meharban Rai, ancestors of Har Kumar Rai and Ishwari Pratap Rai, and also Bahadur Rai and Basti Rai, sons of Meharban Rai, were paying equal land revenue to the government. At the time of the revolt, Ishwari Pratap Rai was the zamindar of Padrauna and was pro-British. Hafiz Ilahi Bakhsh, the tehsildar of Padrauna, wanted to depute Ishwari Pratap Rai for protecting the treasury from the rebels. But Raghupati Rai, son of Bahadur Rai, and Dubri Rai, son of Basti Rai, who were from the other branch and were the descendants of Meharban Rai, wanted a role in protecting the treasury which Ishwari Pratap Rai declined. This was the time when Mr. Bird ran away from Gorakhpur and reached Padrauna. Ishwari Pratap Rai complained to him against these inimical kins. By the time, Raghupati Rai and Dubri Rai had recruited a number of persons in their employ. Their men were going on rampaging the people. Mr. Bird regarded it as a rebellious activity. When the British recaptured Gorakhpur, the government regarded Raghupati Rai and Dubri Rai as rebels, took them prisoners, and confiscated their zamindari. They were sentenced to transportation to life. Raghupati Rai and Dubri Rai died while still in jail.[295] The information compiled by P. N. Chopra is faulty. He has described Raghupati Rai and

Devi Rai (Dubri Rai) as the sons of Ishwari Pratap Rai and said that both were executed.[296]

Mendhu Khan

Mendhu Khan may be regarded as one of the unsung heroes of Rebellion 1857. He was killed at Biskohar, in the north-eastern part of the Bansi estate, while fighting against the British army, along with 200 of his followers. This fighting by the rebels, which resulted in the killing of such a large number of rebels, is one of the noteworthy events in Gorakhpur district.

Mendhu Khan belonged to Biskohar. On 30 August 1858, Mohammed Hasan (the Nazim) had appointed him tehsildar of the eastern part of Bansi and had instructed him to kill the infidel *firangis*. On 5 September 1858, Mohammed Hasan had sent him another edict, instructing him to liberate the Bansi tehsil from the enemies and punish Mr. Peppe, the Deputy Magistrate. Mendhu Khan was very efficiently discharging the role of revenue collection, which the British Government regarded as rebellious activity and sent an army against him. With his men, he valiantly fought against the British army and was killed along with 200 followers.[297]

Pahaad Singh Rajput

Led by the Raja Udai Singh of Nagar, the Babus of Pipra played a notable role in rebellious activities. Pahaad Singh Rajput belonged to this very Pipra village. Along with his supporters, he participated in the battle of Gagaha, led by Mohammed Hasan, to snatch the government treasure being sent to Azamgarh under the Gorkhas' protection. Despite the failure there, he continued his rebellious activities. Feeling harassed, 200 Gorkhas, led by Forbes, attacked the Pipra village and ravaged it to the ground. Pahaad Singh was arrested with a sword and a light loaded gun. He was tried and sentenced to death.[298]

Wali Mohammed

Wali Mohammed belonged to village Tilji, thana Bakhira, pargana Hasanpur-Magahar. He joined the army of Mohammed Hasan when the rebellion began and was made the commander of 500 sepoys. Along with his companions, he launched an attack against Deputy Magistrate Mr. Peppe when the latter had come to Tilji to capture the rebels. After this arrack, Mr. Peppe had to run away for life. His companions, Talib and Sultan, were in the army that attacked the Raja of Gopalpur. Wali Mohammed had become known, during the rebellion, for the loot of enemy properties. Therefore, British documents described him as a rebel and also as a robber. While going to Basti and Nagar, Mr. Burton succeeded in capturing Wali Mohammed en route. He was tried on 1 January 1858 and sentenced to death along with his companions — Fazal, Talib, Sultan and Badal.[299]

Jafar Ali

According to the British records, Jaffar Ali was the son of Raja Abbas Ali of Tanda (Faizabad), and a member of Mohammed Hasan's advisory council.[300] He was counted among the organisers of the rebellion. His name figured among those who led the crowd that killed the British in Mahua Dabar. According to Sir John Kaye, he had shot Lieutenant Ritchie to death.[301]

We know from a letter that he had one thousand sepoys and was involved in rebellious activities at Mohammed Hasan's instructions.[302] No information is available about his end.

Gulab Khan Pathan

Gulab Khan Pathan belonged to village Bhairopur of pargana Nagar. Having formed a group, he was involved in rebellious activities in Nagar area. He was one who had ravaged Bridgeman's indigo factory. He led the crowd that did six British officers to death at Mahua Dabar. For these crimes, he was sentenced to death along with Gulzar Khan Pathan, Nihal Khan Pathan, Badlu Khan Pathan and Ghisa Khan Pathan.[303]

The afore-going narrative is about the heroes of Gorakhpur district (Basti included) about whom some documents are available. This area lies to the north-east of Ghaghra river.

(C) Damman Khan: Inhabitant of Nepal Terai

The *terai* of Nepal, adjoining the northern border of Eastern Uttar Pradesh, not only provided the facility to the rebels of 1857 to take shelter and conduct guerrilla warfare, but also provided courage to a number of people to join the rebellion. Though the Government of Nepal, led by Jang Bahadur Rana, was openly supporting and collaborating with the British Government, it also provided shelter to a number of rebels in its territory. Nay more, a number of Nepalese citizens living in the border areas of Nepal *terai,* openly defied their government and joined the rebellion on the side of Begum Hazrat Mahal of Awadh. Among them, the role of Jagirdar Damman Khan of Jhandanagar, his brother Lal Khan and hundreds of his supporters deserves special mention.

At present, the Nepalese territory adjoining the Badhni border in Siddharth Nagar district of Eastern Uttar Pradesh is known as Krishna Nagar. It is a part of Kapilvastu region (district) of Nepal. It was earlier known as Jhandanagar. At present, Muslims of the place narrate a number of tales about the name of Jhandanagar. The territory which Sa'adat Ali Khan, the Nawab of Awadh had transferred to the Company Government in 1801, included pargana Tilpur and Vinayakpur of Gorakhpur district.[304] This territory fell under the Raja of Butwal's jurisdiction. In 1806, the Government of Nepal captured the Butwal estate.[305] A few members of the Butwal princely family ran away and took shelter in Nichlaul under the Company Government's jurisdiction. Here they received monthly allowances as livelihood and came to be known as the Raja of Nichlaul.[306] In fact, the Anglo-Nepal war of 1814-15 was fought about the border of Butwal.[307] In order to encourage settlement here in view of the inclement weather and forest covered territory, the Nepal Government provided many facilities to the Indians who engaged in cultivation. In 1781, in the mass revolt against Major Hannay in Gorakhpur, about 50,000 people ran away to take shelter in the *terai* of Nepal and a number of them permanently settled there. In brief, numerous Indians were there in the *terai* of Nepal and they had also acquired Nepalese citizenship. It seems Damman Khan's family was one of them, and they were Nepalese citizens at the time of Rebellion in 1857. He was the jagirdar of Jhandanagar and held the responsible position of Diwan in the Land Revenue Department of the Nepal Government. For he has been referred to as "Diwan Damman Khan" while official correspondence too used the word "Dewan."[308]

There is no information about when and wherefrom the family of Damman Khan came to settle in Jhandanagar. But Damman Khan was a Nepalese citizen and jagirdar in 1857. He was a highly influential and prosperous person. Jhandanagar, adjoining the Indian border, was his place of domicile. Maulvi Sarfaraz Ali of Gorakhpur used to go to the Nepal *terai* to deliver sermons. Influenced by him, Damman Khan had become his disciple.[309] Under his inspiration, he joined the Rebellion 1857 on the side of Begum Hazrat Mahal who appointed him the chakladar of Bansi. Discharging his responsibility, Damman Khan collected land revenue from May to June.[310] He also drove away the Britishers and their policemen. According to a report from the Commissioner of Gorakhpur, he attacked Mr. Peppe's factory, attacked the Tharauli thana and drove the policemen from there.[311] He also laid a siege on the pro-British Raja of Bansi's fortress in order to capture it, but retreated on getting the news of the British army's arrival.[312] He was in touch with Mohammed Hasan, the chakladar of

Gorakhpur. Damman Khan had gone to meet Mohammed Hasan when the latter had laid a siege upon the Sonauli fortress of the Raja of Bansi.[313]

Living in Bondi after the fall of Lucknow, Begum Hazrat Mahal was conducting the rebel government of Awadh from there. At the time, Damman Khan helped the Begum economically by collecting land revenue and fines from the zamindars of Bansi and asserted the continued existence of her government. He went to Bondi in company with Maulvi Sarfaraz Ali and stayed there for twelve days. He met Begum Hazrat Mahal and received a robe of honour from Her.[314] From Bondi, he returned to his home in Jhandanagar on 17 July 1858. He was probably entrusted the responsibility of soliciting help from Maharaja Jang Bahadur Rana for Begum Hazrat Mahal. Therefore, along with two disciples of renowned rebel, Jai Kishanpuri, he left for Kathmandu, the capital of Nepal. But the Nepalese authorities detained him,[315] which sent a wave of disappointment among the rebels.[316]

The Government of British India was already in correspondence against Damman Khan through its Resident in Kathmandu. According to the instruction given by G. P. Edmonston, Secretary to the Government of India in the Foreign Department with Governor General, Allahabad, in Letter No. 3183 dated 12 September 1858, C. Wingfield sent to the Assistant Resident at Kathmandu, Captain G.H. Byers, the proofs of crimes committed by Damman Khan of Jhandanagar, and informed about it to the Secretary in a letter on 27 November 1858.[317] Byers, the Assistant Resident based at Kathmandu, then sent a letter to G P Edmonston, Secretary to the government of India in the Foreign Department with Governor General, Allahabad, on 11 December 1858, informing that on the same day he had forwarded the proofs sent against Damman Khan to the Maharaja and that the latter had already acknowledged receipt on 3 December 1858. On the basis of the statements made by various persons, the English Magistrate of Gorakhpur had collected evidences against Damman Khan and his brother, Lal Khan, coming to Burhnee, located in pargana Bansi, capturing some respectable persons of Burhnee and nearby villages, bringing them to Burhnee and extracting money from them through inhuman methods and maltreating them. These are as below in brief:

1. Soorujdeen Gosain, who belonged to Burhnee, tappa Bunjurria, said in his statement that Damman Khan and Lal Khan came to Burhnee, along with two or three hundred persons, in the beginning of June (1858), captured the neighbouring zamindars and compelled them to cough up money. He had seen all those persons

himself and knew them personally as Jhandanagar was close to Burhnee.

2. Toolsee Koormee, who belonged to Surajdeen Gosain's village, confirmed the latter's statement.
3. Ishree Patuck also confirmed the above statement. He was himself captured but, as he was a Brahmin, he was asked for only a cot and released.
4. Ramadeen of village Jandurra, tappa Bunjurria, said in his statement that he was captured and brought to Burhnee and produced before Damman Khan and Lal Khan. There he was physically thrashed, and money was extracted from him.
5. Ramcharan and Ajoodhia of the same village Jandurra, tappa Bunjurria reiterated the statement made by Ramdeen.
6. Bowaneedeen of Piprahawa said in his statement that he was captured and brought to Burhnee in the month of June and produced before Damman Khan and Lal Khan. He was physically tortured until he paid the amount demanded for his release. Damman Khan had gone to Boondi in July.
7. Madho Kurmi, a zamindar of Piprahawa, said he ran away when learnt about Damman Khan's return, but his servant was captured. He sent the required money to get the servant released.

Thereafter Damman Khan and Lal Khan went to village Dohurria in tappa Bunjurria, pargana Bansi where, too, they captured people from the nearby villages and extracted money from them. The following persons made statements about it:

1. Bussunt Koormee, a zamindar of Dohurria, said on oath that Damman Khan and Lal Khan came to his Dohurria village, along with 400 men, on 2 Jyeshth (10 June). Though he managed to escape, these persons ravaged the people and then, spending two days or three there, they went to Rumooapore. He heard all the details from two of his *asamis* (tenants).
2. Sookuee Koormee, who was a co-sharer in the zamindari of Dohurria, endorsed Basant Kurmi's statement and also said he had heard from Damman Khan's men that he had sent all the looted property to his home in Jhandanagar, Nepal.
3. Bugoo Choomar of Dohurria was in his village when Damman Khan and Lal Khan reached there. He saw the two figures with his own eyes. Their men pointed to him while his masters, both the

aforementioned witnesses (Basant Koormee and Sookuee Koormee) had fled away. After ravaging the village, Damman Khan and Lal Khan stayed there for two or three days more and then moved to Kumhurria.

4. Sahay Gurdeen and Bhoor Dhobey made exactly the same statement as the above. The first named (Sahay Gurdeen) was pressed as a cooly by Dummun Khan's people. All sweared to having seen him and his brother).
5. Zamindar Goordutt Singh of Burgaon, whose statement was recorded in detail in the Rumooapore case, said Damman Khan and Lal Khan were present in Dohurria and from there, for the first time, they had sent their men (servants) to demand money.

The following persons tendered evidence that Damman Khan and Lal Khan were present in village Rumooapore, tappa Banjurria, pargana Bansi and looted it:

1. Sadho Mahto of village Sikhoya said in his statement that "at a particular time in the month of Jeth (around 12 to 15 June), Damman Khan and Lal Khan came to Rumooapore along with several hundred followers, which he himself witnessed. They sent their men to apprehend the Tewaris of village Jumouee. These sepoys apprehended me and produced me before Damman Khan in Rumooapore. Damman Khan and Lal Khan asked me for a levy of 600 rupees and presented me as a reputed wealthy man. When I refused to pay, he got me tied up and thrashed and sent me home to fetch money, in his sepoys' escort. From home, I brought 490 rupees and gave it to Damman Khan. I personally saw Damman Khan and Lal Khan as I knew them. They came from Dohurria to Rumooapore, and then went to Kamsar. Fourteen days later, Lal Khan got me captured second time and brought along with him to Burhnee where he held me captive for 21 days. When Damman Khan returned from Boondi, he released me after I paid him another 36 rupees."
2. Hooly Kahar, who belonged to Rumooapore, who carried water for Damman Khan and Lal Khan, and who brought supplies for their personal establishment, had seen Sadho when he was held captive at Damman Khan and Lal Khan's order. He was constantly in contact with the two.

3. Bunnoo Tewarry of Rumooapore stated that Damman Khan and Lal Khan came to his village around 15 June and plundered it. He himself saw Sadho Mahto in the captivity of their sepoys. From Burhnee they came to Dohurria and then went to Karamha. Damman Khan stayed at a place for a few says only and for about 18 days in the district.
4. Munoj Dutt, the zamindar of Juntora, stated that the sepoys of Damman Khan and Lal Khan captured him in the middle of June, and took to Damman Khan in Rumooapore. They put a log of wood in order to torture him and compelled him to pay 400 rupees. He had himself seen Sadho Mahto, the bailiff of Doorga Tewarry, held captive in Rumooapore.
5. Ram Gulam Misra of Sekhua was also captured and taken to Damman Khan and compelled to give out money. During his detention, he himself saw Munoj Dutt in the same condition.
6. Around the middle of June, Bodee Khan, the bailiff of the zamindar of Jumouee, was captured and taken to Damman Khan and Lal Khan in Rumooapore and forced to pay money. He had himself seen both there. He knew Damman Khan very well as he had already paid him toll tax on timber because Damman Khan also had the contract to collect *sair* (a kind of cess) in the Nepalese forests.
7. Meddnee Oopaddia, a resident of Jumouee, was also captured and brought to Damman Khan in Rumooapore and maltreated till he paid money for his release. Here he had seen Sadho Mahto as well. Damman Khan and Lal Khan regularly held a *kachahari* (court) of their own.
8. Ishree Sahai, the zamindar of Maduapur, said that he was captured around the middle of June and taken to Damman Khan in Rumooapore. He was forced to pay 100 rupees. He had seen them and they were pointed out by me.
9. Bal Govind, of the same village Maduapur, made a similar statement.
10. Siree Raam, zamindar of Myudonee, was similarly captured and taken to Damman Khan in Rumooapore. He also stated about ransom payment. Gaya Prasad of the same village made a similar statement.
11. Sheo Sahai of Juhra stated that he was captured in June and taken to Damman Khan and Lal Khan in Rumooapore, 2 miles off, where

he was beaten and a wooden log was put on his chest. He was released after he paid 169 rupees. Palatdeen of the same village was subjected to a similar treatment and 140 rupees were extracted from him.

12. Ram Pershad Oopauddia, resident of Mamtua, was captured and taken to Damman Khan and Lal Khan in Rumooapore where he was beaten up and 12 rupees were extracted from him. Ganga of Naroya village was given a similar treatment.
13. Goordut Singh of Burgaon said that some sepoys of Damman Khan and Lal Khan came to him in the beginning of June and demanded revenue from him. He said he would wait for Damman Khan. The sepoys then went back. He informed the neighbour zamindars about it and asked them to intimate the tehsildar by letter about it, which they did. Two days later, Damman Khan and Lal Khan left Dohurria and came to Rumooapore. Afraid of them, he and some others went there. Peons were recruited to have an eye on them so that money could be collected. He gave 250 rupees. He saw Damman Khan with his own eyes. The other zamindars with him had known Damman Khan before. Damman Khan said that he was going west (Boondi) and that, during his absence, they should pay the remaining amounts to his brother, Lal Khan. They first came to Burhnee, and from there they went to Kumhurria, Dohurria and Rumooapore. From Rumooapore, they went to Karamha. He heard that Damman Khan had left for Boondi while Lal Khan was still in the district. Damman Khan stayed in the district for some 20 days.

The letter to the Tehseeldar alluded in the above disposition was sent by him to Magistrate on 13th June. He had said in his report that Damman Khan had come to Dohurria and committed plunder, oppression and forced revenue collection. The concerned evidence was not recorded till October.

The following persons provided evidence of many acts of oppression and plunder of British subjects, committed by Damman Khan in village Karamha of pargana Bansi.

Zamindar Surdawn Singh of Lahittia village stated that when he returned to his village, he heard that the peons (Karinds) of Damman Khan were still there, demanding revenue. He and other zamindars intimated the tehsildar about it while other zamindars went to meet Damman Khan in Rumooapore and came back, along with the in-charge of Damman Khan's peons in order to make payments. He too went to Damman Khan along with them. Damman Khan had left for Karmaha. He had himself seen Damman Khan and his brother there, whom he knew beforehand. He paid them 150 rupees for release. They came to Rumooapore via Burhnee, Kumhurria and Dohurria and from there they went to Boondi.

Bua Mahout (Mahout), a servant of Surdawn Singh, stated that on the first of Jyeshtha, i.e. in May, he had taken his master's elephant into the Nepal forests where he came across Damman Khan who was then returning from Bootwal. Damman forced him to take the elephant to his own home in Jhandanagar. From Jhandanagar, he accompanied Damman Khan to Sonauli where Damman Khan met Mohammed Hasan. There the latter had laid a siege on the Sonauli fortress of the Raja of Bansi. Then Buwa went to Rumooapore via Burhnee, Kumhurria, Dohurria, Ramooapore and Karamha along with Damman Khan. From Karamha he returned to Jhandanagar, and then, immediately, Damman Khan left for Boondi along with a maulvi. They stayed there for 12 days before returning to Jhandanagar. Shortly afterwards Dumman Khan was apprehended by the Nepalese authorities and the witness (Buwa Mahawat) then made his escape to his master along with his elephant.

The context of the above statement by Buwa makes it clear that Damman Khan had gone to meet Mohammed Hasan when the latter had laid a siege on the Sonauli fortress. The tehsildar of Bansi also informed that Damman Khan had run away when he got the news on 1 June that the British army coming for help. The raja of Bansi too had included Damman Khan among those laying the siege.

Jaygeer, bailiff (karinda) of the zamindar of Karmaha, stated the Damman Khan and Lal Khan had come there. He had himself seen them there. They had taken him prisoner and released only after his master has sent them money. From Karmaha, Damman Khan went to Boondi. The Gorait (chowkidar) also confirmed the statement. But he was not an eye witness as he had run away on getting the news of Damman Khan's arrival.[318]

Lastly, C. Wingfield, the Commissioner of Gorakhpur, wrote in his report that "Several reports of the tehseeldars from the 30th May to 21st June allude, to Dummun Khan being at some or the other of the places specified in the depositions of the above numerous witnesses or elsewhere in the neighbourhood." The tehsildar had said Damman Khan did not stay at a place for long, which was confirmed by the witnesses' statements.[319] C. Wingfield's letter of 27 November also said that "I may observe that the evidence implicates, Lal Khan, his brother equally in all these acts, but there are several other cases of the robbery by open violence clearly proved against him, notably the robbery of Mr. Peppe's factory and the attack and the overthrow of Thanna of Tharowlee."[320]

Captain Byers, Assistant Resident in Nepal, sent a memorandum (letter) to Maharaja Jang Bahadur, Prime Minister and Commander-in-Chief of Nepal, on 2 December 1858. In this letter containing the proofs, he said: "Damman Khan is your citizen, as per the treaty of 1855, British Government cannot demand his extradition and neither any such offer had been made by the Nepal Government. But keeping in mind the relationship between ours (Indian) and Nepal, this is the duty of the Nepal government that a person who had forcibly occupied our area and conducted looting and took the looted money to his home in Jundaanagger, who showed his loyalty towards the Beghum of Lucknow, an enemy of British and accepted gifts from her, should meet his justice." He further wrote: "The Maharaja has assured the Governor General that if the charges against him will be proved, he will be punished. In order to fulfil his promise, he had already taken a first step by ordering to arrest Dummun Khan."

According to Captain Byers, Maharaja Jang Bahadur had said in his letter: "if the British government will run the case against Dummun Khan then the accused will had to face their biasness." He also asked the Governor General: "to suggest his punishment so that Nepal court can punish him." But Captain Byers wrote that "Governor General cannot declare punishment of any criminal whose case is not being run in British court." He further wrote: "Since Dummun Khan is being tried in your country, the punishment should be declared by you only." He assured that "He has got instruction from Governor General side that they do not fear any biasness from your judiciary. You should not hold any doubts regarding this as the Governor General has full confidence in your government. He cannot suggest any punishment for Dummun Khan. You had promised that if his charges were proved he will be punished. Governor General can only ask you to fulfil that. For further actions on this I am attaching of statements of 32 witnesses, collected by Commissioner of Gorackpore in last two months and which cannot be doubt in any way, is being sent as a proof. These statements confirm that charges against Dummun Khan that, in the month of June, he stayed in British region for 20 days." He further wrote that, according to the statement of Bua Mahaut, "he went out of his house in Jundanaggar as a leader of hundreds of rebels and entered British region, set up a kind of court as a Chakladar, appointed by rubber stamp government of Bondee, summoned the zamindars of nearby region in his court and forced them to pay the desired amount. This way he continued to move from one place to another, till he looted all the money from people. When he returned back to his place in Jundanugger, he had 9216 rupees with him. He left his brother Lal Khan in this region for further revenue collection." Captain Byers finally wrote that Damman Khan's case was now in his (Maharaja's) hands.[321]

On 7 December 1858, when Captain Byers was about to leave the Tuni Sports Parade Ground after having watched the parade, Maharaja Jang Bahadur told him that he wanted to have some talk with Byers. So, the next day was fixed for the conversation. Next day he went to the Prime Minister's (Maharaja's) residence in company with Dr Oldfield. The Prime Minister asked his opinion about the kind of punishment to be meted to Damman Khan, which could also satisfy the Governor General. He also said he had carefully read the proofs sent by Mr. Wingfield against Damman Khan and also his (Byer's) own memorandum, and all this proved his crime. But the Maharaja also said that in his opinion Damman Khan's biggest crime was his going over to the Begum of Lucknow who was inimical to the British government and hence of his own government. Yet Damman Khan had not killed anyone in the trans-border excursions, and therefore in his (Maharaja's) opinion his life should not be snatched. If Byers still thought he (Damman Khan) should be given capital punishment, the Maharaja would give him capital punishment. But when God would ask him why Damman Khan was given capital punishment, his reply would be that Captain Byers had thought him deserving for it. Going by law, the Maharaja suggested giving Damman Khan any one of the four harshest punishments in view of the gravity of his crime. These were first, capital punishment; second, one-year imprisonment along with the forfeiture of all his property; third, his release after the forfeiture of all his property; and fourth, three years of imprisonment without the forfeiture of his property. Captain Byers refused to make any suggestion about the due punishment. Then the Maharaja said he was going to give Damman Khan one-year imprisonment with the forfeiture of all his property. He said it was highly harsh punishment as Damman Khan would then lose everything. Moreover, he said if the Governor General thought it lenient, he was ready to change it. But the Maharaja did not promise any kind of compensation to the persons oppressed by Damman Khan in return for their confiscated properties.[322] In the memorandum sent on 9 December 1858, too, the Maharaja had intimated his decision to give Damman Khan the aforesaid punishment.[323]

Maharaja Jang Bahadur instructed General Badri Narsingh to arrest Damman Khan, to be punished with the forfeiture of all his property along with one-year imprisonment.[324] After his arrest, Damman Khan was lodged in the Bootwal Jail. However, when Maharaja Jang Bahadur got information about the entry of Begum Hazrat Mahal, along with her followers, into Nepal, he considered her relations with Damman Khan and sent another instruction to General Badri Narsingh, telling him to shift Damman Khan from Bootwal to Palpa Jail.[325] Apart from losing all his property, Damman Khan faced the punishment of a year of rigorous imprisonment. After his release, he spent a life of travail as a resourceless person. No information is available about his confiscated property,[326] or about his demise. The people of the area showed us the madrasa running there for education of Muslim girls and also the "well of Damman Khan" which is still a reminder of his life, but they do not have any kind of interest or respect for him.[327]

(D) Rebel Leaders from Azamgarh, Banaras, Jaunpur, Mirzapur and Ghazipur Districts and Adjoining Areas

To the south of Ghaghra river lay Azamgarh, Jaunpur, Mirzapur, Banaras and Ghazipur districts. Azamgarh district was a part of Ceded Provinces, where Mahalwari system was introduced. The Western border of Azamgarh and Jaunpur districts adjoined Awadh. Its eastern border was Ghazipur district which also includes the modern district of Ballia. Eastern Ghazipur was influenced by the revolt of Babu Kunwar Singh of Jagdishpur. Besides, Bengal Army had a large number of sepoys of this area. Thus, the rebellion in Bengal army had adverse effect on the people of this district and they turned against British rule. The zamindars, who were ousted from their zamindaris due to the permanent settlement, were also against the British rule. Hence the rebellion in these areas was serious and wide. But it seems that the districts of Benares and Mirzapur were not much affected by the rebellion. The company government had made special security for the safety of the Delhi-Calcutta route, which passed through the Benares and Mirzapur districts. There, the British army crushed the rebellion but even then, it did not remain unaffected by the rising tide of rebellion. The rebel leaders of Eastern Uttar Pradesh made the Britishers felt that their existence is in danger. In this section, the brief description of the leaders of this region and their activities have been given;

Pargan Singh (Azamgarh)

Pargan Singh belonged to village Heerapatti in Sadar tehsil of Azamgarh district.[328] He emerged as a deft organiser and tactician during the Rebellion of 1857. S.B. Chaudhuri wrote about him that "Pargan Singh had formulated many schemes of combined action on different occasions."[329] By his efforts, he had made his village a rebel stronghold. That was why Mr. Venables later attacked his village and got it burnt to ashes.[330] In return, he too attacked

Mr. Venables,[331] and cooperated with the rebels' capture of Azamgarh town.[332] It was with a scheme that Pargan Singh had made the north-western part of the district a stronghold of rebellious activities.[333]

Official narratives tell us that Pargan Singh had formed a group of very many rebels. On 23 April 1858, he looted the Maharajganj market, with his group which included 100 rebel sepoys and, besides, a number of other rebels. On 3 May, he again attacked the town to collect money from traders. On 10 May, he surrounded Koilsa tehsil office but the tehsildar, Sheikh Mamnun, faced him determinedly. In the skirmish between the two sides, three men of Pargan Singh's group were killed and two severely injured while two government *barqandazs* were also injured severely. However, while retreating from there, the rebels set the Koilsa thana afire.[334]

In the beginning of June, Pargan Singh again attacked Koilsa tehsil, but had to retreat again after an encounter for several hours. They then looted the Koilsa market.[335]

Pargan Singh had close relations with Madhav Prasad Singh, the powerful taluqdar of Birhar. According to the police report, he had asked Maho Prasad to provide him two guns.[336] We know from Robert Taylor's supplementary narrative that "Twice did Pargan Singh successfully attack the thannah of Maharajgunje, and it was only after a long and hard fight that he retired from the Tahseeldaree of Koelsa." [337] It was conceded in a government report that while not attacking Koilsa, he had encroached upon the British territory several times.[338] The statement corroborates that Pargan Singh did not lie low and continuously engaged in rebellious actions so that he had become a symbol of revolt. Rumours in his name were also spread in order to scare the Englishmen. For example, some village people once told the British officials and employees that: "He has got a notice printed in Persian and Hindi languages that there will be a revolt again on 21 June, on the day of Dussehra."[339] Pargan Singh had created terror by getting cut off the nose of an informer of the British there.[340] Even after Babu Kunwar Singh had left Azamgarh, some rebel activities did continue in the district. At the time, many groups of rebels were active there, and the most powerful was that of Pargan Singh. It had about 200 rebel sepoys and a large number of the rebellious people, and they had made the Jehangirganj area their base.[341] Pargan Singh went underground after the rebellion had been crushed and escaped the British net. He went in hiding in the Nepal *terai* and breathed his last there in December 1859. This was informed by Captain Holdich on 17 December 1859, after coming back from the Gorkha headquarters.[342]

Sheikh Rajab Ali

Sheikh Rajab Ali was among the top figures who led the common people's revolt in Azamgarh district. He belonged to village Bambhour in Mohammedabad tehsil. He had formed an organisation against the British Government in Mohabbatpur, Sakhia, Parkauli, Meghai, Nainijor, Rudari, Lachhirampur and some other villages, a few miles from Azamgarh.[343] According to the British Government, Kiya Khan and Ummed Ali, zamindars of village Siktee, were his relatives and Rajab Ali had motivated the people for revolt while he was sheltered in their house.[344] At the time, Mohabbatpur was the centre of rebellious activities. Therefore, after recapturing the city of Azamgarh, Mr. Venables attacked Mohabbatpur on 30 June 1857, with the aim of strengthening peace and order there. He arrested a number of rebels and put them behind the bars in Kotwali.[345] Many of these people were Rajab Ali's followers. Hence, demonstrating his valour, Rajab Ali gathered about 400 persons, attacked the Azamgarh Kotwali in broad daylight on 23 July, and got all the prisoners freed.[346] The main ones among them were Mohabbatpur zamindar Jag Bandhan Singh, Araiya zamindar Ram Prasad Rai, Khandya Singh, Mairi Singh, Ajayab Lal, Dhannu Patak, Sunra zamindar Gulab Singh, Sangram Singh, Siuli zamindar Sohan Singh and Baijnath Singh. Mr. Venables could not manage to re-arrest them. The British Government announced a reward of 100 rupees for his arrest.[347]

On 29 December 1857, Mr. Venables got the news of Sheikh Rajab Ali's presence in village Mamruapur. He at once encircled the village, with his armed horsemen, in order to arrest him. But Rajab Ali broke through the British troop's siege and escaped towards the Tons (Tamsa) river. The British soldiers chased him and tried to apprehend him alive. With no escape route in sight, he jumped into the river and, going up and down, he swam up to Hajipur Ghat. There he came out of the river and tried to run away but was shot to death by British soldiers. The British burnt his house to ashes and confiscated all his property.[348]

Prithvipal Singh (Azamgarh)

Prithvipal Singh was the taluqdar of Tighra Estate which was situated in the Awadh territory. But he also had the zamindari of nine villages in Azamgarh district, which he managed from Baramadpur (in pargana Mahul).[349] Being contiguous to the border of Azamgarh, Tighra Estate had become a centre of disturbances (revolt).[350] Prithvipal Singh had cordial relations with Muzaffar Jehan, the Raja of Mahul, and Raja Beni Madho of

Atraulia. He was also the leader of Palwar Rajputs of Azamgarh. To recover some revenue arrears, the British Government had confiscated some of his villages and had this angered him. Hence, he wanted an end of the British Raj. On 3 June 1857, soldiers of the 17th NI revolted, looted the government treasury, and then moved towards Faizabad. The rein of revolt was now in the hands of local heroes. Palwar Rajputs now held high the banner of revolt under Prithvipal Singh. He retained control on Azamgarh town from August 9 to August 25th, 1857 and made a collection of ten thousand rupees. He vacated the town when he learnt about the Gorkhas coming.[351] Earlier, Prithvipal Singh had also participated, along with Raja Beni Madhav and Raja Muzaffar Jehan, in the Koilsa battle with Mr. Venables. The British army had to run away.[352]

Led by Prithvipal Singh, Palwar Rajputs were a constant source of disturbance. Therefore, a Gorkha troop, led by Mr. Bird, was sent to subdue them. The Gorkha troop destroyed his Baramadpur fortress and other properties.[353] Led by Cox, an English troop had already destroyed his Tighra fortress.[354] However, despite all these, he did not deviate from the path of revolt. British officials then adopted the tactic of friendship instead of conflict with Palwar Rajputs, and they succeeded.[355] Prithvipal Singh now had to keep low. He lived long after the rebellion was crushed. He died at Ayodhya on 29 July 1891.[356]

Raja Beni Madho (Atraulia, Azamgarh)

Raja Beni Madho of Atraulia was a resident of village Barahara, under Atraulia, tehsil Phoolpur, district Azamgarh.[357] He had a small estate in Atraulia. His father, Darshan Singh, had been a high official in the Nawab of Awadh's army.[358] His elder brother, Raja Jai Lal Singh, held an important post in the Begum's government, and he was appointed the Nazim of Azamgarh and Jaunpur.[359] Raja Beni Madho had declared himself the Naib Nazim of Azamgarh.[360] He had be-friended his traditional rival, the Pulwar Rajputs, and forged a strong front against the British. Himself, he belonged to the Kurmi caste.[361] Therefore, with a troop, Mr. Venables launched an attack on Koilsa in the south-western part of the district in order to break the hold of the rebels. But his attack went in vain. After three days of confrontation, Raja Beni Madho again occupied Atraulia.[362] Raja Beni Madho then attacked Mr. Venables, and the British had to vacate the Azamgarh town.[363] In August 1857, the British reoccupied Azamgarh after the Gorkha troops came. But Raja Beni Madho was still in control of the western part of the district. After preparations, both sides came face to face and Raja Beni Madho had to suffer defeat in the battle held at a place called Mandauri on 20 September 1857. Hence, he returned to his fortress in Atraulia. But, chasing him, the Gorkhas too reached Atraulia. With his followers, Raja Beni Madho then moved into the Awadh territory. The Gorkha troop then occupied the Atraulia fortress.[364] In November 1857, he succeeded in getting Atraulia back with the help of the Awadh rebels.[365] But the British would not allow him to have a hold again. Hence, a British army from Jaunpur, under colonel Longden was sent against him. It is said that when the British troops came, Raja Beni Madho had to leave Atraulia once again.[366] In the convoy of Begum Hazrat Mahal, he too went into Nepal.[367] The British Government forfeited his zamindari which consisted of 41 villages.[368] No concrete information is available about his last days.

Jag Bandhan Singh

Jag Bandhan Singh was a resident of village Mohabbatpur in pargana Mohammedabad of Azamgarh district. The village was a rebel stronghold. Therefore Mr. Venables attacked the village, arrested a number of rebels and imprisoned them in Kotwali. Jag Bandhan Singh had close relations with rebel leaders like Sheikh Rajab Ali and Pargan Singh. Learning about his arrest, Sheikh Rajab Ali, accompanied by four hundred persons, attacked the Kotwali in broad daylight. The thanedar and the police present there could not defend the Kotwali and the crowd got all the prisoners released. Jag Bandhan Singh continued to engage in rebellious activities. The government announced a reward of four hundred rupees for his arrest.[369] Finally, the government declared him an 'absconder' and confiscated his property.[370]

Madhai Prasad

He was one of the close associates of Raja Beni Madho of Atraulia. Madhai Prasad Yadav was a resident of village Ahiripur in pargana Nizamabad. He had earlier served in the Nawab of Awadh's army. Raja Beni Madho had therefore made him in-charge of cannonry in his army. He was killed while fighting in the Mandauri battle. The British Government got his house burnt down and confiscated all his property.[371]

Raja Muzaffar Jahan (Mahul)

Raja Muzaffar Jahan was the zamindar of Mahul in Azamgarh district. It was a very old zamindari.[372] In the days of Raja Balwant Singh of Banaras, according to *Balwant Nama*, the zamindar here was Shamshad Jehan whom the people addressed with the title of Raja.[373] Raja Didar Jehan of this very family had populated Didarganj after his own name. After his demise, his nephew, Iradat Jehan, inherited the zamindari. Raja Muzaffar Jahan was the eldest son of Raja Iradat Jehan.[374]

When the revolt broke out, Muzaffar Jahan declared himself the Raja on 26 June 1857, and occupied the Mahul thana and tehsil office. Before it, he had occupied government offices on the pretext of providing protection to British officials and had started living therein. With 1,000 of his men, he occupied his zamindari that had been forfeited. He thrashed and drove away the government officer who was the in-charge there.[375] He plundered it in company with Palwar leader Prithvipal Singh and Rajkumar Rajputs. He augmented his strength by recruiting a large number of soldiers, took part in all the anti-British campaigns in all parts of the district and committed the deeds which were most heinous misdeeds in the eyes of the British.[376]

Earlier, Raja Muzaffar Jahan also used to take the contracts for revenue collection from the Awadh Government as well. Therefore, he was on good terms with the Awadh taluqdars. Taking advantage of this he had joined hands with Raja Beni Madho Singh, taluqdar of Birhar in Awadh and the leader of Palwar Rajputs and formed a big group of rebels. With them, he had invaded Azamgarh on 18 July 1857.[377]

On Gorkha army's arrival, the British began a campaign against his father and, after having grabbed and executed him, moved towards Atraulia. Learning about the British moving ahead along with the Gorkha army, Raja Muzaffar Jehan, his followers and supporters, along with Prithvipal Singh, did not resist them. Rather they sneaked into the Awadh border and thus remained safe.[378]

To the British, Raja Muzaffar Jehan was a cruel rebel. Hence, they announced an award of 500 rupees for his arrest.[379] Raja Muzaffar Jehan was apprehended but he met the conditions of clemency included in Queen Victoria's proclamation. He was therefore not awarded death sentence. However, he was tried for some other crimes and sentenced to seven years imprisonment. When he came out of jail after completing his sentence, an allowance was fixed for his livelihood by the British Government. He died some time in 1874-75.[380]

Madho Prasad Singh Palwar (Taluqdar of Birhar in Awadh)

Birhar (Jehangirganj), adjoining the north-western border of Azamgarh, is situated in Awadh (in Ambedkar Nagar district at present). Madho Prasad Singh Palwar was the taluqdar here at the time of the revolt.[381] He had made Azamgarh district the centre of his rebellious activities. In July 1857, he declared himself the chakladar of Azamgarh and entered the district with a big army of rebels.[382] In the beginning, he had made a display of friendly relations with the English by giving shelter to many of the British in Faizabad. Nothing in his conduct was against the British Government before the battle of Koilsa. The government too had not confiscated his zamindari.[383] But at Koilsa, Madho Prasad Singh and his rebel army defeated the army led by Mr. Venables and compelled them to run away.[384] They managed to capture the Azamgarh town and went back after entrusting its administration to Prithvipal Singh.[385] H.C. Tucker, Commissioner, 5th Division, Banaras, wrote a letter on 15 August 1857 to C. Biden, Secretary, Government of India, Fort William, to appeal that the government must attack Madho Prasad Singh who had gone to Azamgarh along with 5,000 persons, and forfeit all of his zamindari, so that no other zamindar of the area could do such misadventure.[386] This underlines the importance of Madho Prasad Singh.

Madho Prasad Singh's rebellious activities continued.[387] His Chandipur fortress on the Ghaghra bank was strategically quite important. From there, rebels launched their invasions in Gorakhpur. Therefore, on 17 February 1858, led by Colonel Rowcroft, a Gorkha troop of 1,000 and a Naval Brigade attacked this fortress of Madho Prasad Singh and razed it to the ground. They also got a number of guns here. Their side too suffered harms.[388]

Palwars were pacified after a friendly gesture was adopted towards them in the last part of the rebellion. Madho Prasad Singh's taluqdari was not confiscated either.[389]

Raja Iradat Jehan (Jaunpur)

Raja Iradat Jehan was the zamindar of Mahul. His zamindari sprawled into Jaunpur district as well. He lived in Garhi Mubarakpur. When the rebellion broke out, he received from the Awadh Government the appointment letter of Naib Nazim's post of Jaunpur.[390] At the main gate of his *garhi* (fortress), which had two gates of the entry, had pasted a notice that "all the taluqdars, zamindars and ryots should come to his court as the Awadh Government had appointed him Naib Nazim, and that disobeying the order would not be in the interest of a person".[391] Raja Iradat Jehan also began large scale preparations for his protection from his enemies. He recruited a large number of persons in his army and began to amass arms and weapons. He also began to strengthen the fortification of his *garhi*.[392]

After the Gorkha army reached Jaunpur, the British decided to begin a military campaign against Raja Iradat Jehan. On 27 September midnight, a strong army moved out to attack Raja Iradat Jehan's strong fortress at Garhi Mubarakpur. Reaching there, the army found that Raja Iradat Jehan too was prepared for a war. His residence had been converted into a fort and sepoys had gathered there. They began the battle by shooting upon the advancing army. The Gorkha army immediately brought cannons to the main gate and began using it. After a brief encounters Raja Iradat Jehan and another rebel leader, Fasahat Jehan, were captured.[393]

The letter sent by the Magistrate of Jaunpur to the Commissioner of Banaras gave the following description of this battle: "On Sunday night, at 12 midnight, a force, consisting of 1000 Gorkhas and four guns, left this place, en route to Moobaruckpore (Mubarakpur). The distance by the road we were obliged to take, on an account of having the guns with us, is not less than fifteen or sixteen miles. Rajah Iradat Jehan, talookdar of Moobaruckpore, has, by numerous acts, testified his disaffection to our government and as he was a man of influence and substance, I deemed it expedient to direct my first operations against him. His spirit of dissaffection will be shown in the sequel of this narrative, by his conduct on our near approach to the stronghold of Moobaruckpore. This stronghold is situated in a comparatively open space, being surrounded at some distanced by heavy dock (dhak) jungle. It is encircled by a mud wall and adjoining it a grove of trees, also enclosed. These walls were loop-holed, and we have a every reason to believe, screened armed men. There are two entrances, one from the north and the other from the west; the former is the main entrance and in front of it earthen moorchas (morchas) had been recently thrown up.

Our force marched to the north of Moobaruckpore and then deployed so as to bring the guns opposite to the principal entrance. Sometime before our arrival before the place, the tocsin was heard sounding the alarm to collect the rebels. These we could distinctly see from the distance running in the direction of the stronghold…."[394]

Padma Jang Bahadur Rana, the son of Jang Bahadur Rana, the Prime Minister of Nepal, has also mentioned the capture of Raja Iradat Jehan after a brief encounter and his execution without any unnecessary delay.[395] Robert Taylor has mentioned the death sentence awarded to Iradat Jehan and Fasahat Jehan by a military court.[396] All the property of Raja Iradat Jehan was confiscated.[397]

Next day, the small Adampur fortress of Amar Singh, the Commander of Raja Iradat Jehan, was also attacked and destroyed. He too was done to death.[398] Some writers have described Raja Iradat Jehan as the first martyr of the rebellion of 1857 from Jaunpur.[399]

Makhdoom Bakhsh (Jaunpur)

Makhdoom Bakhsh was a prominent representative of Raja Iradat Jehan, the Naib Nazim of Jaunpur declared by the Government of Awadh. He kept the flame of revolt alive even after his master had been killed. He had around him a group of rebels and was involved in rebellious activities.[400] After destroying Atraula in Jaunpur, Colonel Longden reached Singramau on 22 November 1857, but only to learn that a rebel army was planning attack under the leadership of Raja Muzaffar Jahan of Mahul, Malik Mehdi Bakhsh and other leaders, and that the rebel ranks were growing very fast. (They were 10,000 on 22 November but had grown to 16,000 by 28 November.) Colonel Longden could not muster courage to fight this rebel army and returned to Jaunpur. Encouraged by it, Makhdoom Bakhsh and his troop attacked Tighra (Khutahan) tehsil. Pandit Kishan Narayan was already there to protect the tehsil from the rebels. From the security point of view, he had got the government records and treasury shifted from there. But he could not withstand the attack of Makhdoom Bakhsh's troop and silently escaped to Jaunpur in the night. Makhdoom Bakhsh thus occupied Tighra tehsil on 2 January 1858.[401] His rebellious activities continued further. On 4 January 1858, he attacked the newly built thana of Badlapur.[402] Raja Mahesh Narayan of Raja Bazaar created many obstacles for the rebels in this area. The British Government could not apprehend Makhdoom Bakhsh to the end and had to content itself with the seizure of his property.

Raja Udwant Singh (Bhadohi)

Raja Balwant Singh of Banaras had annexed Bhadohi to his estate in 1748-49. He defeated Raja Jaswant Singh, a Mona Rajput, occupied the fortress of Bhadohi and began to collect revenue through his employees. Subsequently, during the Company Government, half of the Bhadohi estate had been merged in the estate of Raja of Banaras.[403] But the presence of Mona Rajputs in Bhadohi continued. When the fire of revolt spread in 1857, Raja Udwant Singh, chief of the Mona Rajputs, took a very daring step. In the beginning of June 1857, he formed an army by gathering his caste fellows, in order to liberate Bhadohi from the Raja of Banaras who was enjoying life under British protection. He declared himself the "Raja of Bhadohi" and drove the government employees away. He appointed two "Diwans" to run the administration and to collect revenue. Now he began to collect revenue, occupied the government establishments and sent a troop which occupied the Grand Trunk Road. The Company Rule came to a virtual end because of his activities.[404]

This situation was intolerable to the Company Government and the Raja of Banaras. Therefore, led by Chapman, a British troop reached Gopiganj to arrest Raja Udwant Singh. Munshi Darshan Lal, representative of the Raja of Banaras, was also striving hard to get Raja Udwant Singh apprehended. He succeeded, apprehended Raja Udwant Singh by deceit, and handed him over to the British. Raja Udwant Singh was tried and sentenced to death after a brief hearing, and then the British executed him. This execution led to widespread reaction. Mona Rajputs took the path of rebellion to avenge his killing.[405]

Jhoori Singh (Bhadohi)

Jhoori Singh was a Mona Rajput of pargana Bhadohi. He had taken the pledge to avenge the killing of Raja Udwant Singh and formed a strong group. British Magistrate Mr. Muir and Munshi Darshan Lal, Diwan of the Raja of Banaras, were held responsible for the execution of Raja Udwant Singh. Along with the Raja, his Diwans, Ram Bakhsh Singh and Bhola Singh, too had been executed. The wives of all these three persons had forsaken water and food in their village Abhawali and were demanding from their caste fellows that they bring the severed heads of Mr. Muir and Darshan Lal. The wife (rani) of Raja Udwant Singh had announced an award of 300 rupees on Mr. Muir's head.[406]

Along with his associates, Jhoori Singh decided to murder Mr. Muir. When he learnt that Mr. Muir was staying in an indigo factory at Pali, along with his friends, he thought it was a good occasion to murder him. Along with 200 persons who were well armed, Jhoori Singh and Mata Bakhsh Singh surrounded the factory. Mr. Muir, Mr. Jones and one of the latter's relatives were having their food at the time when the crowd suddenly attacked them. Jhoori Singh killed him, got his head severed and sent it to the Rani in Abhawali.[407]

Jhoori Singh, a criminal in the British Government's eyes, now took up the path of rebellion. His activities soon spread to Gopiganj, the border of Allahabad, Jaunpur and the Awadh region. A letter from Jamaadar Zahoor Ali tells us that, after coming from the Awadh Government's area, Jhoori Singh had put up his camp, along with 1,500 persons, in an orchard at a place called Dasmi; which was situated in the ilaqa of Bhameri in pargana

Mongir.[408] On 15 May 1858, Chowkidar Lotan of village Bardoa informed about his appearance in village Sumri in pargana Machhli Shahar of district Jaunpur.[409] He also told that he (Jhoori Singh) was accompanied by 1,000 persons including eight cavaliers, and that all were armed with guns.[410] We have information about his departure from Sumri to Janghai Bazaar in Allahabad, then his stay in village Kisni,[411] his presence on the Allahabad-Lucknow border,[412] his depredation against Saunders' factory at Sumeeho in pargana Badshahpur,[413] the loot of a market in Ghiswa or Machhli Shahar earlier,[414] his departure for Madiyahu and then for Faizabad.[415] We learn that he died a natural death because of cholera in Awadh in July 1858.[416]

Jhoori Singh was the most active and popular hero of his area. Popular memory and popular songs in this area are full of unmixed praise for him.

Thakur Abhilakh Singh (Dobhi, Jaunpur)

Raghuvanshi Rajputs of taluqa Dobhi in Jaunpur district openly challenged the British Government. After the Sikh troop's revolt in Jaunpur, the Europeans had taken shelter in Hingan Lal's house. But when the Rajputs of Dobhi learnt about it, they drove the Europeans away from there.[417] They also obstructed the Banaras-Azamgarh Road. But the troop sent under Mr. Jenkins crushed them. It is said about this campaign that the British called the Rajput leaders of Dobhi to village Senapur for negotiations, but then they encircled the village by deceit and arrested the rebel leaders. Prominent among these leaders was Thakur Abhilakh Singh who belonged to village Barsar. All these persons were sentenced to death after a brief hearing. Thakur Abhilakh Singh, 12 other Raghuvanshi Rajputs and nine followers were then handed to death from various branches of a mango tree. The British officials then left the bodies as they were and went back. A few days later, the villagers took the bodies down and cremated them properly.[418] Along with Thakur Abhilakh Singh, Thakur Bisesar Singh, Thakur Changur Singh, Thakur Dayal Singh, Thakur Devki Singh, Thakur Jai Mangal Singh, Thakur Madho Singh, Thakur Ram Bharose Singh, Thakur Ram Dular Singh, Thakur Singh and Thakur Yaduvir Singh too had been hanged from the tree.[419] But the Rajputs of the area were soon ready to fight again. In July, they started for an attack on Banaras but had to suffer defeat when they were only nine miles away from their destination.[420]

Meghar Singh or Mengar Singh (Gahmar, Ghazipur)

Meghar Singh or Mengar Singh, who belonged to village Gahmar in pargana Zamania of Ghazipur district, was an important rebel leader. From the statement which he made in the court of William Ordros, the Special Magistrate of Banaras, on 27 November 1860, we learn that "his name was Mengar Singh, he was a Kshatriya by caste, and his father's name was Bhajan Singh. He was a zamindar and numberdar by occupation."[421] According to him, "in the month of Jeth-Baisakh (June) in the second year (1858) of the rebellion, in village Biranji on the Karmanasa river's bank, three *kos* from Gahmar, people of a large number of villages gathered and discussed the rumour that, because of rebellious activities, the British Government was going to burn down six villages, namely, Sherpur, Reotipur, Barha, Gahmar, Ausiya and Khareba, to ashes. Some persons were deputed to find the truth of this rumour, and they informed that only the six said villages would be burnt down. Thereafter, through two or three leading persons of this area, ten to twelve thousand persons were collected in an orchard of Deval village in pargana Zamania, to decide about protection. It was decided there that help should be sought from Babu Amar Singh of Jagdishpur in Shahabad district. "The people sent Lodhi Singh and Mengar Singh together with the eight other persons to Amar Singh with Rs 2000 as '*Nazrana*'. Lodhi Singh fell ill and died on the way. Mengar Singh alone reached the place and handed over the Nazrana and told Amar Singh about the state of affairs. Amar Singh then ordered 500 Tilangas to go with him for help. Mengar Singh then informed those who had sent him that he would be there after five days. They sent reply asking him to reach there immediately with the Tilangas". [422] Fifteen days later, Mengar Singh reached village Kharha in pargana Chausa of Shahabad district, where villagers were staying. Now, they began the plundering and looted the bungalow and godown of the Indigo factory with a body of few hundred men.[423]

Five days later, Amar Singh reached there with a contingent of 15 to 20 thousand, foot soldiers and cavalrymen. Rs 25,000 were collected from the zamindars and traders of pargana Chausa, Zamania, Chainpur, Mhanj and Narwan, and offered to Amar Singh as revenue and *nazrana*. Amar Singh stayed there for five days.[424] But when the British army reached there, Harkishan Singh, the bailiff of Amar Singh, quit the place in the night, along with the troop, and only two sepoys were left with Amar Singh. In the morning, Amar Singh too left for Jagdishpur via the south of Gahmar, while the British army reached Gahmar from the east side.[425]

Along with 500 persons, Mengar Singh then went to village Dewal, four *kos* from there. There, some persons decided to surrender to the government. But Mengar Singh was already a notorious figure in the government's eyes because of his activities. He decided not to surrender. With about 500 Tilangas and 10 to 12 thousand men of zamindars and dignitaries, he stayed in village Khairai for three months. The people of those parganas bore his expenses. However, after the British army reached there, all the men quit the place except the 500 Tilangas sent by Amar Singh. After their defeat, they also fled towards south. Mengar Singh remained with them.[426] He spent a lot of time in Bihar and bought grains from here and there to survive. When no safe place remained in Bihar for protection, they crossed the Ganga and sneaked into Nepal, and joined the forces of Begum Hazrat Mahal, Raja Devi Bakhsh, Raja Beni Madho and other rebels.[427] He had those 500 Tilangas. After his return from Nepal, Mengar Singh remained in hiding here and there for eight months and then surrendered. The British Government had already announced an award of three or six thousand rupees for his arrest dead or alive. His property was also confiscated by the Government.[428]

According to Mengar Singh, about seventy thousand tilangas (sepoys) and other rebels had died in the Gorakhpur territory.[429] This shows the severity and horror of the revolt in Eastern Uttar Pradesh.

Government records tell us about the rebellious activities and leadership qualities of Mengar Singh. According the letter dated 30 May 1858 of Darogha Fazal Khan of thana Dildar Nagar in pargana Bara, Mengar Singh had joined Amar Singh as his ally and told him that he would get all the men of pargana Rhat to rise against the British if he gets adequate help. The letter also informs us that, he got the assistance and he had a troop of 250 to 300 armed men, that a large number of sepoys in Gahmar and Bara had come to join him and had decided to stay in these parganas in order to motivate the public against the British Government. Some people even said that they would be coming to fight against the British.[430]

In yet another letter dated 4 June 1858, a police officer informed about the presence of 500 rebels and also that five strong bungalows had been burnt down to ashes, a night before, on the other side of Karmanasa river. He also said the rebels had gone to burn down thana Chausa and had also decided to go via Oosia and attack the tehsil building. He said Mengar Singh, a zamindar of Gahmar, was their leader, and that other zamindars of Gahmar had also joined him.[431] A letter dated 7 June 1858 tells us that a troop of 400 rebel sepoys, led by Mengar Singh, had burnt down thana Chausa, an indigo godown and a bungalow.[432] From another letter, we learn about the villagers cooperating with Mengar Singh.[433]

Mengar Singh had, in fact, become quite important for the British Government. His activities took place in Bihar also. Hence the government had decided not to grant him clemency. The Commissioner of Patna wrote a letter to the Secretary of the Bengal Government on 23 September 1859 to request that Amar Singh, Harkishan Singh, Jyodhar Singh, Mengar Singh, Sidha Singh, Shiv Prasanna Singh and Devi Ojha should not be granted any clemency.[434]

Mengar Singh surrendered himself. After his surrender, according to the records preserved in the Regional Archives at Allahabad, the British Government tried him for two crimes — one, of leading the revolt and waging a war against the government's army, and, two, of destroying the indigo godown at Gahmar. On 21 January 1861, Mengar Singh was awarded 14 years of imprisonment and transportation for life. He was sent to Port Blair on 2 March. However, a part of his sentence was remitted because of his good conduct and he was released on 22 July 1871. The government had already confiscated his zamindari and his house; now the villages populated by him were also destroyed.[435] He passed his life in hardships and finally got his natural death. Writing Mengar Singh as Makar Singh, Syed Ahmad Ali Shah acknowledged his importance as a rebel by linking him with Sada Singh (Sidha Singh) of Ballia in the rebellion. He wrote:

Makar Singh bhi ek tha bavaqaar
Hue baaghi yeh dono bhi naabkaar.
[One Makar Singh too, who was dignified
Both these malicious ones also became rebels][436]

Bharat Rai (Ghazipur)

Bharat Rai was the zamindar of village Hasanpura, in pargana Zahoorabad of district Ghazipur. He displayed his leadership potential by collecting about 3,000 persons and making an attempt to occupy the tehsil. However, he did not succeed because of the arrival of the British army (musketeers accompanying the tehsildar).[437]

Sada Singh (Seedha Singh)

Among the important rebels of Ballia which was part of Ghazipur district at the time of rebellion of 1857, Syed Ahmad Ali Shah has mentioned only Sada Singh. He wrote:

Sada Singh Zamindaar Ballia suna
Bada naamwar aur purzoor tha
Makar Singh bhi ek tha bavaqaar
Hue baaghi yeh dono bhi naabkaar
[Heard of Sada Singh, the zamindar of Ballia

Was very well renowned and powerful
[One Makar Singh, who was dignified
Both these malicious ones also became rebels][438]

But British records mention Seedha Singh as a dreaded rebel of pargana Ballia in Ghazipur district. For him, the Commissioner of Patna had written a letter to the Secretary of the Government of India, requesting that he should not be granted clemency.[439]

The narrative of events taking place in Azamgarh district, during the week ending 14 August 1858, named as Siddha Singh the person who led the rebel troop occupying the Ghosi tehsil and attacking Bibipur thana. His group consisted of 800 rebel sepoys, 400 cavaliers and 800 commoner rebels. There were also some women and children.[440] The number illustrates the extent of Seedha Singh's influence.

Seedha Singh continued his rebellious activities in association with Amar Singh, a rebel leader of Jagdishpur. A letter dated 19 June 1858 said Seedha Singh had crossed the Ganga river about a fortnight back and had been plundering Ghazipur and Doaba, and had been talking that he and his troop would go back to Shahabad to join hands with Amar Singh.[441] Even after the revolt had been crushed, Seedha Singh continued to roam in Palamu and Shahabad in Bihar, in Ghazipur and Nepal.[442] According to British officials, he continued to receive support from common people including the Nepalese.[443] There is mention of Seedha Singh entering Palamu along with 1,100 rebels on 30 November 1858, and fighting against Captain Davis there.[444] There is no information about the last days of Seedha Singh.

Jyodhar Singh (Ballia)

Jyodhar Singh[445] of pargana Ballia in Ghazipur district also played an important role in the rebellion. Joining hands with Kunwar Singh, his group intensified the rebellious activities.[446] According to government records, he caused a great deal of damage in the vicinity of Masariganj.[447] There is a mention of the presence of Jyodhar Singh, along with 900 rebels, in Palamu in November 1858.[448] The Patna Commissioner's list of rebel leaders not deserving clemency included Jyodhar Singh's name.[449] This shows his importance.

Any narration of rebel leaders would appear incomplete without a mention of Maulvi Ali Kareem of Patna, Babu Kunwar Singh and Amar Singh of Jagdishpur, Mehdi Hasan, an official of the rebel government of Awadh and Raja Devi Baksh Singh of Gonda. They should be included in the list of the heroes who came to Eastern Uttar Pradesh from outside, gave momentum to rebellious activities here and presented a serious challenge to the British. In this list, the name of Rani Ishwari Devi of Tulsipur should also be included. Though she did not come in the region but supported the rebels of the area. Here follows a brief description of these rebels:

Maulvi Ali Kareem (Patna)

Maulvi Ali Kareem was the zamindar of village Dausi near Patna. He was striving to create an organisation for revolt against the British rule. He was a talented organiser.[450] When a person called Waris Ali was arrested on 23 June 1857 for involvement in rebellious activities, he was writing a letter to Maulvi Ali Kareem. The letter remained incomplete.[451] It was from this incomplete letter, the British Government came to know about Maulvi Ali Kareem as a person involved in rebellion. Then he escaped to Patna and went underground. The Nazir of the Criminal Court in Patna gave him shelter. Learning about it, Commissioner Taylor got him arrested, but he managed to escape from Patna and came to Gorakhpur.[452] The British Government confiscated his property and announced an award of two thousand rupees to anyone producing him alive or dead; the award was later raised to five thousand rupees.[453] Maulvi Ali Kareem was, along with his followers, seen fighting against the British army at Sohanpur, which was situated between Mairwa (Bihar) and Salempur (Gorakhpur).[454] Harkishan Singh, the nephew of Babu Kunwar Singh, also fought in this battle. After their defeat, Maulvi Ali Kareem went to Tanda via Gorakhpur. Active in the Tanda area along with his followers (Bhojpuri sepoys), Maulvi Ali Kareem remained a headache to the British Government.[455] He remained in constant touch with Amar Singh and, staying at Kartarpur eight miles to the west of Tanda, he waited for a favourable turn of tide.[456] He was facing difficulties in meeting the expenses of his group and his sepoys wanted to return home. Despite all this, Maulvi Ali Kareem did not surrender to the British.

Babu Kunwar Singh (Jagdishpur, Arrah)

Babu Kunwar Singh of Jagdishpur made an important contribution in stoking the flames of rebellion in Azamgarh district of Eastern Uttar Pradesh. Dividing the rebellion in Azamgarh district into three phases, a writer of modern history considered Kunwar Singh's arrival in Azamgarh as the beginning of the second phase; this was when he reached Atraulia with 6,000 sepoys.[457] He stayed in the district for about 35 days and then, defeated by British army, left for Ghazipur. His military successes in Azamgarh had caused anxiety even to the Governor General, Lord Canning, who was then camping in Allahabad. In view of the severity of the battle, he had then dispatched a big contingent under Mark Kerr of the Crimea War fame and one who was experienced in Indian wars. Besides, a powerful contingent, led by Colonel Lugard, also came from Lucknow. But, through his tactic, Kunwar Singh foiled the British army's moves, crossed the Ganga river with the people's cooperation, and reached Jagdishpur safely.[458] Babu Kunwar Singh's struggle had sent a new wave of ardour among the people of the area. This led to an expansion in the area of the rebellion.

Babu Amar Singh

Babu Amar Singh played a major role in continuation of rebellious activities along the eastern border of the Uttar Pradesh, from Ghazipur to Banaras. Born in 1782, he was the youngest brother of Babu Kunwar Singh. He had come to Ghazipur to help the rebels with his army. In his confession, rebel leader Mengar Singh had acknowledged Amar Singh's help. The writer of *Kashful Baghaavat, Gorakhpur* held Amar Singh responsible for the revolt in Ghazipur which was otherwise a peaceful district. He took the reins of revolt after the demise of Kunwar Singh, his elder brother, and harassed the British for a long time through his guerrilla tactics. Frederich Engels too praised his guerrilla tactics in his article "Mutiny in India," published in *New York Daily Tribune* on 1 October 1858. After Nana Saheb of Kanpur took refuge in Nepal, Amar Singh also reached there with his associates. But Gorkha soldiers of Maharaja Jang Bahadur arrested him in mid-November 1858 and handed him over to the British. He was lodged in Gorakhpur Jail for some time. Bengal Government wanted to try him in his home district. But he developed dysentery on 3 January 1860 and was admitted to the jail hospital in Gorakhpur where he died on 5 February 1860.[459]

Mehdi Hasan (Nazim of Sultanpur)

Mehdi Hasan was the Nazim of Sultanpur, appointed by the rebel government of Awadh.[460] He has been described as a nice, tall and bulky person who played a notable role in anti-British battles.[461] His headquarter was in Hasanpur and he had the support of many taluqdars of Faizabad and Sultanpur.[462] His area of influence spread from Sultanpur to Allahabad, and he had 1,500 men.[463] Colonel Wroughton led a military campaign against him on 31st October 1857. A severe battle was fought at Chanda. According to Colonel Malleson, rebels were defeated, while Mehdi Hasan's version was that he had driven the British army towards Jaunpur.[464] Mehdi Hasan maintained constant pressure on Jaunpur. In February 1858, he had to fight at Chanda again, against General Frank, and Mehdi Hasan had to retreat.[465] He created a powerful, albeit unsuccessful, obstruction against the Lucknow campaign of General Frank and Gorkha army.[466] Yet he still maintained constant pressure on the western borders of Azamgarh and Jaunpur.[467] As a result the British could never feel secure about the western borders of these districts. Finally, after his failure to get Awadh liberated, Mehdi Hasan surrendered along with Ghulam Hussain son of Mohammed Hasan and was compelled to live the rest of his life in Sitapur district, at an annual pension of 200 rupees from the British Government.[468]

Raja Devi Bakhsh Singh (Gonda)

The name of Raja Devi Bakhsh Singh of Gonda is notable for strengthening the rebellious activities on the western border of Gorakhpur district. Raja Devi Bakhsh Singh faced the Gorkha army at Belwa on the Ghaghra bank and forced the Gorkhas to run towards Tanda. He joined hands with Mohammed Hasan, the Raja of Charda and Mehdi Hasan, and raised a big army of 4,000 sepoys, 10,000 irregular sepoys, 300 cavaliers and 9 cannons, to fight the British. He faced Colonel Rowcroft's army at Amorha, which was nine miles from the Belwa Ghat. Though he was defeated in the battle against Rowcroft and the Gorkhas, he maintained constant vigil on the ghats of Ghaghra. In the end, unsuccessful, he went to join Begum Hazrat Mahal in the Nepal *terai* along with 8,000 men and breathed his last there. The British Government confiscated his zamindari.[469]

Rani Ishwari Devi (Rani of Tulsipur)

Rani Ishwari Devi Singh of Tulsipur, also played an important role in the rebellion. This estate, Tulsipur was situated on the north-western border of Eastern Uttar Pradesh. Her husband, Raja Drig Narayan Singh, had died as prisoner in the Residency at Lucknow and she had herself assumed the management of the estate. She took up arms against the British Government during the revolt and sheltered the rebels. She also provided shelter to the absconding soldiers of the 73rd NI and 11th Irregular Cavalry. Besides, the Rani had 4,000 paid rebel soldiers. Joining hands with the fragmented armies of Bala Rao Marhatta, Begum Hazrat Mahal, Raja Devi Bakhsh Singh of Gonda and Mohammed Hasan, the Nazim of Gorakhpur, she put up the last and unsuccessful resistance in the hills. Even after she was driven into the Nepal borders along with the aforesaid persons, she refused to believe the clemency announced by the British Government and did not surrender to the latter. Therefore, the government confiscated her estate and handed it over to the Maharaja of Balrampur as a reward. Rani Ishwari Devi remained a source of shelter and of inspiration for the rebels during the rebellion.[470]

The foregoing narrative does not mention a large number of heroes who raised the voice of revolt against the British government, and whom the British government awarded capital punishment or whom the government could not trace till the last. Their list is not small either. But it is impossible to highlight their roles for want of records and information. Even then, the above description of the heroes of Eastern Uttar Pradesh on the basis of records is enough to demonstrate that people rose above the parochial casteist, communal and regional feelings in order to make serious efforts in 1857 to end the Company Government in the territory.

Notes and References

1. From C. Wingfield, the Commissioner of Goruckpore to William Muir, Secretary to Government, North Western Provinces, 5 July 1858, No. 196 of 1858; Narrative of Events Attending the Outbreak of Disturbances and the Restoration of the Authority in the District of Goruckpore in 1857-58; para 18, p. 3, copy preserved in Regional Archives, Allahabad (now onwards referred to as Wingfield C. Narrative, July 1858); Syed Athar Abbas Rizvi, *Freedom Struggle in Uttar Pradesh* (here to fore as *FSUP*), Vol. IV, p. 152.
2. *FSUP*, Vol. IV, pp. 294, 372-73; *Proceedings of the Indian History Congress*, 69th session, Kannur, 2008, published from Kolkata, 2009, p. 492.
3. *FSUP*, Vol. IV, pp. 244-46; Taylor, Robert, *The Rebellion of 1857 in the Province of Benares*, 15 October 1858, Jaunpur, para 68, p. 20.
4. *FSUP*, Vol. IV, pp. 244-45. According to Robert Taylor, Beni Madho had assumed the title of Naib Nazim. See, *op.cit*, para 43, p. 14.
5. *FSUP*, Vol. IV, pp. 436-38, 444-46, 447-48, 450-51, 457-63; Datta, K K, History of Freedom movement in Bihar, Vol. I (1857-1928), published by Government of Bihar (1957), pp. 47-50. The pro-British Syed Ahmad Ali Shah wrote only this much about Kunwar Singh —

   "Kunwar Singh Babu tha Jagdishpur,
   Hua dur uske bhi chehre ka noor.
   Muqabil na sarkaar se ho saka
   Toh Dilli ka usne bhi rasta liya."
   [Kunwar Singh was the Babu of Jagdishpur
   His face also lost its radiance
   He could not confront the government
   So, he too took the route to Delhi]
   See, *Kashful-Baghaavat, Gorakhpur*, stanza 262-63, pp. 41-42.

6. *FSUP*, Vol. IV, pp. 481-85, 494; Datta, K K, *op.cit*, pp. 58-59. About Amar Singh, Syed Ahmad Ali Shah says that he organised the rebellion in Ghazipur. He wrote —-

 "Ghazipur ab tak bahut saaf tha
 Ke hai tazkirah uska bhi upar likha.
 Vale June mein woh bhi baaghi hua
 Amar Singh ke haanth daaghi hua.
 Jo aaya woh mardak mile wahaan ke log
 Kam aqlee se apni khareeda yeh rog."
 [Uptill now Ghazipur was very clean
 In fact, its accounts have been written above
 But in June it also became mutinous
 It was soiled by the hands of Amar Singh.
 When that mean fellow came, people of that place joined him,
 By their foolishness, they bought and nursed this illness].
 Kashful-Baghaavat, *Gorakhpur,* Stanza no. 1664-66, p. 256.

7. *FSUP*, Vol. IV, pp. 299, 310, 312, 315. Syed Ahmad Ali Shah has described Harkishan Singh's activities in detail. Coming back from Delhi, he fought against the (pro-British) Raja of Gopalpur but could not subdue him. Fleeing from there, he fought against the British at Sohanpur and was defeated. Then he came to Gorakhpur and stayed there for several days. He met the Nazim (Mohammed Hasan) and showed his willingness to fight against the Gorkhas. Mohammed Hasan provided him two cannons, then he fought at Shahbazganj (Gorakhpur) but got defeated. After his defeat, he ran to Lucknow and then never faced the British. Shah wrote —

 "Bhatija jo uska tha ek Harkishan
 Khasumat ki uske hui dil mein daman.
 Gaya apne kaka ke humraah woh
 Ab aage ka ahwaal jo ho so ho."
 [One Harkishan who was Kunwar Singh's nephew
 A detritus of antagonism grew in his heart,
 He went along with his uncle
 Now whatever shape circumstances may take, let them take]
 — *Kashful-Baghaavat*, *Gorakhpur*, stanza 264-65, p. 42.

 *****

 "Phira jab ke Dehli se woh Harkishan
 Giraftaar-e-iza-o-ranj-o-mehan
 Lada Raja se su-e-Gopalpur
 Gaya pesh jab uska us se na zoor.
 Toh bhaaga wahaan se bhi misl-e -Shuaal
 Sohanpur mein ja lada badkhisaal,
 Kiya qasad ladne ka haakim se jab

Tamaache lage ghaib se munh pe tab.
Wahaan se bhi bhaaga hazeemat kashaan
Kushadah dahaan khaakash andar dahaan.
Gorakhpur mein aaya bhaaga hua.
Kai rooz tak yahaan pe sakin raha.
Woh masnui Nazim se jaa kar mila
Ladaai ka dil mein iraadah kiya
Chala ladne English se woh naabkaar
Dil-e-murda ba haal zaar-o-nizaar
Diya toop Zalim ne phir do adad
Gaya ladne haakim se woh bekhirad
Qaza le chali su-e Shahbazganj
Mila wahaan pe usko har ek tarha ranj
Kiya wahaan se bhi aakhir usne faraar
Raha ek dum bhi na usko qaraar
Jo bhaaga toh pahuncha woh ja Lucknow
Hua phir na hukkam se ru-ba ru.

— *Op.cit*, stanza 1386-97, pp. 211-12.

Syed Ahmed Ali Shah had very little knowledge about his activities or he intentionally did not mention them. After his defeat in Gorakhpur, Harkishan Singh joined his Uncle, Kunwar Singh at Ayodhya. He was in command of the Bihar rebel forces during their campaign in Azamgarh and also was with Kunwar Singh at the time of their crossing the Ganges at Sheopur Ghat. After the death of Kunwar Singh, he was the leading man and had on the defeat of Le Grand and re-occupation of Jagdishpur in April 1858. Harkishan Singh helped Amar Singh in re-establishing their Government which appears to have lasted for over four months. He was apprehended at Mauza Dineah in pargana Badhowal of district Banaras on 29th August 1859 and after trial executed in December 1859. See; Datta K.K., Biography of Kunwar Singh and Amar Singh (K.P. Jaiswal Research Institute, Patna 1957), pp. 98-100, 196-197. As for the British records, Colonel Rowcroft's letter dated 20 December 1857 informs us about Harkishan Singh's battle against the British at Sohanpur. See, *FSUP*, Vol. IV, p. 299; Wingfield C. Narrative 5 July 1858, para 43-45, p. 6.

8. Home Department, Public, June 1858; William Fort, Proceedings, 11 June 1858, No. 97, p. 53, Deposition of Uchhraj Singh, (preserved in National Archives of India, New Delhi).
9. Along with his followers, Maulvi Ali Kareem of Patna joined the battle against the combined forces of the British and Gorkhas at village Sohanpur, situated between Majhauli and Mairwa. There was also a rumour about his death in the battle. But he was alive and at Tanda, along with his 600 soldiers, waited for a favourable situation. He was in regular touch with Amar Singh. See, *FSUP*, Vol. IV, pp. 205, 299; Datta, K K, *op.cit*, pp. 20-21, 52.
10. *FSUP*, Vol. IV, pp. 360-61, 363, 367-69, 370. In *Kashful-Baghaavat*, *Gorakhpur*, Syed Ahmad Ali Shah described the rebels' defeat at the hands of the British

army at Tulsipur, saying that all except Mohammed Hasan and Bala Rao were scattered here and there. He wrote —

Mohammad Hasan aur Bala Rao

Siwa unke sab chal diye zaar -e- jaye

See, *Kashful-Baghaavat*, *Gorakhpur*, stanze, 1885, p. 290.

11. *FSUP*, Vol. IV, pp. 345, 347, 350. Also See, the correspondence between the then Nepal Residency and Maharaja Jang Bahadur Rana about Damman Khan. Foreign Department, 31 December 1858, Foreign Consultation, File No. 2086-88 and 11 March 1859, File No. 375-77, preserved in National Archives of India, New Delhi. The record also mentions Jaikishanpuri.
12. *FSUP*, Vol. IV, p. 336. On behalf of Awadh, many rebels like Ashraf Bakhsh Khan and Jawahar Khan were holding control over Domriaganj and other border posts. See, *ibid*, pp. 348, 362, 363-64. Ashraf Bakhsh Khan was the Sardar of Burhapara and, along with the Nazim of Gorakhpur, had launched a campaign against the British. See, Carnegy, P, *A Gazetteer of Awadh* (*A to Z*), reprint: Delhi, 2006, p. 547.
13. *Ibid*, pp. 313, 345, 349, 350, 359, 361, 365. Syed Ahmad Ali Shah has mentioned the Raja of Gonda's defeat. See, *Kashful-Baghaavat*, *Gorakhpur*, stanza 1875-77, p. 288.
14. *FSUP*, Vol. IV, pp. 202, 221-24, 271-72, 361.
15. *Ibid*, pp. 219, 223; Taylor, Robert, *op.cit*, para 72, p. 21.
16. *FSUP*, Vol. IV, pp. 295-96, 321, 337, 340, 353, 354.
17. *Ibid*, p. 247. Maulvi Sarfaraz Ali played an important role during the rebellion at Shahjehanpur, Bareilly and Delhi. See, the details about Maulvi Sarfaraz Ali in Chapter III. Similarly, Pir Ali Khan of Patna was said to hail from Mohammedpur in Azamgarh district. See, Khan, K M S, *Excavations of Truth (Unsung Heroes of 1857 War of Independence): Role of Muslims, Fanatical and Nationalist*, edited by Khan Ahmad Adeel, New Delhi: Kanishka Publishers, 2007, pp. 18, 26. The allies of Pir Ali Khan included Maulvi Ali Kareem who was the rich zamindar of Dausi. See, *ibid*, p. 32.
18. Syed Ahmad Ali Shah, *op.cit*, stanza 1513-17, p. 230. Farhat Nasreen's English rendering of stanza 1516 is defective.
19. Wingfield C. Narrative July 1858, para 38, p. 5; Letter from Colonel Rowcroft to the Secretary ...... Camp Majhauli on the River of Chhoti Gandak, dated 28 December 1857; *FSUP*, Vol. IV, p. 299.
20. Syed Ahmad Ali Shah, *op.cit*, stanza 557-61, 569 -72, 575-83, pp. 89-92.
21. *Ibid*, stanza 592-603, pp. 92-94.
22. Haq, Syed Moinul, *The Great Revolution of 1857*, Karachi, 1968, p. 454 FN 3, p. 455; Hasan, Moinuddin, *Khadang-e-Ghadar*, English translation, p. 90; Haider, Kamaluddin, *Qaisar-ut-Tawarikh*, Vol. 2, p. 304.
23. Syed Ahmad Ali Shah, *op.cit*, stanza 604, p. 94.
24. *Ibid*, stanza 605, p. 94.
25. *Ibid*, stanza 607, p. 94.
26. *Ibid*, stanza 1470-80, pp. 223-24. Tehsildar Haider Husain had devastated the area of Brajmanganj. See, Stanza 1481-82.

27. *Ibid*, stanza 1498, 1501, 1502, 1505, 1506, 1509, pp. 228-29.
28. *Ibid*, stanza 268-69, p. 43.
29. *Ibid*, stanza 444, p. 70.
30. *Ibid*, stanza 1249, p. 191.
31. *Ibid*, stanza 1929, p. 299.
32. Wingfield C. Narrative, 8 July 1858, para 38, p. 5, *FSUP*, Vol. IV, pp. 318, 350-51, 372.
33. *Kashful-Baghaavat, Gorakhpur*, *op.cit*, stanza 232, p. 37.
34. *Ibid*, stanza 236, p. 37.
35. *Ibid*, stanza 468, p. 74.
36. *Ibid*, stanza 469, p. 74
37. *Ibid*, stanza 470, p. 74
38. *Ibid*, stanza 1507, p. 229.
39. Wingfield C. Narrative, 5 July 1858, para 38, p. 5.
40. *Ibid*, para 22, p. 3. The babu of Bakhira was called Ram Pratap Singh. On 10 August 1857, he had beaten the Bakhira thana policemen and driven them away.
41. *FSUP*, Vol. IV, p. 319.
42. *Ibid*, p. 383.
43. *Kashful-Baghaavat, Gorakhpur*, *op.cit*, stanza 1248, p. 191. According to Mengar Singh, Tolia was situated about 20 *kos* from the Nepal Territory (Border). See, *FSUP*, Vol. IV, p. 287.
44. *FSUP*, Vol. IV, p. 350; Narrative of Events for Gorakhpur for the week Ending 8 August 1858.
45. Foreign Department, Political – A, Proceedings, October 1867, No. 21; From Colonel G Ramsay, Resident at Nepal, to the Secretary to the Government of India, in the Foreign Department, with the Governor General, Simla, No. 28, Dated 10 September 1867, preserved in National Archives of India, New Delhi.
46. *FSUP*, Vol. IV, pp. 21-22. 85-90; *Kashful-Baghaavat, Gorakhpur*, *op.cit*, stanza 113-15, p. 18, stanza 162-67, p. 25.
47. Wingfield C. Narrative, 8 July 1858, para 18, p. 3.
48. *Ibid*, para 13, p. 2.
49. *FSUP*, Vol. IV, p. 397.
50. *Ibid*, pp. 306, 348, 357, 369.
51. *Ibid*, pp. 369-70, 380.
52. *Kashful-Baghaavat, Gorakhpur*, *op.cit*, stanza 142, p. 22.
53. Taylor, Robert, *op.cit*, para 41-48, 62-63, 79, pp. 11-15, 19, 20, 22.
54. *Kashful-Baghaavat, Gorakhpur*, *op.cit*, stanza 1668, p. 256.
55. *Ibid*, stanza 1669, p. 257. The real name of Makar Singh was Mengar Singh or Magahar Singh and he was the zamindar of Gahmar village in Ghazipur. The British Government had announced a reward on his arrest.
56. Taylor, Robert, *The Rebellion of 1857 in the Province of Benares;* See, the complete narrative.

57. Oldham, Wilton, *Tenant Rights and Auction Sales in Ghazeepoor and the Province of Benares*, p. 6.
58. *FSUP*, Vol. IV, p. 174.
59. *Ibid*, p. 216.
60. *Ibid*, p. 210.
61. *Ibid*, p. 217. There was a mention of Raja Jai Lal Singh fighting against the Gorkha army at Azamgarh and his defeat. See, *Kashful-Baghaavat, Gorakhpur,* stanza 504-505, p. 79.
62. *FSUP*, pp. 226-27.
63. *Ibid*, p. 230.
64. *Ibid*, pp. 236-37.
65. *Ibid*, p. 266.
66. *Ibid*, pp. 144, 342.
67. Hasan, Moinuddin, *Khadang-e-Ghadar*, Hindi translation, Delhi, reprint: 2006. The translator has inadvertently written "Bahra" for "Barha."
68. Haider, Kamaluddin, *Qaiser-ut-Tawarikh*, Vol. 2, Lucknow, 1879, p. 302. It was republished from Nawal Kishore Press, Lucknow in 1896.
69. *FSUP*, Vol. IV, p. 294 FN 1, Mohomed Husein Khan (Mohd. Hasan Khan) is mentioned on page 371.
70. Badayuni, Maulvi Mohammed Suleman, A Note on Little Known Fighters in the War of Independence, 1857-58, *Journal of Pakistan Historical Society*, Karachi, Vol. V, Part II, 1957-58, p. 125; Haq, Syed Moinul, *The Great Revolution of 1857*, *op.cit*, p. 454.
71. *Ibid.*
72. *Ibid*, pp. 125-26; Haider, Kamaluddin, *op.cit*, p. 305; *FSUP*, Vol. IV, p. 294.
73. Badayuni, *op.cit*, p. 126; Haider, Kamaluddin, *op.cit*, p. 305; *FSUP*, Vol. IV, p. 372.
74. Syed Ahmad Ali Shah wrote —

    "Hilaal-e-Moharram ki yeh baat hai
    Chehattar the Hijri ke sun barah she.
    Ke makkar ek shaks aayaa yahaan
    Woh Nazim na tha afsar-e-dakuaan.
    Bazaahir woh Nazim yahaan aa bana
    Haqiqat mein jaali-o-masnui tha.

    (Evidently by usurpation he became Nazim here. In reality he was fake and false.)

    In other words, he did not regard him as the Nazim but as an officer of dacoits, fake and false. See, *Kashful-Baghaavat, Gorakhpur*, *op.cit*, stanza 540-41, 547, pp. 86-87. The descriptions given by Moinuddin Hasan and Kamaluddin Haider, too, give the impression that he utilised the opportunity to capture Gorakhpur by force. See, *Khadang-e-Ghadar*, *op.cit,* pp. 73-74; *Qaiser-ut-Tawarikh*, Vol. 2, pp. 302, 304. Moinul Haq also wrote that he declared himself the Nazim. See, *The Great Revolution of 1857*, *op.cit*, p. 454.

75. *FSUP*, Vol. IV, pp. 371-72. Kamaluddin Haider, too, mentions that Mohammed Hasan saved Colonel Lennox and his family. See, *Qaiser-ut-Tawarikh*, Vol. 2, pp. 303-04. On the charge of looting the property of Colonel Lennox at Dalpatpur Ghat, Mr. Burton, the Special Commissioner of Gorakhpur, had sentenced, on 19 February 1858, Raghubir Singh Rajput, the *pattidar* of village Darauli in pargana Amorha, to death along with the seizure of his property. See, Pre-Mutiny Records, Gorakhpur Collectorate, List 14, Vol. 177, Bag 27, number illegible, preserved in Regional Archives, Allahabad.
76. *Ibid*, p. 372.
77. *Ibid.*
78. *FSUP*, Vol. IV, pp. 153-54, 373; Haider, Kamaluddin, *op.cit*, p. 304; Badayuni, *op.cit*, p. 126. Mohammed Hasan made his first appearance in Khalilabad.
79. Wingfield C. Narrative, Gorakhpur, 8 July 1858, para 23-25, 29-30, p. 4; *Kashful-Baghaavat, Gorakhpur*, story of Gagaha, stanza 488-503, pp. 77-79.
80. Wingfield C. Narrative, Gorakhpur, 8 July 1858, para 34, p. 5.
81. Wingfield C. Narrative, *op.cit*, para 36, 37 and 38, p. 55; *FSUP*, Vol. V, pp. 156-57. Syed Ahmad Ali Shah, too, mentioned the donning of a robe of honour. See, *Kashful-Baghaavat*, *Gorakhpur*, *op.cit*, stanza 1247-49, pp. 191.
82. Hasan, Moinuddin, *Khadang-e-Ghadar*, p. 137; English translation by H.A. Qureshi, Lucknow, 2007, p. 90. He writes: Here were weavers and carders, there the cobblers.
83. *Qaiser-ut-Tawarikh*, Vol. 2, pp. 304-05.
84. Haq, Syed Moinul, *op.cit*, p. 454 FN 3. The memorandum by Khudabakhsh Khan, too, said that the Nazim's army had five or six thousand people. See, *FSUP*, Vol. IV, p. 385.
85. *FSUP*, Vol. IV, p. 373. Going by the dates, Mohammed Hasan's contention is incorrect. He entered Gorakhpur town as Nazim on 21 August 1857 and left Gorakhpur for Tanda on 6 January 1858 after his defeat by the Gorkha army of Maharaja Jang Bahadur Rana. This comes to about four and a half months. Syed Ahmad Ali Shah, too, said that four months and twenty days were troublesome. See, *Kashful Baghaavat,* Gorakhpur, Stanza 1746, p. 267.
86. Wingfield C. Narrative, *op.cit*, para 40, p. 5.
87. *FSUP*, Vol. IV, petition by Khuda Bakhsh, pp. 384-85; Atkinson, E.T. *Statistical, Descriptive and Historical Accounts of North Western Provinces*, Vol. VI, Part II, Gorakhpur: Government Press, Allahabad, (1881), p. 457.
88. *Khadang-e-Ghadar*, Hindi translation, *op.cit*, p. 74.
89. *Qaiser-ut-Tawarikh*, Vol. 2, pp. 305-06.
90. Under the title "Tashreeh-e-Asbaab," Syed Ahmad Ali Shah has given a detailed description of the things that had been looted from the Imambara of Gorakhpur, of which he was the caretaker. See, *Kashful-Baghaavat*, *Gorakhpur*, stanza 922-72, pp. 142-46. About the moneylenders of Pipraich being looted, he wrote —

    "Mahajan jo ilaaqah ke mere rahe
    Woh becharah na haq pe loote gaye"

[The mahajan was from my region
Helpless, he was unjustly looted]

— *Ibid*, stanza 988, p. 151.

Similarly, he described the vandalism at Mohiuddinpur in stanza 989-1000, pp. 152-53. About the plunder of the kothi of Kusamhi, he wrote —

"Luta jo ke Kosamhi se asbaab-o-maal,
Woh, ghaaratgaraan honge sab paimaal.
[Those who looted property and money from kosamhi,
All these plunderers shall be ruined]

— *Ibid*, stanza 1448, p. 220

About the vandalism against the well-wishers of the British government, he wrote —

Kiya usne taaraaj har ek ko
Na chhoda hai usne kisi nek ko."
[He has plundered everyone,
He has not spared any virtuous person]
"Lute khaas sarkaar ke khairkhaah
Hua maal -o- asbaab unka tabaah."
[All the prominent well-wishers of the Government were looted
Their wealth and properties were destroyed.]

— *Ibid*, stanza 1532-33, p. 234.

Thus, writing about the vandalism against the British government's well-wishers, Syed Ahmad Ali Shah underlined that Mohammed Hasan did not treat his enemies well. However, as against his contention, Mohammed Hasan demonstrated his humaneness by saving Colonel Lennox and his family as well as George Yeoward, the Eurasian head clerk of Gonda. See, Sen, Surendra Nath, *Eighteen Fifty-Seven*, pp. 187 and 366, 237, FN 121.

91. Lari, Ahmar, *Mukhtsar Tarikh-e-Gorakhpur* (Urdu, brief History of Gorakhpur), Gorakhpur, 1972, p. 38.

92. *FSUP*, Vol. IV, p. 302. The intention behind this letter was not only to prevent Nepal's help to the British but also to strengthen the Hindu-Muslim unity. Raja Devi Bakhsh Singh of Gonda, too, had written a letter to the Maharaja, asking him to help Begum Hazrat Mahal. A letter was also sent by Prince Birjis Qadr. See, Foreign Department 1858, Political Consultation No. 75-77, dated 19th November 1858; Padma Jang Bahadur Rana, *op.cit,* pp. 217-18.

93. *Qaiser-ut-Tawarikh*, Vol. 2, p. 305.

94. *Ibid*, pp. 306-07; *Khadang-e-Ghadar*, p. 74. Syed Ahmad Ali Shah too talks of the killing of Mohammed Hasan's soldiers.

"Bahut baaghi dariya pe maare gaye
Bahut khud ba khud duub kar ke muye
Mohammad Hassan tha jo ek bad khisaal
Woh bhaaga hai yahaan se ba-misl-e-shaghaal."

[Many rebels were killed on the river side
Many drowned themselves to their death
Mohammad Hasan who was an evil man,
Fled from here like a Jackal]

— *Ibid*, stanza 1413-14, p. 214.

95. Rana, Padma Jang Bahadur, *Life of Maharaja Sir Jang Bahadur of Nepal*, Kathmandu, second reprint, 1980, p. 206. According to C, Wingfield, "This force defeated Harkishan Singh who had been re-inforced by a large body of Sepoys and Irregulars under Moosharruf Khan from Goruckpore and advanced towards Burhul. Simultaneously the Goorkha army under Maharajah Jung Bahadoor crossed the Gunduk at Peepra and moved on Goruckpore. There was a slight skirmish with the rebels on the bank of that river another at Pipraich, 15 miles from the station, which was occupied by the Gorkha army on the 6th. The rebels attempted to make a stand in the forest but were soon driven from their position and being quickly followed up through the town of Goruckpore, many perished in attempting to cross the Raptee. Mahomed Hussun and his principal officers fled early in the morning and made such speed that by the evening they were across the Gogra at Tanda." See, Wingfield C. Narrative, July 1858, para 44-45, p. 6; Ball, Charles, *op.cit*, Vol. II, pp. 226-27; Haider, Kamaluddin, *op.cit*, Vol. 2, p. 306.
96. *FSUP*, Vol. IV, pp. 312-13, 315.
97. *Ibid*, p. 322.
98. Nevill, H. R., District Gazetteer, Basti, p. 162; Chaudhuri, S. B., *Civil Rebellion in the Indian Mutinies, 1857-58*, Calcutta, 1957, p. 146.
99. Foreign Department, Secret consultation, No. 16, Dated 31 December 1858, preserved in National Archives of India, New Delhi.
100. Haider, Kamaluddin, *op.cit*, p. 307; Badayuni, *op.cit*, pp. 126-27.
101. For details, See *FSUP*, Vol. IV, pp. 386-94; Sen, Surendra Nath, *op.cit*, pp. 363-67.
102. *FSUP*, Vol. IV, p. 385; Sen, Surendra Nath, *op.cit*, p. 366.
103. *FSUP*, Vol. IV, pp. 397, 399; Sen, Surendra Nath, *op.cit*, pp. 366-67.
104. Badayuni, *op.cit*, p. 127. According to S N Sen, Mohammed Hasan was given a pension of 200 rupees and told to remain in Sitapur. See, p. 367. But the pension was actually given to Mehdi Hasan Khan. Thus, his contention is incorrect.
105. See, the details about Raja Udit Narayan Singh in Verma, Nageshwar Prasad Singh, *Nag-Kaushalottar*, Vol. 1, Patna: Bankipur Press, V.S. 1975 (AD 1918). Rudrapur was 27 miles to the south-east of Gorakhpur and was known as the capital of Satasi Raj. In his narrative penned on 28 September 1857, Khuda Bakhsh described Musharraf Khan as a released prisoner, representative of the Raja of Satasi and a leader of the rebels. ("Musharraf Khan, a released prisoner, the agent of the Raja of Satasi and one of the Chief of rebels.") See, *FSUP*, Vol. IV, p. 384.
106. *Kashful-Baghaavat*, *Gorakhpur*, stanza 445-46, pp. 70-71.
107. Commissioner's Office, Gorakhpur, Vol. 74, File 91, Serial No. 58, p. 49: From Deputy Collector, In-charge of Raj Satasi, 26 March 1832, to S. M. Boulderson,

Officiating Commissioner of Revenue, 9th Division, Gorakhpur, preserved in Regional Archives, Allahabad.

108. Verma, Nageshwar Prasad Singh, *op.cit*, details about Raja Pahalwan Singh, Raja Kawalwan Singh, Rani Haniwant Kunwari and Prahlad Kunwari.

109. Wingfield, C. Narrative, 5 July 1858, para 34, p. 5. Syed Ahmad Ali Shah also wrote —

Woh Rajah ki jaanib se mukhtaar ho,
Gaya pesh moozi ke sardaar ho
[He as an agent from the side of Raja
Went before the obnoxious as a leader].

— *Kashful-Baghaavat, Gorakhpur, op.cit*, stanza 447, p. 71.

As a representative of the Raja of Satasi, Musharraf Khan also wrote a letter to Begum Hazrat Mahal. See, *FSUP*, Vol. IV, p. 372.

110. Wingfield, C. Narrative, 5 July 1858, para 38, p. 5. *Kashful-Baghaavat, Gorakhpur, op.cit* also mentions (stanza 647, p. 100) that

"Musharraf jo Naib tha uska bana
Woh sabiq se shaitaan ka ustaad tha"
[Musharraf who had become his deputy
He had always been the master of Satan].

In the above contexts, his appointment as Naib Nazim is mentioned but the cause of this appointment is not given.

111. Wingfield, C. Narrative, 5 July 1858, para 26, 28, p. 4. *Kashful-Baghaavat, Gorakhpur,* also mentions that he was once imprisoned. See, (stanza 445, p. 70).

112. Ball, Charles, *op.cit*, Vol. II, p. 228.

113. *FSUP*, Vol. IV, p. 306.

114. Wingfield, C. Narrative, 5 July 1858, para 38, p. 5.

115. *Ibid*, para 31, p. 4.

116. *Kashful-Baghaavat, Gorakhpur,* stanza 461, p. 73.

117. *Ibid*, stanza 583, p. 91.

118. *Ibid*, stanza 564, p. 89.

119. *FSUP*, Vol. IV, p. 158; Wingfield C. Narrative, 8 July 1858, para 40, p. 5. Lambasting him, *Syed Ahmed Ali Shah,* wrote —

Kiya khoob barbad usne har ek ko
Na chooda tha usne kisi nek ko
[Ravaged everyone thoroughly
He had not spared any noble person]

Kashful-Baghaavat, Gorakhpur — stanza 649, 100.

Again,

Khalish se Musharraf ke, Nazir lute
Diya maal-o-zar ko toh woh jaan se chute
[Nazir was looted due to apprehensiveness of Musharraf Khan

Only when he gave money and gold, was his life spared]

Mahajan se zar naqad usne liya

Sitam mein woh zaalim ke the mubtala

[He hauled Gold and cash from the Mahajan

He was trapped in oppression of the ruthlessness]

- *Kashful-Baghaavat, Gorakhpur* — stanza 1546-47, p. 237.

120. *Kashful-Baghaavat, Gorakhpur* stanza 922-74, pp. 142-48, (Tashreeh-e-Asbab).

121. *Ibid*, stanza 950, p. 145 —

Gharaz maal mera aur hukkaam ka

Liya usne sab kaisi aafat kiya

[Therefore belongings, mine and of the rulers, He took it all

what a disaster he executed]

122. *Ibid*, stanza 1053-58, pp. 162-63.

123. Wingfield, C. Narrative, 5 July 1858, para 42, pp. 5-6. The Raja of Bansi had accepted the tehsildar appointed by Musharraf Khan.

124. *Kashful-Baghaavat, Gorakhpur*, Stanza, 2070-71, p. 321.

125. Wingfield, C. Narrative, 5 July 1858, para 42, pp. 5-6. Musharraf Khan's name does not figure in the details regarding the campaign against the Raja of Gopalpur.

126. *Kashful-Baghaavat, Gorakhpur* narrates the impact of Musharraf Khan's defeat in the battle of Sohanpur. See, Stanza 1326-29, p. 202. For the impact of the defeat, the following are noteworthy -

Musharraf maa fauj apni gaya

Pada phir talaatum me, woh behaya

[Musharraf went with his army,

Then that shameless one become interwined in buffeting] (1328)

Jab aaya Musharraf hue beqaraar

Hue kitne us rooz dariya ke paar

[When Musharraf came, they became restless,

on that day many crossed over the river.] (1329).

127. Ball, Charles, *op.cit*, Vol. II, pp. 227-28 and p. 228 FN; Haq, Syed Moinul, *op.cit*, pp. 456-57 FN.

128. *FSUP*, Vol. IV, p. 305; Proceedings of the Government of India in the Home Department, Judicial, (From July to December 30, 1859), Translation of a Petition from Udit Narayan Singh, former Raja of Satasi, 20 May 1859, point 5, p. 10. According to Charles Ball's description, "We expect the arrival , at Goruckpore, of that consummate villain Mushharaf Khan, who has apprehended few days since by the Ranee of Bustie, but was taken from her by a powerful zamindar of the same district, who is anxious to curry favour with the British government, now that it is again un-mistakenly in the ascendant". See, Ball, Charles *op.cit*, Vol. II, p. 228.

129. *FSUP*, Vol. IV, pp. 305-06; Ball, Charles, *op.cit*. p. 228.

130. *Kashful-Baghaavat, Gorakhpur,* stanza 1469, p. 223. Charles Ball also wrote that "Upon the advance of Jung Bahadur's force, Mr. Bird accompanied it as

joint magistrate of the district and upon the subsequent recapture of Musharraf Khan, he had the satisfaction of hanging his un-invited visitor, whom he first paraded in cart through the streets of Goruckpore, where during the five preceeding months, he had been accustomed to ride about with a species of regal pomp". See, Ball, Charles, *Op.cit*, pp. 227-28.

131. *Kashful-Baghaavat, Gorakhpur*, stanza 1473, p. 223. See, stanza 1470-72 for other names.

132. *Ibid*, stanza 1476, p. 223.

133. Verma, Nageshwar Prasad Singh, *op.cit*, narrative regarding Raja Udit Narayan Singh.

134. Pre-Mutiny Records, Magistrate's Office, Gorakhpur, Bag 141, Serial No. 25, Revenue Letters Issues, Series – I, from E. A. Read, 25 May 1843, List of the Principal Native Gentry in the District of Gorakhpur, Serial No. 1, preserved in Regional Archives, Allahabad.

135. Verma, Nageshwar Prasad Singh, *op.cit*, narrative regarding Raja Udit Narayan Singh, 1. He had also sent a letter to Mohammed Hasan, addressing him as the Nazim. See, *FSUP*, Vol. IV, p. 379, Letter No. 8, Dated 17 August 1857.

136. *FSUP*, Vol. IV, p. 379.

137. Wingfield, C. Narrative, 5 July 1858, para 27, p. 5. He had only sent a representative. *Kashful-Baghaavat, Gorakhpur*, stanza 449-50, p. 71, Shah also writes —

Satasi ka Raja hua pur ghuroor
Woh haakim se karne laga makr-o-zoor.
Rahe muntazir uske hukkam sab
Na haazir hua haif woh beadab.

[The Raja of Satasi became arrogant. He began
exerting deceit and power over the rulers,
All rulers were awaiting him, But alas!
That impudent one did not present himself]

— See, Stanza 449-50, p. 71

138. Home Department, Fort William, Proceedings, 12 August 1859; Judicial, Serial No. 3, No. 1, pp. 1 and 2, preserved in National Archives of India, New Delhi.

139. *Kashful-Baghaavat, Gorakhpur*, stanza 1252, p. 191.

140. Home Department, Fort William, Proceedings, Judicial, 12 August 1859; Serial No. 3, No. 1, p. 1.

141. *Kashful-Baghaavat, Gorakhpur*, stanza 1198-1210, pp. 183-85.

142. Foreign Department, Secret Consultation No. 82-83, 26 March 1858, preserved in National Archives of India, New Delhi; *FSUP*, Vol. IV, p. 304.

143. *Ibid*; C. Wingfield, the Commissioner of Gorakhpur, was sure that Udit Narayan Singh was hiding in the jungles of Gorakhpur, along with his followers. *FSUP*, Vol. IV, p. 305.

144. *FSUP*, Vol. IV, p. 358.

145. Foreign Department, Secret Consultation No. 44; from C. Wingfield, Commissioner of Gorakhpur, to W. Muir, Secretary to Government, NWP, 6 January 1859,

Dispatch No. 4 of 1859, para 7, p. 2, preserved in National Archives of India, New Delhi.

146. Proceedings of the Government of India in the Home Department, Fort William, 15 to 20 July 1859, Judicial, No. 9-10 to 61-63; Fort William Proceedings, 12 August 1859 to 26 August 1859, No. 1 to 6, and 26 August to 4-5 December 1859, No. 1 to 6, (preserved in National Archives of India, New Delhi). Syed Ahmad Ali Shah wrote —

"Satasi ka Raja Muquaiyyad hua

Yehi uske aamaal ki thi sazaa

[The Raja of Satasi was imprisoned,

This was the punishment for his deeds]

See, *Kashful-Baghaavat, Gorakhpur*, stanza 1927, p. 299; Pandey, Rajbali, Gorakhpur Janpad aur Uski Kshatriya Jatiyon ka Itihas, p. 270.

147. Home Department, Public, 1864, No. 382-A, 27 August 1864, p. 7, from Udit Narayan Singh, 28 July 1864, preserved in National Archives of India, New Delhi.

148. Home Department, Public, 9 November 1864, No. 46-47, No. 575 A of 1864, from J. D. Sandford, Joint Secretary, North Western Provinces, to E. C. Bayley, Secretary, Home Department, Fort William, Nainital, 25 October 1864, preserved in National Archives of India, New Delhi.

149. Home Department, Public, 1864, No. 18 of 4 October, No. 583 A, 27 August 1864, from Major V. Ford, Officiating Superintendent of Port Blair, to Colonel A. Fytche, Commissioner of Tenasserim Division, British Burma, No. 32, Dated 12 August 1864, p. 5; Home Department, Public, 9 November 1864, No. 5334, p. 7, (preserved in National Archives of India, New Delhi).

150. Commissioner's Office, Gorakhpur (Pre-Mutiny Records), Revenue Records, Vol. 70, File No. 82, Serial No. 5, pp. 57-58; Vol. 105, File No. 144, Serial No. 7, pp. 107-08; preserved in Regional Archives, Allahabad; Pandey, Rajbali, *op.cit*, 172; Nevill, H. R., District Gazetteer, Gorakhpur, 1909, Allahabad, p. 114.

151. Pre-Mutiny Records, Magistrate's Office, Gorakhpur, Bag No. 141, Serial No. 29, Revenue Letters Issued, Series No. 1, from Reade E.A., 5 May 1843, Serial No. 25.

152. Wingfield, C. Narrative, 5 July 1858, para 7, p. 2; *FSUP*, Vol. IV, p. 145.

153. *FSUP*, Vol. IV, p. 378.

154. *FSUP*, Vol. IV, pp. 160-63. C. Wingfield's Narrative also mentions that the Gorakhpur-Azamgarh Road was closed till 15 June. See, para 9, p. 2.

155. Wingfield, C. Narrative, 5 July 1858, para 18, p. 3; *FSUP*, Vol. IV, p. 152.

156. Wingfield C. Narrative, 5 July 1858, para 38, p. 5.

157. *FSUP*, Vol. IV, p. 385. *Vishwen Vansh Vatika* (Bankipur Press, Patna, 1885) Written by Khang Bahadur Mall, mentions that Raja of Narharpur participated in the battle of Sohanpur. See, p. 81.

158. *Ibid*, p. 436.

159. Home Department, Public, Consultation No. 98, 30 July 1858, No. 20 of 1858, from C. Wingfield, Commissioner of Gorakhpur, to W. Muir, Secretary to

Government, NWP, Gorakhpur, 14 July 1858, para 7, preserved in National Archives of India, New Delhi.

160. Foreign Department, Secret Consultation No. 132, 25 June 1858, No. 153 of 1858; from the Commissioner of Gorakhpur to W. Muir, Secretary to Government, NWP, 28 May 1858, para 2; Foreign Department, Secret Proceedings, 25 June 1858, Vol. 1413 A, p. 3877, para 2.
161. Foreign Department, Political, 11 March 1859, from C. Wingfield, Commissioner of Gorakhpur, to W. Muir, Secretary to Government, NWP, para 6, p. 2.
162. Swinton, Alan, *Manual of the Statistics of the District of Goruckpore*, Allahabad: (NWP & Awadh Government Press), p. 18; Pandey, Rajbali, *op.cit*, p. 272; Nevill, H. R., District Gazetteer, Gorakhpur, 1909, p. 193.
163. Pandey, Rajbali, *op.cit*, p. 272. Rajendra Singh too says that the Raja of Narharpur was executed along with his followers. See, *Land, Power and People*, New Delhi, 1988, p. 139.
164. *Kashful-Baghaavat, Gorakhpur*, stanza 268, 270, p. 43.
165. Rizvi, Syed Najmul-Raza, *Attharahwin Sadi ke Zamindar* (Hindi), New Delhi, 1988, p. 33.
166. Settlement Report of Gorakhpur District, 1871, Allahabad, p. 62; from L. Wynne, Assistant, Settlement Department, to G. Ousley, Collector of Gorakhpur, 9 May 1864, p. 62.
167. Pre-Mutiny Records, Commissioner's Office, Gorakhpur, Vol. 105, File 144, Serial No. 6, p. 83; Settlement Report of Pargana Tilpur, 1 May 1840.
168. Pre-Mutiny Records, Magistrate's Office, Gorakhpur, Bag 141, Serial No. 25, Revenue Letters Issued, Series 1, from E. A. Reade, 5 May 1843, Serial No. 4. According to Mr. Reade "Rajah Bejaie Sen, Niechlowl; caste Nepalese, age 21, commonly called The Rajah of Butwal. He is refugee from Nepaul, and his income from possession in Pergunnah Tilpur, including a government stipend, is about 18000 rupee per annum."
169. Settlement Report of Gorakhpur District, 1871, p. 62.
170. Wingfield, C. Narrative, 5 July 1858, para 38, p. 5.
171. *Kashful-Baghaavat, Gorakhpur*, Stanza 1247, p. 191.
172. *Ibid*, stanza 269, p. 43.
173. *FSUP*, Vol. IV, p. 304.
174. *Ibid*, p. 336.
175. *Ibid*, p. 347.
176. Foreign Department, Secret Consultation No. 3, 24 September 1858, preserved in National Archives of India, New Delhi.
177. Foreign Department, Secret Consultation No. 47, 26 November 1858, preserved in National Archives of India, New Delhi.
178. Nevill, H R, District Gazetteer, Gorakhpur 1909, pp. 193-94.
179. Rizvi, Syed Najmul-Raza, *op.cit*, p. 60.
180. Pandey, Rajbali, *op.cit*, p. 271.
181. Pre-Mutiny Records, Magistrate's Office, Gorakhpur, Bag 141, Serial No. 25, from E. A. Reade, 5 May 1843, Serial No. 11 in the list.

182. *Ibid*, Serial No. 7 in the list.
183. Wingfield, C. Narrative, 5 July 1858, para 38, p. 5.
184. *Kashful-Baghaavat, Gorakhpur*, stanza 1249, p. 191.
185. Home Department, Public, Consultation No. 98, 30 July 1858, para 6.
186. Nevill, H R, District Gazetteer, Gorakhpur 1909, pp. 114.
187. *Ibid.*
188. Pre-Mutiny Records, Gorakhpur Collectorate, Bag 7, Revenue Letters Issued, Series 1, 10 July 1807, pp. 170-71.
189. *Ibid.*
190. Wingfield, C. Narrative, 5 July 1858, para 38, p. 5.
191. Nevill, H R, District Gazetteer, Gorakhpur 1909, p. 193; Om Prakash Srivastava, District Gazetteer, Gorakhpur 1987, p. 39. According to Ahmar Lari, some parts of the Shahpur zamindari, after its confiscation, were given to the Raja of Gopalpur as reward. See, *Mukhtsar Tarikh-e-Gorakhpur*, *op.cit*, p. 40.
192. *Hindustan*, (Hindi) daily, Gorakhpur edition, 12 November 2013.
193. *Ibid.*
194. Foreign Department, Political Consultation, No. 60-62 KW, Dated 27 May 1859. Extract from List of Persons Eminent for Loyalty in District Gorakhpur during the Late Disturbance, Kishan Kishore Chand, Raja of Gopalpur, Kaushik Rajput, Nature of Conduct Given in Detail. The Raja of Nagar was his sister's son.
195. Rizvi, Syed Najmul Raza, *op.cit*, p. 63.
196. Pre-mutiny Records, Magistrate Office, Gorakhpur, BAG No. 141, Serial 25, Revenue letters issued, Series I, From E.A. Reade, 5 May 1843, Serial No. 6: Pandey, Rajbali, *op.cit*, p. 280; *Kashful-Baghaavat, Gorakhpur*, stanza 218-20, p. 34.
197. Wingfield, C. Narrative, 5 July 1858, para 18, p. 3.
198. *Kashful-Baghaavat, Gorakhpur*, Stanza 218, 220, 224, 226-27, pp. 34-35.
199. Wingfield, C. Narrative, 5 July 1858, para 18, p. 3.
200. *FSUP*, Vol. IV, p. 382.
201. *Ibid.*
202. *Ibid*, p. 379, Letter No. 7.
203. *Ibid*, p. 383; Pre-Mutiny Records, Gorakhpur Collectorate, List No. 14, Vol. 177, Bag No. 27, preserved in Regional Archives, Allahabad.
204. Wingfield, C. Narrative, 5 July 1858, para 38, p. 5.
205. *FSUP*, Vol. IV, p. 156; Wingfield C. Narrative, 5 July 1858, para 34, p. 5.
206. *FSUP*, Vol. IV, p. 305.
207. Home Department, Public, Consultation No. 115, from Commissioner of Gorakhpur, May 1858, para 2, pp. 1-2; *FSUP*, Vol. IV, p. 324.
208. *Ibid*, para 9, pp. 3-4; *FSUP*, Vol. IV, pp. 225-26; Foreign Department, Secret Consultation No. 66-69, 28 May 1858, para 9-13, 15-18.
209. Foreign Department, Secret Proceedings, 25 June 1858, Vol. 1413 A, Narrative, 22 May 1858, para 7 and 12, pp. 3877-78, preserved in National Archives of India, New Delhi.

210. *Ibid.*
211. *FSUP*, Vol. IV, pp. 325.
212. Settlement Report of Gorakhpur District, 1871, from P J White, Settlement Officer, Jalaun, On Duty at Gorakhpur, to G P Mony, Officiating Commissioner, Banaras Division, 20 September 1865, pp. 140-41. According to Mr. White, Raja Udai Pratap Singh had committed suicide while in jail.
213. *Kashful-Baghaavat, Gorakhpur*, Stanza 1926-29, pp. 299-300. (30th Shaban 1275 Hijri or 3rd April 1859 AD).
214. Singh, Rajendra, *op.cit*, pp. 119, 137-39.
215. Swinton Alan, *op.cit*, p. 6.
216. Wynne, L, Settlement Report of Gorakhpur District, 1871, from: P. J. White, Deputy Collector of Gorakhpur, to F M Bird, Collector of Gorakhpur, Dated 29 July 1861, para 15, p. 250; In 1843, Rajah Abye Singh, Caste Soorujbunsee, residence Amorha khas, Age 60 years, used to get a Nankar of rupees 9000 and was worth about 18000 per annum, Pre-mutiny Records, Magistrate Office, Gorakhpur, BAG No. 141, Serial 25, Revenue letters issued, Series I, From E.A. Reade, 5 May 1843, Serial No. 5.
217. *Ibid*; *FSUP*, Vol. IV, pp. 318, 350, 351.
218. Chopra, P N, (chief editor), *Who is Who of Indian Martyrs*, Vol. III: 1857, New Delhi, 1973, p. 12.
219. Report on the Settlement of Gorakhpur-Basti District, from P J White, Deputy Collector of Gorakhpur, to F M Bird, Collector of Gorakhpur, Dated 29 July 1861, para 15, p. 250.
220. Singh, Rajendra, *op.cit*, pp. 118, 139; Nevill, H R, District Gazetteer, Basti, 1907, p. 210.
221. Verma, Nageshwar Prasad Singh, *op.cit*, pp. 19-20; List of the Babus of Satasi, No. 12 and the narrative about Raja Roop Narayan Singh.
222. Pre-Mutiny Records, Magistrate's Office, Gorakhpur, Bag 141, Serial No. 25, Revenue Letters Issued, Series I, from E. A. Reade, 5 May 1843, Serial No. 31.
223. Wingfield, C. Narrative, 5 July 1858, para 18, p. 3.
224. *FSUP*, Vol. IV, p. 378.
225. Wingfield, C. Narrative, 5 July 1858, para 29, p. 4.
226. *Ibid*, para 38, p. 5.
227. *Kashful-Baghaavat, Gorakhpur*, Stanza 232-35, p. 37. Syed Ahmed Ali Shah has written Wynyard as "Vineet" and Burton as "Booran Saheb."
228. *FSUP*, Vol. IV, pp. 362-63.
229. *Ibid*, p. 365.
230. *Ibid*, p. 366.
231. Foreign Department, Political Supplement, No. 1165, 30 December 1859, from Narrative of Events up to 19 May 1858, p. 3.
232. Nevill, H R, District Gazetteer, Gorakhpur, 1909, p. 193.
233. Verma, Nageshwar Prasad Singh, *op.cit*, pp. 19-20; List of the Babus of Satasi, No. 13 and the narrative about Raja Sarvadaman Singh.

234. Inscription on Babu Bandhu Singh's statue in Alinagar, Gorakhpur City.
235. Pre-Mutiny Records, Gorakhpur Collectorate, List 14, Vol. 177, Bag 27, preserved in Regional Archives, Allahabad.
236. *Kashful-Baghaavat*, *Gorakhpur*, Stanza 470 and 473, pp. 74-75.
237. *Ibid*, stanza 981-82, p. 150.
238. *FSUP*, Vol. IV, p. 333.
239. Home Department, Public, Consultation No. 116, Governor General's Proceedings May 1858, preserved in National Archives of India, New Delhi; *FSUP*, Vol. IV, p. 334.
240. Foreign Department, Secret Proceedings, 25 June 1858, Vol. 1413, para 11, p. 3878, Foreign Department, Secret Consultation No. 132, 25 June 1858 (preserved in National Archives of India, New Delhi); *FSUP*, Vol. IV, p. 336.
241. Foreign Department, Secret Proceedings, 25 June 1858, Vol. 1413, para 14, p. 3878; Foreign Department, Secret Consultation No. 132, 25 June 1858; *FSUP*, Vol. IV, p. 336.
242. *FSUP*, Vol. IV, p. 341.
243. Foreign Department, Secret Consultation No. 139-140, 25 June 1858, preserved in National Archives of India, New Delhi; *FSUP*, Vol. IV, p. 336.
244. *FSUP*, Vol. IV, pp. 343-44.
245. *Ibid*, p. 365.
246. *Ibid*, p. 347.
247. *Ibid*, pp. 361-62.
248. Foreign Department, Secret Consultation No. 15, 31 December 1858; *FSUP*, Vol. IV, pp. 364-65.
249. *FSUP*, Vol. IV, pp. 362-63.
250. Foreign Department, Political, 11 March 1859, No. 44-45; from C. Wingfield, Commissioner of Gorakhpur, to W. Muir, Secretary to the Government of North Western Provinces, 6 January 1858, para 6, p. 2, preserved in National Archives of India, New Delhi.
251. *Kashful-Baghaavat*, *Gorakhpur*, Stanza 1782, p. 272.
252. Foreign Department, Political Consultation No. 60-62, 27 May 1859, preserved in National Archives of India, New Delhi.
253. Swinton, Alan, *op.cit*, p. 21.
254. Verma, Nageshwar Prasad Singh, *op.cit*, pp. 19-20; also See, the narrative about Raja Basant Singh; Report on the Settlement of Gorakhpur-Basti District, Allahabad, 1871, pp. 199-200.
255. Verma, Nageshwar Prasad Singh, *op.cit*, the narrative about Raja Basant Singh.
256. Wingfield, C. Narrative, 5 July 1858, para 38, p. 5.
257. Home Department, Public B, Consultation No. 17/20, 16 September 1859; from: G. Cooper, Secretary to the Government of the North Western Provinces, to the Secretary of Government of India, Home Department, Nainital, 28 June 1860; Home Department, Public, Consultation No. 5862, Mr. Peppe, Grant of Jagir, 25 March 1861.

258. Report on the Settlement of Gorakhpur-Basti District, Allahabad, 1871; from: J. P. Lumsden, Settlement Officer, Gorakhpur, to A. Shakespeare, Commissioner of Banaras Division, 21 March 1867, p. 200.

259. Home Department, Public, 25 March 1861, No. 58; from G Cooper, Secretary to the Government of the North Western Provinces, 28 June 1860, No. 59; 9 October 1860, No. 60; 31st December 1860, No. 61; from: W. H. Low, Secretary to the Sadar Board of Revenue of North Western Provinces, 19th December 1860, No. 87, 12th January 1861; Home Department, Public B, Consultation No. 17/20, 16 September 1859; from Mr. Peppe to His Excellency the Right Honourable George Ford Canning, Governor General and Viceroy of India, 22 June 1859; Nevill, H R, District Gazetteer, 1909, p. 193.

260. *Kashful-Baghaavat, Gorakhpur*, Stanza 236-41, pp. 37-38.

261. *Ibid*, stanza 1205, p. 184.

262. Swinton, Alan, *op.cit*, p. 11; Atkinson E.T., (editor), *Statistical, Descriptive and Historical Account of North Western Provinces*, Vol. VI, Part II, Gorakhpur, p. 470. (Printed at N.W.P and Oudh, Government Press, Allahabad).

263. Verma, Nageshwar Prasad Singh, *op.cit*, narrative about Raja Gaj Singh.

264. Commissioner's Office, Gorakhpur, Vol. 105, File 144, Serial No. 10, Settlement Report of Pargana Hasanpur-Magahar, para 22, p. 153. According to this report, Bakhira was under the Raja of Bansi (Srinet Rajput) till Fasli 1189 (AD 1779) and it was part of the zamindari of the Raja's younger brother. Babu Sangram Singh, nephew of Raja Sarabjit Singh of Bansi, was the zamindar here. He was dependent upon his uncle and paid him revenue directly. After his demise, his illegitimate son, Balwant Singh, quarrelled with the Raja and succeeded in 1789 in having Bakhira as his independent zamindari. It comprised seven *tappas*. Babu Kshatradhari Singh was the Babu of Bakhira in 1807. See, Gorakhpur Collectorate, Bag No. 121, Serial No. 5, Revenue Letters Issued, Series 1, pp. 578-79, 582, 586 (Preserved in Regional Archives, Allahabad). In 1838, Babu Ram Pratap Singh, then a minor, was the Babu here; Babu Balwant Singh was his grandfather.

265. Babu Ram Pratap Singh was the Babu of Bakhira, according to the Settlement Report. See, Settlement Report of Pargana Hasanpur-Magahar, *op.cit*, para 22, p. 153. According to Rajendra Singh, the Babu of Bakhira was Jaggi Singh, which is incorrect. See, *Land, Power and People*, p. 139.

266. Wingfield, C. Narrative, 5 July 1858, para 22, p. 3.

267. Singh, Rajendra, *op.cit*, p. 119; Nevill, H R, District Gazetteer Basti, 1907, p. 153.

268. *Ibid.*

269. Mehdawal too is a part of Pargana Hasanpur-Magahar. The Babu of Mehdawal was a relative of the Raja of Bansi (a Srinet Rajput) and was in possession of Mehdawal since long. See, Settlement Report of Pargana Hasanpur-Magahar, *op.cit*, p. 152. Thakur Jaggi Singh, whom Rajendra Singh described as the Babu of Bakhira, could be the Babu of Mehdawal.

270. Singh, Rajendra, *op.cit*, p. 119; District Gazetteer Basti, 1907, p. 153.

271. *Ibid.*

272. Commissioner's Office, Gorakhpur, Vol. 105, File 144, Serial No. 10, para 20, p. 152.
273. Home Department, Public, Consultation No. 115, Governor General's Proceedings of May 1858, No. 129 of 1858, From the Commissioner of Gorakhpur to W. Muir, secretary to Government, North Western Provinces, Captainganj Camp, 1 May 1858, para 2 and 3; *FSUP*, Vol. IV, pp. 324-25; Syed Ahmed Ali Shah also wrote,

    "Vo maara use fauj-e Sarkaar ne
    Aur ghaarat kiya usko idbaar ne"
    [He was killed by the army of the government
    Indeed, he was ravaged by misfortune]
    See, stanza 1508, p. 229.
274. Singh, Rajendra, *op.cit*, p. 119.
275. *Kashful-Baghaavat, Gorakhpur*, Stanza 1005-09, p. 154. The location of Haiti is not clear. Perhaps it was in the region of present day Sahjanwa tahsil.
276. *Ibid*, stanza 1515, p. 230.
277. *Ibid*, stanza 557, 565, pp. 88-89.
278. *Ibid*, stanza 593, p. 93.
279. *Ibid*, stanza 1287-92, pp. 196-97.
280. *Ibid*, stanza 777, p. 120.
281. *Ibid*, stanza 959, p. 147.
282. *Ibid*, stanza 1895-97, p. 293.
283. Naqal, Wajib-ul-Arz, Jild Bandobast, 1860, Babat, Mauza (Mohalla) Muftipur, Tappa Qasba, Pargana Haveli, Tehsil Sadar, Zila Gorakhpur. The attested copy of this document mentions the confiscation of Sardar Ali Khan's property. The present author got a photocopy of this document from Sardar Ali Khan's descendants. Also See, Chopra, P N, (chief editor), *Who is Who of Indian Martyrs*, Vol. III: 1857, New Delhi: Government of India, 1973, pp. 131-32.
284. In *Kashful-Baghaavat, Gorakhpur*, the Shah himself wrote —

    "Mohalla milega tumhen Muftipur,
    Kachahri mein yeh hukm hoga sudur.
    [you shall get the lane area of Muftipur.
    This ordered will be issued in the court]
    Humein is khabar se musarrat hui
    Mubaddal yeh mehnat ba raahat hui
    [This news made me happy
    Thus, hard work was exchanged for comfort]
    See, *op.cit*, stanza 1906-07, pp. 295-96.

    This announcement was made on 9 January 1859. See, *op.cit*, stanza 1902, p. 295. Also See, Foreign Department, 1859, Political, 2 May 1859; Extract from the List of Persons Eminent for Loyalty in District Gorakhpur during the late disturbance.

285. The news published on 17 September 2005 in the Gorakhpur editions of Hindi dailies, *Rashtriya Sahara* and *Aaj*.
286. *Kashful-Baghaavat*, *Gorakhpur*, stanza 568, p. 89.
287. *Proceedings of the Indian History Congress*, Kannur session, 2008 (Kolkata 2009), p. 486.
288. *Ibid*, p. 497 FN 22; Pre-mutiny Records, Magistrate Office, Gorakhpur, BAG No. 141, Serial 25, Revenue letters issued, Series I, From E.A. Reade, 5 May 1843, Serial No. 17.
289. *Kashful-Baghaavat*, *Gorakhpur*, stanza 2160-61, pp. 333-34.
290. *FSUP*, Vol. IV, p. 384.
291. *Ibid*, pp. 379-80.
292. *Ibid*, p. 384.
293. *Proceedings of the Indian History Congress*, Kannur session, 2008 (Kolkata 2009), pp. 496-97.
294. *Kashful-Baghaavat, Gorakhpur,* stanza 2162, p. 334.
295. Commissioner's Office, Gorakhpur, Vol. 105, File 144, Serial No. 3, pp. 36-39. For a detailed narrative, See, Farooqi, M. G. A., *Shajra-e-Shadab* (Urdu Press, Gorakhpur: 1900), pp. 102-05, 121, 150-56.
296. Chopra, P. N. (Chief Editor), *Who is Who of Indian Martyrs*, Vol. III, *op.cit*, pp. 35 and 117.
297. *FSUP*, Vol. IV, p. 397; Foreign Political Consultations, 18 March 1859, No. 15, preserved in National Archives of India, New Delhi.
298. Pre-Mutiny Records, Gorakhpur Collectorate, List 14, Vol. 177, Bag 27, preserved in Regional Archives, Allahabad.
299. *FSUP*, Vol. IV, p. 306; Home Department, Public – B, Consultation No. 17/20, Dated 16 September 1859, preserved in National Archives of India, New Delhi.
300. Foreign Department, Secret Consultation No. 355-62, 30 April 1858.
301. Kaye, Sir John, *The History of the Indian Mutiny*, Vol. I, p. 401. According to Seargent Busher "Jaffer Ali, who shot poor Leutinent Ritchie and fired to me (Seargent Busher), See, Chick, N.A; Annals of the Indian Rebellion, 1857-58, Part IV, pp. 471-77.
302. Pre-Mutiny Records, Gorakhpur Collectorate, List 14, Vol. 192, Bag 27, preserved in Regional Archives, Allahabad; *FSUP*, Vol. IV, p. 383 Letter No. 49.
303. Pre-Mutiny Records, Gorakhpur Collectorate, List 14, Vol. 177, Bag 27, preserved in Regional Archives, Allahabad.
304. Aitchison, C. U., *A Collection of Treaties, Engagements and Sanads*, Vol. II, p. 61; Montgomery, Martin, *The History, Antiquities, Topography and Statistics of Eastern India*, Vol. II, Gorakhpur, first Indian reprint: 1976, New Delhi: Cosmo Publications, pp. 308-10.
305. Om Prakash, (State Editor, *Uttar Pradesh District Gazetteers)*, Gorakhpur: UP Government, Allahabad, 1987, pp. 33-34.
306. Wynne, H. L., Supplement Reports and Statements of the Gorakhpur District, Allahabad: Government Press, para 21, p. 62.

307. Shah, Rishikesh, *Modern Nepal: A Political History*, Vol. I, New Delhi: (Manohar Publications, Ansari Road, Daryaganj, New Delhi, 1980), pp. 116-18.

308. Foreign Department, Political, Confidential Proceedings, July, No. 375, From R.C. Lawrence, the Resident in Nepal, 10 July 1868, No. 14, to C U Aitchison, Officiating Secretary to Government of India, Foreign Department with Governor General, para 3, preserved in National Archives of India, New Delhi.

309. *FSUP*, Vol. IV, p. 347; Damman Khan has been said to be a resident of Utraula. See, Singh, Bhagwati Prasad, *Rashtriya Swatantrata Sangharsh aur Gonda Janapad*, Varanasi: Shivam Printers, 1993, p. 80.

310. Foreign Department, 1858-59, No. 13 of 1858; From C. Wingfield, Commissioner of Gorakhpur, to G. P. Edmonston, Secretary to the Government of India, 27 November 1858, para 5, pp. 6-7.

311. *Ibid*, para 6, p. 7.

312. Foreign Department, 1858-59, No. 91, in A letter from the Assistant Resident and Incharge of the Nepal Residency, Dated 11 December 1858, Copy of the Resume in the Case of Damman Khan Forwarded by Mr Wingfield C., Commissioner of Gorakhpur, pp. 17-18.

313. *Ibid.*

314. *Ibid,* p. 27, Foreign Department, 1858-59 No. 3; From, Assistant In-charge of Nepal Residency 11 December 1858, Abstract translation of the Yaddasht from Maharaja Jung Bahadur Rana Jee, Prime Minister and Commander-in-Chief of Nepal to addresee …., dated 9 december 1858, pp. 41-42, No. 91 of 1858, pp. 44-45, *FSUP*, Vol. IV, p. 345.

315. *FSUP*, Vol. IV, p. 350; Wingfield C. Narrative of Events for Gorakhpur for the Week Ending 8 August 1858.

316. *FSUP*, Vol. IV, p. 351.

317. Foreign Department, 1858, No. 2087, 31 December, No. 13 of 1858, From Wingfield C., Commissioner of Gorakhpur, to Secretary to the Government of India.

318. Foreign Department, 1858-59, No. 376, from Captain G H Byers; Copy of the Resume in the Case of Damman Khan Forwarded by C. Wingfield, Commissioner of Gorakhpur, pp. 10-18.

319. *Ibid*, p. 18.

320. Foreign Department, 1858, Political, Copy no. D of 1858, 2 December 1858, No. 13 of 1858, Consultation No. 2087, From C. Wingfield, Commissioner of Gorakhpur, to Assistant Resident of Nepal, 27 November 1858, p. 7.

321. Foreign Department, 1858-59, Abstract Translation of a Yaddasht from Captain G H Byers, Assistant Resident at Nepal, In-charge of the Residency to Maharaja Jang Bahadur, Prime Minister and Commander-in-Chief of Nepal, 2 December 1858, pp. 36-39.

322. Foreign Department, 1858, No. 91 of 1858, from Captain Byers to Secretary, Government of India, Nepal Residency, Dated 11 December 1858.

323. Foreign Department, 1858-59, No. 3, Consultation No. 378, December 1858, Abstract Translation of a Yaddasht from Maharajah Jang Bahadur Ranaji, Prime Minister and Commander-in-Chief of Nepal, to the Address of Captain

G H Byers, Assistant Resident at Nepal, In-charge of the Residency, dated19th of Ughan, Sambut 1915 (Thursday) corresponding with the 9th December 1858.

324. Foreign Department, 1859, No. 8 of 1859, from Captain G H Byers, Assistant Resident at Nepal, Incharge of the Residency, to G. P. Edmonston, Secretary to the Government of India, in the Foreign Department, Fort William, Nepal Residency, 19 January 1859, para 1, p. 55, Dummun Khan was arrested earlier and was kept in Tarragurhee where he then was in the charge of Sardar Hustbeer Sahee. See, *Ibid*, Para I.

325. *Ibid*, para 2.

326. *Ibid*, para 3, p. 56, Maharaja Jang Bahadur Rana had promised to convey the list to Resident, on receiving the details of the confiscated property but the details were not sent to Mr. Byers.

327. The present writer came to this conclusion after holding talks with the people of Jhandanagar and the nearby villages.

328. Singh, Thakur Prasad, *Swatantrata Sangram ke Sainik, Zila Azamgarh*, Lucknow: Information Department, pp. Gh; Singh, Phool Badan, *Azamgarh ka Swadhinata Sangram*, Vol. 1, Azamgarh, 1974, p. 46.

329. Chaudhuri, Sashi Bhusan, *Civil Rebellion in the Indian Mutinies, 1857-59*, Calcutta, 1957, p. 156.

330. Singh, Phool Badan, *op.cit*, pp. 46-47; Singh, Thakur Prasad, *op.cit*, p. Gh; Drake-Brockman, D L, Azamgarh, A Gazetteer being Volume XXXIII of the District Gazetteers of the United Provinces of Agra and Awadh, Allahabad, 1911 (heretofore referred to as District Gazetteer Azamgarh, 1911), Lucknow: Government Press, p. 175.

331. Foreign Department, Secret Consultation No. 355-362, 30 April 1858.

332. Singh, Thakur Prasad, *op.cit*, p. Gh.

333. Taylor, Robert, Supplement to the Narrative of Events in the Banaras Division, 19 November 1858, p. 3.

334. Foreign Department, Fort William Proceedings, 25 June 1858, p. 3201, Foreign Department, Secret Consultation No. 81, 28 May 1858, from Davis, R H, Azamgarh Magistracy, 13 May 1858, pp. 3-4, preserved in National Archives of India, New Delhi.

335. Foreign Department, Secret Consultation No. 143, 25 June 1858, from Davis, R. H., Azamgarh Magistracy, 3 June 1858, preserved in National Archives of India, New Delhi.

336. *Ibid*.

337. Taylor, Robert, 19 Nov 1858, *op.cit* ....., p. 3.

338. Foreign Department, Secret Consultation No. 139, 27 August 1858, from Azamgarh Magistracy, 17 June 1858, preserved in National Archives of India, New Delhi.

339. Foreign Department, Secret Consultation No. 143, 25 June 1858, *op.cit*; *FSUP*, Vol. IV, p. 203.

340. Foreign Department, Secret Consultation No. 139, 27 August 1858, from Davis, R H, Azamgarh Magistracy, 17 June 1858, preserved in National Archives of India, New Delhi.

341. *FSUP*, Vol. IV, p. 205. Pargan Singh's group was present in Jehangirganj. Groups of the Raja of Narharpur and Balli Singh too were present there. Jehangirganj was situated near the Ghaghra river, to the north-west of Azamgarh. From here, it was easy to enter Gorakhpur district.
342. Foreign Department, 1858, Political Supplement, Consultation, 30 December, No. 232, from Camp Dakari, 15 December, from Brigadier Holdich to Military Secretary with Governor General, preserved in National Archives of India, New Delhi.
343. Singh, Phool Badan, *op.cit*, pp. 122-23. Venables has described Rajab Ali as the zamindar of Bamhaur. See, Foreign Department, Secret Consultation No. 355-62, 30 April 1858, p. 5.
344. Foreign Department, Secret Consultation No. 355-62, p. 5.
345. Taylor, Robert, *The Rebellion of 1857 in the Province of Benares*, 15 October 1858, para 41, p. 14, preserved in State Archives, Lucknow; Haq, Syed Moinul, *op.cit*, p. 452.
346. Drake-Brockman, D. L., *op.cit*, p. 86.
347. Foreign Department, Secret Consultation No. 355-62, 30 April 1858, preserved in National Archives of India, New Delhi, Sohan Singh and Baijnath Singh, the zamindars were executed after they were apprehended.
348. Singh, Phool Badan, *op.cit*, p. 123; Oopauddia, Vishwamitra, *San Sattawan ke Bhule-Bisre Shaheed*, Vol. 2, New Delhi: Publication Division, p. 85.
349. Singh, Phool Badan, *op.cit*, p. 114.
350. *FSUP*, Vol. IV, p. 191.
351. Taylor, Robert, *op.cit*, 15 October 1858, para 62, p. 19.
352. *FSUP*, Vol. IV, p. 27; Singh, Thakur Prasad, *op.cit*, p. G; Singh, Phoolbadan, *op.cit*, p. 39.
353. Taylor, Robert, *op.cit*, 15 October 1858, para 65, p. 20.
354. *FSUP*, Vol. IV, p. 191.
355. Taylor, Robert, *op.cit*, para 79, p. 22; Singh, Phool Badan, *op.cit*, pp. 47-48.
356. Singh, Phool Badan, *op.cit*, p. 115.
357. *Ibid*, pp. 111-12.
358. *FSUP*, Vol. IV, pp. 111-12.
359. Verma, Acharya Rajnikant, *1857 ke Vismrit Yoddha*, Allahabad, pp. 93-94.
360. Taylor, Robert, *op.cit*, 15 October 1858, para 43, p. 11.
361. *Ibid*, para 44, p. 15.
362. District Gazetteer Azamgarh, 1911, p. 175.
363. Taylor, Robert, *op.cit*, para 46, p. 15; District Gazetteer Azamgarh, 1911, p. 175.
364. Taylor, Robert, *op.cit*, para 63-64, pp. 19-20; Chaudhuri, Sashi Bhushan, *op.cit*, p. 155; Malleson, G B, *History of Indian Mutiny*, Vol. II, pp. 117-18.
365. Taylor, Robert, *op.cit*, para 80, p. 22; Malleson, G B, *op.cit*, pp. 319-20.
366. Taylor, Robert, *op.cit*, para 80, p. 22.

367. Singh, Phool Badan, *op.cit*, p. 78; The evidences show that Rajah Beni Madho Singh of Shankarpur went to Nepal with Begum Hazrat Mahal.
368. *Ibid*, pp. 111-13.
369. Foreign Department, Secret Consultation No. 355-62, 30 April 1858; Singh, Phoolbadan, *op.cit*, p. 139.
370. *Ibid*.
371. *Ibid*, pp. 131-32.
372. Rizvi, Syed Najmul-Raza, *Attharahwin Sadi ke Zamindar*, New Delhi: People's Publishing House, 1988, pp. 54-55.
373. Reid, J. R, Report on the District of Azamgarh, Compiled in Connection with the Completion of Sixth Settlement, Ch I, Section VIII, para 213, p. 67.
374. *Ibid*, para 213, p. 68; *FSUP*, Vol. IV, p. 247.
375. *FSUP*, Vol. IV, pp. 189, 247; Taylor, Robert, *op.cit*, 15 October 1858, para 41, p. 14.
376. *FSUP*, Vol. IV, p. 247.
377. *Ibid*.
378. *Ibid*, p. 102.
379. *Ibid*, p. 247.
380. Reid, J. R., *op.cit*, para 213, p. 68.
381. Taylor, Robert, *op.cit*, 15 October 1858, para 43, p. 15; Agrawal, Ruchi, *Taluqdars of Awadh and the Revolt of 1857*, Agra: S R Scientific Publications, 2013, p. 127.
382. Taylor, Robert, *op.cit*, para 43, p. 15.
383. *Ibid*, para 45, p. 15.
384. *Ibid*, para 46, p. 15; *FSUP*, Vol. IV, p. 108.
385. Taylor, Robert, *op.cit*, para 46-48; pp. 15-16; *FSUP*, Vol. IV, p. 108.
386. *FSUP*, Vol. IV, p. 182.
387. *Ibid*, pp. 189-90.
388. *Ibid*, p. 190.
389. Agrawal, Ruchi, *op.cit*, p. 129.
390. *FSUP*, Vol. IV, pp. 243-45; Taylor, *op.cit*, para 68, p. 20.
391. *FSUP*, Vol. IV, p. 242.
392. Taylor, *op.cit*, para 68, p. 20.
393. *Ibid*.
394. *FSUP*, Vol. IV, pp. 219-20.
395. Rana, Padma Jang Bahadur, *op.cit*, p. 201.
396. Taylor, *op.cit*, para 68, p. 20.
397. Reid, J. R. *op.cit*, para 213, p. 68. According to Phool Badan Singh op "Raja Iradat Jehan lost a zamindari whose annual revenue was about 24,000 rupees). *op.cit*, pp. 116.
398. Taylor, *op.cit*, para 69, p. 20.

399. Jaunpuri, Syed Iqbal Ahmad, *Sharqi Rajya Jaunpur ka Itihas*, Jaunpur: Sheeraz-e-Hind Prakashan Bhavan, 1968, pp. 292-94.

400. Makhdoom Bakhsh went into hiding after his defeat. See, *ibid*, p. 295.

401. Taylor, *op.cit*, 15 October 1858, para 82, p. 23; Nevill, H R, Jaunpur, A Gazetteer being Volume XXVIII of the District Gazetteers of the United Provinces of Agra and Awadh, Allahabad: Government Press, 1908, p. 183.

402. *Ibid.*

403. Rizvi, Syed Najmul-Raza, *Attharahwin Sadi ke Zamindar*, *op.cit*, pp. 48-50.

404. Taylor, *op.cit*, para 55, pp. 17-18; Drake-Brockman, Mirzapur, A Gazetteer being Volume XXVIII of the District Gazetteers of the United Provinces of Agra and Awadh, Allahabad: Government Press, 1911, p. 241; *FSUP*, Vol. IV, pp. 29-30.

405. *Ibid.*

406. *FSUP*, Vol. IV, p. 83; Taylor, *op.cit*, para 56, p. 18.

407. *FSUP*, Vol. IV, pp. 82-83; Taylor, Robert, *op.cit*. para 56, p. 18.

408. *FSUP*, Vol. IV, pp. 231-32.

409. *Ibid*, p. 232.

410. *Ibid.*

411. *Ibid*, p. 233.

412. *Ibid.*

413. *Ibid*, p. 234.

414. *Ibid.*

415. *Ibid.*

416. *Ibid*, p. 235.

417. Taylor, *op.cit*, 15 October 1858, para 35, p. 13.

418. Chopra, P. N., (Chief Editor) *Who is Who of Indian Martyrs*, Vol. III: 1857 details about Thakur Abhilakh Singh, pp. 2-3.

419. *Ibid*, pp. 25-153.

420. Taylor, *op.cit*, para 35, p. 13.

421. Deposition of Mengar Singh, on 27 November 1860, in the Court of William Ordros, Special Commissioner, Banaras; *FSUP*, Vol. IV, pp. 283-84.

422. *FSUP*, Vol. IV, pp. 284-85.

423. *Ibid*, p. 285.

424. *Ibid,* pp. 285-86.

425. *Ibid*, p. 286.

426. *Ibid.*

427. *Ibid*; Ghazipur, Mutiny Records Series, Bag 74, preserved in Regional Archives, Allahabad.

428. *Ibid*, pp. 287-88. According to Mengar Singh, the government had announced a reward of three or six thousand rupees on his capture.

429. *Ibid*, 289.

430. *Ibid*, pp. 280-81.

431. *Ibid*, p. 281. Details are available about Mengar Singh crossing the Karmanasa river and creating disturbances in Ghazipur. See, Home Department Proceedings, 6 August 1858, Fort William, 20 August 1858 (Public), p. 336.

432. *Ibid*, pp. 281-82; Foreign Department, Secret Consultation No. 147, 27 August 1858, preserved in National Archives of India, New Delhi.

433. *Ibid*, p. 282.

434. Datta, K.K, *Freedom Movement in Bihar, Vol. I*, (1857-1928) (published by the Bihar Government, Patna, 1957) pp. 57-58.

435. Ghazipur, Mutiny Records Series, Bag 74, page number not mentioned.

436. *Kashful-Baghaavat, Gorakhpur*, stanza 1669, p. 257. Makar Singh could also be read as Mengar Singh. This could be a printing error.

437. Foreign Department, Secret Consultation No. 355-62, 30 April 1858, preserved in National Archives of India, New Delhi.

438. *Kashful-Baghaavat, Gorakhpur,* stanza 1668-69, pp. 256-57. Seedha Singh belonged to village Bariya, pargana Ballia, district Ghazipur, and served in Kunwar Singh's army. See, Home Department (Public), Fort William Proceedings, 11 June 1858, preserved in National Archives of India, New Delhi, p. 53; Datta K.K, Biography of Kunwar Singh and Amar Singh (K.P. Jaiswal Research Institute Patna, 1957) p. 215.

439. Datta, K. K, *op.cit*, Part 1, pp. 57-58.

440. *FSUP*, Vol. IV, p. 207.

441. Home Department, Public Proceedings, 16 July 1858, No. 474, 19 June, p. 377.

442. Datta, K.K, *op.cit*, p. 58.

443. *Ibid.*

444. *Ibid*, p. 68; Datta K.K, Biography - *op.cit,* p. 126.

445. According to Datta, Joodhur Singh was the resident of Khumiani, pargana Arwal, See, Datta K.K *op.cit* Vol. I; p. 53.

446. Home Department, Public, June 1858, Fort William Proceedings, 11 June 1858, No. 97, preserved in National Archives of India, New Delhi, p. 53.

447. Fort William Proceedings, Public, No. 2801, 20 August 1858, p. 336; Datta K. K, *op.cit*, p. 62.

448. Datta, K.K, *op.cit*, Vol. I. p. 65, Also See, Datta K.K. Biography, *op.cit* p. 123.

449. *Ibid*, pp. 57-58.

450. Khan, K M S, *Excavation of Truth: Unsung Heroes of the 1857 War of Independence*, edited by Khan Ahmad Adeel, New Delhi, 2007, pp. 46-47.

451. *Ibid*, According to K.K. Datta, Ali Kareem was the Scion of very respectable and wealthy zamindar family of village Doomri in the Patna district. See, Biography of Kunwar Singh and Amar Singh, p. 101.

452. Datta, K.K, *op.cit*, p. 21; According to K.K Datta, Ali Kareem at the time of his flight from Bihar stayed for some time with Kunwar Singh and probably, an earlier contact with him. See, Biography of Kunwar Singh and Amar Singh, p. 101.

453. Datta, K.K, *op.cit*, Vol. I, p. 21.

454. *FSUP*, Vol. IV, p. 299.

455. *Ibid*, p. 205.
456. Datta, K.K, *op.cit*, Vol. I, p. 52; Also See, Biography of Kunwar Singh and Amar Singh, p. 101.
457. Singh, Mahendra Pratap, "1857 ka Maha Sangram aur Purbi Uttar Pradesh" Itihas Drishti Joint Issu No. 8-9, Gorakhpur, June 2013, pp. 123-24; Datta K.K, *op.cit*, Vol. I pp. 46-47.
458. Savarkar, V.D, *op.cit,* pp. 340-351; Datta K.K, *op.cit*, Vol. I, pp. 47-50; Sen, Surendra Nath, *op.cit*, pp. 306-08; Chaudhari, Rashmi, *1857 ke Amar Senani Veer Kunwar Singh*, (Publications Division, New Delhi, 2007), pp. 18-21; Datta K.K., Biography of Kunwar Singh and Amar Singh, *op.cit,* p. 108, Appendix V, p. 209.
459. Datta, K.K, *Biography of Kunwar Singh and Amar Singh*, pp. 24-25, Chapter IX pp. 160-87; Datta K.K, *op.cit*, Vol. I pp. 51-52, 58-59; Chaudhuri, Sashi Bhusan, *op.cit*, p. 63; *Kashful-Baghaavat, Gorakhpur*, stanza 1664-65, p. 256; Sen, Surendra Nath, *op.cit*, 308-10; Marx and Engels, *The First Indian War of Independence, 1857-58* (Progress Publishers, Moscow, 1978), pp. 161, 209; Husain, Iqbal, *Karl Marx on India*, pp. 282-83 and FN 1.
460. *FSUP*, Vol. IV, p. 173.
461. Agrawal, Ruchi, *op.cit*, p. 129.
462. *Ibid*.
463. *Ibid*, p. 129.
464. *Ibid*, pp. 129-30.
465. *Ibid*, p. 130.
466. *Ibid*, pp. 130-31.
467. *FSUP*, Vol. IV, pp. 174, 211, 223-25, 271-72, 333.
468. Agrawal, Ruchi, *op.cit*, p. 131.
469. *Ibid*, pp. 142-45; Foreign Department, 1859, Political Consultation No. 466, 30 December, from Camp Dakari, 15 December, Brigadier Holdich, No. 232.
470. *Ibid*, pp. 141, 145; *FSUP*, Vol. IV, pp. 314, 364. M. L. Ferar, C S Assistant Commissioner, a Gazetteer of the Province of Awadh Vol. III, A to Z, reprint: Delhi, 2006, pp. 504-06.

Chapter - 6

Limitations, Consequences and Significance of the Rebellion

The mass rebellion, which started in Eastern Uttar Pradesh from Paina village of Gorakhpur district on 31 May 1857, came to an end — after Queen Victoria's grant of clemency for the rebels on certain conditions — with the surrender of Raja Udit Narayan Singh of Satasi and some other prominent rebels in the first week of January 1859 and then the return of rebel Nazim, Mohammed Hasan, with 150 of his followers from his hideout in Nepal and his surrender at the British army camp in Bootwal. Delhi and Lucknow had already fallen, and their resistance had already stopped. But the rebel leaders of this area continued the mass rebellion here through the guerrilla war tactics for around a year and a half. This period also included the four months and twenty days of an independent government. Thus, from the viewpoint of time period, the Great Revolt of 1857 continued for the longest duration in Eastern Uttar Pradesh.

In its long-duration struggle, the area also suffered the maximum loss of life and property. While surrendering himself after the end of the rebellion, Mengar Singh (Mengar Rai or Magahar Rai), rebel hero of village Gahmar in Ghazipur district, had said in his confessional statement that about 70,000 sepoys (Tilangas) and other rebels had died in the Gorakhpur area alone.[1] Mengar Singh's rebellious activities spread over Ghazipur and Bihar, till he took shelter in Nepal, and the government had also announced an award for his arrest. Mengar Singh's figure was based on his own estimate. The loss of life was still greater, as the figure did not include the number of the dead in Azamgarh, Jaunpur, Ghazipur, Banaras and Mirzapur. Agriculture and other activities suffered in that period of disturbance and anarchy, but no figures are available, nor can be, about the losses therein. Thus, only a guess may be hazarded about the catastrophe. Its extent cannot be calculated.

To uproot and overthrow the foreign rule was the aim of the rebellion, even though the aim of Mohammed Hasan and his supporters was confined to liberating the State of Awadh.[2] Rebel leaders fought with utmost zeal and high morale to achieve their aim, though they failed in the end. Historians like R.C. Majumdar and S.N. Sen have underlined the causes of the rebellion's failure at the national level, and other historians have expressed agreement with it. However, in this region level study, attempt has been made to trace out the causes that led to the rebellion's failure in this area.

The biggest cause of the rebellion's failure was the superior armed strength of the British. They had experienced military commanders and a trained army which was armed to the teeth. On the contrary, around sixty-two regiments of the Bengal Army revolted in several parts of the country at various times.[3] Of these, however, most of the regiments had been disarmed before they could revolt. Most of the rebel sepoys lacked weapons, and therefore the sepoys' revolt did not have any notable impact on the military power and weaponry of the British. In Gorakhpur and Azamgarh districts, it was sepoys of the 17th NI who had revolted. But most of its sepoys had left for Lucknow.[4] At Banaras, sepoys of the 37th NI revolted when they were being disarmed, and they could not withstand the British cannons and ran helter skelter.[5] Sikh soldiers of the Ludhiana Regiment, stationed in Jaunpur, had already left for Lucknow with the treasury and arms.[6] Hence the role of the rebel sepoys was only minimal in this territory, though sepoys absconding from other areas did participate here. On the contrary, coming from other areas, the British troops did act to crush the rebellion in this territory. Bengal Yeomanry Cavalry was dispatched to assist them. They played an important role in the rebellion in the Basti and Bansi areas, particularly in the battle at Belwa.[7] The British Government asked for Nepal to send Gorkha soldiers, and 200 of them immediately came forth at their request.[8] It was in their protection that government treasury was sent from Gorakhpur to Azamgarh.

A comparative study of the two sides in the battle at village Sohanpur for capturing the Majhauli Raj, and of the rebel army's situation at the time the Gorkha army captured Gorakhpur, does give an idea of the British armed strength and its superiority. Babu Kunwar Singh's nephew had created a front, along with 500 soldiers, for the capture of the Majhauli Raj. Maulvi Ali Kareem had come from Patna with a few hundred men, and Naib Nazim Musharraf Khan had come to fight, along with six to seven thousand persons wherein soldiers numbered only eleven or twelve hundred. Though the number was ostensibly very high, describing them as a zealous crowd instead of an organised troop would be more appropriate. On the other hand, besides 1,100 of his own men, Colonel Rowcroft of the Saran Field Force had 30 soldiers of the Royal Marines, 130 of the Naval Brigade, 350 of the Gorkha regiment, four Howitzer guns of 12 pounds each (including two Mountain Batteries), and 50 Sikh soldiers from Captain Rattray's troop.[9] Thus, there was a zealous crowd on one side and a trained armed force on the other. The France of Napoleon Bonaparte had already proved that a small trained force could drive a big crowd away. Here too, rebels ran away after a few hours of the battle. Nazim Mohammed Hasan of Gorakhpur had started from Tanda with a few hundred men and had started recruiting an army in August 1857 end, after he had captured the city of Gorakhpur. According to Moinuddin Hasan, he had recruited 25,000 persons from all castes in his army, while Kamaluddin Haidar and other sources say he had recruited five to six thousand persons. But these sepoys had received training for four months only.[10] It means their training in this small period was inadequate. Yet they had to face a superior, well trained and well-armed army of ten thousand Gorkhas, being led by Maharaja Jang Bahadur Rana of Nepal. To withstand the Gorkha army's attack was not possible for them. Hence, they had to run away after a brief encounter and the Gorkhas captured Gorakhpur city on 6 January 1858. On 11 January, they handed it over to British officials.[11]

During the guerrilla actions in Gorakhpur district in the subsequent days, Colonel Rowcroft had superior strength compared to the rebels, and, moreover, he received help from the Yeomanry Cavalry and Naval Brigade from time to time.[12] Besides, 6th Madras Light Cavalry had been sent from Allahabad to help him.[13]

In Azamgarh district, the British began their campaign against the rebels only after Gorkha soldiers reached there. Gorkha army played a notable role in crushing the rebellion in Jaunpur too. It was Gorkhas who fought against Raja Iradat Jehan's strength.[14]

After Babu Kunwar Singh captured Azamgarh district, renowned Commander Mark Kerr reached Banaras with 372 soldiers and 19 officers, and then reached the vicinity of Azamgarh with the Royal Artillery and the Second Dragon Guard.[15] Besides, Colonel Sir Lugard was sent from Lucknow to Azamgarh with 700 Sikh cavaliers, 500 Europeans, 450 Gorkha soldiers, 18 cannons.[16] Against the Nazim of Sultanpur who was planning to attack Jaunpur, General Frank was sent with 3,200 Gorkha soldiers, 2,300 European soldiers and 20 cannons.[17] Colonel Neill was already stationed in Banaras, with his Madras Fusiliery (artillery), to crush the rebellion.[18] Any rebel resistance against such powerful armies could not but have its own limitations. The sad plight of the rebel heroes was also evident from the fact that in the Gorakhpur region, Mohammed Hasan's sepoys had deserted him at a point and he had to borrow 200 sepoys from Raja Devi Bakhsh Singh of Gonda.[19] However, he did not feel deterred by such adverse circumstances and continued the struggle. This reflected the firm determination of the rebel heroes.

Crunch of economic resources was the biggest problem facing the rebel leaders. Money was needed to have the rebel sepoys in service. Means of transport were needed for moving from one place to another; reliable persons were needed to have a tab on the British troops' movements and locations; arms and weapons had to be procured clandestinely, and all this required money. Mobilisation of resources was utmost necessary to pay to the soldiers for their livelihood. Rebel sepoys were always in search of economically well-off leaders. Raja Devi Bakhsh Singh of Gonda was economically better-off than others. Hence, we see him trying to win over 500 to 600 soldiers of Ayodhya and Faizabad, who had a horse battery of six cannons, with the proposal of paying them more money. He, however, failed.[20] But persons like Mohammed Hasan had no source of income. His capital consisted of whatever money he could collect, as Nazim, from Gorakhpur, and that too was dwindling because of the unending struggle. It was thus that he had a quarrel with his sepoys for the payment of salary arrears and he was, in a way, encircled by them. He solved the problem by somehow raising money and paying them, but yet his men left him after the event.[21]

Rebel rajas and zamindars had to quit their zamindaris for their safety. Hence, they were seen unable to collect revenue from their ryots. Now only traditional followers or caste fellows remained with them. Raising money for their livelihood was also a big problem. Therefore, given a chance, they were compelled to plunder the village markets, rich zamindars and peasants to raise resources. But this plunder, committed out of compulsion, only added to their adversary ranks. Besides, this made the common people afraid of and abhorrent about the rebels.

Rebel sepoys did not lack in the feelings of sacrifice. They could remain content with the minimal of salary as was absolutely essential for survival. Armed sepoys of Babu Kunwar Singh used to get only two rupees in a fortnight while those fighting with lathis and lances got nothing.[22] On the contrary, British Government's sepoys got five rupees a month. The government also sanctioned them more money in special circumstances. In order to foil the rebels' activities in Azamgarh, 2,325 persons of Gopalpur were recruited for six rupees as the monthly wage; every official per 25 sepoys was given 12 rupees a month, and an in-charge of 100 persons was given 50 rupees a month. Thus, the British Government had appointed 2,325 persons, including 24 big and 93 small officials, at a monthly expenditure of 16,266 rupees.[23] Nazim Mohammed Hasan used to pay every sepoy a monthly wage of 5 rupees and 13 annas. Hence the British had hiked the monthly wage to 6 rupees in order to attract the sepoys.[24] This is enough to demonstrate the economic problem facing the rebel leaders vis-a-vis the government's economic prosperity. As such, continuing the struggle for a year and a half was no small achievement.

The rebels of the area had high hopes of getting help from Nepal. Mohammed Hasan, the Nazim of Gorakhpur, Raja Devi Bakhsh Singh of Gonda and Birjis Qadr, son of Begum Hazrat Mahal and heir apparent of Awadh, wrote a number of letters to Maharaja Jang Bahadur of Nepal, asking for help against the British and for protection of religion.[25] Attempt was also made to send Damman Khan, jagirdar of Jhandanagar, to Nepal to seek help for the rebels.[26] Major G Ramsay, British Resident at Kathmandu, wrote in his narrative that rebels had even dangled the allurement of making Maharaja Jang Bahadur Rana the emperor of Awadh.[27] This offer of rebels was a reflection of their farsightedness. But all these efforts failed. Referring to Nepal's treaty with the British Government, Maharaja Jang Bahadur Rana asked the rebels to surrender. S N Sen has mentioned the letter sent by Jang Bahadur Rana to Begum Hazrat Mahal on 15 January 1859. Padma Jang Bahadur Rana has, in his book *Life of Maharaja Sir Jang Bahadur of Nepal*, reproduced the English translation of the letters written by Begum Hazrat Mahal and the replies sent to her by the Maharaja. On 15 January, the Maharaja wrote to Begum Hazrat Mahal: "Be it known, that an intimate friendship exists between the British Government and the Nepal State, and both of them are bound by the Treaty to apprehend and surrender to the other the enemies of either. I therefore, write to you, that if you remain or seek an asylum within my Territory and frontier, the Goorkha troops will most certainly, in pursuance of the treaty agreed upon by both the high states and make war on you. And be it also known, that the Nepal State will neither assist, show mercy to, nor permit to remain in its territories or within its frontier those who have been so faithless and ungrateful as to do mischiefs, and raise animosity and insurrection, against of having taken part in a murders are to be answered by a communication of or reference to the Queen's Proclaimation without further comment."[28] In reply to the letters written by other persons, Jang Bahadur Rana denied the charge of the British Government harming the religions of the Hindus and Muslims, and refused to accept it. In the light of the correspondence, it seems S N Sen was right to contend that the Nepal Government had decided that rebel chiefs must be made to surrender, by request or else by force.[29]

It would be appropriate to discuss here the causes behind the said decision of the Nepal Government, as the Government of British India did not view Nepal as a good neighbour. The British Government viewed Nepal's interest in Indian affairs with a sense of apprehension. Yet Maharaja Jang Bahadur Rana sided with the British Government for his own advantage. He had come to realise the British might after his return from Europe in 1850 and he firmly believed that the British would definitely win and therefore Nepal should help the British in this hour of crisis (Rebellion 1857), as it would be advantageous to him. He had clearly put forward his objectives behind providing military help to the British. In his farewell speech before leaving Kathmandu, on December 10, 1857, he had said "I have three motives for acting as I am now doing. First, to show that Gorkhas possess fidelity and will shed their blood in defence of those who treat them with honour and repose confidence in them. Second, I know the power of the British government and were I to take part against it, although I might have temporary success, my country would afterwards be ruined and the Gorkha dynasty annihilated. Third, I know that upon the success of British arms and the re-establishment of British Power in India, its government will be stronger than ever and that I and my brothers, and my country will all then benefit from our alliance."[30] However, in his address, he said nothing about the policy of remaining neutral. His address makes it clear that he had decided to take advantage of all sorts from the crisis of the revolt. Therefore, he paid no heed to the rebels' entreaties and preferred the benefits that were safe from all angles.

The Nepal Government's decision was contrary to the expectations which the rebel leaders of Eastern Uttar Pradesh, adjoining the Nepal border, had harboured. Disappointment gripped them and this too reduced the life of rebellion in this region. It was their despondency due to the Nepal Government's action that compelled Mohammed Hasan, Mengar Singh and others to surrender before the British Government.[31]

Those having loyalty to the British Government caused maximum harm to the rebel world in this territory. Whatever might have been the cause of their behaviour, they weakened the rebellion and harmed the cause. The Company Government rewarded them for their help. British officials have mentioned such people in their narratives. In the narrative of events sent to William Muir, Secretary to the Government of North Western Provinces, on 5 July 1858, Gorakhpur Commissioner C. Wingfield mentioned that most of the government employees did not cooperate with Mohammed Hasan, that the Rajas of Gopalpur, Bansi, Tamkuhi, Salempur-Majhauli and the Rani of Basti did not recognise his government and cooperated with the British Government. About the Raja of Gopalpur, C. Wingfield wrote that he had defeated and driven away the rebel troop which had been sent to demand revenue from him, but he was compelled to run away and take shelter in Azamgarh when a superior force was sent against him, and he remained there from October till the British reoccupation of Gorakhpur district.[32] Similarly, he wrote about the Raja of Bansi that he had refused to recognise the government of the so called Nazim and hand over to him the government treasury of the tehsil. Moreover, he even defeated a big rebel contingent that was sent to punish him. However, when the rebels made large scale preparations against him, discouraged by the fate of the Rajah of Gopalpore, he accepted subordination for the time being and welcomed the tehsildar appointed by the rebels.[33] C. Wingfield wrote about the Rani of Basti that remaining steadfast on her loyalty, she did not allow the rebel thanedar enter her town. However, she was allowed much leeway by the rebels as she was Kunwar Singh's niece.[34] Another reason was that Raja Udit Narayan Singh of Satasi was her son-in-law.

He similarly wrote about the Raja of Tamkuhi that the rebels did not take any immediate step against him despite his loyalty for the British as his was a far-flung area.[35] About the Raja of Majhauli, C. Wingfield wrote "the Raja of Majhauli's refusal to recognise the rebel government and provision of protection to the government employees." At the same time, he also wrote that his loyalty was not sufficiently strong to induce him to run any risk.[36]

Strategically, the support and cooperation of the aforementioned pro-British rajas proved highly beneficial for the British. Most of the northern border from Bahraich to Gorakhpur, which adjoined the Nepal border, was under the control of the rajas of Bansi and Balrampur. As exceptions, a small part of the border was in the hands of Rani of Tulsipur and rebel Raja of Nichlaul. As such, most of the rebel activities took place in the zamindari area of Raja of Nichlaul, to the east of Tulsipur and Bansi, from where rebels had the ease of sneaking into Nepal and conducting a guerrilla war from there. On the contrary, British army had the advantage of conducting anti-rebel campaigns in Balrampur and Bansi. These pro-British rajas created maximum obstacles to the rebels taking strategic advantages of the Nepal borders. In the same way, in Gorakhpur district, the Rajas of Padrauna and Tamkuhi in the east, and of Majhauli in the south-east, created obstacles in their having contacts with the Bihar rebels and continuing the struggle.

Among the government employees of Gorakhpur, Commissioner C. Wingfield recognised the Nazir's services as invaluable and recommended the government reward for him.[37] Yet another record mentions Har Sahai as the name of Nazir of the Gorakhpur Collectorate or Magistrate court, and award of landed property that could fetch him a revenue of seven thousand rupees.[38] The same record mentions the help offered to the British Government by Raja Kishan Kishore Chand of Gopalpur, Dervish Ahmad Ali Shah, the Rani of Basti and Har Sahai, and the government's proposal of rewards for them. In his work *Kashful Baghaavat, Gorakhpur*, Dervish Ahmad Ali Shah has himself described in detail the services he had rendered to the British and the reward of Muftipur mohulla which he got in return.[39] Besides, the English Commissioner rewarded him with the area of Gagaha and village Islampur. Shah has also mentioned the British supporters in detail.[40]

In his *Manual of the Statistics of the District of Goruckpore*, Alan Swinton, who was the Acting Commissioner of Goruckpore, has given some details which tell us that, for their help to the British during the rebellion, Raja Lal Mahendra Singh of Bansi and Sahebzada Mahipal Singh were rewarded with the estates of Raja of Nagar and his uncle, Ranmast Singh, which had been confiscated. Similarly, Kaushik Raja Krishna Kishore Chand of Gopalpur was rewarded by the government with the Raja of Narharpur's estate, some other villages and a robe of honour worth 5,000 rupees. Raja Udai Narayan Mall of Majhauli was rewarded with the *mahal* of Paina. For the help rendered to the British during the revolt by his grandmother, Raja Shitla Bakhsh Singh of Basti was rewarded with a grant of land out of the confiscated lands of rebel leaders. For the help rendered to the British Government, Ramlal Pandey of pargana Amorha was given a land grant bringing in 2,000 rupees as revenue, and his bailiff, Gopal Singh Rajput, got a land grant bringing in 1,500 rupees as revenue. Syed Ahmad Ali Shah, caretaker of the Imambada in Gorakhpur city, got land grants for his loyalty to the British Government. For siding with the government in Banaras, Sardar Surat Singh got half of the Dumri taluqa while the remaining half went to Babu Ram Prakash Singh.[41]

Besides, most of the Company Government's employees did not side with the rebels. They went into hiding in their houses or elsewhere instead of joining the government of Mohammed Hasan. They remained fully committed to the British and re-joined the government service after the

British recaptured Gorakhpur. The available list of such native officials working in the Magistrate's office of Gorakhpur district corroborates this fact. The list includes the following names — Jamuna Prasad (peshkar), P Lal (naib peshkar), Gorakh Prasad (record keeper), Zahoor Ashraf (jailor), Pheru Prasad (muharrir), Ramdutt Singh (thanedar of Basti), Sheel Chand (muharrir of Basti), Bisheshar Dubey (thanedar of Bansi), Safdar Khan (thanedar of Dumariyaganj), Jagannath Prasad (muharrir of Dumariaganj), Kalab Khan (thanedar of Tharauli), Ghulam Nabi Khan (thanedar of Bakhira), Jitan Dubey (jamadar of Bakhira), Guptar Prasad (jamadar of thana Rudhauli), Bhawani Dubey (jamadar of thana Mahuli), Thakur Prasad (muharrir of thana Mahuli), Pandit Chhote Lal (jamadar of Gaayghat chowki), Sheikh Hussin Bakhsh (thanedar of Bansgaon), Inayat Ali (muharrir of Bansgaon), Madad Ali (thanedar of Sikriganj), Devi Dayal Lal (muharrir of Sikriganj), Rasool Khan (thanedar of Sikriganj), Bindeshwari Prasad (thanedar of Gopalpur), Talis Bakhsh Khan (jamadar of Gopalpur), Khalilulla (thanedar of Mansurganj), Lakshman Prasad (muharrir of Mansurganj), Yousuf Khan (thanedar of Pipraich), Nand Kumar Awasthi (thanedar of Pipraich), Digbandhan Lal (thanedar of Misraulia), Chandi Prasad (muharrir of Misraulia), Khairuddin (jamadar of thana Misraulia), Tulsi Ram (muharrir of thana Kothibhar), and Lakshman Prasad (muharrir of thana Padrauna). The list also provides information about the positions in which the above persons served before the rebellion, their activities during the rebellion, and their places of domicile.[42] It is difficult to estimate the number of such native officials and employees who helped the British by remaining inactive during the rebellion, and cooperated in the restoration of British administration after the rebellion had been crushed.

In 1835, in order to weaken the hereditary rajas and big zamindars, the Company Government had recognised the Birtia zamindars, who numbered about ten thousand, as full-fledged and independent zamindars and had pitted them against 18,000-odd zamindars. Therefore, during the revolt, they either remained inactive or helped the British Government.

In Azamgarh district, similarly, the number of those assisting the British during the rebellion was no smaller. The names of Raja Mohammed Mubarak Khan of Azamgarh,[43] Ali Bakhsh Nazir, Safdar Hussein, the tehsildar of Nagra, Maulvi Ali Hussein, Abdul Majeed Munsif, Mohammed Taqi, the peshkar of Mohammedabad tehsil, etc, figure in the list. The narrative of events sent by F.B. Gubbins, Commissioner of the Banaras Division, from Machhli Shahar (Jaunpur) on 6th November 1858, to William Muir, Secretary to the Government of North Western Provinces, mentions the names of persons in Banaras Division whose services to the British

Government were particularly important and notable. He mentioned the names of — Pundit Gokuul Chund, the Nazir of the court of the judge of Benares, Zamin Shah Khan (Kotwal of the city), Moonshee Sheo Sahai, Sarishtahdar of the Magistrate's court, Nusseer-oollah Khan (thanedar of Dushashwamedh), Meer Ibadut Alee, Darogah of the jail, among the government employees of Benares. Among those un-connected with the government, were, Deo Narayan Singh, Sirdar Soorut Singh, Meer Rayet Ali, a vakeel of the judge's court, Babu Devee Singh, Raja of Banaras, Raja Deo Narayan Singh, Babu Gooroodass Mitter, Babu Huruck Chand, Babu Narain Das, Babu Devi Dayal Singh, Babu Ram Kishoon Dass, son of Babu Hunooman Dass.

In Jaunpur District: Hingun Lall of Kerakut, Madho Singh zamindar of Bishruthpoor, Raja Muhesh Narain, Raja Sheo Ghoolam Doobey.

In Mirzapur District: The Raja of Kuntit and his brother.

Azamgarh: The government employees who rendered excellent help included Ali Bakhsh Khan (Nazir of the Magistrate's court), Asghar Ali (thanedar of Nagra), Safdar Hussein (sarishtadar of the Magistrate's court), Mohammed Taqi (naib tehsildar of Mohammedabad).

Ghazipur: Sheikh Khairuddin (Deputy Collector, Ballia), Abdur-Rehman Khan (munsif of Ballia); the list mentioned the Raja of Haldi among the unconnected persons.[44]

Narratives by British officials, too, mention some names who assisted the British Government. Robert Taylor, for example, mentioned the name of Pandit Kishan Narayan in Khutahan tehsil of Jaunpur.[45] These people obstructed the rebels' attempts to challange the British in Eastern Uttar Pradesh, and served to reduce the extent and duration of the rebellion here. But we have also to keep in view the fact that the feeling of nationalism had not yet fully developed among the Indians in this period. On the contrary, the British were full of feelings like nationalism and racial superiority. The formation of Bengal Yeomanry Cavalry on 23 July 1857 and the active role it played in crushing the rebellion in Eastern Uttar Pradesh, the way Mr. Peppe staked his life in Gorakhpur and Mr. Venables and Mr. Dunes did so in Azamgarh to face the rebels, proved this point.[46]

The end of the rebellion in Eastern Uttar Pradesh was, in a sense, its end in the whole country. Though the rebellion failed in achieving its ultimate goal of freedom from the foreign yoke, it almost shook the British rule in India. It compelled the British government to end the rule of East India Company and to take the administration directly in its own hand by passing the act of 1858. So, one cannot underestimate its importance. As R. C. Majumdar said about it underlines its importance: "But even though, the great outbreak of 1857 ended in failure, it would be a mistake to minimise its importance or underrate the gravity of its danger to the British. In spite of all their defects and drawbacks, the sepoys and Indian rebels, by their number and favourable situation, threatened to destroy the whole fabric of the British empire. Its fate hung on a thread, as it were, and it was almost a touch and go."[47]

The sacrifices made together by the Hindus and Muslims in the Rebellion 1857 did make the British feel that any time they could be driven out of the country. As Peter Hardy wrote: "After 1857, the British believed they could be driven from India — and this was never dismissed as impossible — by a union of the "Twin Fanaticisms" of caste and Islam."[48] The policy which the British Government adopted in order to pre-empt this possibility was what led to the country's vivisection. But it was the sacrifices made by Indians during the Rebellion of 1857 that motivated the next generation to initiate the national movement which adopted the policy of non-violence and succeeded in wresting the country's independence.

Notes and References

1. *FSUP*, Vol. IV, pp. 283-89; Ghazipur Collectorate Mutiny Records, File No. 74; Trial Proceedings in the Case Government versus Mangor (Mengar) Singh, Deposition of Meghar Singh, dated 27 November 1860, in the Court of William Ordros, Special Commissioner, Banaras.
2. *FSUP*, Vol. IV, p. 390; Letter from Mahomed Hussain Khan to Khairuddin, 24 October 1858.
3. The Nepali poem talks of a revolt by sixty thousand black (Indian) soldiers. See Pant, Dinesh Raj (editor), *op.cit*, p. 50. According to Professor Irfan Habib, the Bengal Army sepoys taking up arms against the British Raj numbered about one lakh (1,00,000). Not only a large number of armed sepoys joined the rebellion; it was also the most modern army of its kind. See Habib, Irfan, *160 Saal Baad 1857*, p. 39.
4. Taylor, Robert, *The Rebellion of 1857 in the Province of Benares*, 15 October 1858, para 23, p. 11.
5. *Ibid*, para 12, p. 9.
6. *Ibid*, para 25, p. 11.
7. Nash, J. T, *Volunteering in India*, Ch VII to Ch XV; *FSUP*, Vol. IV, pp. 313-14, 316, 322.
8. Wingfield, C, Narrative of Events, 5 July 1858, para 17, p. 3.
9. *FSUP*, Vol. IV, pp. 296-300, 297 FN; Ball, Charles, *The History of the Indian Mutiny*, Vol. II, London Printing & Publishing Company Ltd., London 1858, pp. 228-30.

10. Hasan, Moinuddin, *Khadang-e-Ghadar*, (Hindi as Gadar), p. 74; *FSUP*, Vol. IV, p. 385; Haider, Kamaluddin, *Qaiser-ut-Tawarikh*, Vol. 2, pp. 302, 304-05.
11. Wingfield, C, Narrative of Events, para 44, p. 6; Rana, Padma Jang Bahadur, *op.cit*, p. 206; Ball Charles, *op.cit*, Vol. II, pp. 225-26.
12. *FSUP*, Vol. IV, pp. 316, 340.
13. *Ibid*, p. 332.
14. Rana, Padma Jang Bahadur, *op.cit*, p. 201; Taylor, Robert *op.cit*, para 68, p. 20.
15. Ball Charles, *op.cit*, Vol. II p. 286; Drake-Brockman, D.L, District Gazetteer Azamgarh, 1911, p 182. According to Malleson "Lord Mark Kerr started with his wing, 391 strong for Banaras, picked up there troop – fifty five men and two officers – of the Queen's Bays, 17 gunner and one officer, with 2 Six Pounder guns and two, five and half inches Motors and set out for Azamgarh. His entire force consisted of 22 Officers and 444 men". See, Malleson, Colonel G.B, The *Indian Mutiny of 1857*, (Seelay and Co. Limited, Essex Street Stand, London, 1891, p. 371; Savarkar Says that "Lord Mark Kerr arrived within eight miles of Azamgarh with 500 men and eight guns", see Savarkar, V. D. *op.cit,* p. 343.
16. *FSUP*, Vol. IV, p. 193; Ball, *op.cit*, p. 286; Drake-Brockman, D.L, *op.cit*, p. 184; According to Malleson, "The Commander in chief despatched at once. General Lugard, with three English Regiments, 700 Sikh Sabres and eighteen guns, to march by way of Atraulia, to Azamgarh, to deal with Kunwar Singh". See, Malleson, Colonel G.B, *Op.cit* p. 371.
17. Nevill, H R, *District Gazetteer, Jaunpur*, 1908, p. 184.
18. Taylor, Robert, *op.cit*, para 12, p. 9.
19. *FSUP*, Vol. IV, p. 343.
20. *Ibid*, p. 320.
21. *Ibid*, p. 312.
22. Home Department, Public, Fort William Proceedings, 11 June 1858, p. 55.
23. Home Department, Judicial, No. 20-25, 9 April 1858, from A R Pollock, Officiating Magistrate, Azamgarh, to H. C. Tucker, Commissioner Fifth Division, Banaras, letter No. 52, pp. 8-10.
24. *Ibid*; from A R Pollock, Officiating Magistrate, Azamgarh Camp, 14 January 1858, to H C Tucker, Commissioner Fifth Division, Banaras, Letter No. 17, para 9, p. 26.
25. In his book, Padma Jang Bahadur Rana has provided a English translation of the correspondence between Birjis Qadr and Maharaja Jang Bahadur Rana. See, *The Life of Maharaja Sir Jang Bahadur of Nepal*, *op.cit*, pp. 217-18. In *Qaiser-ut-Tawarikh* (Vol. 2, p. 305), Kamaluddin Haider says Mohammed Hasan wrote a letter soliciting help from Nepal. For an English translation of the letter written by Raja Devi Bakhsh Singh of Gonda to Maharaja Jang Bahadur Rana on 19 September 1858, see Foreign Department, 1858, Political Consultation No. 75-77, November 19th, 1958. In this letter, he requested for help to Begum Hazrat Mahal and talked of defilement of religion by the British.
26. *FSUP*, Vol. IV, pp. 350-51.
27. Hasrat, Bikramjit, *op.cit*, p. 336.

28. Sen, Surendra Nath, *Eighteen Fifty- Seven*, pp. 367-68 (Ist Edition, May 1957).
29. *Ibid*, p. 368.
30. *c.f.* Adrian Sever, Nepal under the Ranas (Oxford and IBH publishing Company Pvt. Ltd. New Delhi, 1993), pp. 125; Shaha, Rishikesh, *Modern Nepal, A political History, 1765-1955*, Vol. I (Manohar Publications, New Delhi, 1990), Page 252.
31. In his confession, Mengar Singh said: "When we saw that there was no place of protection and safety in Bihar, we crossed over to the Ganges and went to the Nepal side, where we joined the forces of the Begam, Raja Devi Bakhsh, Raja Beni Madho and other rebels. I had those 500 tilangas with me. After one year and three months, Raja Jang Bahadur came to our place with his troops, disarmed all the rebels, took a large number of rebels as captive and sent them to the British. Some of the rebels fled away. Sickness had broken into the rebel camp because change of climate and a number of rebel chiefs had died by the time Raja Jang Bahadur came with his army. This was why, the rebel army made no resistance. I do not know the names of the rebel Rajas who died. Those who survived were Raja Beni Madho, Raja Devi Bakhsh, Raja Hardas Rai, Raja Nana Rao, Raja Bala Rao, Raja Narharpur (name not known), and Nawab of Azeemabad (name not known) and Nawab of Farrukhabad (name not known). Raja Jang Bahadur took Amar Singh captive and sent him to the British. He died after being taken captive." Mengar Singh also told that "some of my tilangas were taken captive with Amar Singh, some of them died and others had fled away. See *FSUP*, Vol. IV, pp. 286-87.
32. Wingfield, C. Narrative of Events, 5 July 1858, para 41, p. 5; *Kashful-Baghaavat, Gorakhpur*, stanza 215, p. 32. For the services of Raja of Gopalpur, see Home Department, Judicial, No. 20-25, 14 January 1858, from A R Pollock, Officiating Magistrate, to H C Tucker, Commissioner, Banaras.
33. Wingfield, C. Narrative of Events, *op.cit*, para 42, pp. 5-6; *Kashful-Baghaavat, Gorakhpur*, stanza 270-74. p. 321.
34. Wingfield C. Narrative of Events, *op.cit*, para 42, pp. 5-6.
35. *Ibid*, para 43, p. 6.
36. *Ibid*, para 50, p. 6.
37. *Ibid*, para 46, p. 6.
38. Foreign Department, 1859, Consultation No. 60-62, KW, 27 May, from Officiating Secretary to Government, North Western Provinces, April, No. 405, Extract from the List of Persons Eminent for Loyalty in Zila Gorakhpur, during the Late Disturbances. This includes the names of Kishan Kishore Chand, Raja of Gopalpur, Ahmad Ali Shah Dervish, Rani of Basti, and Magistrate and Nazir of Collectorate Court Har Sahai. It also mentions their services and the rewards they were given.
39. *Kashful-Baghaavat, Gorakhpur,* pp. 26-28, 57-65, 207-210, 295, 324-26.
40. *Ibid*, pp. 19, 21, 32-33, 34, 155, 185, 263-65, 287, 285, 289, 295, 298, 315-18, 319, 321-22, 328-43. Rajendra Singh has also mentioned the pro-British persons of Basti. See *Land, Power and People*, pp. 141-43.
41. Swinton, Alan, *Manual of the Statistics of the District of Goruckpore*, Allahabad: (Government Press, 1861).

42. Pre-Mutiny Records, Gorakhpur Collectorate, List 14, Vol. 177, Bag 27, Return Showing the Conduct during the Late Insurrection of the Native Officials of Magistrate Department (Now Employed in the Gorakhpur District). *Kashful-Baghaavat, Gorakhpur*, mentions the appointment of Hussein Bakhsh as tehsildar, his nephew as darogha, and Zahoor Bakhsh as darogha. See p. 303. Besides, it gives the names of several British supporters. See pp. 313-17.
43. *FSUP*, Vol. IV, p. 106.
44. Narrative of Events Attending the Outbreak of Disturbances and the Restoration of Authority in the Division of Benares in 1857-58, No. 323 of 1858, by F B Gubbins, Commissioner Office, Benares, 6 November 1858; Malleson and Kaye, *op.cit*, Vol. II, pp. 230-31. Sir John Kaye has mentioned the services rendered by Sardar Soorut Singh, Pundit Gokul Chand, Raja Dev Narayan Singh, and the Raja of Banaras.
45. Taylor Robert, *op.cit*, 15 October 1858, para 82, p. 23.
46. Nash, J. T, *op.cit*, pp. 1-2, Ch IV to Ch XVII, Home Department, Public B, Consultation No. 17/20, 16 September 1858; Home Department, Public, 13 March 1861; Taylor, Robert, *op.cit*, 15 October 1858, para 37, 39, 40,46, pp. 13-15.
47. Majumdar, R C, *The Sepoy Mutiny and the Revolt of 1857*, second edition, Calcutta, 1963, p. 484.
48. Hardy, Peter, *The Muslims of British India*, New Delhi: Cambridge University Press, First Indian Edition, p. 89.

Appendices

Appendix - A

Names of Rebels Mentioned in *Kashful-Baghaavat, Gorakhpur*, a Contemporary Source

Sl. No.	*Rebel's Name, Position, Designation, Place*	*Page No.*
1.	Babu of Pandeypar	37
2.	Babu of Rajpur-Paniya	37
3.	Kunwar Singh	41, 42
4.	Harkishan Singh	42, 211
5.	Raja of Narharpur	43, 87
6.	Raja of Tilpur	43, 191
7.	Salamat Ali	49
8.	Murtaza Khan	49
9.	Abul Qasim	50
10.	Hikamatullah Khan	50
11.	Sardar Khan and his brother	50
12.	Nana Rao of Bithur	50
13.	Raja of Satasi	70, 71, 191
14.	Musharraf Khan	70, 71
15.	Babu of Madapar-Belwa (Madanpur-Belwa)	74
16.	Mawari of Talibabad	74
17.	Babu of Bhowapar	74, 184
18.	Bandhu Singh of Dumri	74, 150
19.	Raja Jay Lal	79, 98
20.	Abbas Ali (guide of Mohammed Hasan)	87
21.	Bali Singh	87
22.	Sardar Ali Khan, his relatives and associates	88, 89, 196
23.	Ali Hasan	88, 89
24.	Navanda Rai	88
25.	Mirza Fateh Ali and his relatives	88
26.	Mohd Saeed	88
27.	Tehsildar of Rajhe	89
28.	Sons of Mirza Hasan Ali	299
29.	Ulfat Ali	90

(*Contd...*)

30.	Amir Ali (muharrir)	90
31.	Mohd Saeed (Amir Ali's risaledar)	90
32.	Kaman Khan (jamadar of thana)	90
33.	Bandhu Singh (tumandar)	90
34.	Imdad Ali	90
35.	Abid Ali	90
36.	Mazhar Ali	90
37.	Wajid Ali	90
38.	Ahmad Khan risaledar	90
39.	Ibrahim Beg[1]	91
40.	Kallu Beg	91
41.	Brij Mohan	91
42.	Anup Bari	91
43.	Mansoor Ali	91
44.	Makhdoom Bakhsh	91
45.	Faiz Bakhsh (army's subedar)	91
46.	Najaf Ali (spy for the British artillery's location)	92
47.	Sardar Ali (incharge of cavalry)	93, 120, 196
48.	Nawab[2]	93
49.	Gauhar	93
50.	Shamsher Ali	93
51.	Ehsan Ali	93
52.	Khurshid Ali Khan	93
53.	Wazeeran	93
54.	Kallu Beg (cavalry officer)	93
55.	Dildar Khan	93
56.	Hasan Khan	93
57.	Ram Bahal	93
58.	Ghaziuddin Khan and his son	93
59.	Walidad Khan and his brother	94
60.	Raheemdad Khan	94
61.	Abid Ali (cavalier)	94
62.	Aali Hasan	108, 116, 120
63.	Fazl-e-Ali	111, 112, 120
64.	Jafar Ali	116
65.	Nusrat Beg (havildar)	119
66.	Mirza Humayun	119
67.	Ramzan Khan	119
68.	Abd-e-Khaliq	119
69.	Allahdad Khan	119
70.	Mohd Fakir	120
71.	Bihari	120
72.	Rawat of Haiti	154
73.	Doon Singh	154

(Contd...)

74.	Babu of Belwa	184
75.	Gosain of Tolia	191
76.	Raja of Barhyapar	199
77.	Raja of Nagar	299
78.	Amar Singh (Jagdishpur, Arrah)	256
79.	Sada Singh (zamindar of Ballia)	256
80.	Makar Singh (Mengar Singh)	257
81.	Alivardi Khan	326
82.	Palwar Caste	22, 97
83.	Sepoys of Tuman (army)	94
84.	Ram Lal	50
85.	Mohammed Hasan (Nazim)	124

Notes:

(1) Number 39 to 43 were representatives of Raja Udit Narayan Singh of Satasi.

(2) Number 48 to 51 and 55 to 57 were cavaliers.

Source: *Kashful Baghaavat*, Gorakhpur, Urdu, Arifeen Press, Mirzapur, 1860

English Transliteration and Translation by Nasreen Farhat, Rupa Publications India P Ltd, New Delhi, 2010.

Appendix - B

Details of Punishments Meted out to Some Rebels, according to *Kashful-Baghaavat, Gorakhpur*

(I)

Sl. No.	*Name*	*Punishment*	*P. No.*
1.	Musharraf Khan (Naib Nazim)	Hanged to death	223, 224, 228, 229
2.	Rasool Ali	Hanged to death	223, 224, 228, 229
3.	Aulad Ali	Hanged to death	223, 224, 228, 229
4.	Navanda Rai	Hanged to death	223, 224, 228, 229
5.	Wahid Ali	Hanged to death	223, 224, 228, 229
6.	Pashupati Nath	Hanged to death	223, 224, 228, 229
7.	Ramzan Ali Khan	Hanged to death	229
8.	Lal Khan (Sepoy)	Hanged to death	223
9.	Walidad Khan	Hanged to death	224
10.	Kareemdad Khan	Hanged to death	224
11.	Haidar Hussein (Tehsildar of Brijmanganj)	Hanged to death	224
12.	Inayat Ali (Army leader)	Hanged to death	228
13.	Sitaram (Jamadar of Mansoorganj)	Hanged to death	228
14.	Haider Khan	Hanged to death	229
15.	Umar Khan	Hanged to death	229
16.	10 unknown persons	Hanged to death	228
17.	Shiv Ghulam Singh (Babu of Rudhauli)	Killed in battle	229

(*Contd...*)

18.	Khairat Ali	Ten years imprisonment	224
19.	Sheikh Faizu	Ten years imprisonment	224
20.	Fateh Ali	Imprisonment	299
21.	9 unknown persons	Hanged to death	229
22.	Raja of Nagar	Died in jail	299
23.	Mirza Fateh Ali	Imprisonment	299
24.	Raja of Satasi	Imprisonment	299

(II)

Persons Who were Granted Pardon

Sl. No.	*Name*	*P. No.*
1.	Faiz Bakhsh	292-93
2.	Wazir Ali Khan	293
3.	Sardar Ali Khan's relatives and associates	293

Source: *Kashful Baghaavat*, Gorakhpur, Urdu, Arifeen Press, Mirzapur, 1860.

English Transliteration and Translation by Nasreen Farhat, Rupa Publications India P Ltd, New Delhi, 2010.

Appendix - C

List of Rebels who Played an Active Role in the Rebellion of 1857 in Eastern Uttar Pradesh, according to an Unpublished Contemporary Document in English

Sl. No.	*S No in Govt Record*	*Name*	*Designation or Position*	*Clan and Lineage*	*Place*	*Remark*
1. 2. 3. 4.	5 6 7 8	Jhoori Singh, Mata Bheekh Singh, Mata Bakhsh Singh, Sarnam Singh	Zamindars and chiefs of various villages	Unknown	Gopiganj	Killed W R Mr. Muir, Deputy Magistrate of Mirzapur, in the Pali factory at Gopiganj. The government had announced a reward of 1,000 on each one's arrest.
5. 6.	77 78	Fakir Chand, Ramdeen	Unknown rebel, agent of Vijay Bahadur Singh	Unknown	Gopiganj	Both had attacked, with a troop, at Phoolpur
7.	83	Kunwar Singh	Zamindar	Unknown	Jagdishpur (Arrah)	Rebellious role in Azamgarh
8.	84	Amar Singh	Zamindar	Unknown	Jagdishpur (Arrah)	Rebellious role in Ghazipur
9.	92	Madho Singh (Ram)	Sepoy in Private Light Company, 17th NI (Bhondu Singh's son-in-law)	Unknown	Azamgarh	Shot the first bullet in rebellion, killing Lt Huchinson. Also injured others. Govt announced reward of 2,000 rupees for his arrest.

(*Contd...*)

10.	93	Bhondu Singh	Subedar, 17th NI	Unknown	Azamgarh	After revolting, the 17th NI proceeded for Faizabad under his leadership. Govt announced reward of 1,000 rupees for his arrest.
11.	94	Pargan Singh	Pattidar (zamindar) of village Hirapatti	Unknown	Azamgarh	Collected people to attack Venables at Azamgarh
12.	95	Madho Prasad Singh	Birhar	Unknown	Azamgarh	Gathered Palwar Rajputs in large numbers against the British
13.	98	Mansoor Ali	-----	Unknown	Azamgarh	Sided with rebels against British
14.	99	Sahebdad Khan	Tehsildar	Unknown	Azamgarh	
15.	100	Jagbandhan Singh	Rich zamindar	Unknown	Azamgarh	Sided with rebels
16.	101	Siyadeen Singh	Zamindar of Kudari	Unknown	Azamgarh	Sided with rebels
17.	102	Dhiranjan Singh	Zamindar of Kudari	Unknown	Azamgarh	Sided with rebels
18.	103	Harchand Singh	Zamindar of Kudari	Unknown	Azamgarh	Sided with rebels
19.	104	Harku Singh	Zamindar of Kudari	Unknown	Azamgarh	Sided with rebels
20.	105	Jayshri Singh	Zamindar of Bhagwa	Unknown	Azamgarh	Sided with rebels
21.	106	Ram Ghulam Singh	Zamindar of Bhagwa	Unknown	Azamgarh	Sided with rebels
22.	107	Ramcharan Singh	Zamindar of Bhagwa	Unknown	Azamgarh	Sided with rebels
23.	108	Bindeshwari Singh	Zamindar of Bhagwa	Unknown	Azamgarh	Sided with rebels
24.	109	Ram Prasad Rai	Zamindar of Araiya	Unknown	Azamgarh	Sided with rebels
25.	110	Khande Singh	Zamindar of Araiya	Unknown	Mohabbat pur, Azamgarh	Sided with rebels
26.	111	Bhairav Singh	Zamindar of Araiya	Unknown	Mohabbat pur, Azamgarh	Sohan Singh and Baijnath Singh were hanged to death on charge of looting some villages
27.	112	Ajaib Lal	Zamindar of Araiya	Unknown	Mohabbat pur, Azamgarh	
28.	113	Jag Bandhan Singh	Zamindar of Araiya	Unknown	Mohabbat pur, Azamgarh	Rajab Ali freed Jagbandhan Singh and four others from jail. Hence the govt announced 100 rupees for the arrest of each.
29.	114	Gulab Singh	Zamindar of village Sunra	Unknown	Mohabbat pur, Azamgarh	
30.	115	Sangram Singh	Zamindar	Unknown	Mohabbat pur, Azamgarh	Sohan Singh and Baijnath Singh were hanged to death on
31.	116	Karamat Ali	Zamindar of Siuli	Unknown	Mohabbat pur, Azamgarh	

(Contd...)

32.	117	Sohan Singh	Zamindar	Unknown	Mohabbat pur, Azamgarh	charge of looting some villages
33.	118	Baijnath Singh	Zamindar	Unknown	Mohabbat pur, Azamgarh	
34.	119	Rajab Ali	Zamindar of Bamhaur	Unknown	Mohabbat pur, Azamgarh	Venables, Deputy Magistrate of Azamgarh, described Rajab Ali as the zamindar of Bamhore. Staying at the houses of two other zamindars, he collected people for revolt.
35.	120	Kiya Khan	Zamindar of Sikti	Unknown	Mohabbat pur, Azamgarh	
36.	121	Ummed Ali Khan	Zamindar of Sikti	Unknown	Mohabbat pur, Azamgarh	
37.	122	Bhawani Singh	Subedar, 41st NI	Unknown	Azamgarh	Commandant of the Azamgarh chakladar's army
38.	123	Kishan Prasad	Zamindar	Unknown	Azamgarh	Brother of Azamgarh rebel Madho Prasad. On behalf of his brother, he attacked Venables' troop.
39.	124	Shiv Prakash	Zamindar	Unknown	Azamgarh	
40.	125	Beni Madho	Unknown	Unknown	Azamgarh	Openly revolted against the Company Government.
41.	126	Prithvipal Singh	Unknown	Unknown	Azamgarh	
42.	127	Muzaffar Jehan	Unknown	Unknown	Azamgarh	
43.	128	Raja of Atraulia	Unknown	Unknown	Azamgarh	
44.	129	Chandresh Singh	Rajput	Unknown	Azamgarh	Fought against the government.
45.	130	Amaresh Singh	Rajkumar	Unknown	Azamgarh	
46.	191	Bharat Rai	Zamindar	Unknown	Ghazipur	He was zamindar of village Hasanpura in pargana Zahoorabad and lived in Kusera. He collected about two thousand people and surrounded the tehsil. But he retreated after the tehsildar reached there with 70 musketeers.
47.	192	Zamindar of Chaura	Zamindar	Unknown	Ghazipur	Leader of rebellious Rajputs. They looted a factory and fired. They conducted rebellious activities in the nearby villages.
48.	194	Mohammed Hasan	Former Nazim of Gonda-Bahraich	Unknown	Gorakhpur	He was the main rebel of Gorakhpur district. He immediately occupied the district when British officials vacated it. He declared himself the Nazim of Gorakhpur and Azamgarh.

(Contd...)

49.	195	Faiz Ali Khan	Unknown	Unknown	Gorakhpur	They were Mohammed Hasan's counsellors.
50.	196	Fakir Khan	Unknown	Unknown	Gorakhpur	
51.	197	Jafar Ali	Naib Nazim	Abbas Ali's son	Gorakhpur	
52.	199	Raja of Nagar	Unknown	Unknown	Gorakhpur	All of them sided with Mohammed Hasan during the revolt and ended the government's tehsildari.
53.	200	All zamindars in north western part, led by Balli Singh	Unknown	Unknown	Gorakhpur	
54.	202	Meer Madad Ali	Unknown	Unknown	Gorakhpur	All these people corresponded with rebel leader Mohammed Hasan.
55.	203	Najmul Burhan	Unknown	Unknown	Gorakhpur	
56.	204	Faizalli Khan	Unknown	Unknown	Gorakhpur	
57.	205	Raja of Amorha	Raja	Unknown	Gorakhpur	
58.	206	Raja Udit Narayan Singh of Satasi	Zamindar	Unknown	Gorakhpur	
59.	207	Sheikh Abdullah	Jamadar of Chowki Mehdawal	Unknown	Gorakhpur	They had welcomed Chakladar Mohammed Hasan on his arrival in Gorakhpur.
60.	208	Najaf Ali	Musketeer of Kotwali	Unknown	Gorakhpur	
61.	209	Shiv Ghulam Singh	Babu of Rudhauli	Unknown	Gorakhpur	Killed while fighting against British army.
62.	210	Babus of Pandeypar	Unknown	Unknown	Gorakhpur	
63.	211	Raja of Chillupar	Unknown	Unknown	Gorakhpur	
64.	213	Gangadutt and others of Digrapur	Unknown	Unknown	Gorakhpur	
65.	214	Govind Bali Singh	Prominent Babu of Pandeypar	Unknown	Gorakhpur	Openly involved in the rebellion.
66.	215	Zamindar of Bhowapar	Unknown	Unknown	Gorakhpur	
67.	216	Bailiff of Raja of Nagar	Unknown	Unknown	Gorakhpur	
68.	217	Kisun Sahay	Wasil Baqi Navees of pargana Amorha	Unknown	Gorakhpur	
69.	219	Wasil Baqi Navees of pargana Anola/Andia	Unknown	Unknown	Gorakhpur	
70.	220	Mohammed Nawaz	Unknown	Unknown	Gorakhpur	
71.	221-222	Mohd Hussein Bakhsh and his brother	Tehsildar of Bansi	Unknown	Gorakhpur	
72.	223	Mohd Sami	Unknown	Unknown	Gorakhpur	
73.	224	Mirza Fateh Ali	Unknown	Unknown	Gorakhpur	
74.	225	Ali Hasan	Unknown	Unknown	Gorakhpur	
75.	226	Surat Singh	Zamindar of Shivpur in pargana Amorha	Unknown	Gorakhpur	
76.	227	Devideen	Unknown	Unknown	Gorakhpur	
77.	229	Hussein Ali	Unknown	Unknown	Gorakhpur	

(Contd...)

78.	230	Raja Jay Lal Singh	Unknown	Unknown	Gorakhpur	
79.	232	Baqar Hussein	Unknown	Unknown	Gorakhpur	
80.	233	Faiz Ali alias Sheikh Bheekha	Unknown	Unknown	Gorakhpur	
81.	235	Daulat Ali	Unknown	Unknown	Gorakhpur	
82.	236	Sher Ali	Unknown	Unknown	Gorakhpur	
83.	238	Musharraf Khan	Unknown	Unknown	Gorakhpur	He led the army troop that was to attack the Raja of Mahuli.
84.	239	Reet Bhuwan Singh	Unknown	Unknown	Gorakhpur	
85.	240	Zulfiqar Ali	Unknown	Unknown	Gorakhpur	
86.	242	Devki Prasad	Was appointed tehsildar of Salempur by rebels			
87.	243	Madad Ali	Was appointed tehsildar of Padrauna			
88.	244	Wahid Ali Khan	Deputy Magistrate			
89.	245	Meer Ali Nasar	Tehsildar of Bansgaon			
90.	246	Son of Raja of Mahul				
91.	247	Babu of Ganeshpur Pipra				
92.	248	Banwal of pargana Nagar				
93.	249	Babu Vansh Bahadur Singh	Zamindar of Badokhar			
94.	250	Chhatar Dhari Singh	Zamindar of Badokhar			
95.	252	Jagarnath Singh of Aniya				
96.	252	Babu of Belghat				
97.	253	Abbas Ali of Tanda				
98.	254	Babu of Bootwal				
99.	255	Babu of Bansgaon				
100.	256	Sarfaraz Ali				
101.	257	Faiz Ali	A rebel commander			
102.	278	Kalab Ali	Kotwal	Unknown	Jaunpur	Appointed Kotwal by the city people
103.	280	Jagesar Bakhsh	Badlapur	Unknown	Jaunpur	Appointed thanedar of Badlapur by rebels
104.	281	Makhdoom Bakhsh		Unknown	Gorakhpur	Chakladar (an appointed officer)
105.	282	Iradat Jehan	Raja of Mahul			Leader of rebellion in Jaunpur
106.	283	Two sons of Iradat Jehan	---	---		
107.		Hasan Yar Khan	Rebel Naib Nazim of Jaunpur			

Source: Foreign Department, Secret Consultation No. 355-362, 30 April 1858, pp. 1-12, printed record preserved in National Archives of India, New Delhi.

Appendix - D

List of Rebels in Eastern Uttar Pradesh, according to Published Documents

Sl. No.	*Name*	*Place*	*Designation/ Position*	*P. No.*
1.	Rani of Amorha	Gorakhpur	Zamindar	318, 372
2.	Babu of Rudhauli (Shiv Ghulam Singh)	Gorakhpur	Zamindar	157, 324, 330-331
3.	Babu of Pandeypar (Govind Bali Singh)	Gorakhpur	Zamindar	362, 379
4.	Zamindar of Paina	Gorakhpur	Zamindar	144, 150, 152, 342
5.	Babu of Bakhira	Gorakhpur	Zamindar	153
6.	Raja of Barhyapar	Gorakhpur	Zamindar	157, 372
7.	Raja of Nichlaul	Gorakhpur	Zamindar	157, 304, 306-307, 336
8.	Raja of Shahpur	Gorakhpur	Zamindar	157
9.	Raja of Satasi (Udit Narayan Singh)	Gorakhpur	Zamindar	152, 156, 305
10.	Zamindar of Amorha	Gorakhpur	Zamindar	152
11.	Raja of Nagar	Gorakhpur	Zamindar	152, 305, 326
12.	Raja of Narharpur	Gorakhpur	Zamindar	150, 152, 305
13.	Mohammed Hasan	Gorakhpur	Chakladar	155, 156, 185
14.	Musharraf Khan	Chakla Gorakhpur	Naib	157, 299, 305, 384
15.	Pratap Singh	Gorakhpur	Zamindar	162
16.	Narayan Dayal	Gorakhpur	Qanungo	300
17.	Babu of Tighra	Gorakhpur	Zamindar	157
18.	Sangram Lal	Gorakhpur	Zamindar	300-301
19.	Wali Mohd	Tilji	Zamindar	306
20.	Babu of Chillupar	Gorakhpur	Zamindar	319
21.	Babu of Dumri (Bandhu Singh)	Gorakhpur	Zamindar	333, 34
22.	Balli Singh	Gorakhpur	Zamindar	354, 357, 358, 365, 383
23.	Balikaran	Gorakhpur	Zamindar	354, 357, 365
24.	Rajivan Singh	Gorakhpur	Zamindar	365
25.	Mendhu Khan	Gorakhpur	Zamindar	359, 397
26.	Damman Khan	Gorakhpur	Zamindar	345
27.	Surat Singh	Amorha Gorakhpur	Zamindar	380
28.	Mohd Hussein Bakhsh	Gorakhpur	Zamindar	379
29.	Mirza Fateh Ali	Gorakhpur	Zamindar	379, 384
30.	Mirza Ali Hasan	Gorakhpur	Zamindar	151,379
31.	Jafar Ali	Gorakhpur	Zamindar	383
32.	Mohd Nawaz	Gorakhpur	Zamindar	383
33.	Faiz Ali alias Sheikh Bhikha	Gorakhpur	Zamindar	381
34.	Ghulam Hussein	Belwa, Gorakhpur	Zamindar	207
35.	Bailiff of Raja of Nagar	Gorakhpur	Zamindar	326, 331
36.	Maulvi Sarfaraz Ali	Gorakhpur	Zamindar	345
37.	Babu of Pipra	Gorakhpur	Zamindar	383
38.	Bhondu Singh	Azamgarh	Subedar, 17th NI	89
39.	Ram Tahal/Ram Taul son of Bhondu Singh	Azamgarh	Sepoy in 17th NI, First Company	89
40.	Madho Ram, Bhondu Singh's son-in-law	Azamgarh	Sepoy in 17th NI, Light Company	89
41.	Muzaffar Jahanson of Raja Iradat Jehan	Azamgarh	Zamindar	101, 246-247

(Contd...)

42.	Fasahat Jehan	Azamgarh	Zamindar	101, 102
43.	Faiz Ali Khan	Azamgarh	Servant of Zamindar Muzaffar Jehan	101
44.	Dhawan Mal	Azamgarh	Servant of Zamindar Muzaffar Jehan	101
45.	Jivan Mishra	Azamgarh	Servant of Zamindar Muzaffar Jehan	101
46.	Ramphal Mahajan	Tehsil Sagdi, Azamgarh	Moneylender	104
47.	Ram Niwas Singh	Chiraiyakot, Azamgarh	Civilian	107
48.	Madho Prasad Singh	Birhur (Awadh), Azamgarh	Taluqdar	108, 174,182, 189
49.	Prithvipal Singh	Tighra (Awadh), Azamgarh	Taluqdar	108, 187, 191
50.	Pargan Singh	Azamgarh	Zamindar	141, 142, 177, 202, 203, 204
51.	Raja Beni Madho	Azamgarh	Zamindar	187, 244
52.	Seetal Prasad	Azamgarh	Unknown	190
53.	Indrajit Singh	Nainijor, Azamgarh	Zamindar	161, 162, 195
54.	Zamindar of Dhanauli	Azamgarh	Zamindar	163
55.	Raja Jay Lal Singh	Jaunpur and Azamgarh	Chakladar	217
56.	Syed Mohd Hussein	Azamgarh	Chakladar	217
57.	Balki Singh	Azamgarh	Unknown	205
58.	Kanhaiya Singh	Azamgarh	Subedar	206
59.	Son of a maulvi of Tanda	Azamgarh	Civilian	205
60.	Seedha Singh	Azamgarh, Jaunpur	Commander	207
61.	Amar Singh	Adampur, Jaunpur	Army chief of Raja Iradat Jehan	32
62.	Makhdoom Bakhsh	Jaunpur	Agent of Raja Iradat Jehan	35
63.	Malik Mehdi Bakhsh	Jaunpur	Zamindar	35
64.	Sarabjit Singh	Jaunpur	Civilian	123
65.	Harnandan Singh	Jaunpur	In Raja Iradat Jehan's employ	124
66.	Jattan Singh	Jaunpur	In employ of Amar Singh of Adampur	124
67.	Shivnath Singh	Jaunpur	Employee of a Nilha Englishman	124
68.	Shivnandan Singh	Jaunpur	Employee of a Nilha Englishman	124
69.	Ashraf Khan	Jaunpur	Artisan in indigo factory	125
70.	Janki Singh son of Amar Singh	Jaunpur	Rebel	125
71.	Ghasitan	Jaunpur	Tailor	126
72.	Udresh Singh	Jaunpur	Zamindar, Rajkumar Rajput	138, 174, 189
73.	Chandresh Singh	Jaunpur	Zamindar, Rajkumar Rajput	174
74.	Jagesar Bakhsh	Badlapur, Jaunpur	Taluqdar	210, 211, 213-214, 216

(Contd...)

75.	Arjun Singh	Jaunpur	Taluqdar	211, 213-214
76.	Bindeshwari Prasad	Jaunpur	Zamindar	215
77.	Bhawani Singh	Jaunpur	Subedar in 41st NI	217
78.	Raja Iradat Jehan	Mubarakpur, Jaunpur	Zamindar	219-221, 242-244
79.	Hasan Yar Khan	Jaunpur	Chakladar	223
80.	Sangram Singh	Madiahu, Jaunpur	Zamindar	229, 230, 235-236
81.	Ghulam Hussein son of Mohammed Hasan, Chakladar of Gorakhpur	Madiahu, Jaunpur	---	230
82.	Bhairo Prasad	Banaras	Moneylender	236-237
83.	Khudabakhsh Khan	Jaunpur	Commander (?)	226-227
84.	Phooli Singh	Badlapur, Jaunpur	Zamindar	216-217
85.	Nazar Hussein	Jaunpur	Bailiff of Raja Iradat Jehan	245
86.	Mengar Singh	Gahmar, Ghazipur	Zamindar	277
87.	Jawahar Singh	Gahmar, Ghazipur	Zamindar	287
88.	Nishun Khan	Bara, Ghazipur, Mirzapur	Rebel	122
89.	Raja of Singrauli	Mirzapur	Zamindar	263
90.	Randhir Singh (cousin of Raja of Singrauli)	Mirzapur	Zamindar	263
91.	Raja Lakshman Singh	Vijaygarh, Mirzapur	Zamindar	36, 350
92.	Ganesh Prasad Singh	Bhadohi, Banaras	Zamindar	67, 82
93.	Balbhadra Singh	Bhadohi, Banaras	Zamindar	67, 82
94.	Dhawan Singh	Bhadohi, Banaras	Unknown	80
95.	Hanuman Brahmin	Bhadohi, Banaras	---	80
96.	Raja Udwant Singh	Bhadohi, Banaras	Zamindar	67, 79
97.	Bhola Singh	Bhadohi, Banaras	Raja Udwant's Diwan	79
98.	Ram Bakhsh Singh	Bhadohi, Banaras	Raja Udwant's Diwan	79
99.	Shiv Dayal Singh	Bhadohi, Banaras	---	80
100.	Mabusia (female)	Bhadohi	Raja Udwant Singh's widow	81
101.	Mata Bheekh Singh	Bhadohi, Banaras	Zamindar	64
102.	Mata Bakhsh Singh	Bhadohi, Banaras	Zamindar	64, 72
103.	Jhoori Singh	Bhadohi, Banaras	Zamindar	64, 69, 72, 80
104.	Sarnam Singh	Bhadohi, Banaras	Zamindar	64, 72, 80
105.	Shivadin Singh	Bhadohi, Banaras	Zamindar	83
106.	Bindeshwari Singh	Bhadohi, Banaras	Zamindar	83
107.	Shiv Tahal	Bhadohi, Banaras	Zamindar	83
108.	Musai Singh	Bhadohi, Banaras	Zamindar	84
109.	Sanwal Singh/Sanwaal Singh	Bhadohi, Banaras	Zamindar	84
110.	Najai (Vijayi) Singh son of Indrajit Singh	Bhadohi, Banaras	Zamindar	84
111.	Musai Chamar	Bhadohi, Banaras	Zamindar's servant	84
112.	Ashraf Bakhsh Khan	Utraula, Awadh	Taluqdar	348
113.	Jawahar Khan	Utraula, Awadh	Unknown	348

Appendix - E

PART - I

List of Martyrs of Rebellion 1857 in Eastern Uttar Pradesh

Sl. No.	Name	Domicile/Place	P. No.
1.	Thakur Abhilakh Singh	Village Barsar, taluqa Dobhi, dist Jaunpur	2-3
2.	Thakur Amar Singh	Village Adampur, Jaunpur	9
3.	Angadu Singh	Badlapur, Jaunpur	10
4.	Awadhoot Singh	Haraiya, Basti	12
5.	Ayodhya	Jaunpur	12
6.	Babu Sohan Singh	Bakhira, Basti	13
7.	Bahadur	Village Hauz, Jaunpur	14
8.	Varun (sentenced to death along with 14 others)	Village Hauz, Jaunpur	19
9.	Bhanu	Village Hauz, Jaunpur	21
10.	Bhawan Bheekh	Jaunpur	22
11.	Thakur Bishesar Singh	Dobhi, Jaunpur	25
12.	Thakur Chhangur Singh	Dobhi, Jaunpur	28-29
13.	Thakur Dayal Singh	Dobhi, Jaunpur	32-33
14.	Thakur Devki Singh	Dobhi, Jaunpur	34
15.	Devi Rai?	Padrauna, Deoria	35
16.	Dharam Raj Singh	Ama, Basti	35
17.	Diteha?	Jaunpur	37
18.	Fasahat Jehan	Mahul, Jaunpur	40
19.	Harpal Singh	Dharauli ka Babu, Basti	53
20.	Ishwari Shukla	Haraiya, Basti	60-61
21.	Thakur Jay Mangal Singh	Dobhi, Jaunpur	66
22.	Jhoori Singh	Pappaur, Jaunpur	66
23.	Jivaram Ahir	Dobhi, Jaunpur	67
24.	Kishun Ahir	Dobhi, Jaunpur	77
25.	Bakht Singh	Kunwarpur, Jaunpur	70
26.	Lakshman Prasad	Ghazipur	80
27.	Thakur Madho Singh	Dobhi, Jaunpur	84
28.	Mangaru (sepoy)	Basti	88
29.	Maan Singh (sepoy)	Deoria	90
30.	Merhi	Jaunpur	92
31.	Mohai	Jaunpur	94
32.	Mukhi	Jaunpur	101
33.	Raja of Nagar	Basti	104
34.	Prasanna	Hauz, Jaunpur	115
35.	Raghupati Rai?	Padrauna, Deoria	117
36.	Raghubir Singh	Chirauli, Haraiya, Basti	118
37.	Thakur Ram Bharos Singh	Dobhi, Jaunpur	119
38.	Thakur Ram Dular Singh	Dobhi, Jaunpur	120-121
39.	Ramdin Singh	Chirauli, Haraiya, Basti	123
40.	Rameshwar	Hauz, Jaunpur	123
41.	Ramzan Ali Khan	(Risaladar in Awadh cavalry) Gorakhpur	123-124

(Contd...)

42.	Sangram Singh	Badlapur, Jaunpur	131
43.	Seetal	Jaunpur	133
44.	Sardar Ali Khan	Gorakhpur	131-132
45.	Thakur Shivbrat Singh	Dobhi, Jaunpur	136-137
46.	Shivdeen	Hauz, Jaunpur	137
47.	Shivlal	Hauz, Jaunpur	138
48.	Sukhlal	Hauz, Jaunpur	141
49.	Sukhraj Singh	Mustafabad, Jaunpur	141
50.	Thakur Singh	Dobhi, Jaunpur	144-145
51.	Thakuri	Hauz, Jaunpur	145
52.	Thakur Yadubir Singh	Dobhi, Jaunpur	153

Note: All the above were either hanged to death or they died fighting.

Source: P N Chopra (Ed), *Who is Who of Indian Martyrs of 1857*, Vol. III, Government of India, New Delhi, 1973.

PART - II
List of Martyrs and Those Transported to Life in Azamgarh District

Sl. No.	Name	Address	Date of Punishment	Nature of Punishment
1.	Raja Jay Lal Singh son of Darshan Singh	Village Bawandara, thana Atraulia, tehsil Phoolpur	01-10-1859 (at Faizabad)	Execution, confiscation of property
2.	Raja Syed Iradat Jehan	Vill Shamsabad, thana Ahraula, tehsil Phoolpur	---	Execution, confiscation of property
3.	Raghubar Singh	Vill Katta, thana Ahraula, tehsil Phoolpur	02-02-1858	Execution, confiscation of property
4.	Sheikh Rajab Ali	Vill Bamhaur, thana Mubarakpur, tehsil Mohammedabad	29-12-1857	Was shot to death at Hajipur Ghat; property was confiscated
5.	Sheikh Mubban	Vill Bamhaur, thana Mubarakpur, tehsil Mohammedabad	02-07-1857	Execution, confiscation of property
6.	Sheikh Bechai	Vill Bamhaur, thana Mubarakpur, tehsil Mohammedabad	02-07-1857	Execution, confiscation of property
7.	Chamru Barber	Vill Bamhaur, thana Mubarakpur, tehsil Mohammedabad	02-07-1857	Execution, confiscation of property
8.	Durgpal Singh	Vill Pasipur, thana Maharajganj, tehsil Phoolpur	06-01-1858	Execution, confiscation of property
9.	Bhimal Singh	Vill Pasipur, thana Maharajganj, tehsil Phoolpur	06-01-1858	Execution, confiscation of property
10.	Gulab Singh	Vill Pasipur, thana Maharajganj, tehsil Phoolpur	06-01-1858	Execution, confiscation of property
11.	Sangram Singh	Vill Pasipur, thana Maharajganj, tehsil Phoolpur	06-01-1858	Execution, confiscation of property

(*Contd...*)

12.	Shitla Bakhsh Singh	Vill Pasipur, thana Maharajganj, tehsil Phoolpur	06-01-1858	Execution, confiscation of property
13.	Madhav Singh	Vill Pakraul, thana Ahraula, Tehsil Phoolpur	08-02-1858	Execution, confiscation of property
14.	Swami Prasad Singh	Vill Pakraul, thana Ahraula, Tehsil Phoolpur	08-02-1858	Execution, confiscation of property
15.	Shiv Tahal Singh	Vill Pakraul, thana Ahraula, Tehsil Phoolpur	08-02-1858	Execution, confiscation of property
16.	Gopal Singh	Vill Pakraul, thana Ahraula, Tehsil Phoolpur	08-02-1858	Execution, confiscation of property
17.	Shiv Ghulam Singh	Vill Pakraul, thana Ahraula, Tehsil Phoolpur	08-02-1858	Execution, confiscation of property
18.	Bakkas Pasi	Vill Pakraul, thana Ahraula, Tehsil Phoolpur	08-02-1858	Execution, confiscation of property
19.	Govind Singh	Vill Lohra, thana Ahraula, tehsil Phoolpur	12-05-1858	Execution, confiscation of property
20.	Daljeet Singh	Vill Lohra, thana Ahraula, tehsil Phoolpur	17-12-1857	Execution
21.	Sheikh Buddhu	Vill Pakrauli, thana Maharajganj, tehsil Sagdi	28-10-1857	Execution
22.	Harnam Singh	Vill Bhilampur, thana Atraulia, tehsil Phoolpur	20-09-1857	Martyred in battle at Maduri
23.	Bhola Singh	Vill Bhilampur, thana Atraulia, tehsil Phoolpur	20-09-1857	Martyred in battle at Maduri
24.	Mardan Singh	Vill Bhilampur, thana Atraulia, tehsil Phoolpur	20-09-1857	Martyred in battle at Maduri
25.	Sheelwant Singh	Vill Bhilampur, thana Atraulia, tehsil Phoolpur	20-09-1857	Martyred in battle at Maduri
26.	Harpal Singh	Vill Bhilampur, thana Atraulia, tehsil Phoolpur	20-09-1857	Martyred in battle at Maduri
27.	Hardutt Singh	Vill Bhilampur, thana Atraulia, tehsil Phoolpur	20-09-1857	Martyred in battle at Maduri
28.	Madhai Prasad Yadav	Vill Bahiripur, thana Nizamabad, tehsil Sadar	20-09-1857	Martyred in battle at Maduri
29.	Shivdihal Rai	Vill Maduri, thana Kandhrapur, tehsil Sagdi	20-09-1857	Was killed by a dagger
30.	Mitai Kahar	Vill Maduri, thana Kandhrapur, tehsil Sagdi	20-09-1857	Was killed by a dagger
31.	Wife of Mandil Rai	Vill Maduri, thana Kandhrapur, tehsil Sagdi	20-09-1857	Was shot dead in home
32.	Durg Singh	Vill Meghai, thana Jiyanpur, tehsil Sagdi	20-09-1857	Tortured to death in jail
33.	Shiv Ghulam Rai	Vill Mudahara, thana Ahraula, tehsil Phoolpur	02-02-1858	Execution, confiscation of property
34.	Zalim Singh	Vill Paradaha, thana Mau, tehsil Mohammedabad	03-12-1857	Execution, confiscation of property
35.	Ramhit Singh	Vill Paradaha, thana Mau, tehsil Mohammedabad	03-12-1857	Execution, confiscation of property
36.	Daswant Singh	Vill Hirapatti, thana Kotwali, tehsil Sadar	03-12-1857	Execution, confiscation of property
37.	Harakh Singh	Vill Dubari, thana Madhuban, tehsil Ghosi	03-12-1857	Execution, confiscation of property
38.	Hulas Singh	Vill Dubari, thana Madhuban, tehsil Ghosi	03-12-1857	Execution, confiscation of property
39.	Goga Sahu	Vill Azmatgarh, thana Jiyanpur, tehsil Sagdi	03-12-1857	Transportation for life, confiscation of property

(Contd...)

40.	Bhikho Sahu	Vill Azmatgarh, thana Jiyanpur, tehsil Sagdi	03-12-1857	Transportation for life, confiscation of property
41.	Shiv Ratan Rai (Singh)	Vill Kisunpur, thana Jehanaganj, tehsil Mohammedabad	03-12-1857	Transportation for life, confiscation of property

PART - II

List of Azamgarh Rebels (Absconding) whom British Govt could not Arrest

Sl. No	*Name*	*Father's Name*	*Address*
1.	Raja Beni Madho Prasad (Singh)	Darshan Singh	Vill Atraulia, tehsil Phoolpur
2.	Thakur Prithvipal Singh	Govind Dayal Singh Palwar	Vill Tighra, thana Ahraula, pargana Mahul, Azamgarh
3.	Thakur Pargan Singh	Girdhari Singh	Vill Hirapatti, thana Kotwali, tehsil Sadar
4.	Jagbandhan Singh	Pratap Singh	Vill Mohabbatpur, thana Mubarakpur, pargana Mohammedabad
5.	Ram Ghulam Singh	Bihari Singh	Vill Mohabbatpur, thana Mubarakpur, pargana Mohammedabad
6.	Ram Tilak Das	Bichak Das (Kayastha)	Vill Mohabbatpur, thana Mubarakpur, pargana Mohammedabad
7.	Pratap Singh	Shiv Dayal Singh	Vill Mohabbatpur, thana Mubarakpur, pargana Mohammedabad
8.	Motilal Ahir	Radhe Ahir	Vill Mohabbatpur, thana Mubarakpur, pargana Mohammedabad
9.	Kunjan Singh	Mahabal Singh	Vill Mohabbatpur, thana Mubarakpur, pargana Mohammedabad
10.	Ammar Singh	Ram Dihal Singh	Vill Mohabbatpur, thana Mubarakpur, pargana Mohammedabad
11.	Bhairav Singh	Hirab Singh	Vill Mohabbatpur, thana Mubarakpur, pargana Mohammedabad
12.	Qayam Ali	Nahar Khan	Vill Sakhia
13.	Medan Ali	Ghaus Khan	Vill Sakhia
14.	Madhav Prasad Singh	Munna Singh	Vill Bidahar (Awadh region), thana Maharajganj
15.	Kisun Prasad Singh	Munna Singh	Vill Bidahar (Awadh region), thana Maharajganj
16.	Shiv Prasad Singh	Ishwari Dayal Singh	Vill Birhur (Awadh region), thana Maharajganj
17.	Ram Newas Singh	Unknown	Vill Munja, pargana Sikandarpur, Azamgarh
18.	Meer Mansab Ali	Syed Ali	Vill Sarai Meer, thana Sarai Meer, tehsil Sadar
19.	Syed Muzaffar Jahan(went through seven years of imprisonment)	Raja Iradat Jehan	Vill Mahul, pargana Mahul, thana Ahraula
20.	Balwant Singh	Chunni Singh	Vill Farrukhabad, pargana Nizamabad, Azamgarh
21.	Sheikh Jawwad Ali (went through five years of imprisonment)	---	Vill Mau, pargana Mohammedabad, Azamgarh

(*Contd...*)

22.	Rashil Ali Khan (went through three years of imprisonment)	---	Vill Mau, pargana Mohammedabad, Azamgarh
23.	Hiralal Mishra (suffered 100 hits of a cane)	---	Vill Lohra, thana Atraulia, tehsil Phoolpur, Azamgarh
24.	Naipal Singh	---	Vill Lohra, thana Atraulia, tehsil Phoolpur, Azamgarh
25.	Baror Singh	---	Vill Lohra, thana Atraulia, tehsil Phoolpur, Azamgarh
26.	Swayambar Singh	Nanhku Singh	Vill Khatabpur, thana and pargana Nizamabad, tehsil Sadar
27.	Ram Bahal Singh		
28.	Amresh Singh	Harnandan Singh (Rajkumar Kshatriya)	Region Awadh, thana Maharajganj
29.	Chandresh Singh	---	Region Awadh, thana Maharajganj
30.	Awadhesh Singh (Rajkumar Kshatriya)	---	Region Awadh, thana Maharajganj
31.	Jagbandhoo Singh	---	Vill Nagraul, pargana Mahul, Azamgarh
32.	Harnam Singh	Prithvipal Singh	Vill Kartalpur, thana Kotwali, pargana Nizamabad, Azamgarh
33.	Indrajit Singh	Raja Bahadur Surahna	Vill Nainyjor, pargana Sagdi, Azamgarh
34.	Ayodhya Singh	Jagannath Singh	Vill Bidahardiha, region Maharajganj, tehsil Sagdi
35.	Bisar Singh	Thakur Dayal Singh	Vill Bidahardiha, region Maharajganj, tehsil Sagdi
36.	Tapsi Bahadur Singh	Ayodhya Singh	Vill Bidahardiha, region Maharajganj, tehsil Sagdi
37.	Thakur Dayal Singh	Hargovind Singh	Vill Bidahardiha, region Maharajganj, tehsil Sagdi
38.	Dashgrah Singh	Harkhu Singh	Vill Bidahardiha, region Maharajganj, tehsil Sagdi
39.	Ram Adhar Singh	Dashgrah Singh	Vill Bidahardiha, region Maharajganj, tehsil Sagdi
40.	Ram Narayan Singh	Harkhu Singh	Vill Bidahardiha, region Maharajganj, tehsil Sagdi
41.	Antu Singh	Devi Singh	Vill Nariyaon, thana Atraulia, Azamgarh
42.	Harihar Singh	Dal Thamman Singh	Vill Nariyaon, thana Atraulia, Azamgarh
43.	Ram Bali Singh	---	Vill Barohi, thana Maharajganj, Azamgarh
44.	Gaya Singh	---	Vill Barohi, thana Maharajganj, Azamgarh
45.	Jantri Singh	---	Vill Barohi, thana Maharajganj, Azamgarh
46.	Narayan Rai	---	Vill Sethwal, pargana Nizamabad, Sadar
47.	Udit Rai	---	Vill Sethwal, pargana Nizamabad, Sadar
48.	Ramhit	---	Vill Unchagaon, pargana Nizamabad, Sadar
49.	Shah Asad Ali	---	Vill Chhatwara, thana Kotwali, Sadar
50.	Ram Narayan Mishra	---	Thana Madhuban, pargana Ghosi
51.	Birli or Murali Singh	---	Pargana Mohammedabad

(Contd...)

51.	Birli or Murali Singh	---	Pargana Mohammedabad
52.	Madhav Singh	---	Vill Chikraul, Ahraula, Phoolpur
53.	Sitasaran	---	Vill Chikraul, Ahraula, Phoolpur
54.	Gulab Mishra	---	Vill Chikraul, Ahraula, Phoolpur
55.	Hargun Singh	---	Vill Gaurdiha, Ahraula, Phoolpur
56.	Saltnat Singh	---	Vill Sonadih, pargana Ghosi
57.	Fasahat Jehan (was sentenced to death)	---	Vill Mahul, Ahraula, Phoolpur
58.	Syed Ali Jehan	---	Vill Mahul, Ahraula, Phoolpur
59.	Lappan Singh	---	Vill Meghai, thana Jiyanpur, tehsil Sigdi
60.	Shivjor Singh	---	Vill Meghai, thana Jiyanpur, tehsil Sigdi
61.	Ram Bahal Singh Kurmi	---	Vill Khatabpur, thana and pargana Nizamabad, tehsil Sadar
62.	Bihari Singh	---	Vill Dubari, thana Madhuban, tehsil Ghosi
63.	Salamat Ali	---	Vill Dubari, thana Madhuban, tehsil Ghosi
64.	Balwant Singh	---	Nizamabad, tehsil Sadar

Source: Phoolbadan Singh, *Azamgarh ka Swatantrata Sangram* (Freedom Struggle in Azamgarh, Hindi), Vol. I, Published by District Freedom Fighters Association, Azamgarh, 1974.

Appendix - F

List of Main Supporters and Collaborators of the British in Eastern Uttar Pradesh

PART - I

Sl. No.	*Name*	*P. No.*
1.	Ali Bakhsh	19
2.	Safdar Hussein	21
3.	Raja of Bansi	32, 185, 263
4.	Raja of Gopalpur	32, 185, 236
5.	Raja of Padrauna	33
6.	Qadir Bakhsh Jamadar	34
7.	Amanullah	34
8.	Ram Nawaj	155, 170
9.	Jamuna Prasad	168
10.	Niranjan	168
11.	Bechan Lal (Qanungo)	168
12.	Ganga Prasad	168
13.	Bhawani Prasad	169
14.	Bechan Lal (Mukhtar)	169
15.	Devi Charan	169
16.	Kanhaiya (Mudarris)	169, 266
17.	Grandson of Devidutt	170

(*Contd...*)

18.	Pandey of Ahata	170
19.	Dhanpat Rai (Tehsildar)	170
20.	Mohd Lateef (Sadr-us-Sudoor)	170
21.	Hadi Ali Khan (Deputy)	170
22.	Hafiz Ilahi Bakhsh (tehsildar of Padrauna)	171, 319
23.	Hidayat Ali	171
24.	Meer Wahid Ali	171
25.	Khudabakhsh	171
26.	Hussein Bakhsh	171
27.	Ahmad Ali son of Mehar Ali	171
28.	Hussein Ali	171
29.	Mehboob Ali	171
30.	Nawazish Ali (Hakim)	172, 329
31.	Maan Khan (Mukhtar-e-Kul)	175
32.	Brij Lal (Munshi)	176
33.	Yahya Khan	177
34.	Raja of Majhauli	185
35.	Raja of Tamkuhi	185, 263
36.	Shiv Bakhsh Lal	188
37.	Babu of Paikauli	264
38.	Babu of Rampur	264
39.	Babu of Bishanpur	265
40.	Himmat Ali (Assistant to Lorein)	265
41.	Fazl-e-Ali	319
42.	Bandhal Gosain (Gosain of Mathiya in Padrauna)	320
43.	Shah Ali Gauhar	329
44.	Khairuddin Khan	300

Source: *Kashful Baghaavat, Gorakhpur*, by Nasreen Ahmad, Rupa Publications P Ltd, New Delhi, 2010.

PART - II

List of Main Collaborators of the British

Sl. No.	*Name*	*Place*	*Position*	*P. No.*
1.	Raja of Gopalpur	Gorakhpur	Zamindar	34, 155, 160
2.	Sardar Surat Singh	Banaras	---	44
3.	Ali Hussein	Azamgarh	Head Clerk of Mohammedabad tehsil	104, 106
4.	Raja Mohd Mubarak Khan	Azamgarh		106
5.	Maulvi Najmuddin	Azamgarh	Grandee of Chiraiyakot	106, 109
6.	Hussein Bakhsh	Azamgarh	---	107
7.	Hasan Ali	Azamgarh	---	107
8.	Murtaza Khan	Azamgarh	---	108
9.	Sheikh Mamnoon Khan	Azamgarh	Tehsildar	109
10.	Raja Salamat Shah	Azamgarh	Zamindar	110
11.	Raja of Bansi	Gorakhpur	Zamindar	152, 160

(*Contd...*)

12.	Mohammed Bakhsh	Gorakhpur	Zamindar	153
13.	Rani of Basti (Digambar Kunwari)	Gorakhpur	Zamindar	158, 160
14.	Nazir of Gorakhpur (Krishna Sahay)	Gorakhpur	Employee	159
15.	Raja of Tamkuhi	Gorakhpur	Zamindar	160, 210
16.	Raja of Salempur	Gorakhpur	Zamindar	160, 210
17.	Devi Dayal	Gorakhpur	Zamindar	213
18.	Rustam Sahay	Jaunpur	Pleader	213
19.	Murtaza Bakhsh	Jaunpur	Thanedar	213
20.	Hingan Lal	Jaunpur	---	213, 214
21.	Shiv Ratan Singh	Jaunpur	---	227
22.	Rani of Mahto	Gorakhpur	---	305
23.	Ahmad Ali Shah	Gorakhpur	---	384
24.	Khudabakhsh Khan	Gorakhpur	---	384
25.	Pandit Kishan Narayan	Jaunpur	---	35
26.	Naib Nazir of Gorakhpur	---	---	164
27.	Khairuddin Khan	Deputy Magistrate	---	263
28.	Raja Man Singh	Shahganj, Jaunpur	---	309, 312
29.	Raja Mahesh Narayan Singh	Jaunpur	---	234
30.	Khwaja Hidayatullah	Azamgarh	---	108
31.	Randhir Singh	Singramau	---	210
32.	Pheku Singh	Saidpur, Ghazipur	Zamindar	120

Source: Syed Athar Abbas Rizvi, *Freedom Struggle in Uttar Pradesh*, Vol IV, Publication Department, Uttar Pradesh Government, Lucknow, 1959.

Glossary

Babu: Younger brother of a zamindar

Bigha: Unit of land measurement; it was not uniform in all areas; at the time of settlement in Banaras, a *bigha* was considered to be equal to 3,136 square yards

Chaudhari: Chief of a village or profession; the term denoted a zamindar at places

Domkatar: A Kshatriya caste

Jagir: Grant of land revenue of the territory assigned; was allotted for the services rendered or to be rendered

Maafi: Exemption from revenue payment

Mahal: A unit of land for revenue administration, equivalent to a pargana

Pargana: Part of a *sarkar* or district for revenue administration

Pattidar: Owner of a portion of a divided zamindari

Raja: There was a tradition of calling a big zamindar as a raja

Resident: Representative appointed by the East India Company in another state

Ryot: Cultivators, public

Taluqa: A subordinate territory; for revenue purposes, a cluster of several villages under a zamindari or a zamindar family; from the viewpoint of land revenue, a smaller area than a pargana

Taluqadar: Holder of a taluqa, landlord or revenue collector

Birt: Land granted for one's livelihood

Birtia: Holder of the land granted as a *Birt*

Bibliography

Unpublished Documents

National Archives, New Delhi

(1) Foreign Department: Political and Secret Consultation, files for 1857, 1858 and 1859.

(2) Foreign Department: Political – A, files for October and December 1857 and for May and July 1868.

(3) Foreign Department: Governor General's Dispatch to Secret Committee, files for 1857, 1858 and 1859.

(4) Home Department: Public and Judicial Consultations, files for 1857, 1858, 1859, 1860, 1861, 1862, 1863 and 1864.

(5) Home Department: Governor General's Proceedings (Fort William), files for 1857, 1858 and 1859.

State Archives, Lucknow

(1) Narrative of Events Attending the Outbreak of Disturbances and the Restoration of Authority in the Division of Benaras in 1857-58, No. 523 of 1858 (printed), 06 Nov. 1858.

(2) The Rebellion of 1857 in the Province of Benaras (printed), 15 Oct. 1858.

(3) Supplement to the Narrative of Events & C. in the Benaras Division (printed), 19 Nov. 1858.

(4) Proceedings Abstracts, North Western Provinces, Judicial (Criminal), 1859.

(5) Abstracts of Proceedings, NWP (General).

Regional Archives, Allahabad

(1) Commissioner's Office, Gorakhpur — Revenue Records (Pre- and Post-Mutiny).

(2) Commissioner's Office, Banaras — Post-Mutiny Records.

(3) Gorakhpur Collectorate — Mutiny Records under List No. 14.

(4) Ghazipur Collectorate — Mutiny Records under List No. 13 and Post-Mutiny Records Series.

(5) Mirzapur Collectorate — Mutiny Records under List No. 17.

Printed Documents

(6) Narrative of Events Attending the Outbreak of Disturbances and the Restoration of Authority in the District of Gorakhpur in 1857-58, No. 196 of 1858.

(7) Tenant Rights and Auction Sales in Ghazeepoor and the Province of Benares (Printed for Author by John Falconer, 53 upper Sackville streets, Dublin, 1873).

Published Documents: Settlement Reports, Manuals and Gazetteers

(A)

1. Bennett, W.C. - Report of the Final Settlement of Gonda District, Allahabad.
2. Conybeare, H.C.A. – Note on Pargana Dudhi of the Mirzapur district with special references to its Land Assessment.
3. Dale, G. – The Final Report on Completion of the Revision of records of that portion of Mirzapur District, commonly described as Gangetic Valley, Allahabad, 1887.
4. Duthoit, W. – Report upon the Position of Munzooreedaars of Pergunnah Bhudohee in the family domain of Maharaja of Benares.
5. Hooper, J. - Final Report of the Settlement of the Basti District, Allahabad.
6. Irwine William – Reports on the Revision of Records and Settlements Operations in the Ghazipur District, 1880-85, Allahabad, 1886.
7. Oldham, Wilton – Historical and statistical Memoir of the Ghazeepoor District, Part -I, Allahabad, 1870 & Part II, Allahabad 1876.
8. Porter, F.W. – Final Report on the Survey of Revision of Records, recently compiled for the Benares District, Allahabad 1887.
9. Reid, J.R. – Report on the District of Azamgarh: Compiled in the connection with the completion of the Sixth Settlement, Allahabad, 1887.
10. Thomas, J. – Report of the Collector of the Azimgarh on the Settlement of Ceded Portion of the District, commonly called as Chuklah Azimgarh, Agra, December 1837.
11. Wheeler P.C. – Report on the Revision of Records and Settlement Operations in the District of Jaunpur, from 1877 to 1886, Allahabad, 1886.
12. Wynne H.L. – Settlement Report and Statements District of Goruckpore, 1868.
13. Wynne H.L. – Report on Statements of Goruckpore – Bustee District, Allahabad 1871.

(B) Manual

1. Swinton, Alan, *Manual of the Statistics of the District of Goruckpore*, Allahabad, 1861.

(C) Gazetteers

(a) The Provincial Gazetteers of North Western Provinces

1. Atkinson, E. T. (ed), *Statistical, Descriptive and Historical Account of the North Western Provinces of India*, Vol. VI, Part 2: Gorakhpur, Part 3: Basti, Allahabad.

2. Fisher, F. H. (ed), *Statistical, Descriptive and Historical Account of the North Western Provinces of India*, Vol. XIII

Part 1: Azamgarh, Allahabad, 1883

Part 2: Ghazipur, Allahabad, 1884

Part 3: Ballia, Allahabad, 1884

3. Fisher, F. H. and Hewett, J. P. (ed), *Statistical, Descriptive and Historical Account of the North Western Provinces of India*, Vol. XIV

Part 1: Banaras, Allahabad, 1884

Part 2: Mirzapur, Allahabad, 1883

Part 3: Jaunpur, Allahabad, 1884

4. Bennett, W. C.; Harrington, A. H.; and Ferrer, M. L. (ed), *Gazetteer of the Province of Awadh*, 3 volumes bound in one, Delhi, 2006.

(b) District Gazetteers of the United Provinces of Agra and Oudh

1. Drake-Brockman, D. L., *Mirzapur: A Gazetteer Being Volume XXVII of the District Gazetteers of the United Provinces of Agra and Awadh*, Allahabad, 1911.
2. *Azamgarh: A Gazetteer Being Volume XXXI of the District Gazetteers of the United Provinces of Agra and Awadh*, Allahabad, 1911.
3. Nevill, H. R., - *Banaras: A Gazetteer Being Volume XXVI of the District Gazetteers of the United Provinces of Agra and Awadh*, Allahabad, 1909.

   - *Ballia: A Gazetteer Being Volume XXX of the District Gazetteers of the United Provinces of Agra and Awadh*, Allahabad, 1907.

   - *Basti: A Gazetteer Being Volume XXXII of the District Gazetteers of the United Provinces of Agra and Awadh*, Allahabad, 1907.

   - *Ghazipur: A Gazetteer Being Volume XXXI of the District Gazetteers of the United Provinces of Agra and Awadh*, Allahabad, 1909.

   - *Gorakhpur: A Gazetteer Being Volume XXXI of the District Gazetteers of the United Provinces of Agra and Awadh*, Allahabad, 1909.

   - *Jaunpur: A Gazetteer Being Volume XXVIII of the District Gazetteers of the United Provinces of Agra and Awadh*, Allahabad, 1908.
4. Prakash, Om (State Editor), *Gorakhpur: Uttar Pradesh District Gazetteers*, Lucknow, 1987.
5. Varun, D. P. (State Editor), Gorakhpur, 1985, Ghazipur 1982, Deoria 1988.

ENGLISH BOOKS

1. Agrawal, Ruchi, *Taluqdars of Awadh and the Revolt of 1857*, S R Scientific Publications, Agra, 2013.
2. Anderson, Clare, *The Indian Uprising of 1857-58: Prisons, Prisoners and Rebellion,* Anthem Press, Wimbeldon Publishing House, London, 2007.
3. Ball, Charles, *The History of the Indian Mutiny*, Vol. I & II, The London Printing and Publishing Company Limited, London, 1858.
4. Ballhatchet, Kenneth, *Race, Sex and Class under the Raj: Imperial Attitudes and Policies and Their Critics 1793-1905*, Vikas Publishing House, New Delhi, 1979.

5. Bates, Crispin (ed), *Mutiny at the Margins*, Vol. 7, Sage Publications, India, P Ltd, New Delhi, 2014.
6. Bayley, C. S. (ed), *The Indian Revolt of 1857*, Clarendon Press, London, 1986.
7. Bhargava, Meena, *State, Society and Ecology: Gorakhpur in Transition, 1750-1830*, Manohar Publishers & Distributors, New Delhi, 1999.
8. Bhargava, M. L., *The Saga of 1857: Success and Failure*, Reliance Publication House, New Delhi, 1992.
9. Bhargava, M. L., *Architects of Indian Freedom Struggle*, Deep and Deep Publications, New Delhi, 1981.
10. Bhattacharya, Sabyasachi (ed), *Rethinking 1857*, Orient Blackswan, New Delhi, 2010.
11. Chanda, S. N., *1857: Some Untold Stories*, Sterling Publishers, New Delhi, 1976.
12. Chand, Tara, *History of the Freedom Movement in India*, Vol. I, Information & Broadcasting Department, Government of India, Delhi, 1961.
13. Chattopadhyaya, Hara Prasad, *The Sepoy Mutiny 1857: A Social Study and Analysis*, Book Land Pvt. Ltd, Calcutta, 1957.
14. Chick, N. A., *Annals of the Indian Rebellion, 1857-58*, Part IV, Saunders, Kons & Co, Calcutta, 1859.
15. Chopra, P. N. (ed), *Who is Who of the Indian Martyrs of 1857*, Vol. III, Government of India, New Delhi, 1973.
16. Chaudhuri, Sashi Bhusan, *Civil Rebellion in Indian Mutinies (1857-59)*, The World Press P Ltd, Calcutta, 1957.
17. Chaudhuri, Sashi Bhusan, *Theories of the Indian Mutiny (1857-59)*, The World Press P Ltd, Calcutta, 1965.
18. Dalrymple, William, *The Last Mughal: The Fall of a Dynasty, 1857*, Penguin Books, New Delhi, 2007.
19. David, Saul, *The Indian Mutiny 1857*, Penguin Books, New Delhi, 2002.
20. Dharmapal, *The Purabia Soldier: The Hero of India's War of Independence 1857*, Delhi, 1957.
21. Datta, K. K., *Reflections on the Mutiny*, University Press, Calcutta, 1967.
22. Datta, K. K., *Biography of Kunwar Singh and Amar Singh*, K P Jaiswal Institute, Patna, 1957.
23. Datta, K.K., *History of the Freedom Movement in Bihar*, Vol. I, Government of Bihar, Patna, 1957.
24. Edwards, Michael, *Red Year: The Indian Rebellion of 1857*, Hamish Hamilton, London, 1973.
25. Edwards, Michael, *Battles of the Indian Mutiny*, new edition, Macmillan, London, 1963.
26. Edwards, Michael, *A Season in Hell: The Defence of the Lucknow Residency*, Hamish Hamilton, London, 1973.
27. Embree, Ainslie Thomas (ed), *1857 in India: Mutiny or War of Independence ?*, D C Heath & Co, Lexington, 1963.

28. Embree, Ainslie T, *India in 1857: The Revolt against Foreign Rule*, Chanakya Publishers, Delhi, 1992.
29. Fitchet, W. H., *The Tale of the Great Mutiny*, John Murray, London, reprint: 1939.
30. Forrest, G. W., *A History of the Indian Mutiny* 1857-58, Vol.I, William Blackwood & Sons Edinburgh and London, MCMIV, New Delhi, 2006.
31. Frykenberg, Robert Eric, *Land Control and Social Structure in Indian History*, first Indian edition: Manohar Publications, New Delhi, 1979.
32. Ganguli, A. B., *Guerrilla Fighters of the First Freedom Movement*, Janki Prakashan, Patna, 1980.
33. Gooptu, Sharmishtha and Mazumdar, Boria (ed), *Revisiting 1857: Myth, Memory & History*, Lotus Books, New Delhi, 2007.
34. Gubbins, Martin Richard, *An Account of the Mutinies of Oudh and of the siege of Lucknow Residency,* Richard Bentley, New Burlington Street, London, 1858.
35. Haq, Syed Moinul, *The Great Revolution of 1857*, Pakistan Historical Society, Karachi, 1968.
36. Hardy, Peter, *The Muslims of British India*, Cambridge University Press, New Delhi, 1992.
37. Hasrat, Bikramjit, *History of Nepal as told by Its Own Contemporary Chroniclers*, B B Research Institute, Hoshiarpur, 1970.
38. Hibbert, Christopher, *The Great Mutiny: India 1857*, Penguin Books, New Delhi, 1980.
39. Holmes, T. R., *History of the Indian Mutiny*, Macmillan & Co, London, 1898.
40. Husain, Imtiaz, *Land Revenue Policy in North India*, New Age Publishers, Delhi, 1967.
41. Husain, Iqbal, *Religion and Ideology of the Rebels of 1857*, Primus Books, New Delhi, 2013.
42. Husain, Iqbal, *Karl Marx on India*, Tulika Books for Aligarh Historians Society, 2008.
43. Husain, Iqbal, *The World of The Rebels of 1857*, Primus Books, Delhi, 2019.
44. Husain, Syed Mahdi, *Bahadur Shah II and the War of 1857 with Its Unforgettable Scenes*, Atmaram & Sons, Delhi, 1958.
45. Jafri, Saiyid Zaheer Husain, *Delhi and Awadh During 1857, Studies, Images and Documents*, Gyan Publishing House, Daryaganj, New Delhi 2020.
46. Joshi, P. C. (ed), *Rebellion 1857*, National Book Trust, New Delhi, 2013 reprint.
47. Kaye, Sir John William, *A History of the Sepoy War in India*, Vol. I & II. W.H. Allen & Co. Ltd., 13 Waterloo Place London, 1880.
48. Khan, K. M. S., *Excavation of Truth*, Kanishka Publishers & Distributors, New Delhi, 2007.
49. Khan, Syed Ahmed (Sir), *The Causes of the Indian Revolt*, Oxford University Press, London, 2000.
50. Kaye's & Malleson, G B, *History of the Indian Mutiny,* Edited by Colonel Malleson, By Sir John Kaye, Second Edition, W.H. Allen & Co. Ltd., 13 Waterloo Place, London, 1892.

51. Malleson, G. B., *The Indian Mutiny of 1857*, reprint: Seelay & Co. Ltd. Essex Street Stand, London 1891.
52. Marx, Karl and Engels, Frederich, *The First Indian War of Independence*, Progress Publishers, Moscow, fifth edition: 1978.
53. Majumdar, R. C., *The Sepoy Mutiny and the Revolt of 1857*, second edition, Firma K L Mukhopadhyaya, Calcutta, 1963.
54. Majumdar, R. C., *History of the Freedom Movement in India*, Vol I, Firma K L Mukhopadhyaya, Calcutta, 1988.
55. Mehta, Asoka, *1857: The Great Rebellion*, Hind Kitabs, Bombay, 1946.
56. Metcalfe, C. T. (ed), *Two Native Narratives of the Mutiny in Delhi*, reprint: Kessenger Publishing Series, 2010.
57. Metcalfe, Thomas R, *The Aftermath of the Revolt in India, 1858-1870*, Princeton University Press, 1964.
58. Mishra, Anand Swaroop, *Nana Saheb Peshwa and the Fight for Freedom*, Information and Publication Department, Uttar Pradesh, Lucknow, 2007.
59. Mishra, Kamla Prasad, *Banaras in Transition*, Munshi Ram Manohar Lal Publishers P Ltd, New Delhi, 1973.
60. Montgomery, Martin, *The History, Antiquities, Topography and Statistics of Eastern India*, Vol. II (reprint), 1976.
61. Moosvi, Shirin (ed), *Facets of the Great Rebellion*, Sahmat/Tulika Books, New Delhi, 2008.
62. Mukherjee, Rudragnshu, *Awadh in Revolt, 1857-58*, Oxford University Press, 1984.
63. Nash, J. T., *Volunteering in India*, George Phillip & Son, Liverpool and London, 1893.
64. Nasreen, Farhat (Transliterator & Ttranslator), *Kashful Baghaavat, Gorakhpur*, Rupa Publications India P Ltd, New Delhi, 2010.
65. Nehru, Jawahar Lal, *The Discovery of India*, (6th Impression, Oxford University Press, Delhi 1994).
66. Nizami, Farhan Ahmad, *Madrasas, Scholars and Saints: Muslim Response in the British Presence in Delhi and Upper Doab*, 1805-1857, Oxford University Press, London, 1983.
67. Norgate, James Thomas & Fillet, D C (translator): *From Sepoy to Subedar: Being the Life and Adventures of Subedar Sita Ram, A Native Officer of the Bengal Army, Written and Related by Himself*, Lahore, 1873.
68. Pandey, Smita, *Vision of Rebels during 1857*, Rupa Publications P Ltd, New Delhi, 2005.
69. Pemble, John, *The Raj, the Indian and the Kingdom of Oudh*, Oxford University Press, New Delhi, 1979.
70. Powell, Avril Ann, *Muslims and Missionaries in Pre-Mutiny India*, Curzon Press Ltd, London, 1993.
71. Rag, Pankaj, *1857 in Eastern Uttar Pradesh and Adjoining Areas*, Rupa Publications, New Delhi, 1992.

72. Rana, Padma Jang Bahadur, *Life of Maharaja Sir Jang Bahadur of Nepal*, Ratna Pustak Bhandar, Kathmandu, reprint: 1980.
73. Rizvi, Syed Najmul Raza, *Zamindars and Revenue Farmers of Eastern Uttar Pradesh*, Anamika Publishers & Distributors, New Delhi, 2004.
74. Rizvi, Syed Najmul Raza and Jaffri, Saiyid Zaheer Husain (ed), *The great Uprising of 1857*, Anamika Publishers & Distributors, New Delhi, 2008.
75. Russell, Sir William Howard, *My Indian Mutiny Diary*, Castel & Co, London, 1857.
76. Savarkar, V. D. (An Indian Nationalist), The Indian War of Independence of 1857, (London, S.N. 1909, Columbia Universities Library, Digital collections), Veer Savarkar, The Indian War of Independence, 1857, Abhishek Publications, Chandigarh, 2019, first Edition.
77. Sengupta, K. K., *Recent Writings on the Revolt of 1857: A Survey*, Indian Council of Historical Research, New Delhi, 1975.
78. Sen, Snigdha, *The Historiography of the Indian Revolt of 1857*, Punthi Pustak, Calcutta, 1992.
79. Sen, Surendra Nath, *Eighteen Fifty Seven*, First Edition, May 1957 and Second Edition 1977; Publications Division, Government of India, New Delhi, second edition: 1977.
80. Sever, Adrien, *Nepal under the Ranas*, in 2 volumes, Oxford and IBH Publishing Co. Pvt. Ltd. New Delhi, 1999.
81. Shah, Rishikesh, *Modern Nepal*, Vol. 1, Manohar Publications, New Delhi, 1990.
82. Spilsbury, Julian, The Indian Mutiny, A Weidenfeld and Nicolson, e-book, 2007.
83. Srivastava, K. V., *The Great Indian Revolt of 1857*, Regal Publications, New Delhi, 2007.
84. Srivastava, M. P., *The Indian Mutiny of 1857*, Chug Publishers, Allahabad, 1979.
85. Siddika, Shamima, *Muslims of Nepal*, Publisher Ghazala Siddika, Kathmandu, 1993.
86. Singh, Rajendra, *Land, Power and People*, Sage Publications, India, New Delhi, 1988.
87. Stokes, Eric, *The Peasant and the Raj*, Cambridge University Press, New Delhi, 1978.
88. Stokes, Eric, *The Peasant Armed: The Indian Revolt of 1857*, edited by C. A. Bayley, Oxford University Press, New Delhi, 1984.
89. Taqi, Roshan, Lucknow 1857: *The Two Wars at Lucknow, The Dusk of an Era*, New Royal Book Company, Lucknow, 2001.
90. Taylor, P. J. O., *What Really Happened during the Mutiny*, Oxford University Press, New Delhi, 1997.
91. Taylor, P. J. O. (chief editor), *A Companion to the Indian Mutiny of 1857*, Oxford University Press, New Delhi, 1996.
92. Tiwari, Ramashankar, *The War of Independence in Awadh, 1857-58*, Kashi Prakashan, Kanpur, 2012.
93. Yadav, K. C., *Delhi in 1857*, Vol. I: *The Trial of Bahadur Shah*, The Academic Press, Gurgaon, 1980.

94. .... : *The Stories of Indian Mutiny 1857-58*; Edinbergh, W.P. Nimmo, Hay & Mitchell, 1898.

95. .... : (by one who had Served under Sir Charles Napier): *The Mutiny of Bengal Army,* London, Bosworth and Harrison, Regent Street, MDCCCL VIII, London.

HINDI BOOKS

1. Chand, Tara, *Bharatiya Swatantrata Andolan ka Itihas* (History of India's Freedom Movement), Vol. I, Publications Division, Govt of India, New Delhi, second edition: 1977.
2. Chandra, Moti, *Kashi ka Itihas* (History of Banaras), University Publications, Varanasi, third edition: 2003.
3. Chaubey, Devendra; Narayan, Badri and Patel, Hitendra (ed), *1857: Bharat ka Pehla Mukti Sangharsh* (1857: India's First Liberation War), Prakashan Sansthan, New Delhi, 2006.
4. Chaudhari, Rashmi, *Vir Kunwar Singh*, Publications Division, Govt of India, New Delhi, 2007.
5. Datta, K. K, *Bihar mein Satantraya Andolan ka Itihas* (History of Freedom Movement in Bihar), Vol. 1, Bihar Hindi Granth Academy, Patna, 1988.
6. Ganguli, Ashok, *Bharatiya Swadhinata Sangram ka Itihas* (History of India's Freedeom Struggle), Radhakrishna Prakashan, New Delhi, 2012.
7. Habib, Irfan, *160 Saal Baad 1857* (1857: 160 Years Later), Tulika Books, New Delhi, 2017.
8. Hasan, Moinuddin, *Khadang-e-Ghadar: 1857* (The Disturbance of Rebellion 1857), Hindi translation by Abdul Haq, as *Gadar 1857* (Hindi Madhyam Karyanvayan Nideshalaya), Delhi University, 2006.
9. Jaunpuri, Syed Iqbal Ahmad, *Sharqi Rajya Jaunpur ka Itihas* (History of Jaunpur the Sharqi Kingdom), Shiraz-e-Hind Prakashan Bhavan, Jaunpur, 1968.
10. Joshi, P C (ed), *Inquilab 1857* (Rebellion 1857), National Book Trust, New Delhi, fourth reprint, 2014.
11. Mall, Lall Khanga Bahadur, *Vishwen Vansh Vatika*, Bankipur Press, Patna, 1887
12. Mishra, Amaresh, *Mangal Pandey*, Rupa and Co, New Delhi, 2006.
13. Mishra, Daya Shankar, *Azamgarh ka Itihas* (History of Azamgar), Azamgarh, V 2012 (1956)
14. Mishra, Jagannath Prasad, *Bihar Kesari Babu Kunwar Singh* (Babu Kunwar Singh: The Lion of Bihar), Delhi, 1965.
15. Namboodiripad, E M S, *Bharat ka Swadhinata Sangram* (India's Struggle for FReadeom), Granth Shilpi, Delhi, 2010.
16. Narayan, Badri; Chaudhari, Rashmi and Nath, Sanjay (ed), *1857 ka Mahasangram* (Great War of 1857), Adhar Publications, Panchkula, 2009.
17. Nehru, Jawaharlal, *Hindustan ki Kahani* (Discovery of India), Sasta Sahitya Mandal, New Delhi, 2011.
18. Pandey, Rajbali, *Gorakhpur Janapad aur Uski Kshatriya Jatiyon ka Itihas* (History of Gorakhpur District and Its Kshatriya Castes), Thakur Mahatam Rao Publishers and Booksellers, Gorakhpur, VS 2003 (AD 1946).

19. Raza, Rahi Masoom, *1857 Kranti Katha* (Saga of Revolution 1857), Vani Prakashan, New Delhi, 1999.
20. Rizvi, Syed Athar Abbas, *Sangharshkaleen Netaon ki Jivaniyan* (Biographies of Fighting Leaders), Vol. I, Information Department, Uttar Pradesh, Lucknow, 1957.
21. Rizvi, Syed Athar Abbas, *Swatantra Dilli* (Liberated Delhi), Information Department, Uttar Pradesh, Lucknow, 1968.
22. Rizvi, Syed Najmul Raza, *Attharahwin Sadi ke Zamindar* (Zamindars of the Eighteenth Century), People's Publishing House, New Delhi, 1988.
23. Saxena, Pradeep (ed), *1857: Mahakranti ya Vidroh?* (Great Revolution or Mutiny?), Praveen Prakashan, Delhi, 2008.
24. Savarkar, Vinayak Damodar, *1857 ka Swatantrya Samar* (1857 War of Independence), Prabhat Paperbacks, New Delhi, 2011.
25. Sen, Surendra Nath, *Attharah Sau Sattavan* (Eighteen Fifty-Seven), Publications Division, Government of India, New Delhi, second edition: 2005.
26. Sharma, Ram Bilas, *Swadhinata Sangram: Badalate Pariprekshya* (War of Independence: Changing Perspectives), University of Delhi, Delhi, 1992.
27. Singh, Ayodhya, *Bharat ka Mukti Sangram: Atharahwin aur Unnisawin Sadi ke Vidroh* (India's War for Liberation: Revolts of the Eighteenth and Nineteenth Centuries), Prakashan Sansthan, New Delhi, 2006.
28. Singh, Bhagawati Prasad (ed), *Rashtriya Swatantrata Sangharsh aur Gonda Janapad* (National War of Independence and Gonda District), Shivam Printers, Varanasi, 1993.
29. Singh, Durga Prasad, *Babu Kunwar Singh*, Vidya Bhavan, Patna, 1962.
30. Singh, Kanhaiya, *1857 ka Swatantrata Sangram* (1857 War of Independence), University Publications, Varanasi, 2004.
31. Singh, Murali Mahohar Prasad and Awasthi, Rekha (ed), *1857: Baghaavat ke Daur ka Itihas* (History of the Days of the Rebellion), Granth Shilpi, New Delhi, 2009.
32. Singh, Phoolbadan, *Azamgarh ka Swadhinata Sangram* (Freedom Struggle in Azamgarh), District Association of Freedom Fighters, Azamgarh, 1974.
33. Singh, Thakur Prasad, *Swatantrata Andolan aur Banaras* (Independence Movement and Banaras), University Publications, Varanasi, 1990.
34. Singh, Thakur Prasad, *Swatantrata Sangram ke Sainik: Zila Azamgarh* (Soldiers of the War of Independence: District Azamgarh), Govt of Uttar Pradesh, Lucknow, n d.
35. Soni, Ved Prakash, *Bharat ka Pratham Swatantrata Sangram: 1857* (India's First War of Independence), Part 1, Delhi, 2008.
36. Upadhyaya, Vishva Mitra, *San Sattavan ke Bhule-Bisre Shaheed* (Forgotten Martyrs of the Year 1857), Publications Division, Govt of India, New Delhi, 2004.
37. Verma, Acharya Rajnikant, *1857 ke Vismrit Yoddha* (Forgotten Fighters of 1857), Allahabad, 2000.
38. Verma, Nageshwar Prasad Singh, *Nag-Kaushalottar*, Bankipur Press, Patna, V.S. 1975 (AD 1918).

Unpublished

Ansari, Mohd Lateef, Discovery of Mahua Dabar, typescript, in Hindi.

URDU BOOKS

1. Farooqi, Syed Abdul Ghafoor, *Shajra-e-Shadab* (Genealogy), Gorakhpur, 1900.
2. Haider, Kamaluddin, *Qaiser-ut-Tawarikh* (The Lords of History), Vol. 2, Nawal Kishore Press, Lucknow, 1896.
3. Haider, Kamaluddin, *Sawanihat-i-Salatin-i-Awadh*, Lucknow, 1889.
4. Hasan, Mujahidul, *Mecca Muazamma se Muazammabad tak* (From the Holy Mecca to Gorakhpur), Kakori Press, Lucknow, 2010.
5. Khan, Najmul Ghani, *Tarikh-e-Awadh* (History of Awadh), in 3 volumes, Nawal Kishore Press, Lucknow, 1919.
6. Khan, Syed Ahmed, *Asbab-e-Baghaavat-e-Hind* (Causes of the Revolt in India), Mufassilat Gazette Press, Agra, 1859.
7. Lari, Ahmar, *Mukhtsar Tarikh-e-Gorakhpur* (Brief History of Gorakhpur), Adabistan, Gorakhpur, 1972.
8. Mehar, Ghulam Rasool, *1857 ke Mujahid* (Fighters of 1857), Kitab Manzil, Lahore, 1957.
9. Mian, Maulana Mohd, *Ulema-e-Hind ka Shandar Mazi* (Glorious Past of the Indian Ulema), Vol. IV, Lahore.
10. Qadri, Mohd Ayub, *1857: Jang-e-Azadi, Waqiyat-o-Shakhsiyat* (1857 War of Independence, Events and Personalities), Pak Academy, Hyderabad and Karachi, 1976.
11. Rizvi, Syed Khurshid Mustafa, *Tarikh-e-Jang-e-Azadi-e-Hind: 1857* (History of India's War of Independence: 1857), Raza Library, Rampur, 2000.
12. Shahabi, Mufti Intezamullah, *East India Company aur Baghi Ulema* (East India Company and the Rebellious Ulema), Maktaba Rizwan, Lahore.
13. Shah, Syed Ahmad Ali, *Kashful Baghaavat, Gorakhpur* (An Exposition of the Rebellion in Gorakhpur), Arifeen Press, Mirzapur, 1860.
14. Shah, Syed Ahmad Ali, *Mehboob-ul-Tawarikh* (Beloved of History), Hyderabad, 1863.
15. Sharar, Abdul Haleem, *Guzishta Lucknow* (The Past of Lucknow), Delhi.

NEPALI BOOKS

1. Upadhyaya, Ramji, *Nepal ko Itihas* (History of Nepal), Subba Homnath Kedarnath, Kathmandu, 1950.
2. Pant, Dinesh Raj, *Dhadingma Phela Pareka Nepali Kavita*, Rajiv Lochan Joshi Memorial Foundation, Kathmandu, V 2061 (AD 2004).

Important Papers, Journals and Proceedings

ENGLISH

1. *Journal of Pakistan Historical Society*, Karachi, Vol. V, Part 2, 1957-58.
2. *Proceedings of the Indian History Congress*, Kannur session, 2008.

3. *People's Democracy,* 22-28 January 2007.
4. *Social Scientist*, January-April 1988, Tulika Print & Communication, New Delhi.
5. *Studies in People's History*, editor: Irfan Habib and Shirin *Moosvi*, Vol. IV, No. 1 June 2017, Sage Publications India, New Delhi.
6. The Kathmandu Post, 24 September 2019 and 23 April 2020, kathmandu.com/awadh.

HINDI

1. *Anbhai Sancha,* special number on Rebellion 1857, quarterly, Guest Editor: Murali Manohar Prasad Singh, July-December 2007, New Delhi.
2. *Ajkal*, special number on 1857 struggle for independence, editor: Yogendra Datta K.K. Sharma, May 2007, Publications Division, Govt of India, New Delhi.
3. *Itihas Drishri*, No. 1 to 13, December 2008 to March 2015, editor: Syed Najmul Raza Rizvi, Gorakhpur.
4. *Proceedings, UP History Congress*, Hindi section, 2005, 2008, 2009 and 2011, Anamika Publishers and Distributors, New Delhi.
5. *Samayantar*, monthly, editor: Pankaj Visht, February 2007.
6. *Samkaleen Janmat,* chief editor: Ramji Rai, November 2006.
7. *Vartman Sahitya* (1857: Mass Resistance), editors: Kunwar Pal Singh and Namita Singh, November-December 2006, Aligarh.
8. *Yojana,* editor: Anurag Mishra, August 2007, New Delhi.

URDU

- *Sadiq-ul-Akhbar*, No. 4, H 1273, Delhi, July 1857.

Index

C

D

G

N

O

P

Q

R

S

V

W

Z